COMMUNIST REGIONS OF
CHINA, 1944
CHAHAR
JEHOL
HOPEI
SHANTUNG
KIANGSU
ANHWEI
CHEKIANG
KIANGSI
FUKIEN
TAIWAN
Mukden
Peiping
Tientsin
Tsinan
Tsingtao
Chengchow
Nanking
Shanghai
Hangchow
Hankow
Nanchang
Foochow
Amoy
Canton
Hong Kong
Taipei
120°
110°
30°
40°
20°
Kilometers
0
200
400
600
Miles
0
100
200
400
D0712780

HONORABLE SURVIVOR

JAILED IN U. S.
SPY CHARGES

Amerasia
Vital Sec
Contents

FBI Will Not Release
Service-Jaffe Record

Serv
Ame
FBI
Rep
By
U. S

MAY 18, 1950

Work

ow FBI Linked 6
Amerasia Case

al, Page 34)

of its most intensive surveillance jobs, the FBI linked Philip J. Jaffe with his five as case.

movements were watched in an attempt to learn how large quantities of Governmen falling into the possession of the Communist magazine editor.

Cast

Mr. Jaffe

rsen

Jaffe, editor of Amer figure in case, pleaded paid $2500 fine.

uel Sigurd Larsen, State nt China expert, paid without contesting

In 11 weeks' work the puzzle was put together. Six arrests followed, involving charges of conspiracy to steal official documents.

In the windup Jaffe got off with a $2500 fine. One co-defendant, Emmanuel Sigurd Larsen, paid a $500 fine. Charges against the rest were dropped.

Meeting

in Amerasia office. Later dined at Jaffe's apartment, 49 E. Ninth-st. Jaffe drove her to train.

April 15. Lieut. Roth left Navy Building office around 9 a. m. Met Larsen on corner 18th and nw and handed him Larsen

Building.

Another Me

Service May
Be Reassigned
By S

The S
ported
ing can
John St
cases of
vestigat

Loyalty
Diplomat
Five Red

WASHINGTON

5-18-50

Service Loaned
Jaffe Reports

Diplomat Helped Amerasia Editor

ERICK WOLTMAN Scripps-Howard Staff Writer

week after he arrived in America in 1945, recalled from China by the State ment, John Stewart Service, career diplomat, met Philip J. Jaffe. e, key figure in the Amerasia case, was under surveillance at the time by the

State Department officer available to the Communist editor official reports he prepared on Yenan, then headquarters of the Chinese munists.

Mr. Service loaned copies of them Jaffe, to take back to New York

A few days later, the State Department official picked them up in Jaffe's Amerasia headquarters. Six weeks later, on June 6, FBI arrested Jaffe. In Amerasia's

J. S

Dis

A

Service
To Diplo

SERV
FOR

ying before the
Committee in

Officer
Is No
Depar

FBI Testimony
On John Service
Is Kept Secret

Unfair to Release
Portion of Recording,
Senators Decide

Service Asks Court
To Restore Him to Job,
Quash Loyalty Ruling

John Stewart
career State Dep
yesterday asked a
restore his job,
ay and quash a
ere was "reasonal

JOHN S. SERVIC
BUT HE REMAI

WASHINGTON, June 14.—The U.S. Court of Appeals today upheld the Government's 1951 firing

High Court's 8-0
Voids Firing of

HONORABLE SURVIVOR

Mao's China, McCarthy's America, and the Persecution of John S. Service

LYNNE JOINER

NAVAL INSTITUTE PRESS
Annapolis, Maryland

Naval Institute Press
291 Wood Road
Annapolis, MD 21402

Library of Congress Cataloging-in-Publication Data
Joiner, Lynne.
The honorable survivor : Mao's China, McCarthy's America, and the persecution of John S. Service / Lynne Joiner.
p. cm.
Includes bibliographical references and index.
ISBN 978-1-59114-423-6 (alk. paper)
1. Service, John S. (John Stewart), 1909-1999. 2. Diplomats—United States—Biography. 3. United States—Foreign relations—China. 4. China—Foreign relations—United States. 5. United States—Foreign relations—1945-1989. 6. Anti-communist movements—United States—History—20th century. 7. McCarthy, Joseph, 1908-1957. I. Title.
E748.S413J65 2009
973.9092—dc22
[B]

2009027765

Printed in the United States of America on acid-free paper

14 13 12 11 10 09 9 8 7 6 5 4 3 2
First printing

To my mother and father,
who always encouraged me—and taught me the
value of the application of the seat of the pants
to the seat of the chair.

CONTENTS

PREFACE

When I was growing up in California, my family had one of the first television sets in our neighborhood. I remember watching news reports about the Korean War, the newscaster talking excitedly about our troops being overrun by the Chinese "Yellow horde." Years later, as a high school student working in a bookstore, I noticed a new arrival: *China: The Country Americans Aren't Allowed to Know.* The title expressed my own sense of frustration, although the book was pure propaganda.

As a student at Cornell University, I finally began to learn about this mysterious country of millions of people, hidden behind a Bamboo Curtain. In my Chinese political science class, I was first introduced to the story of John Service, an American diplomat in China during World War II. Chalmers Johnson, a China scholar, called his reporting "probably the single most important source in any language on the fateful decade of the 1940s in Chinese politics."

In 1970 ping-pong games became part of an unusual diplomatic dance between Mao's China and Nixon's United States—the first direct contact between Chinese and American citizens made me realize I might one day be able to visit this forbidden country. As a young broadcast journalist in 1975, after taping an interview with President Ford in San Francisco, I impetuously asked if I could go on his upcoming trip to China. After explaining my reasons to his press secretary, I managed to get credentialed for the trip. But when the thorny issue of Taiwan could not be resolved, Ford's ten-day working trip was downgraded to a four-day photo-op visit—and my boss refused to send me.

Soon, however, I was assigned to cover the first diplomatic mission made by the women of the U.S. Congress: a trip to China at the invitation of Vice Premier Deng Xiaoping. I was allowed to take a documentary cameraman along. We were the only Americans in China when Premier Zhou Enlai died, and I filed news reports for all three American television networks on the Chinese reaction to his death.

At a Stanford conference on U.S.–China relations a few months later, I first met Caroline and John (Jack) Service, who told me they had seen—and admired—*Flowers From Horseback*, the documentary I had produced about the congressional trip. Our shared professional interest in China soon developed into a warm personal friendship that lasted more than twenty years. The Services allowed me to read their fascinating oral histories at the UC Berkeley library, ten years before their stories were open to the public. And in December 1978, on the day following the announcement about the breakthrough in recognition of the People's Republic of China (PRC), together we happily toasted U.S.–China friendship. That was when Jack first told me about talking with Mao in Yenan about his desire for friendly relations with the United States.

In 1989 the three of us sat together once again, now in stunned silence—watching on television as Chinese tanks rolled through Tiananmen Square. Jack expressed deep disappointment in the evolution of the Chinese revolution, whose early years he had witnessed. It was then that I became determined to tell the story of John Service and the United States' struggle over the two Chinas.

ACKNOWLEDGMENTS

I know this epic would never have been written without the help of many people—and divine providence. You see, I must admit, this is more than a labor of love: I truly feel it was my destiny to write this book.

First and foremost, I must thank Jack and Caroline Service for sharing their story with me. And to their children, especially Bob, I have deep appreciation for their wholehearted support of the project over more than a decade. I am grateful to Val Chao Wu for sharing her story and to Annie Chang and Margaret Sun for helping with translations. I must also thank the staff at UC Berkeley's Bancroft Library, especially Mary Morganti, who organized John Service's collected papers. Staff at the Franklin D. Roosevelt Presidential Library and Harry S. Truman Presidential Library also provided important assistance—and research grants. I was also greatly aided in my research by staff at the National Archives in College Park, Maryland. Without the dogged and persistent help of Linda Colton, now a retired FBI public relations officer, I would never have been successful in prying loose important documents from Service's thick file. The Freedom of Information office at the State Department also worked hard to get its security office to finally admit it had never sent Service's security file to the National Archives (as required by law, twenty-five years after Foreign Service officers retire) and to make sure the files finally were transferred and open to scrutiny.

I have faced some very serious health issues that threatened to derail my effort to finish this project; I am indebted to my doctors; massage therapists; and Gregory Lemenov, my healer, for helping me recover and be able to finish the work.

My friends have been extremely helpful in offering their loving support and wise counsel. I would particularly like to thank my "readers"—Robert Gomperts, Tess Johnston, Tom Keaney, Sharon Silva, and Jerry Youcha—for plowing through the rough drafts, and Clare Wolfowitz for extraordinary editing assistance that sculpted the final manuscript. To my agent, Don Gastwirth, and the people at the U.S. Naval Institute, especially Susan Brook, who were willing to take a chance on an unknown author, I owe a special debt of gratitude.

Finally, I would like to thank my father and mother, Mel and Lucille Shavelson, who both passed away during my writing of the book but who inspired, encouraged, criticized, and supported me every step of the way. And to my son, Scott Joiner, for always being there for his mom.

NOTE ON ROMANIZATION

The modern system of Romanization of Mandarin Chinese is called Pinyin. At the time most of the events depicted in this book took place, however, different Romanizations were in vogue. Transcription of Chinese names and terms in this volume essentially adheres to Pinyin forms, except in direct quotes and in referring to names of certain well-known people and places. Please be aware that Beijing traditionally was known as Peking, except to the Nationalist Chinese government, which changed the name to Peiping when it moved the capital to Nanking—now known as Nanjing.

Romanization of certain key people and places:

Old Romanization	New Romanization (Pinyin)
Chiang Kai-shek	Jiang Jieshi
Chou En-lai	Zhou Enlai
Chu Teh	Zhu De
Dairen	Dalien
Chungking	Chongqing
Mao Tse-tung	Mao Zedong
Nanking	Nanjing
Peking (Peiping)	Beijing
Sian	Xian
Suchow	Suzhou
Tai Li	Dai Li
Yenan	Yanan

PROLOGUE

The handshake on February 21, 1972, between Chinese Communist Party chairman Mao Zedong and U.S. president Richard Nixon—a politician who had launched his national career as an anti-Communist—symbolized a spectacular geopolitical turnabout. For the previous quarter-century, the love–hate pendulum in U.S.–China relations had pointed squarely at mutual mistrust and suspicion. Now, "panda-mania" was sweeping the United States, and Mao caps were trendy. The love affair between the United States and China was on again, and within five years the courting dance would be consummated by the "normalization" of diplomatic relations between the world's most powerful nation and its most populous.

Twenty-seven years earlier, China's Nationalists and Communists had renewed their bloody civil war with a vengeance. In 1949 the Chinese Communists declared victory in the bitter struggle that had raged off and on for more than twenty years, and Chiang Kai-shek's battered Nationalists retreated to an island fortress on Taiwan. On October 1 of that year, China's newest emperor proclaimed the birth of the People's Republic of China (PRC). A year later, as American and Chinese Communist troops faced each other in the Korean War, Taiwan's defense became part of the United State's anti-Communist commitments.

Nixon's historic 1972 visit to Beijing was the first diplomatic opening in the Bamboo Curtain. Nervous supporters of Chiang Kai-shek and Taiwan knew the PRC would now insist that the United States abandon diplomatic relations with the Nationalist regime—still calling itself the Republic of China (ROC).

This was the political backdrop for a very special luncheon held at the Department of State on January 30, 1973, in honor of John Service and other Foreign Service officers who had been vilified in the 1950s for having "lost"

China to the Communists. News of the event set off a flurry of controversy. Rep. John Ashcroft of Ohio complained on the floor of the House that he found the idea of honoring Service "as the 'symbol' of American diplomatic 'integrity, courage, and loyalty' incredible in light of his known serious violations of the Federal Government's security regulations."[1] After all, Sen. Joseph McCarthy had named Service at the top of his list of Communists inside the State Department. One conservative magazine alleged the luncheon hoped to "nail down a pro-Communist policy in Asian affairs."[2] *Human Events* claimed (inaccurately) that Service had once been "caught red-handed slipping secret material to an identified Communist."[3]

Demand for tickets ran so high that closed-circuit television was set up for an overflow crowd that nearly filled the three-hundred-seat auditorium downstairs. "The luncheon was needed to convince people in the department that McCarthyism was really dead," David Biltchik of the American Foreign Service Association (AFSA) recalled years later.[4] One of the few who declined the invitation was National Security Advisor Henry Kissinger. Although he had secretly asked Service's advice about the Chinese Communists, he needed to protect his new China initiative from the wrath of the China Lobby.

McCarthy's witch hunt had not been put to rest: an anonymous flyer appeared on every table, with a list of embarrassing questions for John Service. "In 1945, you admitted having given Philip Jaffe, editor of *Amerasia*, a number of highly classified reports. You justified this on the ground that they were your own reports. Is it your view that Foreign Service officers have a right to give classified material which they have produced to anyone they please?"

The keynote speaker at the luncheon, historian Barbara Tuchman, praised the courage of the Foreign Service China hands: "No matter how much evidence was reported indicating that the collapse of the Kuomintang (Nationalists) was only a matter of time, nothing could induce Washington to loosen the silver cord tying us to Chiang Kai-shek nor rouse the policymakers from what John Service in a courageous report accurately called their 'indolent short-term expediency.'"

When it was his turn to speak, John Service—a tall, thin, distinguished-looking, white-haired sixty-three-year-old—kept his emotions in check as he gently reminded his audience:

> There are still countries—in Latin America, Africa, and parts of Asia—where the situation is not unlike that in China during the 1940s. If we keep ourselves in ignorance and out of touch with new popular movements and potentially revolutionary situations, we may find ourselves again missing the boat. . . .

> The measure of the need for such reporting is not popular sentiment in the United States as reflected in some segments of the press, or by some Congressional committees not charged with foreign relations. . . . The legacy of Senator Joe McCarthy still needs, in some respects, to be shed.[5]

When John Service finished his remarks, there was sustained standing applause for this former Foreign Service officer. Fired for "reasonable doubt as to his loyalty" in 1951, he had spent twenty-two years trying to restore his reputation. CBS news reporter Marvin Kalb reported that the luncheon had the "atmosphere of a class reunion": "When it was all over there was still the question, did the lunch clean the slate? China 20 years ago, Vietnam right now. What has the Foreign Service officer learned? Does he have the courage today to disagree with the White House line about, say, Vietnam or perhaps the Middle East? Does the White House have the courage to listen to disagreement without punishing the dissenter no matter how high or low his rank?"[6]

John Service remained a convenient lightning rod. He would still attract partisan passions in the United States' love–hate relationship with China. The State Department luncheon was intended to mark the end of Service's long fight to restore his reputation—but the pendulum would swing again.

This is his story.

MAP OF PEOPLE'S REPUBLIC OF CHINA, 2009

CHAPTER 1
THE KNOCK ON THE DOOR

The knock at the door came precisely at 5:03 PM.[1] It was a knock that would change the course of John Service's life. The thirty-four-year-old Foreign Service officer, just returned from China, was about to go out to dinner when he opened the door to find two men dressed in dark suits and crisp white shirts. "We're from the FBI," one of them announced, "and you're under arrest."

The agents asked to search the apartment. "I was a bit stunned," Service recalled, "and not being smart or experienced, I said 'yes.' They said, 'Where are the papers?'" Service explained that he kept copies of his China reports in his desk at the State Department—never suspecting that other FBI agents had already been dispatched to his office to confiscate his papers. He was handcuffed and taken out to an unmarked car, along with materials seized from the apartment: his address book, personal letters, a booklet called "Revolutionary China Today," Chinese paper money—and what appeared to be a small code book. This most tantalizing bit of evidence would be especially prized by the FBI agents' boss, J. Edgar Hoover.

The young diplomat—considered one of the department's best and brightest—was certain the FBI had made a terrible mistake. Recently recalled to Washington, he had been providing background briefings to officials and journalists about the tenuous situation in war-torn China, and about his recent talks with the Chinese Communist leadership. He was unaware that the FBI had been watching several of his government and press contacts for more than a month. He had no idea that he had walked into a web of intrigue, suspicion, and controversy that would last nearly half a century.

Service's arrest was part of an elaborately orchestrated FBI operation that netted six suspects and hundreds of government documents in Washington,

D.C., and New York on June 6, 1945. The other suspects were two editors of *Amerasia* (a journal specializing in Asian affairs), a freelance journalist, a State Department researcher, and a Navy intelligence officer. The FBI, always eager for favorable publicity, made sure that the sweep made the national radio news—and was publicly announced at that evening's Washington Senators baseball game, where many prominent politicians were in attendance.

During the war years, when the Soviet Union was our ally, the FBI had been hunting Nazis, not Communists. To most Americans, the idea of Communist spies was a new and shocking threat—especially since President Roosevelt had carefully cultivated the image of Joseph Stalin as a benign "Uncle Joe." But FDR was dead, the war in Europe had just ended, and Stalin was proving uncooperative. Now an "Iron Curtain" was rolling down over Eastern Europe, the Soviets were threatening to scuttle efforts to establish the United Nations, and Russia still refused to commit troops to war in the Pacific.

Harry Truman, the inexperienced new president, had been assured by his advisers that if Stalin sent forces into China—and forced the Chinese Communist guerrillas to support Chiang Kai-shek—Japan's defeat would be hastened and China would emerge as a strong democratic bulwark. In reality, war-ravaged China was a jigsaw puzzle of disparate geopolitical pieces and players: Japan's occupation forces, Chiang's Nationalists, Mao's Communists, and a motley assortment of old-style warlords who bargained away their allegiance to the highest bidder.

In this chaotic war zone, it was Service's job to report to the American military commander on China's bubbling geopolitical cauldron. When suspicions first arose about *Amerasia*, he was on assignment in Mao's stronghold, deep inside Japanese-occupied territory. Back in Washington to report on his secret mission, the unsuspecting diplomat was soon introduced to *Amerasia*'s editor—and was swept up into the FBI's spy case. *Amerasia* would become a harbinger of the Cold War, shattering the dream of a peaceful postwar era.

* * *

In Berkeley, California, Caroline Service heard the news of her husband's arrest from her oldest childhood friend. "Jean, it's impossible!" she exclaimed into the phone. "It can't be true." Jean simply replied, "Turn on the radio. I'm coming right over."[2] Since their evacuation from Shanghai in 1940, amid the widening Sino-Japanese conflict, John Service's wife and their two small children had lived with her parents. When the news of his arrest broke, she had been preparing to join him in Washington, D.C., after nearly five years' separation, to set up house as a family again.

FBI interrogators questioned Service for many hours following his arrest. It was an experience he never forgot. "I kept trying to find out what it was all about," he recalled. "They kept saying, 'We're asking the questions.'"[3] Confident that he had nothing to hide, he explained that providing background information to American journalists was one of his duties and that, since his return, he'd been "much in demand" by both government officials and the media. He was at a loss to explain how copies of some of his China reports had come into the hands of other *Amerasia* suspects, but he freely admitted giving personal copies of some of his recent reports to *Amerasia*'s editor.

More than eight hours after his arrest, John Service signed off on an eight-page typewritten personal statement. The agents noted in their report for the FBI director that Service "might wish to become a witness in the case against other subjects . . . if by so doing it would be to his advantage."[4] The FBI knew such testimony might prove crucial to the prosecution. "Be certain we now bear down on *all* angles of the investigation," J. Edgar Hoover scrawled on the bottom of their report the next morning. "Assign as many agents as necessary."[5]

After straightening his tie and putting on his suit coat and hat, Service was taken for arraignment at 1:30 AM. At the U.S. Commissioner's office, he was astonished to find two casual acquaintances also under arrest: a State Department employee and a lieutenant in the Office of Naval Intelligence. As they waited for the commissioner to arrive, the door suddenly opened and a swarm of press photographers popped flashbulbs in their faces. The FBI had alerted the press.

Because none of the three suspects was able to post the ten-thousand-dollar bail, they were booked at the District of Columbia jail. After being ordered to strip and shower, Service was handed a jail jumpsuit with a large rip in the crotch. "Can't I get another one?" Service asked the guard. He quickly learned it was not just his clothes that had been taken away. "You better take it," the guard advised with a nasty laugh. "It gets pretty cold up there in the cell block."

The next morning, newspapers across the nation carried news of the arrests on their front pages. "FBI Seizes Six as Spies, Two in State Dept.—Secrets Stolen" trumpeted The *New York Times* headline. Later editions included a statement from a top State Department official praising the FBI for "catching the foxes in the chicken coop." "How could one possibly come back from this sort of public degradation?" Service remembered thinking more than fifty years later, as tears filled his eyes. "I was pretty low."[6]

While waiting for family and friends to arrange bail, Service persuaded a guard to give him paper and a pen. "I am innocent of the charges and am confident that I will be cleared," he wrote his widowed mother, "but a trial seems necessary." After more than thirty-five years in China, Grace Service now lived in a California retirement community for missionaries. In 1906 her husband had been sent to Sichuan to establish the first YMCA in that remote region. Thanks to a strong sense of duty and a staunch refusal to "whimper, cry, snivel or complain," Grace had risen above the hardships of pioneer life in China. Her son felt confident she could bear the news of his mistaken arrest. "I am sure the Service escutcheon will remain untarnished," he told her. "So keep your head up and tell the neighbors you don't need their commiserations if they offer them." He signed off, "Very much love and admiration knowing that you will take this crisis as you have taken all the others, Jack."[7]

PART I
CHINA MAN

CHAPTER 2
THE ROAD TO CHUNGKING

John Service was more familiar with China's chaotic landscape than with the power politics of Washington, D.C. When the epic battle to restore his reputation began, he had spent most of his thirty-four years in China. His hometown was Chengdu, a town where little had changed in five hundred years, and where his parents first arrived to establish the YMCA in 1906. Chengdu, the capital of remote Sichuan Province, was a walled city patterned after Peking—with massive gates that were closed every night and an inner city reserved for the highest officials. The dark, narrow streets were crowded with jostling people and animals that scurried out of the way of the sedan chairs of the elite, carried on the shoulders of hired coolies. Each morning human waste was collected in huge ceramic "honey pots" from open, unscreened latrines, to be carried out to the countryside where the "night soil" was carefully ladled onto the fields. The stench mingled with the pungent smell of chili peppers, garlic, and ginger frying in every wok. "All we could do was simply to put ourselves back into the Middle Ages," his mother wrote, "and then settle down to be happy under medieval conditions."[1]

It was a pioneer life that required self-reliance and fortitude. The Services lived in a traditional walled Chinese compound built around two courtyards, with a gateman and several servants who performed the daily chores: fetching well water, keeping fires going, and battling the tropical climate's perennial mold. One retainer served as a human telephone line, carrying notes across town and bringing back the replies. Here Grace Service birthed and raised their sons—Jack, Bob, and Dick—doling out castor oil and deworming them as needed. Ever mindful of the death of her six-month-old baby daughter, Virginia, during their arduous three-month journey to this remote outpost, she worked tirelessly to create a protective shield around her growing family. She rendered soap, ironed her husband's starched collars, and sewed clothes for the children. Grace preserved fruits; pickled a variety of homegrown vegetables; trained the cook to make bread, biscuits, and other American-style food; and forbade the servants to feed her children the treats sold by passing peddlers.

"Peddlers were always plying their trade and we knew all their cries and signals; the barber, scissors sharpener, tinsmith, cloth merchant, and food sellers of many kinds," Jack remembered. "Our cocoon was not impermeable. Just on the other side of the wall was the teeming, crowded life of a Chinese city [where] dogs barked, children cried . . . [and] weddings and funerals passed."[2]

In 1911, when John Service was two years old, China's last imperial dynasty crumbled, and the country descended into even greater disarray. After months of unrest and uncertainty, Chengdu's small colony of foreigners was ordered by the British consul-general to seek safety "down river." Reluctantly, Bob and Grace Service packed up Jack and his new baby brother, Bob, to set out with 140 others for the 900-mile journey to Shanghai. "I looked around and wondered when and how I would see the place again," Grace remembered.[3]

The Services felt a strong duty to keep the YMCA open. Young patriots anxious to modernize China had flocked to the new Y programs around the country. The Chinese president of their local Y sent a big paper lantern inscribed with a large red character, *ren* (people), to be hung at the Service household gate—"a sign known to the revolutionaries as a signal that our place was not to be molested."[4]

This was the first of many evacuations under siege that the family would make during China's turbulent passage into the twentieth century. Their return trip upriver was often even more hazardous. Houseboats and junks were laboriously pulled through the roaring rapids of the Yangtze by hundreds of coolies harnessed together like animals; over the centuries, their ropes wore grooves in the stone walls of the narrow gorges.

But by 1916, when the family returned from their first home leave, there were modern coal-burning steamships equipped with powerful twin engines and four rudders. Even so, each rapid was a battle to be won, as numerous wrecks strewn along the river rocks testified. The steamers took only four or five days—instead of four weeks—to make the trip from Yichang to Chungking, but they were strenuous days filled with drama. "We could hear the captain's urgent shouts for more steam," Jack later recounted. "Sometimes the ships would literally have to pull themselves upstream by putting a cable ashore and using the capstan to gain more power."[5]

Chungking was the last port of call. From here, the family still faced a 10-day, 250-mile overland trek to Chengdu—with the ever-present danger of brigands. The bandits might be local outlaws taking advantage of the breakdown of law and order, or former soldiers from defeated or bankrupt warlord armies. "The hoodlums, if caught, might lose their heads," Jack explained matter-of-factly, as if everyone had childhood memories of seeing the heads of outlaws displayed prominently on poles. "[But] the soldier-bandits had a fair chance of instant redemption by being absorbed into one of the many competing warlord armies."[6]

By the time Jack was ten, he shunned riding in a sedan chair and could walk thirty miles a day on the overland trail. "Father was not given to lavish praise, but I knew he was pleased."[7] As eldest son, Jack was always treated deferentially and called *Lao Da* (literally, "old big") by family servants and his father's Chinese associates. By the time he turned eleven, Lao Da had completed eight grades of schooling, through mail-order lessons taught by his mother. "I realize that I was not only a bookworm," Service later mused. "I also had an exaggerated opinion of my maturity and importance."[8]

Unlike most foreigners, Jack's father had learned to speak the Sichuan dialect, and he cultivated contacts among all the various military and civilian factions. Bob Service was widely respected and a natural organizer. "He was able to make these men feel that he was not partisan, and sought the welfare of all, the peace of the city, and the good of everyone," Grace explained proudly.[9]

A few years after their arrival, Bob established a retreat for Chengdu's missionary families to escape the hot, humid summer's threat of cholera and other diseases. Their mountaintop retreat was fifty miles away and took two days to reach. As soon as the Service boys arrived at the family bungalow, they happily shed the hated pith helmets, exchanged city shoes for straw sandals, and raced around to see who else had arrived before checking out their favorite hiding places. One of Jack's best friends was John Paton Davies, the son of Baptist missionaries, whom he would one day follow into the Foreign Service.

The highlight of the summer season was the annual family camping trip to explore the surrounding ten-thousand-foot mountain ranges. "The trips each summer became longer and more ambitious," Jack recalled. "I truly learned to walk by matching strides with countless load-carrying Chinese coolies."[10] These experiences became an unforgettable part of Service's young life and well prepared him for later adventures as the embassy's self-described "outside man" in China.

In the summer of 1921, as Jack turned twelve, he was allowed to join his father and two of his friends on a "men only" expedition. For years, Bob Service had talked about his dream of trekking across uncharted mountain peaks to the beautiful forests on the eastern edge of the Tibetan plateau, where a Chinese friend owned a logging operation. Now the YMCA had ordered him to take a long vacation before relocating the family to Chungking to establish a new branch. Preparation for the trip took many weeks: Grace Service even made their sleeping bags by sewing wads of silk floss into quilts and sealing them inside oiled cloth covers. In late July, porters were hired and the expedition set off.[11]

The guide hired for the trek claimed to know a secret "smugglers' trail" across the mountains. The shortcut, he insisted, would take only four days. Rain began falling on the second day and continued relentlessly all the next as the group slowly ascended along a streambed that had become a raging mountain torrent. "Very often the overgrowth made it impassable without hacking out a new path . . . or scrambling around or over a cliff," Jack remembered.[12] On the sixth day, they finally reached the top of the first pass—at 15,000 feet, much higher than expected. It was Jack's twelfth birthday, and he was given the honor of stepping across the summit first.

As the party descended, a torrential rain driven by an icy wind made travel impossible. Jack's father supervised the building of a crude shelter, and they spent a miserably cold, wet night, sharing lukewarm tea heated over sterno cans. The next morning, the group lost their trail in a heavy fog. Several days later the icy fog finally lifted, and Bob Service spurred them to move quickly. They had now been on the trail eight days. "Speed was vital. That night's camp had to have fire," Jack explained. "We had to get over the pass and far enough down the other side to reach timberline." At the end of the eighth day, as they finally shared a hot meal around a roaring fire, they learned that two porters had failed to make it into camp. The search party the next day found that the pair had fallen off the trail—one of them dead, the other suffering from hypothermia. Jack's father never forgave himself for the fatal accident. "However badly Father may have felt," Jack later observed, "the rest of us—including the Chinese—knew that if it had not been for his calm, steady leadership the outcome might have been far worse."[13]

Jack left for his second year as a boarding student at the Shanghai American School soon after the Service family moved to Chungking in the fall. Being allowed to travel the river by himself was a major milestone. As the steamship passed through the narrow gorges, bandits fired across the bow. And at Yichang, where the passengers transferred to a new ship, a local warlord launched a surprise nighttime attack on his rivals, imperiling everyone in the harbor. The captain of the new ship herded his passengers into the steel-plated bridge area for protection —but the young boy was somehow forgotten. Awakened by a barrage of bullets,

Jack "decided to simply stay where I was: in bed." The gun battle lasted four hours. The next morning, when young Service appeared for breakfast, there was "a sudden silence" from surprised passengers and crew, embarrassed to see him.[14]

Shanghai in the 1920s was the liveliest outpost of imperialism in Asia. Divided into international and Chinese settlements, each with its own administration, the "Paris of the East" served up an exotic cultural stew of Eastern and Western extravagance and exploitation. Russian showgirls entertained wealthy champagne-sipping Chinese couples; opium dens and brothels flourished under the noses of constables on the take; hapless drunks awakened as "Shanghaied" crewmen on the high seas; and the bodies of the most destitute were carted off the streets early each morning. Shanghai boasted Asia's tallest buildings, its finest hospital, and its best symphony orchestra, thanks mainly to the support of an active Jewish community comprised of refugees from Europe's pogroms and the Bolshevik Revolution. As China's major cultural, banking, and manufacturing center, the city also became a magnet for Chinese revolutionaries intent on ending foreigners' special privileges and exploitation of their countrymen.

Shanghai first became an international port following Britain's victory in the so-called Opium Wars of the 1840s. The emperor was forced to open a number of "treaty ports" to foreign traders, who wanted to sell opium as a way of paying for China's coveted silk, porcelain, and tea. Other foreign demands followed, further encroaching on Chinese sovereignty.

In World War I, the German-held areas of Shandong and Manchuria were seized by the Japanese. At war's end, the Allies' decision permitting Japan to retain these territories triggered a massive patriotic reaction. Outraged citizens, humiliated by China's impotence, staged an unprecedented series of mass demonstrations, strikes, and boycotts of foreign goods, sparking a new national debate on cures for "the sick man of Asia."

This was the exciting and turbulent milieu that John Service first entered at age eleven. Shanghai had electric trolley cars, bicycles, and cement sidewalks—amazing to the boy from upriver. Two years younger than his classmates and accustomed to being treated with respect, Jack had been appalled by the school's hazing rituals. Now, as a returning sophomore, he began to enjoy living in this fascinating city.

His boarding school was located in the British-controlled International Settlement, where trading companies, shipping lines, and banks lined the bustling riverfront. Jack joined the Boy Scouts and loved going on patrol in the city, mapping the maze of alleys in the old Chinese sector and prowling the Shanghai docks. He watched armies of coolie laborers, straining under the heavy cargo loads piled on their backs, moving back and forth to the ships docked at the floating river pontoons. Occasionally he snuck out after curfew to continue his explorations, using a cast iron drain pipe as his "own private exit and entry." Once, when caught and given a stern lecture about the dangers of Shanghai's waterfront, he confessed: "the idea that I was in any personal danger had never occurred to me."[15] Even as an adult, that idea would rarely occur to him.

The young schoolboy had no inkling of the tectonic changes under way in Chinese society. Sun Yat-sen, whose efforts helped topple the decadent Qing Empire in 1911, had failed to unite the country after a decade of struggle. Peking—still recognized as China's official capital—changed hands constantly among local warlords. Sun and his followers set up a rival capital in Canton, which floundered amid general chaos.

Rebuffed by the West, Sun Yat-sen turned to the Soviet Union to finance his revolutionary cause. His Nationalist Party, the Kuomintang (KMT), now joined forces with the newly established Chinese Communist Party (CCP) in a marriage of convenience. Both parties had been outlawed, forced to operate secretly in territory controlled by feudal warlords and privileged foreigners. Soon covert Soviet military aid and advisers began arriving. Both political parties (and their militias) were reorganized on the Russian model, ruled by party committee elites. Josef Stalin instructed the CCP membership to join the Nationalist Party and become "a bloc within" that could eventually take over the revolution and "drop their KMT allies like so many 'squeezed-out lemons.'"[16]

While John Service was still a high school student in Shanghai, Sun's top military aide, Chiang Kai-shek, was sent to Moscow for advanced training. After his return, Chiang established the Whampoa Academy, a modern military training school with Russian funding and instructors. A top Communist named Zhou Enlai became chief of the school's propaganda department. But Chiang secretly recruited many of the new cadets from Shanghai's mafia—associates from his days with the Green Gang—and these gangster recruits later became the backbone of his officer corps.

John Service spent an unhappy senior year in Berkeley, California, during his family's second home leave. At the end of the school year, he happily returned with his family to Shanghai, where his father was now assigned as a regional Y secretary. Young Service got a job working as an apprentice draftsman in the Y's building bureau and dreamed of becoming an architect. Eighteen months later, the seventeen-year-old set off on a six-month journey back to the United States by ship, train, bus—and a used bike that he pedaled a thousand miles through Britain—before entering Oberlin College.

This was also the year that the uneasy alliance between the Nationalist Party and the Chinese Communist Party unraveled completely. After Sun Yat-sen died in 1926, Chiang Kai-shek married the sister of Sun's widow, immediately gaining respectability and legitimacy as his heir apparent. Now the KMT's military campaign against warlords and imperialists finally got under way. As commander-in-chief of the "Northern Expedition," Chiang ordered a two-prong offensive: the alliance's liberal and Communist elements were to seize Wuhan while Chiang's forces moved toward Shanghai. Secretly, however, Chiang allied with the city's underworld bosses and its foreign businessmen, who looked to him for protection from Communist-inspired labor and property reforms. On the night of April 12, 1927, Chiang's troops quietly entered Shanghai. Together with Green Gang gunmen, they tracked down and killed their unsuspecting allies—the members of the Communist underground and their supporters in the labor movement. More than five thousand Communists were slaughtered by Chiang's loyalists.

Chiang's campaign then moved north, and after subduing the Peking warlords, he renamed the imperial city Peiping ("Northern lights") and established Nanjing ("Southern capital") as the Nationalists' new capital. Soon all remaining Communists in the government were purged. KMT forces ruthlessly hunted down the "Communist bandits" and their sympathizers. Sun Yat-sen's veteran Russian advisers escaped to Moscow. The CCP was decimated and its members scattered. Mao Zedong fled to his home province of Hunan, where he began to plot a new revolutionary road to power. The Shanghai massacre—and Chiang's betrayal—would never be forgotten.

In the United States, John Service soon became a big man on the Oberlin campus. He was captain of the track team and a star long-distance runner, winning the all-conference mile event three years in a row. "It's not merely a matter of who's the best runner or the stronger," he later reflected, "but who's got the most determination, resolve, and guts. One guy has to break. If you've got the control and discipline, you'll be the lucky guy that doesn't."[17] And he met his future wife, Caroline Shultz, the daughter of an Army Corps of Engineers colonel, who never forgot their first date. Jack asked her whether she had singed her eyelashes! "I said, 'Why no, what do you mean?' He said, 'Because you have the shortest eyelashes of any girl I've ever seen.' That was a romantic beginning, wasn't it?"[18] Service considered the colonel's daughter "a potent blend of sex, personality, and intellect."[19]

The college sweethearts graduated in 1931, as the Great Depression was deepening. The jobless rate stood at nearly 16 percent and soon would reach

24 percent. It was no time for an unemployed economics graduate to propose marriage. A broken-hearted Caroline headed to Washington, D.C., where her father commanded nearby Fort Humphreys. Service stayed at Oberlin to study art history on a one-year tuition scholarship, with the ambition of becoming a professor.

During the fall semester, the Japanese instigated an incident in Manchuria and quickly took over, setting up the new puppet state of Manchukuo. On January 18, 1932, Japanese marines attacked Chinese districts in Shanghai, killing an estimated 18,000 civilians. The outside world, however, took little notice of angry Chinese demonstrations and the toothless protests of the League of Nations. The city remained under siege for many months.

Jack's parents escaped the crisis. They had already sailed for the United States on home leave. After his school year ended, Service joined his family in California for a reunion—their first in five years. From family friends, young Service learned that his boyhood pal John Davies had embarked on a career as a diplomat in China, and he decided to follow in his footsteps. After two months of preparation, Jack passed the two-day written Foreign Service exam and was ordered to report to the State Department for oral exams in January 1933. He passed easily, only to discover there was a federal hiring freeze and his name would be placed on a waiting list. Disappointed, Service decided to return to Shanghai with his father and apply for a job as a consulate clerk, hoping to earn priority on the Foreign Service list.

But the trip to Washington, D.C., also provided an opportunity to renew his romance with Caroline Shultz. She invited Jack and his visiting parents to a Sunday supper at Fort Humphreys to meet her parents. And a few days later, after Jack had passed his exams, Caroline joined the Services for a celebration dinner in Washington. Returning to their hotel, Jack asked her to marry him, and Caroline happily agreed. Boldly, he suggested they go together to her room. Caroline demurred but was soon persuaded. "It had been quite a day," Jack mused in his memoirs—"passing the oral, becoming engaged, and getting into bed."[20]

In the morning, the couple announced their engagement to his parents. It was decided Caroline would accompany Jack's mother when she returned to China in the fall. By then, Jack assured Caroline, he would be suitably employed. "I used to think I was too self-centered and self-reliant, and wondered how people could say that they couldn't get along alone, but in the last year I've been turned all around," Jack wrote Caroline. "And living without you seems tolerable only to make possible living with you. I'll do my best to make it possible."[21]

In March of 1933 Jack and his father boarded a freighter bound for Shanghai, leaving their women behind. Jack applied for a Foreign Service clerkship at the U.S. consulate. Within six weeks, he was assigned to Yunnanfu (now Kunming), the smallest and most remote of the sixteen American consular offices. A medieval Chinese city much like Chengdu, Yunnanfu had none of the glamour of the international port cities Jack had described to Caroline. It was a dismal prospect, but it paid eighteen hundred dollars a year. He hoped it would be acceptable to his fiancée and her parents.

Caroline's father was dismayed about Yunnanfu and urged her not to accept the proposal. The future Mrs. John Service defiantly announced she was going anyway. She and Jack's mother arrived in Shanghai in September, and there she remained for more than a month. Caroline had intended to travel on to Haiphong, where she and Jack would marry before continuing by train to Yunnanfu. Instead, she had an emergency appendectomy and needed a month of recuperation.

Finally, in late October, Caroline boarded a coastal steamer to Hong Kong, where she spent two days as the guest of the American consul general. After sailing for French Indochina, a typhoon forced her ship to harbor, delaying her yet again. On November 9, 1933, Caroline finally made it to Haiphong, where Jack was waiting nervously, his leave time almost up. Later that same afternoon they were married by the French mayor in his office.

Early the next morning, Mr. and Mrs. John Service caught the train for the daunting three-day ascent to Yunnanfu (elevation six thousand feet). Jack had assured Caroline's parents that her arrival would be "quite an event" in the town's small international community, confidently predicting she would "get to like it." In fact, she hated it. Shanghai had been civilized; Hong Kong had been alluring and exciting. Yunnanfu, however, was remote and squalid. They lived on the outskirts of town, sharing living quarters with the vice consul, an aging bachelor who insisted on being formally addressed even at the breakfast table. There was no running water or electricity, and—apart from a few scattered missionaries—there were no other American women. Social life revolved around the small group of diplomats and other foreigners, who maintained a rigid social pecking order. The bride soon became terribly homesick.

Caroline was overwhelmed by the dirt and the degradation of the Chinese population, many of them addicted to opium (the province's illegal but lucrative cash crop). Its sickly sweet smell was pervasive. Most appalling, Yunnan's capital had no schools and no public health care, and "little girl children were still often let die."[22] After six months, the couple decided she should return to Shanghai to stay with Jack's parents; she confessed she was "glad to go." This was the first of their many long separations—and the only time Caroline was eager to leave.

By the time Caroline returned to Yunnanfu in the autumn, Jack had been promoted to vice consul—although with no raise in pay. Nevertheless, they could move into their own home in the city center where other foreigners were living, and Caroline's life improved. Jack continued to master the basic tools of his trade: coding cables, writing reports, filing dispatches. He would always credit this experience for his later reputation as an effective Foreign Service officer who knew how to get things done in the trenches.

In the spring of 1935 the city was alarmed by rumors of approaching bands of Chinese Communist outlaws. Missionaries seeking refuge in town reported their colleagues being held for ransom. Wealthy landlords told of being robbed and their land being confiscated. But John Service also heard accounts from peasants of being politely treated and even paid for provisions they supplied to the Reds. "It made a tremendous impression," he explained, "because people were not used to being paid for anything that was provided to soldiers."[23] The Communists had been on the run for six months, after Chiang's troops closed in on their mountain camps in southeast China. To survive in the countryside, the Communists learned to rely on the support of the peasants—a revolutionary approach that helped Mao and his followers gain widespread support.

As the city prepared for the worst, Yunnanfu's walls were fortified. The small diplomatic community evacuated its women and children to Haiphong. But the Communists bypassed the city like so many ghosts, to secretly cross the Yangtze River farther to the north. The crisis was over in two weeks, and Caroline returned along with the others.

On July 3, 1935, Virginia Service was born in Yunnanfu and named for her father's sister, who had died in infancy. The baby was barely two months old when Jack was urgently called to Shanghai. His father was dying. Bob Service's whole world had collapsed when he was laid off by the YMCA during the Depression. He had been quickly recruited to run the International Famine Relief Commission's Shanghai office; nevertheless, he believed he must have failed the Y brotherhood in some unfathomable way. As Grace later put it, "The spring of his life had been broken." He died within eighteen months of his discharge.

Shortly after the memorial service, John Service got the news he had been waiting for: the federal hiring freeze was finally over. He was being appointed to the China unit of the U.S. Foreign Service and ordered to report to the embassy in Peking for intensive language training. "Everybody here says that we'll love it up there," he wrote Caroline. "Best place in China. I hope we find it so."[24]

Peking was a refreshing change from Yunnanfu. The Services, warmly welcomed into the tight-knit American diplomatic community, came to know writers, artists, and adventurers living the privileged life of foreigners in the ancient capital. Caroline greatly enjoyed dancing in the rooftop garden of the swank Peking Hotel: "We didn't know it was the end of an era."[25]

Jack's language study was intense: his tutors criticized his "backwoodsy Sichuan dialect." He had to learn the Peking dialect and memorize thousands of Chinese characters. Just to read a newspaper required knowledge of three thousand written characters, but he was training to decipher official Chinese documents and to act as a translator and interpreter at official functions.

Near the old palace complex of China's emperors, the Forbidden City, the Services rented a house with traditional front and interior courtyards and a gated wall surrounding the compound, much like Jack's Chengdu home. In the autumn of 1936 they invited a group to hear American journalist Edgar Snow report on his recent trip to the Communists' base camp in Shaanxi Province. Snow had defied a Nationalist travel ban to become the first Western reporter to interview the "Red bandits." He was eager to share their story, which he turned into his first book, *Red Star over China*. Snow reported that the Communists wanted to join with the Nationalists in a "united front" against the Japanese invaders of their country. Even Snow did not understand that Stalin, fearing a Japanese attack on the Soviet Union's eastern flank, had ordered his propagandists to promote the Chinese "united front" concept. Nevertheless, as Service put it, "There was this possibility, a rather exciting one, that the civil war might end."[26]

A few months after Snow's talk, two Chinese warlords in the Nationalist camp refused to obey orders to attack the Communists and instead kidnapped Chiang Kai-shek himself. Their stated aim was to persuade the Nationalist leader to end the civil war against the Reds and to lead a national fight against the Japanese invaders.

Chiang was in Xian to rally his forces for the next campaign against the Communist "bandits." As he stood in his nightshirt at the window of his hotel suite on the night of December 12, 1936, four army trucks pulled up carrying 120 soldiers who opened fire on his 50 bodyguards. Barefoot, Chiang raced to escape, leaving his false teeth on the bed table. Loyal attendants boosted him over the garden wall. Four hours later a search party discovered the toothless Generalissimo hiding in a shallow cave, cold, exhausted, and in pain from a sprained ankle. His captors took turns carrying him piggyback down the hill.[27]

The humiliated Nationalist leader was driven into the courtyard of the regional military headquarters, now controlled by his mutinous officers, where a military band was waiting to serenade him. The rebel leaders respectfully presented their list of demands: an end to the civil war; a reorganized government that included Communist representatives; and a unified patriotic war effort under Chiang's command. But the coup quickly began to unravel, and the Nationalist defense minister (who headed the government's pro-Japanese faction) prepared to attack Xian.

For ten days in early December 1936, the entire country—and the world—was riveted by the unfolding kidnap drama in Xian. Students staged daily "unity" rallies in major Chinese cities. News of Chiang's capture sparked heated debate among the Communists, with Mao insisting that Chiang should be put on trial for his treachery in the 1927 Shanghai massacre. Instead, the central committee decided to dispatch Zhou Enlai, the urbane, French-educated cadre, to convince the rebel warlords to release the Generalissimo and to push for a patriotic united front war effort.

"Apart from the Generalissimo, there was no one capable of being the leader of the country at this period of [its] existence," Zhou Enlai told Madame Chiang upon his arrival. She agreed that, since "we are all Chinese," their differences must be settled be peacefully—and all patriots should unite under her husband's leadership.[28] Although he had himself barely escaped death in the Shanghai massacre, Zhou joined the negotiations for Chiang's release, urging Chiang (his former colleague at Whampoa Military Academy) to lead the resistance to Japan's occupation. At last Chiang Kai-shek was persuaded to accept the rebels' demands, although their agreement was never put in writing.

"I remember seeing Chinese weep when Chiang was released," Service recalled.[29] The rebel commanders were paid a large undisclosed amount of money by T. V. Soong, the minister of finance, who happened to be Madame Chiang's brother. To guarantee Chiang's safety and to help restore his "face," one rebel warlord agreed to accompany Chiang and his entourage back to Nanjing—where he was promptly put under house arrest.

* * *

On July 7, 1937, seven months after the "Xian incident," fighting broke out between Chinese and Japanese troops at the Marco Polo Bridge, about ten miles from Peking. John Service heard the shooting as he lay in a city hospital suffering from yellow fever. The skirmish signaled the start of a war that would last eight years. "Guns may have been roaring overhead, but we had a feeling of total unreality," Caroline remembered. The embassy ordered all personnel and dependents to crowd into its compound. Then one day the Chinese troops simply disappeared, and the Japanese "came riding into town on these enormous, big horses."[30]

But even as the Japanese forces expanded their control over north China, there was little international protest, and American public opinion remained solidly isolationist.

About a month later, Chiang Kai-shek's troops staged an attack on the Japanese garrison in occupied Shanghai. For the first several days the battle favored the Chinese, but when bombers arrived from Japanese bases on Taiwan, the battle decisively turned against them. Even with hundreds of thousands of casualties, the Chinese forces still held out for two months against hopeless odds. According to *Time* correspondent Theodore "Teddy" White, their courage and sacrifice "kindled a spreading bonfire of patriotic fervor" throughout the country, generating international sympathy for the plight of the heroic Chinese.[31]

As the battle for Shanghai raged, the neutral U.S. government ordered the evacuation of all American dependents from China. Caroline and the children—two-year-old Virginia and five-month-old Bob—sailed across the Pacific to wait out the crisis with her parents in Berkeley, California. It was a voyage across a darkening world. Hitler's Luftwaffe was bombing the antifascist forces in Spain's savage civil war; and Germany and Japan had recently signed their nonaggression pact.

In Peking, the embassy worked around the clock to relay the latest war news to Washington. After long days of studying for his language exams, John Service spent his nights on duty in the code room. Soon the Japanese forces had outflanked the Chinese defenders at Shanghai and pushed south to Nanjing, the Nationalists' capital. In a murderous rampage that lasted six weeks, more than 300,000 civilians were slaughtered, and many thousands of women and girls were repeatedly violated by Japanese soldiers. Foreigners tried to create a sanctuary for Chinese refugees inside their settlements, but the Japanese ignored those extraterritorial boundaries in an orgy of violence that became known as the Rape of Nanjing.[32]

On December 12, 1937—the same day the Nanjing atrocities began—a squadron of Japanese aircraft bombed, strafed, and sank the USS *Panay* as it evacuated American officials and citizens from the city. Sixteen were wounded. The clearly intentional attack was captured on film by a news cameraman on board the sinking American gunboat. When the newsreel reached the United States, it caused widespread outrage. The United States quietly accelerated the build-up of its armed forces "with the thought that *Panay* might indeed be just a prelude to something bigger."[33]

Under Japan's continuing offensive, the besieged government of "Free China" retreated four hundred miles farther up the Yangtze, to Hankou. Thousands of

Chinese refugees from Japanese-occupied territories soon followed. A magical sense of camaraderie pervaded the overcrowded boomtown despite frequent Japanese air raids that presaged the city's doom. The small international press corps wrote glowing stories about the bravery of the Chinese people's defiant resistance, finding sympathetic readers around the world. *Time* magazine even anointed Chiang and his American-educated wife "Man and Wife of the Year 1937." Hankou had become—if only temporarily—a beacon of hope in the struggle against Fascism. And a mythology about Free China began to grow, fed by Chiang's loyalists and his American admirers.

But only the Union of Soviet Socialist Republics (USSR) offered any material aid to Chiang's beleaguered government. Stalin even sent Russian pilots and planes. Madame Chiang hired Claire Chennault, a retired American pilot known for his unorthodox dog-fighting maneuvers, to train Chinese pilots and to help lobby Washington for more aircraft.

As the Sino-Japanese war escalated, the U.S. embassy's military attaché, Col. Joe Stilwell, began traveling to forward positions to observe Japanese tactics and strategy. He visited Communist units (now operating under Chiang's authority) and was impressed with their fighting ability despite the lack of modern weaponry. Meanwhile, John Davies, posted in Hankou, actively sought out contacts with Zhou Enlai and other Communists who now held positions in Free China's newly reorganized government. For the first—and only—time in the twentieth century, there was a real sense of unity and common purpose among China's rival political forces.[34]

By the time Caroline and the two children rejoined Jack six months after their evacuation, he had passed his final language exams and was assigned to the consulate in Japanese-occupied Shanghai. Already one of the United States' largest and busiest diplomatic posts, the Shanghai consulate's workload increased dramatically after Britain and France declared war against Hitler, in September 1939. As the consulate's "utility outfielder," Jack rotated through every department, substituting for diplomats on home leave; at this critical moment he was in charge of the overworked visa section. Desperate European refugees, including many Jews, were flocking to Shanghai—one of the few places in the world accepting stateless persons—and swamping the consulate with thousands of visa requests.

Hitler's blitzkrieg continued to roll across Denmark, Norway, the Netherlands, and Belgium and was poised to capture Paris that spring. The United States' consulate in Shanghai now had a staggering 2,700 visa cases on its waiting list, even after Jack reorganized the system to triple the rate of visas issued. It was a frustrating and wrenching experience: applicants begged, pleaded, and tried to bribe their way to the United States. "This business of having to decide is this poor man going to be able to make a living in the States. . . . We tried to apply the law as leniently as we could, as we felt that we could get away with," he later explained, with tears in his eyes, "at least as long as I was running the visa special unit."[35]

Inevitably, Hankou fell to the Japanese war machine. China's east and northeastern regions were now occupied by the invaders, who controlled the major industrial centers, rail lines, and ports. Still, Free China refused to surrender. The government and thousands of refugees once again retreated farther up the Yangtze. Their destination was Chungking, well above the river's seemingly impregnable gorges. And once again, the U.S. government ordered American women and children out of harm's way.

Service was assigned to help supervise the evacuation from the same Shanghai waterfront he had first known as a boy. He secured passage for Caroline and their children, his widowed mother, and his sister-in-law on the SS *Monterey* in November 1940. "It is hard on all the husbands too, but I think they're all secretly hoping there'll be some excitement," Caroline wrote a friend. "For Jack's sake, I hope he will be in an interesting spot if anything happens."[36] John Service would soon embark on the most important and dangerous adventure of his life.

CHAPTER 3
CHINA ODYSSEY

As soon as his family had been safely evacuated, John Service volunteered for hazardous duty at the U.S. embassy in Chungking. Just getting to the besieged city proved a challenge: Japanese forces controlled the main railroads and the major ports on the Yangtze, as well as most of eastern China. From occupied Shanghai, Service took an armed coastal steamer to Hong Kong and then flew seven hundred miles at night, over enemy territory, to reach the wartime capital high on the cliffs between the Yangtze and Jialing rivers.

The airstrip, on a tiny sandbar island in the Yangtze, was useable only in low water season. "The pilot flipped us over the hills so close we seemed to shave the trees, circled out over the city and set us down neatly in what I'm sure was the steepest landing I've ever made," Jack reported in his first letter home, in May 1941. A U.S. Navy motorboat ferried him to the American Embassy, across the river from the old walled city. "We hadn't been at the office long this morning when the first alarm for an air raid went off. Everybody seems to take it calmly enough around here . . . nobody does anything till the second alarm. Then they gather up their work, put it in the safe and 'stand by.'"[1]

Ever since the Nationalists' retreat to Chungking in late 1938, Japanese bombers attacked the city relentlessly. An ingenious air raid warning system had been developed: A network of spies in enemy territory watched for bomber squadrons and radioed city civil defense towers to hoist warning signals as the bombers approached. An air raid siren then alerted residents to take cover in caves in the surrounding hillsides.

Jack watched the stream of people disappearing into the tunnels across the river. There was a "waiting, expectant silence," followed by "the low, menacing hum" of approaching bombers. Antiaircraft artillery fired, "seemingly from all around us, spotting the sky with white puffs," but there were no Chinese airplanes to challenge the attackers. The falling bombs made "an indescribable whistling sound" as they floated down on the city. A piece of shrapnel fell right on the embassy grounds—and when Service unthinkingly picked it up, he burned his hand.

"It's almost impossible to concentrate or get anything done," he wrote his family weeks later, after experiencing hours in one of the shelter tunnels. "On fine mornings, even before the alarms start, you find yourself looking out the window to look for the signal and wondering when they'll come."[2]

At the all-clear signal, the people of Chungking would reemerge from the dank air-raid caves to begin again the task of rebuilding their smoldering city. The residents, swollen by half a million war refugees, patiently lined up for the meager daily ration of water. People tried to live normal lives despite the raids and the punishing weather—hot and sticky in summer and cold, damp, and foggy in winter. Malaria, cholera, and dysentery were common, and rats grew bigger than alley cats. Still the residents refused to quit. But by 1941, the war conditions were taking a toll: Chungking's cost of living had jumped 1,000 percent. The war-weary city was "absolutely isolated and barricaded and beleaguered."[3]

John Service arrived in Chungking just as the embassy staff (including the veteran ambassador) was being reassigned. The round of farewell events offered him the opportunity to meet many important people, including Chiang Kai-shek and his wife, Soong May-ling. "Service—what a lovely name," cooed the Wellesley-educated Madame Chiang. "We hope you'll be of service to China."[4]

Service was also introduced to Zhou Enlai, the top Chinese Communist representative in the capital. Relations between the Nationalists and Communists were going steadily downhill, and any hope of a serious united front against the Japanese had evaporated. The Communists in 1940 had launched a daring offensive behind enemy lines simultaneously in five provinces, to widespread public approval. Now, fearing their growing strength, Chiang had excluded them from both the government and the war planning council. Nevertheless, both sides continued to maintain the rhetoric of a united front effort for their own political purposes, and the Communists were allowed to maintain offices in Chungking and publish a closely censored newspaper.

A recent incident had destroyed any prospect of further cooperation against the Japanese. Chiang Kai-shek had ordered the Communists' army to relocate north of the Yangtze in January 1941. One large contingent—including headquarters staff, the wounded, and women—failed to cross the river by the December deadline. Nationalist troops promptly surrounded the Communist units and wiped them out, killing thousands and capturing thousands more. Protests against the barbaric treatment of these captives were ignored. The shocking "New Fourth Army incident" threatened to set off a new round of civil war, and the Generalissimo assigned his best-equipped and most loyal troops to blockade the borders of Communist-held territories.

Service began to extend his growing network of contacts by reviving his family's connections in the region. He began to hear of growing disillusionment among young government officials, students, teachers, and progressives in response to the increasingly rigid Nationalist Party rule. He heard reports of widespread domestic spying that made it dangerous to criticize government policies. Outspoken college professors had begun to disappear overnight. Journalist Annalee Jacoby spoke of hearing the screams of tortured inmates emanating from the regime's prison downtown and described her horror when a local United Press messenger showed up at the press compound "with his tongue torn out, cigarette burns festering over all visible skin, and his mind gone."[5]

Americans, however, were still protected from the grim events taking place in Asia and Europe. In mid-1941, the U.S. Army ranked eighteenth in the world—and its 500,000 soldiers were no match for Hitler's nearly 7 million storm troopers. The United States was still focused on peacetime concerns, captivated by Yankee slugger Joe DiMaggio's fifty-six-game hitting streak and by the big band sound of Glenn Miller. But after Germany bombed the British Parliament and invaded the Soviet Union (despite their nonaggression pact), President Roosevelt secretly speeded up the nation's rearmament program.

In July, the Imperial Japanese Army launched a murderous rampage through occupied north China known as the "Three-All" campaign ("burn all, kill all, loot all"). Nearly 20 million civilians were killed. Japanese troops occupied French Indochina and began to threaten British colonies in Southeast Asia. In response, the United States froze Japanese assets, forbade (at last) the sale of strategic products to Japan, and demanded that Japanese troops withdraw from China.

Despite its official neutrality, the United States quietly began serious talks with Britain about the worsening warfronts. In early August, President Roosevelt set sail on his yacht for a highly publicized fishing vacation—and was secretly transferred to the USS *Augusta* that night for a rendezvous with Winston Churchill in Newfoundland. To conceal the president's whereabouts—especially from patrolling German submarines—a Secret Service agent outfitted with fedora and cigarette holder played decoy host for the presidential fishing party.

The two leaders hit it off immediately. Although Roosevelt was not yet prepared to declare war, Churchill was relieved to learn that Roosevelt, too, considered the defeat of Germany their top priority; war with Japan, the president felt, was "the wrong war in the wrong ocean at the wrong time."[6] Roosevelt agreed to send Navy escorts to protect British shipping in the North Atlantic. Their meeting concluded with the signing of the "Atlantic Charter," which disavowed any territorial ambitions and set out lofty postwar goals, including the right of all captive people to choose their own form of government and the establishment of a new international security system.

The United States was not yet prepared to go to war, but FDR was determined to keep both China and Russia in the fight. He decided to extend Lend-Lease—the ingenious aid plan devised for supplying the beleaguered British—to both countries. Highest priority was given to Soviet needs, in keeping with the United States' "Europe First" strategy (which deeply offended Chiang). But Roosevelt finally approved the secret transfer of American aircraft to China, and he allowed one hundred U.S. Army pilots to resign from active duty to "volunteer" for Claire Chennault's new Chinese air force, which would become famous as the "Flying Tigers." Their salaries would be secretly paid by the American government in a clandestine act of belligerency against Japan.

After his first meeting with Lauchlin Currie, the newly designated head of Lend-Lease for China, T. V. Soong cabled Chiang, "He is fully alive to necessity of expediting decision on aircraft, particularly on bombers, in view of the general situation and the continuous bombing of Chungking."[7] Currie helped Soong (Madame Chiang's Harvard-educated brother) to set up the China Defense Supply Company as the authorized conduit for U.S. supplies. Another veteran New Dealer, attorney Thomas "Tommy the Cork" Corcoran, served as the company's general counsel—and Roosevelt's own uncle was appointed its president.

As Roosevelt's point man on China policy, Currie had returned from a fact-finding mission with an unusual recommendation for the president: "Go out of your way to say nice things about China and to speak of her in the same terms now used toward England" to encourage Chiang "to choose democracy over a dictatorship." Currie also recommended sending a special adviser to assist Chiang. "My own experience has led me to believe that an American liberal adviser, backed by his government and able to deliver or withhold dollars and technicians . . . might be able to exert enormous influence in instituting thoroughgoing political and economic reforms."[8] This dubious assignment was accepted by Owen Lattimore, a respected Asian scholar who joined Chiang's personal staff in Chungking and kept Currie informed of developments in China.

By the time Lattimore arrived, the new team was in place at the U.S. Embassy. The new ambassador was Clarence Gauss, Service's former boss at the U.S.

Consulate in Shanghai. Gauss was a no-nonsense, cigar-smoking, three-decade veteran of China's international treaty ports, who spoke no Chinese and had few personal connections in Washington. His new deputy chief of mission, John Carter Vincent, was a polished China specialist; he had spent the previous three years at the State Department combating the pro-Japan faction and warning that Japan's aggressive militarism would not stop with China. Now, in the summer of 1941, Vincent's views were gaining traction with his good friend, Laughlin Currie, and his assignment to Chungking signaled that American support was finally on the way.

The embassy was composed of five career diplomats and four clerks. Vincent and Service were its Chinese language specialists, but only Service was completely fluent. On his own initiative he prepared a daily digest of Chinese editorial opinions that was eagerly read by Gauss and his colleagues. Soon the thirty-two-year-old junior diplomat became indispensable. As the ambassador's translator at official functions, he typed up meticulous meeting reports from memory while performing the routine office work of a junior staffer and managing the residence he shared with Gauss and Vincent. Although the ambassador could be dour and "touchy," he developed an almost paternal interest in this bright young officer.

By September, U.S. and Japanese negotiators were meeting in Washington. The Japanese strongly objected to the United States' new economic embargo and its assistance to China. The U.S. continued to demand the removal of Japanese troops from the Chinese mainland. Chiang Kai-shek feared the United States might buy peace for itself by "tacitly encouraging the Japanese 'to make a little war on us because we are able to stand such a lot.'"[9] Ambassador Gauss could provide little reassurance. For security reasons, he was not kept informed by Washington. He had no idea that Operation Magic had cracked Japan's diplomatic code. He could only bear the brunt of Chiang's frustration and warn Washington that "China's resistance to Japan must not be taken for granted."[10]

On December 7, 1941, Japan's sneak attack on Pearl Harbor transformed the geopolitical landscape. "I never wanted to have to fight this war on two fronts. We haven't got the Navy to fight in both," Roosevelt confided to his wife. "We will have to build up the Navy and the Air Force and that will mean that we will have to take a good many defeats before we can have a victory."[11] The following day, Roosevelt declared war on Japan.

In Chungking, there was jubilation. "The Chinese were beside themselves with excitement and pleasure," Service later recounted. "To them this meant assurance of victory. . . . They sat back after that and didn't do much."[12] In the Communist stronghold of Yenan, Mao strongly urged all Chinese to cooperate with American and British forces in defeating Japan. Hoping to obtain American aid for his guerrillas, he no longer denounced the "imperialists' war."

Churchill urgently telephoned Roosevelt for reassurance that the war in Europe remained his top priority. "To have the United States at our side was to me the greatest joy," Churchill later wrote. "Britain would live . . . the Empire would live."[13] And when Japan's allies, Germany and Italy, declared war on the United States on December 11, the news was received with great relief in Moscow. Stalin quickly dispatched his ambassador in Washington to request expedited Lend-Lease supplies for Soviet troops to support their courageous resistance in the brutal siege of Leningrad—but he resisted any suggestion that Russia declare war against Japan.

The United States' entry into the war affected every aspect of the Chungking embassy's operation. To handle the increased communications with Washington, 12,000 miles away, the cable room was now staffed around the clock; Service volunteered for the first graveyard shift. When he learned that the ambassador had purchased a new automobile in Rangoon—a key target of advancing Japanese forces—Service eagerly volunteered to retrieve it before the expected invasion.

Arriving in Rangoon on Christmas Day, Service and his assistant found the city almost deserted. There were plenty of rooms available at the best hotel in town. "We were just unpacking when the air raid alarm went off," Jack later recalled, "so we went downstairs and found the air raid shelter was a ballroom . . . with mattresses up against the windows."[14] On New Year's Day 1942, they set out again to take the new car back to Chungking over the treacherous Burma Road, the only overland route into China. Before departing, Service had scoured the city to purchase extra gas, spare tires, and motor parts—and to buy out the tobacco store's entire stock of three thousand cigars for Ambassador Gauss, who smoked a dozen a day.

The Burma Road zigzagged through mountainous jungle terrain and across rickety canyon bridges, climbing to elevations of eight thousand feet before passing through China's "back door" into Yunnan Province. Built by local tribesmen who had never seen a proper road, its unbanked hairpin turns were made more daunting by the necessity of dodging straggling bands of refugees and the wrecked supply lorries hidden behind every curve. "The Chinese themselves officially would overload the truck," Service explained, "but then the driver would take extra illicit cargo and a lot of illicit passengers called 'yellow fish.'"[15] The inexperienced cargo drivers often coasted downhill to save gasoline. Some lost their loads—and their lives—tumbling down steep ravines. Service managed to complete the harrowing journey to Chungking in three weeks. Although delighted with his new car and cigars, Ambassador Gauss said only, "You'll look better when you get that beard off."[16]

By the time Service returned, Japan had run up a series of shocking victories. Hong Kong had fallen, followed by a string of South Pacific islands, most of the Philippines, and the Dutch East Indies. Japanese troops were rapidly moving down the Malayan Peninsula through jungle once thought impenetrable to threaten Singapore, a key colonial trading center and a base of the British navy.

Over the glum Christmas holidays of 1941, Britain's prime minister and America's president held their second round of face-to-face meetings. For nearly three weeks, Churchill stayed at the White House as an honored guest who required special attention. "I must have a tumbler of sherry in my room before breakfast, a couple glasses of scotch and soda before lunch," Churchill announced to the president's butler, "and French champagne and ninety-year-old brandy before I go to sleep at night."[17] In late-night sessions over cigars and cognac—with the assistance of Harry Hopkins, the president's indispensable aide—the two leaders hammered out agreements on a joint global strategy for conduct of the war. Unconditional surrender of *all* the Axis powers was the ultimate goal—but Hitler would be defeated first. China must be kept in the war, but the prime minister made it plain that he did not expect much. "I told the President how much I felt American opinion overestimated the contribution which China could make to the general war," Churchill later wrote. "I said I would of course always be helpful and polite to the Chinese, whom I admired and liked as a race and pitied for their endless misgovernment, but that he must not expect me to adopt what I felt was a wholly unreal standard of values."[18] The two leaders and their military staffs agreed to set up an Anglo-American Combined Chiefs of Staff as well as a Combined Munitions Board in Washington, but they never would reach agreement on a joint strategy for the war in the Pacific. Their Chinese and Russian allies were excluded from these new central command councils, feeding Stalin's and Chiang's fears.

On New Year's Eve Roosevelt sent a coded message of reassurance to the Chinese leader, inviting him to exercise "supreme command over all the forces of the united powers" in the Chinese war zone—knowing, however, that no major allied campaigns were planned there and no sizable contingents of GIs were to be sent.[19] The Generalissimo quickly agreed and asked FDR to send an American to serve as his chief of staff in the new allied command. Accordingly, the United States' top officer for the newly designated China-Burma-India (CBI) Theatre, Maj. Gen. Joseph W. Stilwell, was now also assigned to Chiang's staff. Stilwell had first visited China in 1911 when the Manchu dynasty toppled. He had served as a 15th Army Infantry officer in Tientsin alongside his friend, Gen. George Marshall, during Chiang's rise to power in the 1920s; in the mid-1930s he served as the embassy's military attaché while John Service was there.

Standing only five feet nine inches, "Vinegar Joe" Stilwell was acerbic, blunt, and impatient with fools. He was one of the few Western military attachés who braved frontline hardships to observe the Sino-Japanese war. He had witnessed the fighting prowess of Communist guerrilla units and the venality of some Nationalist warlord generals who starved their conscripted peasant soldiers and sold their supplies on the black market. His experiences had convinced him that, with American help, Chinese soldiers—properly fed, equipped, and led—could fight effectively.

Unlike the American officer, the Generalissimo rarely visited the war fronts. For information he relied on a coterie of loyalists who, in Stilwell's view, "gave him a distorted view of everything." After the first meeting of these two stubborn, strong-willed men, Stilwell reported to Washington that Chiang's top priority would be maintaining control over his best troops and their supplies to prevent rivals from threatening his position as supreme leader.[20]

Without major U.S. divisions of his own, Stilwell needed to persuade Chiang to allow him to turn the Nationalists' poorly-trained and ill-fed forces into a modern army capable of beating their formidable foe—and he needed to convince the British to fight alongside them. It was a daunting challenge. If China were to capitulate, Stilwell understood, the million Japanese troops now stationed in China could be redeployed elsewhere. His major objective, therefore, was to keep the Chinese in the war—and that meant protecting the overland supply line from Burmese ports into China. Burma was thus the linchpin of American strategy.

At their first official meeting, General Stilwell found Chiang Kai-shek and his military staff "courteous, friendly, and plan-less." He recommended a strong counteroffensive against the Japanese in Burma—and quickly discovered that "relations between the British, the Indian Government, the Chinese, and the Burmese were of such a nature that fighting the Japs was a very minor secondary operation."[21] Nevertheless, Stilwell flew to Burma, determined to rally the Chinese and British troops to make a stand against the advancing Japanese. But the allies continued to bicker and delay, and they soon were overrun and forced to retreat.

Stilwell refused to be airlifted out of the debacle. Instead, he personally led a group of demoralized survivors on a brutal three-week escape through the

Burmese jungle highlands into India. When food became scarce, the tough sixty-one-year old general ordered half-rations for all—and he himself always stood last in the chow line. "By the time we get out of here," he promised, "many of you will hate my guts."[22] The entire group survived, but for Stilwell, the bitter defeat was unacceptable. "We got run out of Burma and it's humiliating as hell," he told a New Delhi press conference. "I think we ought to find out what caused it, go back and retake it."[23] Vinegar Joe's straight talk made him an instant hero to an American public in desperate need of one.

In early 1942 the news from the Pacific warfronts was grim. In the Philippines, 76,000 American troops and their Filipino comrades trapped on the Bataan peninsula were finally forced to surrender. Singapore fell. The British fleet was lost in the Battle of the Java Sea, which Churchill called "the worst disaster and largest capitulation in British history." And after the Japanese juggernaut cut off the Burma Road, China was completely isolated. A perilous airlift over the towering Himalayas was begun, connecting supply depots in India with airstrips in China—but flying "The Hump" would claim many lives and aircraft. Cargo that made it safely to Chinese bases often wound up in the thriving black market run by profiteering Chinese military officers and government officials. Such corrupt activities fueled resentment among their American allies throughout the war.

In Chungking, an official shroud of censorship and secrecy made it difficult for the embassy to provide Washington with an accurate picture of what was happening in China. Travel for most foreigners was severely restricted, requiring advance approvals from a maze of government bureaucracies and risky passage through checkpoints controlled by rival warlords. Most foreigners simply relied upon official briefings by official Chinese handlers who ingratiated themselves by hosting lavish banquets that belied the worsening conditions of everyday life. Censorship ensured that official reports carried only stories of self-sacrifice and battlefield bravery, and none of worsening corruption, war profiteering, and repression.

One of the few foreigners able to puncture the government's protective wrapping was John Service. "He associated with everybody and anybody in Chungking that could give him information, and he pieced together this puzzle that we had constantly before us as to what was going on in China, and he did a magnificent job at it," Ambassador Gauss later remarked.[24] An ever-expanding network of official and unofficial contacts—and his exceptional language skills—soon provided Service with unusual opportunities to travel outside Chungking's medieval walls.

When a missionary friend of his parents recommended Service to the public works commissioner, he was invited to join a tour of Sichuan's irrigation projects. He accompanied American Lend-Lease officials on an inspection tour of the small munitions and weapons factories hidden in the foothills. In early July, China's minister of economics requested Ambassador Gauss to send Service with a delegation to inspect a top secret oilfield in China's remote northwest that was in need of a prefabricated refinery from the United States. "The ambassador, always touchy, thought it a little odd that Dr. Weng should be choosing the embassy representative," Service recalled, "but he conceded that the trip was important and that I was probably the logical man to go. I was delighted."[25]

The delegation, including its lone foreigner, set off on a thousand-mile journey in a small bus that ran on vegetable oil and often needed to be pushed uphill. Neither Service nor the other passengers—ten engineers and three journalists—had ever seen this territory, where much of China's fabled history had unfolded. "There was almost continual discussion relating to towns or sites we were passing," Service remembered. These lively, modern young Chinese insisted that he call them by their first names or even nicknames. "For the first time, I was being completely accepted as a friend by Chinese on a very intimate basis."[26] The group ate savory dumplings and street food, slept in flea-infested inns, and bathed at public bathhouses—"all the things strictly forbidden to me in childhood."[27]

In Lanzhou, the group transferred to a cargo truck for the final 450 miles to the remote oilfield. The dirt track, which once had carried Silk Road camel caravans, was pockmarked by hazardous washouts and mudslides. Within a few days, their driver refused to drive any further. To everyone's relief and surprise, Service volunteered to take the wheel of the ten-speed truck. The American gained "plenty of 'face'" with his traveling companions for saving their trip.

On the night of their arrival at the oilfield headquarters, Service once again came to their rescue. Sparks from a worker's campfire had ignited a stream of oil that flowed down a ditch toward their quarters. Awakened by the commotion, Service ran outside to see a flaming river headed right in his direction. Quickly he roused his sleeping companions and grabbed his own bedroll. "The last ones out of the building had to run between flames on the oily water," he remembered. They all survived, but their quarters were completely destroyed.[28]

The inspection tour of the oilfield continued without further mishap, but the results were disappointing. Service's report concluded that merely transporting the oil from this remote region to where it was needed would consume most of the oil the small field might produce. His detailed analysis of the operations was later assessed in Washington as "exceedingly thorough and comprehensive" and "all the more commendable since it was not written by an oil technician."[29] The United States decided not to airlift a refinery.

During the eight-week trip Service earned the respect and trust of his traveling companions, and he discovered the depth of their disenchantment with the increasingly repressive Nationalist regime and their fears for the future. All assumed that the United States would easily defeat Japan—and that Chiang Kai-shek would then renew his civil war against the Communists.

Very little was known about the Communists, isolated behind enemy lines, although they had gained respect for their resistance to Japan's occupation. "Nobody had thought of them as being . . . a competitor for power with Chiang," Service explained. When Americans looked beyond the defeat of Japan, most simply took it for granted that Chiang Kai-shek's government would assume control over a liberated and unified China. "This idea that the Communists might be important enough to contest that power, to be cause of a civil war, was new and somehow rather surprising."[30]

As a result of these candid conversations, another Chinese puzzle piece suddenly fell into place for the diplomat. Chiang's reluctance to embrace General Stilwell's plan for a strong counteroffensive might reflect his desire to preserve his troops—and stockpile American arms and equipment—for a renewed battle against the Communists. Until American observers could reach Communist-controlled areas to assess their capabilities, the China puzzle would never be fully understood. "I felt that I had a special kind of linkage and insight," Service later observed. "Was this a seed of hubris? Possibly."[31]

When the delegation headed back to Chungking, Service decided to take a public bus to visit Xian instead. This was the main Nationalist garrison base at the border with Communist territory. As always, Jack made a point of visiting the local missionaries and YMCA representatives at towns along the way. "These people knew from their own church members a lot of what went on, bribes, entertainment, efforts made to get your land classified in lower [tax] categories . . . and conscription."[32] On the road he saw lines of emaciated conscripts chained together. American-made jeeps, ostensibly donated to the war effort, were being used to chauffeur the families of high-ranking officers. One missionary mentioned that local stores routinely sold products pilfered from donated American supplies. When Service went to investigate, the pharmacist proudly showed off bottles of quinine colored a distinctive green, which Service recognized as donated by the American Red Cross. At a tailor's shop he saw donated "Roosevelt cloth," dyed and sold as fabric for expensive suits.

Typically, foreign travelers stayed at official hostels and were immediately reported to the local police, but Service confounded police surveillance by residing at local missionary compounds. (The Catholic missions, he noticed, always seemed to have the best homemade wine.) In Xian, his hosts eagerly briefed him about deteriorating local conditions, including "secret police activity against students, political repression, and thought reform camps."[33] They also talked of a terrible famine in neighboring Honan Province, where a persistent drought was exacerbated by the undisciplined behavior of the Nationalist troops.

Determined to investigate, Service took the hazardous night train—braving Japanese artillery—to Honan's capital, Loyang, where the railroad station was jammed with frantic refugees hoping to flee westward to Xian. The city itself was filled with "wan, half-starved, begging peasants" from around the province, now bordered by Japanese occupation zones on three sides.

Bishop Thomas Megan, an American Catholic, offered him food and shelter because he was the first American official to enter the city since the war started in 1937. Megan painted a grim picture of desperate conditions in the countryside. Thousands of starving peasants had been seized as laborers, carrying supplies for the Nationalist army and digging its expanding network of trenches for little or no pay. The network of Chinese parish priests provided intelligence on everything—from the current price of young girls sold by starving peasants, to the cost of bribes paid to military officers to protect draft-age sons from certain death, to the lucrative drug-smuggling rings and black market deals being made across enemy lines.[34]

Discontent was deepening among tenant farmers over the draconian grain taxes, enforced despite the drought. Relief workers told Service that army officers would inflate their troop numbers to collect extra grain, which was then sold on the black market—or to the Japanese across the border—at exorbitant prices. Angry peasants were ambushing soldiers and battling them with pitchforks. "There would be hunger, but no real famine, if it were not for the war and its background in Honan of brutal and oppressive treatment of the farmers by their own government and army," Service reported to the embassy. "Some [relief workers] went so far as to call this 'a man-made famine.'"[35]

Service had been away from Chungking for three and a half months when a peremptory cable from the ambassador ordered him to return immediately. Gauss was furious about his "unnecessarily protracted absence"—until he received an urgent State Department request for information about the rumored famine in Honan. The ambassador cabled back that an embassy officer had just returned from the afflicted area and would file a report forthwith.

Service's official report about the Honan famine vividly recounted the tragic dimensions of the suffering: "One hears many reports of districts where the inhabitants are eating grass, bark and roots, and the relief workers are seeing corpses of starved refugees along the roads." He reported that an estimated 10 million people would ultimately be affected by the famine, with the greatest suffering expected in early 1943, before the next wheat harvest. Service bluntly criticized the Nationalist government's taxation policy and its belated and meager efforts to deal with the crisis. "That there would be a serious grain shortage was known to the blindest government official in the early spring, after the failure of the wheat crop." His report also assessed the deeper consequences of the famine on neighboring provinces: panic hoarding, rising prices, and a mounting influx of starving refugees. The "man-made famine" was causing the wholesale slaughter of animals and the destruction of good farmland by erosion, threatening the future viability of the entire region. But the most serious effects, Service concluded, would be "the changes in the attitudes and state of mind of the people . . . the atmosphere of longing for peace and of dislike of the government and army which are supposed to protect them."[36] His firsthand investigation left the diplomat deeply disturbed with "the way that conditions in Kuomintang [Nationalist] China were going downhill."[37]

With Ambassador Gauss's permission, John Service showed his confidential Honan report to a few trusted foreign correspondents in Chungking on a "background only" basis. "The press and I were not rivals," he later explained, "but rather allies in trying to learn the truth of what was going on or likely to happen."[38] His journalist friend Teddy White soon afterward traveled to the famine area to report on the humanitarian disaster. "Nothing in my notes can transmit the horror of the entire province," White wrote, ". . . or the sense of doom created by countless miles strewn with unburied bodies, or the haunted look in the peasants' eyes sunk deep from hunger." Despite heavy Chinese censorship, his *Time* article greatly shocked the American public when it hit the newsstands in March 1943. The full, uncensored version of his story was quietly sent in the embassy's diplomatic pouch to Lauchlin Currie at the White House.

CHAPTER 4
CHINA ROMANCE

Stilwell's campaign to reopen the Burma Road was again delayed. A confidential cable from George Marshall, the Army chief of staff, informed him that the long-promised delivery of supplies and equipment was being diverted to other war zones. "Peanut [Chiang Kai-shek] and I are on a raft, with one sandwich between us, and the rescue ship is heading away from the scene," Stilwell lamented in a letter to his wife.[1] His predicament was made all the more frustrating by the lack of cooperation from his Chinese allies. Nevertheless, the general continued to prepare for the counteroffensive. He established a training camp in India for the token forces Chiang had finally assigned to the effort, and he started building a road from India into unoccupied northern Burma.

Stilwell's Chungking staff was left to deal with the swarm of new U.S. wartime agencies, eager to set up shop in China in the wake of Pearl Harbor. One of these was the Office of Strategic Services (OSS), a newly formed espionage agency headed in Washington by "Wild Bill" Donovan with wide authority and unlimited funding from the White House. Another new arrival was Milton "Mary" Miles, a short, stocky Navy officer assigned to establish weather stations and to recruit coast watchers for anticipated U.S. naval operations. Unfamiliar with China's complex political landscape, Miles and the OSS representative soon allied themselves with Gen. Tai Li, the notorious chief of Chiang's secret police, whom Stilwell's staff called "China's Himmler."

Tai Li flew the newcomers to a secret meeting with an astonishing array of his special agents, saboteurs, and propagandists from throughout the Far East. Suddenly a squadron of Japanese bombers swooped down on their conclave, sending everyone diving for cover. "Here I was, sitting out a bombing attack in a rice paddy with the country's most inaccessible general," Miles later mused, ". . . and he was actually offering a most unexpected kind of partnership in a 50-thousand man army."[2] General Stilwell gave his consent to the unusual partnership, and in the fall of 1942 Miles was designated the combined Navy-OSS commander in China—an alliance that would have large consequences for U.S.–China relations and for John Service's fate.

In exchange for American training, arms, and supplies, including modern radio and cryptographic gear, Tai Li promised to share intelligence reports and gather weather information for the U.S. Navy and the OSS.[3] This venture quickly evolved into something more ambitious—the Sino-American Special Technical Cooperation Organization (SACO) headed by Tai Li with Miles as deputy director and funded by the OSS with secret approval by the president and his military staff. The OSS set up generous bank accounts for Miles' expenses in China and India. The program soon began to commandeer precious cargo space on Hump aircraft, delivering tons of plastic explosives, a hundred thousand assassination pistols, demolition equipment, and a radio broadcasting station, as well as paramilitary trainers and FBI interrogators. Naively, Miles agreed to Tai Li's stipulations: none of the American advisers could speak Chinese, and no independent American intelligence operations could be carried out without Tai Li's express consent. Bill Donovan, the OSS's Machiavellian director, agreed. However, he always intended to launch independent espionage activities in due course—counting on Roosevelt, who "handled secrecy as great sport," to back him up.[4]

President Roosevelt maintained his own confidential information channels within the various war zones. After Lauchlin Currie's second fact-finding visit to China for the president in August 1942, he urged Roosevelt to replace both General Stilwell and Ambassador Gauss: both were unpopular with the mercurial Generalissimo, who had become "a prisoner of the cliques and factions that surround him." Roosevelt became convinced that the China problem could be solved if they could just find "the right people" to "bridge the gaps on both sides."[5]

Finding the right people proved no easy task. General Marshall told Currie there was no "suitable successor" to Stilwell; to replace Gauss, Currie proposed himself. Roosevelt accepted his offer, but the Chinese raised objections when they learned of the plan. It would be two more years before FDR replaced his top military and diplomatic officials in China—and his choices would prove disastrous for U.S.–China relations as well as for John Service.

In December 1942 Service was ordered back home for consultations and family leave. Just to reach Miami was a treacherous ten-day journey, crossing the Himalayas and the Indian subcontinent, and then stopping in the Middle East, Africa, and South America. At last he arrived in California for a Christmas reunion with the family he had not seen in two years. In Washington, D.C., after the holidays, Service was surprised to be treated like a celebrity in policy-making circles. As the first Foreign Service political reporter from China since the Pearl Harbor attack, he was invited to give briefings at the Military Intelligence Service (MIS), the Office of Naval Intelligence (ONI), and the OSS as well as the State Department. This exhilarating reception seemed to confirm that his new insights on China were indeed significant.

Most gratifying was the opportunity to express his views to a White House insider: John Carter Vincent arranged for Service to meet with Currie. Service candidly expressed his deep concern about the United States' "unquestioning support" for Chiang and the Nationalists. He spoke of the worsening rural situation, and he advised sending American observers to the Communist base to learn more about Chiang's "united front" partners. Currie commented that Zhou Enlai had made a similar suggestion to him on his first China visit in early 1941, and he indicated general agreement with the young diplomat's views—even implying that "'the man across the street' shared his thinking."[6]

Both men agreed that Chinese censorship had blinded both the American public and decision makers to the reality of China's predicament. "He mentioned that he was trying to make material available to columnists, commentators and writers," Service later testified. Currie asked him to send material to him and "he would see that it did get out and was used."[7] He then arranged meetings for Service with other officials, politicians, and journalists, including the influential columnist Drew Pearson.

Currie also asked Service to prepare a written summary of his observations and recommendations, and—to make the assignment official—he phoned the head of the China desk at the State Department. That a White House aide would order up a report from an outspoken junior officer caused considerable resentment. Service's resulting memo boldly discussed the likelihood of Chinese civil war. Bluntly, he reported that the highly publicized "united front" of Nationalists and Communists against the Japanese "is now definitely a thing of the past" and that countering Communism had become the Nationalist regime's prime preoccupation:

> There is not only a rigorous suppression of anything coming under the ever-widening definition of "Communism" but there appears to be a movement away from even the outward forms of democracy in government. . . . It

> is now no longer wondered whether civil war can be avoided, but rather whether it can be delayed at least until after a victory over Japan. . . . The question is raised whether it is to China's advantage, or to America's own interests, for the United States to give the Kuomintang [Nationalist] government large quantities of military supplies which . . . are not likely to be used effectively against Japan but will be available for civil war to enforce "unity" in the country by military force.[8]

He went on to suggest that it would be difficult for the Nationalists to defeat the Communists in a war if (as the Communists claimed) they were winning the support of the population in the guerrilla war zones.

No one in Washington had ever heard a prediction that Chiang would restart the civil war once the United States had defeated the Japanese. No one considered the Communists serious rivals for power in China. Years later, Service's report would be cited as evidence not of his prescience but of his sympathy for the Communists.

The report concluded with a radical suggestion. Based on the current assumption that an invasion of the Japanese islands would be necessary to end the war, Service pointed out that such an offensive would probably be launched from the areas of northeast China that the Communists claimed to control. Therefore, "the possible positive military value of the Communist army to our war effort should not be ignored." He recommended sending official American representatives to Communist guerrilla base areas to assess the political and military situation—"preferably Foreign Service officers of the China language service." The few journalists who had managed to visit Communist territory, he noted, did not speak Chinese, and they appeared to have "a bias favorable to the Communists." Clearly Service felt he was capable of making an objective appraisal of the revolutionaries and hoped to be picked for the mission even though such an American mission would undoubtedly upset Chiang.[9]

When the Secretary of State's special China adviser Stanley Hornbeck read Service's memo, he wrote a scathing review: "Seldom, if ever, have I ever seen any document by a responsible officer . . . expressive of such complete self-assurance that he knew the facts, all of the facts, and he was prescribing the remedy, the one and only remedy." He had the memo given a new conclusion: because the Nationalists would strongly oppose any attempt to send Americans into Communist-held territory, no such request should be made. In a quiet act of defiance and disobedience, however, Service made sure to give several important people outside the department carbon copies of his original memo, with its bold recommendations.[10]

A bitter schism was developing between the old guard Far East specialists in Washington and their field officers. Hornbeck's experience in China was limited to an academic sojourn during the 1920s, when he became an admirer of Chiang Kai-shek's effort to reunify the chaotic country. Despite the tumultuous changes that had taken place since then, his support for Chiang never wavered. John Vincent, now posted in Chungking, knew that Hornbeck and Maxwell Hamilton (chief of the Chinese Affairs Bureau, and Hornbeck's protégé) "ignored all reports that questioned the ability of Chiang and the Kuomintang to govern China."[11]

This was a key reason for sending Service to meet with Currie. Well aware that the major military and diplomatic decisions were made in the White House, Vincent wanted to ensure that the president heard the views of those closest to the situation on the ground. At the State Department, too, many veteran Foreign Service staff quietly cheered Service's forthright memo. But it was common knowledge that dissenters were "isolated and ignored while Hornbeck continued to give Secretary Hull and President Roosevelt optimistic reports of Chinese military and political progress."[12]

Officials at OSS headquarters saw a new opportunity in John Service's memo. Norwood Allman, the Far East chief of secret intelligence (who had first met Service in Shanghai), invited him to lunch. Service told him the embassy hoped to get permission to open eight consular listening posts throughout Free China—and that he was advocating the inclusion of Yenan, the Communists' stronghold. If that assignment came through, the young diplomat would be willing to report secretly for the OSS. If not, rather than return to Chungking to do "routine clerical work," Service told Allman, he "would be interested in joining OSS."[13]

The spy agency's overtures came at a time when Service was becoming frustrated with his career prospects. Apart from the chilly reception of his memo—Hornbeck had commented in the margins, "preposterous," "ridiculous," and "scandalous"—there was other disappointing news. His name was once again missing from the annual Foreign Service promotion list, despite high praise from his ambassador, who lauded "the abundance of common sense, the energy, the efficiency, and sense of responsibility" of "the best younger officer that I have found in the Foreign Service."[14]

In early February, Service met directly with the OSS chief. It would be of "great value," Bill Donovan wrote confidentially to the State Department after their meeting, "if Mr. Service could be returned to the North China area by the Department of State as soon as possible."[15] Donovan was disappointed when his request was turned down by the head of the Chinese Affairs bureau, Max Hamilton, who made it clear he would not offend the Nationalist government by sending Service or anyone else to Yenan.

While Service was making the rounds in Washington, Mme. Chiang Kai-shek arrived at the White House, bringing along her own silk sheets. The distinguished guest was first flown secretly to New York, where she spent eleven weeks in treatment for hives and nervous exhaustion and two weeks recuperating at Roosevelt's Hyde Park estate. The administration, sensitive about its many broken promises to China, was determined to show the utmost courtesy to its First Lady. One night at dinner, Roosevelt asked how her government would handle a labor leader like John L. Lewis, who had recently launched a coal miners' strike. May-ling silently drew an eloquent lacquered fingernail across her own throat. Eleanor Roosevelt later remarked, "She can talk beautifully about democracy, but does not know how to *live* democracy."[16]

Madame Chiang was a captivating speaker who charmed Americans. Wearing a beautiful, form-fitting cheongsam, she addressed the U.S. Congress on February 18. In perfect English, she argued that defeating Japan first was more important than the defeat of Germany. Recalling how China had resisted Japanese aggressors alone for more than five years, she declared that China was prepared "not to accept failure ignominiously, but to risk it gloriously." An emotional four-minute ovation filled the Capitol. Publisher Henry Luce, the son of China missionaries, featured her on the cover of *Time*; his other publication, *Life* magazine, gushed about her "grace, charm and intelligence."[17]

Madame Chiang continued her charm offensive in official Washington, urging the adoption of Chiang and Chennault's plan to use American air power to strike a decisive blow against Japan. The promised aircraft and supplies must be immediately sent over the Hump, even at the expense of Stilwell's long-planned Burma ground operations. She then embarked on a triumphant fundraising tour across the United States for United China Relief. Twenty thousand people heard her at Madison Square Garden, and another thirty thousand at the Hollywood Bowl. "Madame aroused a greater outpouring of admiration and welcome than anyone since Lindbergh flew the Atlantic," observed historian Barbara Tuchman. Caroline Service later reflected that "everybody just thought the Chinese were sprouting wings of a sort," whereas her husband spoke about "how weak the Chiang Kai-shek regime was and how corrupt." It was hard to sort out these opposing views. "The thing that shocked me was that Jack was already saying that there was going to be civil war in China . . . something which I had never heard of or read of in the paper. . . . I could not believe it. He said, 'Well, you ask other people who have been there.'"[18]

President Roosevelt helped reinforce the China myth. With Madame Chiang at his side, he told a press conference that China "has become one of the great Democracies of the world." Hollywood had helped maintain the heroic fantasy with such popular films as *The Good Earth*, *The Flying Tigers*, and *Thirty Seconds over Tokyo*. The pervasive "fairy tale spirit" obscured the realities: the Nationalist dictatorship, the corrupt diversion of American lend-lease supplies, and the ineffectual fighting of China's warlord armies.

Newspaper and magazine journalists in China had to contend not only with Chinese censors but also with editors who were invested in the China myth. On March 22, *Time* magazine ran a severely edited version of White's Honan famine report, giving vivid descriptions of starving peasants reduced to eating tree bark. But Luce and his foreign editor, Whittaker Chambers, had carefully excised all references to Chinese officials' failures and corruption, widespread profiteering, draconian tax collection, and the growing hatred of the regime. Criticism of the Nationalists would have been bad for morale. White was so upset with the edited version that he posted a sign on his door at the Chungking Press Hostel: "Any similarity between what I write and what appears in *Time* is purely coincidental."[19]

After a farewell visit with his family in California, Jack Service headed back to China, arriving in Chungking in April 1943. Currie had instructed him to write whenever "he had something interesting."[20] The request struck him as highly unusual. "This is the way the White House operates," John Carter Vincent explained. "You might as well go along." Other members of Roosevelt's circle, Service was assured, had their own China pen pals to help them influence White House decision making. Service "never felt very comfortable" about using Currie's proffered back channel, and he claimed that he "never wrote very many letters."[21] But he had now become "personally engaged, in the sense of being much more involved in trying to make sure that what I thought was the correct picture got back to the States, and more interested in American policy."[22]

One of Harry Hopkins' most prolific China correspondents was the journalist Joseph Alsop, a Roosevelt relative who served as Gen. Claire Chennault's admiring aide. During the spring of 1943, Alsop's confidential letters to Hopkins complained bitterly about General Stilwell's wrong-headed Burma campaign plans, his rude "tough uncle" treatment of Chiang and his military, and—especially—his tight-fisted control of the supply line over the Hump, which hampered Chennault's buildup of an air force. "The only simple, easily available military opportunities in China are . . . for use of air power, which Stilwell does not understand, and therefore grossly under-rates." Alsop concluded: "Stilwell's approach to the problem can only end in something very close to disaster for all of us."[23]

By early March, Alsop's drumbeat was having an impact. The president sent General Marshall a memo saying he thought Stilwell had used the "wrong approach" to the Generalissimo. He should remind Stilwell that Chiang was the leader of 400 million people, and "one cannot speak sternly to a man like that or exact commitments from him the way we might do from the Sultan of Morocco." Roosevelt ordered greater emphasis on the "strategic value of Chennault's air operations" and decreed that "Chennault, with Stilwell's approval, will have complete control over his operations and tactics."[24]

Marshall, however, saw a serious flaw in this shift of strategy. "As soon as our air effort hurts the Japanese, they will move in on us, not only in the air, but also on the ground"—and without U.S. training and equipment, the Chinese troops would not be able to defend Chennault's forward air bases. Marshall passed along Stilwell's report of his recent inspection tour. The Chinese army units were "in desperate condition, underfed, unpaid, untrained, neglected, and rotten with corruption. . . . It is the gang of army 'leaders' that is the cause of all our grief."[25] Much later, General Marshall would reflect, "Stilwell had been right, but unfortunately [he was] much too outspoken and tactless."[26]

When John Service returned to Chungking, he learned that Ambassador Gauss had finally persuaded the Chinese to let the embassy open listening posts in several strategically important towns—although not in Yenan. Service was assigned to Lanzhou, not far from the border with Communist territory. As he was preparing to leave for the new post, Mary Miles of SACO met with the embassy's new deputy chief (Vincent having been recently reassigned to Washington). He handed him a suitcase stuffed with 200,000 Chinese dollars (US$10,000), with orders for John Service to deliver the money secretly to the OSS operative who would meet him in Lanzhou. Service objected to being used as SACO's delivery boy but was merely told to protect the cash from roadway bandits. Because he expected to stay in Lanzhou for at least a year, Service packed such staples as coffee, powdered milk, and sugar as well as boxes of tea to dispense as gifts. Now he bought extra tea. "[I] took the tea out of the boxes, filled the boxes with bank notes, and then mixed them in with my groceries and other stuff in a couple of wooden boxes . . . and then I forgot them, paid no more attention to them."[27]

A more significant secret assignment was issued by the ambassador, who was keenly interested to learn more about the Communists. "In Hornbeck's Washington I had been out of line," Service later observed, "but back in Chungking, I was mainstream." The embassy staff shared his concern that civil war would be disastrous, and that "American policy should be to try to avoid a civil war . . . [and] to get the Kuomintang to reform." As Service noted later, "We didn't know much about the Communists, and we hadn't gotten to the point which we eventually reached—of expecting the Communists to win."[28] Service's instructions were clear: if there was "a chance to evade the Kuomintang blockade . . . to seize it." The embassy, however, insisted on deniability for such a politically explosive and risky mission, so no official orders were issued. If he succeeded in his assignment, he noted in his unpublished memoir, "there would inevitably be a strong Kuomintang protest. . . . [The embassy] would then be able to disown me by saying that I was acting without embassy authorization."[29]

Service got a ride to Lanzhou in a truck owned by the China Tea Corporation. After he hosted their first dinner on the road, the two truck drivers quickly accepted him as a friend. When their truck broke down, he bided time in a nearby teashop, listening to carters and drivers complain about bandits, rising prices and taxes, corrupt landlords, and conscription. Finally he found another trucker headed to Lanzhou, who agreed to take him as a paying passenger—a "yellow fish," like those he had seen in trucks on the Burma Road. After a two-week journey, Service arrived in Lanzhou and found lodging with American Seventh Day Adventist missionaries—much to the consternation of the local gendarmes, who had a hard time keeping track of this foreigner who refused to stay at the town's official hostel.

Service's ability to establish a wide-ranging network of contacts freed him from depending on Chinese government sources, and his Lanzhou field reports soon earned him a rare State Department commendation for excellence. He filed dispatches about the lucrative drug trade across the frontier between Japanese-occupied areas and free China, and about the large illegal shipments of gold. He detailed the main trafficking routes and fingered specific army units on the take. After learning that landlords, gentry, and secret societies had joined with the peasant uprisings against the Nationalists' corrupt rule, he predicted "further disturbances" in Gansu Province, noting that "troops and recruits are steadily being brought into the province." He even analyzed the propaganda slogans plastered on walls along the roads as good indicators of serious problems like grain collection, conscription, and opium use.[30]

Soon after Service settled into Lanzhou, two OSS agents arrived from Tibet. Ilya Tolstoy (a relative of the famous Russian writer) was clearly in charge. And when he received the tea boxes stuffed with money, he insisted on counting every last bill. "After counting and recounting, we were $300 [Chinese dollars] short," Service recalled. "Tolstoy felt that he was to receive $200,000, so I made up the difference."[31]

Service quickly made friends with the two agents. Characteristically, he trusted these newcomers with a daring plan for reaching the forbidden Communist stronghold, disregarding any personal risks involved in the venture. Together they would travel by raft down the Yellow River and—to avoid both Nationalist and Japanese checkpoints—trek southward across remote desert on foot to reach Communist territory. They would claim to be setting up weather stations. Weather reporting, after all, was part of Miles' mission with SACO—and Service knew OSS Washington was keenly interested in getting intelligence from Yenan. But the plan was vetoed by Miles himself. Service always suspected that his own participation was the reason, because he knew Miles kept "no secrets" from General Tai, who already had him on his watch list.[32]

After fewer than three months in Lanzhou, John Service was called back to Chungking to take an unusual new position: serving on Stilwell's staff as one of the general's political advisers. The transfer came as a result of a letter from Secretary of War Stimson to Secretary Hull, which explained that the general urgently needed trained political observers to supplement the work of his military intelligence. Ambassador Gauss was not consulted, and he resented losing the best junior officer he had known during his forty-year career.

The new assignment had been engineered by John Vincent. Their colleague, John Paton Davies, had talked his way onto Stilwell's staff the previous year and was now one of the general's most trusted aides, and his chief public relations man. Freed from diplomatic protocol, Davies was able to mingle with every sort of character in China, India, and Burma. He quickly discovered that "all kinds of indiscretions were excused in the military on the grounds that they advanced the war effort." To help give Stilwell "political guidance" in the dysfunctional China-Burma-India Theatre, Davies brought in Service along with two other Asian specialists from the Foreign Service. Their task was to improve relations between the distrustful allies as well as among rival American agencies—a task as critical as actually fighting the enemy.

One of Service's first assignments was to keep Ambassador Gauss informed about affairs at Army headquarters, including Stilwell's ongoing military negotiations with Chiang Kai-shek. "Both were crusty old men . . . and rather prickly," Service explained. "Each took the attitude, 'Well, if he wants to talk to me, I'm available.'"[33] Soon he was also advising officials at other American agencies about all things Chinese while functioning as Stilwell's information officer to deal with the small international press corps in Chungking.

At his first meeting with Stilwell and Davies, Service was also designated the commander's special liaison to the Chinese Communists. Despite the breakdown of the "united front" war effort, the Communists were allowed to maintain political and military offices in Chungking and to publish a newspaper. Their main office and living quarters occupied a downtown building not far from the headquarters of the Nationalist government. Its upstairs floors housed agents of Tai Li's secret police, and plainclothes agents were always posted across the street to observe visitors to the Communist headquarters. Since Stilwell's military officers were forbidden to pay calls there, the task fell to Service, dressed in Army khakis with a distinctive triangular shoulder patch that designated him as a noncombatant civilian. The agents made special note of this uniformed American who frequently met with Chiang's internal enemies. "I was not particularly concerned about being conspicuous as the Army's sole contact with the Communists," Service recalled. "I was already in the [Nationalists'] black book."[34]

Service was told that Davies was helping set up a separate OSS contingent for China, based in India, with the approval of both Stilwell and OSS chief Donovan. This would circumvent Tai Li's prohibition on working with the Communists—or conducting independent espionage operations. By now the idea of sending U.S. observers to the Communist-controlled zone had won favor. War Department strategists were planning to establish air bases in north China for bombing raids against Japan, and even to land American troops in occupied territory controlled by Communist guerrillas. Getting solid intelligence from the guerrillas was now vitally important, and Service was assigned to keep Stilwell's headquarters updated on all matters regarding the Communists.

The top Communist official in Chungking, Zhou Enlai, had already indicated to Davies his willingness to consider military cooperation, and a channel was now established for submitting intelligence requests. Service would pass on to Zhou all U.S. requests for intelligence on specific Japanese divisions; Zhou's staff then radioed the request to Yenan, and relayed the response back to Service. The Communist intelligence soon proved far more reliable than the reports the U.S. Army was receiving from Nationalist sources.

As part of his reassignment to Stilwell's Chungking headquarters, Service moved from the ambassador's comfortable residence to the cramped Army officers' quarters across the river, on the outskirts of the city. He reported to Stilwell's son

Joe, who now headed G-2 (military intelligence). When young Stilwell learned of Service's firsthand experience of the Burma Road, he assigned him to write a report about its condition, bridges, ferries, terrain, and cover—and then a report on all the other roadways he had traveled inside China. Service spent two months with an Army engineer, scouting abandoned roads in the southern provinces bordering Japanese-occupied French Indochina. Once, spotted by Japanese fighter dive bombers, they took cover in an ancient cemetery. "We lay down between the grave mounds and peppered away with our carbines," he recounted, "but we didn't do any damage."[35]

* * *

Meanwhile, the strategy of reopening the Burma Road had become a subject of top-level Allied talks in Quebec. Roosevelt and Churchill and their top military advisers had agreed on a D-day strategy for France, but they could not agree on a strategy for the CBI Theater. Churchill did not share the United States' strong commitment to a united and democratic China. Jabbing the air with his cigar, he argued strongly against Stilwell's plan for a major Burma campaign, which would involve British naval operations and a march through disease-infested mountainous jungle: "The enormous expenditures of man-power and material would not be worthwhile . . . across the most forbidding fighting country imaginable."[36] In the end, the Allies agreed only to build more warehouses and larger air bases in India and China, which would speed up air transport of additional supplies over the Hump. Stilwell's Burma campaign was downsized and delayed again.

By October little progress had been made in delivering more supplies to the isolated Chinese. "I am still pretty thoroughly disgusted with the India-China matter," the president wrote General Marshall. "Everything seems to go wrong. But the worst thing is that we are falling down on our promises every single time."[37] The situation threatened Roosevelt's vision for a secure postwar world with a strong, unified China as the major Asian power. He resolved to try to build up, and buck up, both China and its nominal leader, Chiang Kai-shek. Accordingly, at the Foreign Ministers Conference held in Moscow in late October, China was formally designated a great power over the protests of Britain and the Soviet Union. The United States insisted on including China as a signatory of the "Four Power Declaration," which pledged to establish a new "united nations" security organization for the postwar era.

Determined to secure cooperation, not only in the war effort but also in a postwar global security organization, Roosevelt set up back-to-back Allied summit meetings with Chiang Kai-shek (in Cairo) and Stalin (in Tehran). Once again, the president bypassed the State Department and sent his own advance man:

Maj. Gen. Patrick J. Hurley, a Republican lawyer from Oklahoma and Hoover's former secretary of war, who sometimes now acted as Roosevelt's special envoy. He was a man who had risen to prominence on the strength of his engaging personality and his connections.

Attired in a tailored uniform covered with ribbons, the grandly mustachioed emissary arrived in Chungking on November 7, 1943, to brief Chiang and his wife about the upcoming Cairo talks. Hurley also met with General Stilwell—who was now back in favor because his help was urgently needed to draw up a credible military plan for presentation at Cairo. The crusty CBI commander was amused to be told that many Americans considered him "China's Savior," and he deeply appreciated Hurley's hearty expression of personal support for his efforts. Stilwell later wrote in his diary, "The scarcity and unexpectedness of such an attitude is overwhelming."[38]

The Cairo conference took place in a posh British colonial hotel with an impressive view of the Pyramids. Chiang clearly basked in the illusion of greatness, but his capricious behavior began to erode Roosevelt's patience and his confidence. In long, private meetings between the two men and with Madame Chiang acting as interpreter, promises would be made one day and recanted the next. Winston Churchill became increasingly disdainful: "The talks of the British and American Staffs were sadly distracted by the Chinese story, which was lengthy, complicated and minor," he wrote in his memoir.[39] Agreement was eventually hammered out for a Burma counteroffensive with a commitment of both Chinese and British forces.

Churchill and Roosevelt then flew to Tehran, where Josef Stalin strongly urged them to open a second front in France as soon as possible. Churchill agreed on the condition that Roosevelt drop his insistence on a British amphibious assault in southern Burma, arguing persuasively that those landing craft were more urgently needed for D-day in Europe. Stalin assured his Anglo-American allies that, as soon as Germany was defeated, the Soviet Union would join the war against Japan. No one seemed concerned about Soviet intentions in northeast Asia. After meeting both Chiang and Stalin face to face, Roosevelt judged that the USSR might prove a more trustworthy ally than China, and Stalin a more reliable postwar partner for peace.

The promises made at Cairo were thus reversed in Tehran, a disappointment that served to deepen Chiang's distrust of his Western allies. He again pulled back from committing sufficient troops for Stilwell's Burma campaign, and rumors of Japanese peace feelers resurfaced. Chiang's demand for another billion-dollar loan was viewed in Washington as a blatant attempt at blackmail by an ungrateful

China, the newly anointed Great Power. And General Stilwell was left to soldier on without active support for a Burma campaign from either the British or Chinese.

When the presidential party stopped in Cairo on its way home, Stilwell and Davies met privately with Roosevelt and his confidant, Hopkins. The president reassured Stilwell that the supply airlift would grow, and he vaguely endorsed the Stilwell–Chiang proposal to eventually arm and train ninety Chinese divisions under American supervision. Roosevelt confidently declared that the Soviets would keep the Chinese Communists in line and that they had no expansionist desires in northeast Asia. When asked to assess Chiang's staying power, Stilwell bluntly told the president that Chiang might not last much longer. "Well then," Roosevelt replied, "we should look for some other man or group of men to carry on."[40]

Following the meeting, Hopkins asked Davies to keep in touch. In his initial report, Davies minced no words: "The Generalissimo is probably the only Chinese who shares the popular American misconception that Chiang Kai-shek is China." The Chinese leader, once such a heroic symbol of resistance against Japanese aggression, had become, according to Davies, "a hostage of the corrupt forces he manipulates." The United States needed to adopt a more realistic policy of tough bargaining, providing supplies in exchange for solid commitments—and pressuring for a new, reform-minded coalition government that would include the Chinese Communists. In another memo to Hopkins, Davies suggested that the president formally request Chiang Kai-shek to permit American representatives to cross the blockade into Communist-held territory. "An American observers' mission would break [Communist] isolation, reduce their tendency toward dependence upon Russia and serve to check Chiang's desire to attempt liquidation of the Communists by civil war."[41]

* * *

In the aftermath of Cairo and Tehran, the political atmosphere in Chungking shifted. Service reported that "the artificial inflation of Chiang's status, only adds to his unreasonableness." Returning from his road inspections, Service met with his new intelligence boss, who encouraged him to prepare informal memos on any topics he felt might be significant or useful—especially any news of insurrections or clashes indicating imminent civil war. Tapping his superb network of contacts, Service soon pieced together the details of a failed plot to overthrow Chiang upon his return from Cairo. Sixteen officers had been executed as alleged conspirators by Tai Li's secret agents. And now, he reported, Tai Li was trying to blame the trouble on the Communists.

Typically, Service now spent his mornings reading the Chinese language press, typing reports, and preparing—on his own initiative—an informal "Miscellaneous News Items" memo that summarized daily Chinese news stories and editorials and was packed with news items gleaned from his own news gathering. After finishing these chores, Service left the office for the rest of the day to make his rounds as roving political reporter. Soon the G-2 chief was distributing Service's daily memo to top Army officers, the embassy, and other U.S. field offices around town. A copy always went to Davies in New Delhi, who often sent the memos to his key contacts in Washington.

"Tied to no desk or telephone, without limitation or assignment," Service later observed, "everything was grist for my reporting mill."[42] Once, while dining with Chinese friends, Service overheard a conversation in Shanghai dialect about the supposedly secret construction of American B-29 airbases in the Chengdu area. After introducing himself, he discovered that the diners were contractors out from occupied Shanghai who hoped to cash in on this building bonanza. When he reported his discovery to Army headquarters, he was assigned to make a fact-finding mission to Chengdu.

Once there, his father's former Y associates put him in contact with disgruntled locals. Land, he learned, was being seized without payment for construction of the airbases; special taxes were levied unfairly; and wages were so low for conscripted peasant laborers that they could not feed their families. Although local Chinese administrators were currently being blamed, Service warned in his report that the authorities might try to turn the growing resentment into an anti-American furor.

Service often shared his news-gathering results with trusted journalists. "These people were interested in exactly the same sort of thing I was interested in. . . . We were all living and breathing the politics of Chungking. And they were able to talk to a lot of people I couldn't see." If a reporter landed an important interview with a high official, he would often seek Service's advice on questions to ask—and later share his interview notes as well as the uncensored version of his story. Both Stilwell and Davies encouraged Service's open relations with the press. "We got out of the habit of thinking of [the reports] as classified," he later admitted, "or at least I did."[43]

In Chungking, news stories about the personal life of Chiang Kai-shek and his wife were strictly forbidden, but when rumors started circulating about why they were rarely seen in public together, Service addressed the "domestic troubles in the Chiang household." Gossips claimed the Generalissimo had taken a mistress who was now pregnant, and that madame had thrown a flower vase at her husband's head. Service felt "duty-bound" to report the matter because of China's special circumstances—"where the person concerned is a dictator and where the relationship between him and his wife's family is so all-important."[44]

* * *

They first met on an overcrowded bus in February 1944. Standing in the aisle of the jammed bus, Service chuckled loudly as he read a humorous news story over the shoulder of a seated passenger. Turning around, the young woman was astonished to see a tall young American eying her Chinese-language newspaper. That was all, but when they later met again, they both remembered the brief encounter on that foggy day.

Valentine "Val" Chao was a vivacious twenty-four-year-old stage actress with bright almond-shaped eyes. She had arrived in Chungking several years earlier, having fled Changsha along with her drama school classmates and teachers. They were part of the mass exodus of war refugees who trudged nearly a thousand miles under the constant threat of being robbed by bandits—or raped and killed by patrolling Japanese soldiers—to reach Free China's new capital. When Val and her colleagues at last arrived, they reestablished their National Academy of Dramatic Arts.

A second encounter on the same bus route two months later was almost as brief as the first. But when Val got off the bus, Jack got off, too—and asked her name. "I said, 'I'm not used to telling a stranger my name.' So I kept walking," Val recalled, many years later. "He said [in Chinese], 'Please, I'm sincere. I wouldn't harm you or anything.' Then I look at him and really laugh. I say, 'Okay go to Yi Yuen Theater and see my show.'" The thirty-four-year-old diplomat was unaware that Val Chao was an acclaimed actress, accustomed to favorable attention—and had even been feted by Chiang Kai-shek and his wife at a private cast party.

A few nights later, Service went to the theater and at intermission sent her a handwritten note: "I'm the guy you met on the bus. I'd like to see you after the show. Please. I'll be waiting." Their first conversation took place over a steaming bowl of noodles. "We talk and talk and talk and forget about the time," she recalled. "He was very honest and told me he was married with two children. So I'm glad to know him as a friend." Soon, they were seeing each other once or twice a week, usually late at night after work. He discovered that Val knew many of his journalist friends, and she introduced him to a new circle of theatrical, literary, and government people.[45]

* * *

No American official had been to the Chinese Communists' stronghold since 1937; now, with Stilwell's blessing, Davies and Service were spearheading an effort to reestablish contact. Service's work focused on recruiting the best U.S.

military and intelligence men for a secret mission to Yenan. After Chiang Kai-shek's petulant performance at Cairo, President Roosevelt's attitude had changed. He now agreed with Stilwell and Marshall on a policy of conditional support: if Chiang would not commit the necessary troops for the Burma counteroffensive, the United States would threaten to cut off Lend-Lease supplies. In February 1944, FDR formally asked Chiang to allow U.S. observers to visit the Communist stronghold in Yenan. Chiang reluctantly agreed to let Americans go, but only to the northern areas along the border, controlled by his own troops. It would be several more months before the group, code-named "Dixie Mission," received official permission to fly to Yenan.

* * *

With a tinge of resentment, Caroline Service recognized that the war years were providing her husband with "the most interesting days of his whole life." After their 1940 evacuation from the war zone, Caroline and their two children had moved into her parents' home in Berkeley, California. She worked part-time as a telephone operator, to have "a little something to do." Mail delivery from China over the Hump was slow and undependable. But Jack never had been a prolific letter writer, "so it wasn't only the fault of the mail." Sometimes Caroline wondered if she would ever see her husband again.[46]

* * *

In Chungking, Service moved from the crowded bachelor officers' quarters into the comfortable downtown apartment of his friend Sol Adler, the U.S. Treasury Department representative. The three-story apartment house was owned by Finance Minister H. H. Kung—who was married to Madame Chiang's sister, a woman considered the "brain" of her family's lucrative business operations. The top floor was occupied by Kung's close adviser, Chi Chao-ting, who served on the Chinese Monetary Stabilization Board along with Adler. The British member of the monetary board occupied the ground floor.

Prodigiously well informed and articulate with a great sense of humor, Adler had become Service's good friend, favorite bridge partner, and influential adviser. Service's move to his quarters facilitated their collaborative reporting on economic and financial matters. "He tapped an entirely different layer from what I was reaching," Service explained. "We compared notes and worked together very closely."[47] Service knew nothing of Adler's Communist ties—but had he known, it would have raised no concern. This was a time when "Uncle Joe's" Communists were the United States' allies, and their common enemies were Japanese and German fascists. Nor did Service have any inkling their upstairs neighbor, Chi Chao-ting, was a mole for the Chinese Communist Party.

When Val Chao returned from a three-city theater tour in the late spring of 1944, her relationship with the American diplomat deepened. Sitting with him at a party, she asked Service if he were ever homesick—and was stunned by his reply. Jack confessed that he had volunteered for duty in Chungking in part to stay away from his "dead, unhappy marriage" that had "soured right from the start."[48] His wife, on her return voyage to Yunnanfu from her extended stay in Shanghai, had stopped in Hong Kong, and there she was seduced by a diplomat she met at a party. Her confession of this brief affair, he claimed, had deeply disillusioned him and strained their marriage bond—and led to his own intimate transgressions years before he ever met Val on the bus.

"I was in love long before he told me such things, but . . . I would never intrude to break his marriage." Chao said softly years later. "After I heard his story, I knew it was not my fault." Soon afterward, she agreed to move in with him.[49]

Sol Adler had no objection to the new living arrangement in his apartment. But Amb. Clarence Gauss, who had become like a father to Service, issued a blunt caution: "Don't be a damn fool!" He warned him that the romance could destroy his promising career. Service, however, insisted that Val was "the love of his life," and he wrote his wife asking for a divorce. If he lost his job in the Foreign Service, he told Val, he would simply take a job as a war correspondent in China.[50]

Service's friends in both Nationalist and Communist camps were uneasy about his love affair. "I was warned from both sides that she probably was a dangerous person. . . . Each side thought she was . . . working for the other side." He knew it was a vital concern that he "not become the dupe of an agent for either faction." Some Chinese friends worried that Chao might be motivated by a desire to get to the United States. Service rejected all their apprehensions, insisting that his relationship with Val Chao was extremely valuable "as a release from high tension, constant political news gathering and day-long 'shop talk.'"[51] "I was in love with China and with the hopes and aspirations of my young intellectual friends," he later reflected. "It was not surprising perhaps that I made this more personal by falling in love with a Chinese woman." In later life, however, he judged his wartime romance "probably unwise."[52]

* * *

That same spring, the Japanese launched a major offensive code-named "Ichigo." The objective was to seize control of the north-south rail line, all the way to Canton, and to destroy the American air bases in eastern China. The successful bombing raids of Chennault's Flying Tigers against Japanese targets were now jeopardized, much as Stilwell had predicted. Infantry troops were desperately needed to protect the vulnerable airbases. Too late, Chennault offered to give up his allotment of aviation supplies over the Hump to allow for emergency Army shipments. Stilwell bitterly noted in his diary that the ace flyer still "tried to duck the consequences of having sold the wrong bill of goods, and put the blame on those who pointed out the danger long ago and tried to apply the remedy."[53]

Ichigo began with a three-week sweep through Honan in mid-April 1944. Ill-trained and ill-fed, the Chinese soldiers broke ranks and ran. The local peasants, after suffering so cruelly at the hands of corrupt Nationalist officials and army officers during the manmade famine of 1942–43, now sought revenge. "Never before had the unorganized peasants turned in cold blood against their national troops while they were fighting the enemy," reported war correspondent Teddy White. "Even Chiang Kai-shek, insulated within his court of flattery, became infected with a sense of dangers."[54] Using only pitchforks, bird guns, and knives, the peasants disarmed nearly 50,000 Chinese soldiers.

Ichigo's success finally broke the spell. For nearly seven years, the American public had been led to believe that the brave Chinese were successfully battling the common enemy. In the early years of the Japanese assault, China's courageous and lonely resistance had indeed been remarkable. But after Pearl Harbor brought the United States into the war, the Nationalists' war effort had entered a state of suspended animation.

Roosevelt and his key advisers were jolted by the series of distressing Chinese defeats just a month before the D-day invasion of France. The president decided to send another personal representative to carry a strong message to the Generalissimo: accept U.S. military advice on how to fight the advancing Japanese; reform the one-party government; and permit a group of U.S. military observers into Yenan, where Communist fighters were reportedly eager to cooperate with the United States against the Japanese. Roosevelt's choice of messenger, however, had more to do with domestic American politics than with foreign policy expertise. The president was running for an unprecedented fourth term, and his supporters were pressing him to name a fresh (and less controversial) running mate—a key reason why Roosevelt selected Vice President Henry Wallace for the special mission in China.

CHAPTER 5
THE GENERALISSIMO

The old black Cadillac careened through Chungking's teeming streets, weaving around packed buses and scattering the scurrying pedestrians, rickshaws, and sedan chairs out of its way. After slowing down to pass through the narrow city gate, the limousine roared out into the countryside. A scrawny little dog trotted toward the car, its tail wagging over its back; without diminishing speed, the Chinese chauffeur steered with extra care. John Service was aware of only a slight bump, as the tires crushed the dog into the pavement.

There was no further incident as the limousine raced toward Chiang Kai-shek's hillside villa. On the Generalissimo's orders, the horde of refugee beggars had been rounded up, roped together, and force-marched far beyond the city walls in preparation for this visit by Henry Wallace, vice president of the United States.

Wallace, President Roosevelt's special envoy, had arrived three days earlier, on June 20, 1944, for confidential talks with the Generalissimo. Accompanying him were two China experts: Owen Lattimore, now with the Office of War Information, and John Carter Vincent from State. At this morning's session, Chiang had surprised them all by announcing his willingness to allow official American military observers finally to visit Yenan—but under the auspices of his National Military Council, not the U.S. Army.

There was great excitement at lunch at the ambassador's residence, as Wallace and his advisers recounted this breakthrough. They were interrupted by an urgent top secret cable delivered by Stilwell's chief of staff accompanied by John Service. Roosevelt had just approved a stern message—originally suggested by Service—giving Wallace "strong ammunition" for pressuring Chiang to permit the dispatch of an American group to Yenan. Now that the Nationalist leader had agreed to the trip, the lunch group debated whether FDR's strongly worded message was needed.

The group decided to use the president's message as leverage to put the mission under army sponsorship. Brig. Gen. Benjamin Ferris and Service would participate in the afternoon session to nail down some important details. "Everyone there was considerably bucked up," Service recalled. "I remember the glint in Gauss' flinty eye."[1]

This was the group inside the speeding limousine on the hit-and-run drive out to the Generalissimo's country estate that afternoon. Service and John Carter Vincent were perched on the car's jump seats, choreographing talking points with Ferris, Lattimore, and Wallace—who showed a quick and impressive grasp of the problems and implications. Service's assigned role was "to sniff out hidden technicalities and roadblocks" that the Chinese might raise. When the Cadillac arrived at Chiang's well-guarded compound, "everybody was well primed and knew his lines."

The Generalissimo, dressed as always in his stiff Mandarin-collared uniform, looked "like a stick of wood" as he greeted this expanded Wallace entourage. When Madame Chiang entered the room and spotted Service, she gave him an icy look that he long remembered. "My presence that afternoon," Service later reflected, "associated me firmly with the [Dixie Mission] scheme in Chinese eyes and was another nail in my coffin."[2]

John Service was already a thorn in the side of the Nationalist regime. His independent travels and frequent visits to the Chinese Communist headquarters marked him as "unfriendly" and had been duly noted in a secret police file. Chiang Kai-shek was probably referring to Service when he remarked earlier to Wallace that "some Americans were being swayed badly by Communist propaganda." This unexpected appearance at Chiang's villa only heightened suspicions.

At their initial meeting on June 21, Wallace informed Chiang of the U.S. concern that strained relations between the Nationalists and Communists were seriously hampering the war effort. He delivered Roosevelt's glib—and astonishingly naïve—message that since they were all Chinese, they must be "basically friends," and "nothing should be final between friends." If unable to resolve their differences, Roosevelt suggested, "they might call in a friend"—and the president had indicated his willingness to be that friendly mediator.[3]

Chiang listened politely without interrupting and then complained forcefully that the United States did not appreciate the complex relations between his Nationalists, Mao's Communists, and the Soviets. The Communists were secretly tied to the Soviet Union, he insisted, and were intent on undermining Chinese morale and seizing power. Now that the United States was encouraging Stalin to enter the war against Japan, he feared Russian designs on Manchuria and North China, where the Chinese Communists had their stronghold. Vice President Wallace tried to reassure Chiang by relaying Joseph Stalin's recent remark to visiting Americans: The Chinese Communists were not real Communists, merely "margarine Communists." With a sardonic laugh, Chiang retorted that the Chinese Communist were "more Communistic than the Russian Communists." He urged the United States to remain aloof and cool toward representatives of the Chinese Communist Party.[4]

* * *

Nevertheless, Chiang Kai-shek was now prepared to yield to presidential pressure on Yenan. After a small group of foreign journalists was permitted to go to Yenan in May, Chiang's continued refusal to allow official U.S. observers to travel there began to seem bizarre.

Wallace explained to the Generalissimo that to avoid any misunderstanding about their mission, he had brought along Stilwell's staff members who were most familiar with the project. General Ferris then explained that, with the new airfields around Chengdu now operational and long-range B-29 bombing raids ramping up, there was an urgent need for timely intelligence on weather conditions and enemy troop concentrations in north China. Rescue of any American flyers downed in enemy territory would be essential, and the Communists might be able to provide valuable assistance. He assured Chiang that the Americans would share whatever enemy intelligence their observers obtained.

Chiang reminded his guests that he could not guarantee their protection in "bandit" areas. It was agreed that the Americans could set up radio communications back to their Chungking headquarters. Chiang would give a direct order to his minister of war to work out final details and expedite their departure. The Nationalist Chinese leader then focused on the name to be given to this group: he objected to "mission." After some discussion about the correct translation of various Chinese and English terms, it was agreed the group would be known simply as the "United States Army Observer Group." Left unspoken was the fact that—no matter what it was called—the group represented tacit American recognition of the other China.

With these issues settled, Service and Ferris were excused. Returning to headquarters, Service typed up a three-page memo detailing the remarkable conversation with the Generalissimo, his wife, and T. V. Soong. Copies were delivered (as usual) to Army headquarters, Gauss' embassy, and John Davies at CBI headquarters in India.

Service was quickly dispatched to inform the local Chinese Communist representatives about the new developments. In New Delhi, Davies immediately sent a message to important contacts in Washington (including Currie at the White House), enthusing: "Jack and I are, of course, immeasurably cheered about the permission for the Observer's Group to [go to] Yenan. I think it is about the most damned important thing we have gotten across since Little Sister [Madame Chiang] was given her Wellesley education."[5]

* * *

In preparation for Wallace's visit, John Service had written a detailed briefing paper on the Chinese political and economic situation, including some policy recommendations. "It was assuming a good deal on my part," Service noted in his unpublished memoirs, "but Ambassador Gauss and Joe Dickey [the new G-2 chief] thought it a good idea." He had the assistance of his housemates: Sol Adler of the Treasury Department revised his drafts and their third-floor neighbor, Chi Chao-ting of the Ministry of Finance, offered expert advice. Often Val Chao would arrive home from a theater performance to find the three men engaged in a heated discussion that would continue long after she retired.

Service never learned whether Wallace actually read the report, but his thought-provoking analysis and recommendations received considerable attention in Washington. Officials at army headquarters and the embassy had forwarded it, as did Davies, through their own channels.

"The Situation in China Is Rapidly Becoming Critical" was the alarming title. If the current deterioration continued, Service warned, China would be unable to play an effective part in the war against Japan. Far from evolving into a stable, unified, and democratic cornerstone for U.S. policy in postwar East Asia, China was in danger of complete collapse—and might soon become a major liability to the United States' war effort: "China *is* dying a lingering death by slow strangulation. China *does not* now constitute any threat to Japan. And China *cannot*, if the present situation continues, successfully resist a determined Japanese drive to seize our offensive bases in East China."[6]

Service boldly outlined many reasons why Chiang and his Nationalists were as much to blame as the Japanese invaders for the military crisis, the economic misery, and political disintegration. He bluntly described Chinese leadership as "a congeries of conservative political cliques interested primarily in the preservation of their own power against all outsiders and in jockeying for position among themselves." Chinese officials persistently refused to institute necessary reforms to curb inflation, end corruption, or stop army officers' cruel treatment of conscripts and peasants. Instead, he wrote, the regime increasingly relied on a repressive web of secret police agents and informers "as its last resort for internal security."[7]

Service's stark assessment gave voice to the concerns of many progressive groups in China, people afraid to express their views, who looked to the United States for help. A Chinese commentator, writing seven years after the war ended, endorsed Service's report: "I do not think that the most fervent supporters of Chiang Kai-shek can take exception to this able analysis of the pathological political condition of China during the war."[8]

Civil war—that Service had first predicted in early 1943—seemed closer than ever. "Despite the pretext—to meet foreign and Chinese criticism—of conducting negotiations with the Communists," Service pointed out, the Nationalists were actually stepping up preparations for civil war. This ominous development, he warned, carried serious consequences for the United States' war effort in China.[9]

Only real political reform could help restore the Chinese will to fight, unify the country, and bring about a government actually supported by the people. Service bluntly criticized what he called the "disjointed and absent-minded manner" in which American policy was currently executed by rival U.S. agencies. The United States could play a positive role as "a catalytic agent" if it took a series of steps to encourage reform, including ending a collaboration with Chinese secret-police outfits that enabled the torture of political prisoners. A more vigorously coordinated policy of conditional support for Chiang's government was in the United States'—and the Nationalists'—best interest. "This democratic reform does not necessarily mean the overthrow of the Generalissimo or the Kuomintang," he wrote. "On the contrary, if they have the vision to see it, their position will be improved and the stability of the Central Government increased, if they were pressured to reform and allow a multi-party United Front government to emerge."[10]

Service's confidential briefing paper reached Washington at an opportune moment. Ichigo (Japan's brutal offensive in China) was making headlines back home. American forward air bases in eastern China were now being threatened. China's precarious economy was staggering under runaway inflation, and official Washington was desperately looking for answers.

At the State Department, the Service report was the subject of heated debate. The pro-Chiang faction was outraged by Service's damning indictment of the Nationalists as well as by his presumption. Other diplomats, however, were impressed by Service's cogent analysis and pragmatic recommendations. An official copy was sent to the White House by Secretary of State Cordell Hull, and Service was ultimately awarded a rare State Department commendation for excellence. Sol Adler sent a copy to his boss at Treasury (without Service's knowledge) noting that Ambassador Gauss believed the briefing paper "should be read entirely by all personnel having anything to do with China."[11] But in the summer of 1944, John Service had no idea that his confidential Wallace report was being so widely circulated in Washington. He was busy preparing for the mission to Yenan, scrambling to obtain the necessary Chinese approvals.

The Office of War Information, ignoring security regulations, provided a copy of the Service brief "on deep background" to a freelance journalist named Mark Gayn, who was working on a China story for the popular weekly *Collier's*. When Service eventually saw Gayn's published piece, he was astonished. "Almost whole paragraphs were lifted out from my report," Service recalled. "I said, 'Good God, I know where this came from.'"[12] He could not have imagined that, a year later, Gayn's account would become one of the threads leading to his own arrest.

* * *

After four days of talks on a wide range of topics, Vice President Wallace was driven to the Chungking airstrip by the Generalissimo and Madame Chiang in their Cadillac limousine. Offering their scathing opinion of General Stilwell, they beseeched Wallace to have President Roosevelt appoint a personal representative with whom they could discuss military and political issues. "I was deeply moved by the cry of a man in great trouble," Henry Wallace later recalled. "It was very clear to me from the tone and language of the Generalissimo, that he and Stilwell could not cooperate." During the hour-long ride to the airport, Wallace was convinced the China situation would be completely unmanageable if the American commander could not "genuinely help the Generalissimo in the hard times through which he was passing."[13] Vincent and Lattimore agreed: the president should consider Chiang's request for a special advisor. During their stopover at Chennault's Fourteenth Air Force headquarters, Wallace worked with Vincent and Joe Alsop (Chennault's trusted advisor and Wallace's long-time friend) to draft a long cable for Roosevelt. He recounted Chiang's complaints and recommended replacing General Stilwell—a man he had never met. Stilwell himself, stuck at the Burma front during Wallace's whirlwind tour, never had an opportunity to tell his side of the story.

The vice president wanted to propose the charismatic and charming Claire Chennault as Stilwell's replacement, but Alsop cautioned that the maverick air boss was too unpopular at the War Department to be approved. As an alternative, Alsop suggested Gen. Albert C. Wedemeyer, then deputy commander of allied forces in Southeast Asia: Chiang had once expressed admiration for this spit-and-polish officer. Wallace agreed immediately to the change. "With the right man to do the job," Wallace cabled FDR, "it should be possible to induce the Generalissimo to reform his regime and to establish at least the semblance of a united front, which is necessary to the restoration of Chinese morale."[14]

Wallace informed the president that Chiang had finally agreed to permit American military observers to go to Yenan, but talks between the Nationalist government and Communists were "so imbued with prejudice" that he saw "little chance of a satisfactory long-term settlement." He found conditions in China "extremely discouraging": China's leader appeared "bewildered regarding the economic situation, and obviously distressed regarding military developments." Wallace had strongly urged the Generalissimo to initiate agrarian reforms as a first step in fixing the economy and raising morale, but Chiang stubbornly refused to regard such measures as vital, insisting that such reforms must await the end of the war.[15]

With the vice president now enlisted as their spokesman, the China hands of the Foreign Service were hopeful that, as Vincent put it, "China might at last become a subject of major concern to the White House." At the very least, the vice president's visit boosted the morale of many frustrated and increasingly cynical Americans serving in China.

Upon his return, Wallace wrote an official trip report for the president. It was the most critical analysis of Chiang Kai-shek ever made by a senior American official. Chiang Kai-shek, the report concluded, was only "a short-term investment" who had neither the intelligence nor political strength to run postwar China. "The leaders of post-war China will be brought forward by evolution or revolution," Wallace wrote, "and it now seems more likely the latter."[16] He recommended that the United States broaden its efforts to encourage and support "a new coalition" of progressive banking and commercial leaders, Western-trained men, and military officers who were "neither subservient to the landlords nor afraid of the peasantry."[17]

But Wallace soon became a lame duck, and his report was never given serious consideration. By the end of July, the Democratic Convention had chosen Harry Truman as Roosevelt's new running mate. Wallace's highly classified report was relegated to the presidential files, where it gathered dust for years—and when it was finally declassified, during the turbulent McCarthy era, his critical remarks about Chiang Kai-shek had been heavily censored.[18]

* * *

At the same moment Wallace concluded that General Stilwell must be replaced, the War Department had successfully persuaded President Roosevelt that "Vinegar

Joe" himself was the only man capable of dealing with the deteriorating military situation in China. He had proven his worth by prevailing in the grueling jungle campaign in Burma against horrific odds and had demonstrated that Chinese soldiers could fight effectively if properly trained, fed, and led. War Department officials wanted Stilwell promoted to full general and put in command of *all* Chinese forces—including Mao's guerrilla forces.

Before presenting these bold recommendations to Roosevelt, General Marshall cabled Stilwell, his old comrade from their early days with the 15th Infantry in Tientsin, asking if he would accept such a position. "Even with complete authority, the damage done is so tremendous," Stilwell cabled back, "that I can see only one chance to repair it." He proposed staging a surprise counteroffensive in the north—from Shansi Province with an attack through Loyang. "The Communists should also participate," he told Marshall, "but unless the G-mo [Generalissimo] makes an agreement with them, they won't. Two years ago they offered to fight with me. They might listen now. . . . Outside of this one shot, I see no chance to save the situation."[19]

With Stilwell's conditional acceptance, General Marshall brought the Joint Chiefs of Staff proposal to Roosevelt. On July 6, even as Wallace was finishing his formal trip report, a blunt presidential cable was fired off to Chungking army headquarters for immediate delivery to the Chinese leader: "I recommend . . . that you charge [Stilwell] with the full responsibility and authority . . . to stem the tide of the enemy advances. . . . I feel that the case of China is so desperate that if radical and promptly applied remedies are not immediately effected, our common cause will suffer a disastrous setback."[20] When the cable arrived at army headquarters in Chungking, General Ferris ordered John Service to accompany him as official translator of this "eyes only" message to Chiang Kai-shek. Service had experience providing informal translations of conversations and speeches for the ambassador and others; he was often seen at diplomatic events whispering a running summary into an official ear. This cable, however, required a precise, word-for-word translation. For years, translations for Chiang had been handled by one of his American-educated relatives or aides, but experience had taught that the text would often be softened in translation—or sometimes not even delivered. Roosevelt's cable was too important to trust to others, and John Service was the only American diplomat with adequate translation skills. Nevertheless, to have such a blunt message delivered by this young and low-ranking diplomat was an extraordinary humiliation for Nationalist China's supreme leader. This loss of face would not be forgotten.

The president's cable came as a complete surprise to John Service. Nevertheless, Chiang and his supporters later would blame him personally for the president's unprecedented request. In fact the idea had been hatched by military strategists sitting at their desks in Washington, with no understanding of China's culture or its complex politico-military situation. Service was well aware that the proposed military command was unrealistic. Even in Burma, where Stilwell had overall command, there were often critical delays in carrying out American battlefield orders because Chinese officers still felt obliged first to check with Chiang, who (as Stilwell put it) "was still driving from the back seat." Chiang Kai-shek's power rested on his selective distribution of supplies to warlords and their armies, and he would quickly lose support if he lost overall command. "Chiefs of state with totalitarian control," Service noted grimly, "do not ordinarily commit suicide."[21]

Within a week, Service and Ferris were back again to meet with the stony-faced Chiang, delivering a second "eyes only" cable from the president. In the interim, Chiang had replied to Roosevelt, saying that "in principle" he accepted the command proposal but asking that a trusted personal representative be sent to work out the details. Roosevelt's new cable informed the Generalissimo that a special envoy would soon be appointed—but, due to the urgent and dangerous military situation, FDR insisted Stilwell be put in charge of all Chinese forces expeditiously.[22]

Given the current military emergency, President Roosevelt assumed that the details could be worked out after Stilwell took on his new role. His new cable brushed aside Chiang's two crucial stipulations: that the Communists not be included in Stilwell's overall command; and that Chiang, not Stilwell, control the distribution of Lend-Lease supplies.

Their positions reflected a total misunderstanding between the two allies, which perhaps was inevitable. The Americans, narrowly focused on the short-term goal of winning the war against a common enemy, confidently assumed they could keep internal Chinese politics separate from their military requirements. The Chinese leader, on the other hand, faced the enormous task of maintaining and expanding power in a country at war—a country that had not known unity since before the fall of the Qing Dynasty in 1911. Chiang's American ally seemed amazingly insensitive to his desperate needs, and he targeted his anger on the messenger: John Service. "I was always the bad news guy," Service recalled in testimony before a U.S. Senate subcommittee in 1950. "[The Nationalists] had repeated experience with my being sort of the bearer of bad tidings." His presence on these unpleasant occasions, he said, "helped to contribute to Chinese animosity toward me and to their conviction that I was again the instigator of a very unwelcome demand."[23]

Nevertheless, back in the summer of 1944 the diplomat must have felt great personal satisfaction in delivering these strong presidential messages to the Chinese leader. Perhaps the tide was finally changing and divided China could be brought together. At long last, it seemed that the United States was no longer going to "mollycoddle" the Nationalist leader. In his unusual role as political adviser to the commanding American general in the war zone, the young diplomat was both an eyewitness and a participant in the profound events shaping the land of his birth.

Within a few weeks, Gen. Patrick J. Hurley was picked as Roosevelt's special representative to work out the details of Stilwell's command. Even Stilwell thought well of the president's choice; but as the United States' struggle over the two Chinas sharpened, it would prove disastrous.

* * *

At 8:05 AM on July 22, 1944, the U.S. Army Air Force transport lifted out of the heavy, humid gloom of Chungking, heading north toward Yenan. It had been a month since Chiang met with Wallace and gave the green light for the United States Army Observer Group—informally dubbed the "Dixie Mission" (for a popular song, "Is It True What They Say about Dixie?"). John Service had been busy helping mission commander Col. David Barrett recruit men and supplies, and spending long days at the minister of war's office to obtain travel permits and the official "chops" (stamps) on documents.[24]

At army headquarters, various U.S. military outfits scrambled to offer volunteers for the most exciting action in China since America's entry into the war. For the OSS, the mission to Yenan represented a golden opportunity: it had long been looking for ways around Tai Li's ban on independent intelligence operations with the Communists.

John Davies had been working with OSS India, trying to establish a separate group of agents for insertion into China. Now he began recruiting secret agents for the Dixie Mission—men from special sabotage operations in the Burmese jungle, or from Chennault's weather and communications sections. He adamantly refused to consider any OSS or naval personnel from the SACO organization headed by Captain Miles and Tai Li. In the recruitment process, Davies also made new enemies in Washington. When he discovered that yet another OSS unit, headed by Ilya Tolstoy, was independently planning a trek to Yenan, he used his political clout to squelch it.[25]

The C-47 carried eight U.S. Army men (five of them with secret OSS ties, approved by Davies) plus John Service, the lone diplomat. These nine were merely the vanguard. Within a few weeks, a second contingent of nine more would fly to Yenan. All eighteen had been carefully selected for their specialized skills, and quite a few spoke Mandarin or other Chinese dialects. Many had years of experience in the country. Several, like Service, were the sons of missionaries in China. Others had worked as teachers or, like Barrett, were career military officers in China service. Many had secret affiliations to the OSS.

On the day before their departure, Colonel Barrett realized he had never been given formal orders regarding their mission. Hastily, the G-2 intelligence chief at headquarters typed up general instructions for reporting weather conditions and rescuing downed fliers along with a laundry list of topics to be thoroughly investigated, including a who's who of Communist officials; their forces' equipment, training, and operations; target intelligence; enemy operations and order of battle (Japanese weaponry, troops, and positions); plus an evaluation of present and potential "contribution of Communists to war effort."[26] "No other instructions of any kind, oral or written, secret or non-secret were ever given me," Barrett later insisted.

But everyone on the mission must have known that their findings would influence the strategic decision on whether to supply American weapons and supplies to the Communists. And both Barrett and Service must have been aware of the overarching, and secret, OSS objective: to set up an intelligence network in cooperation with Communist guerillas, deep behind enemy lines in north China, and eventually to conduct joint sabotage operations against the Japanese.

CHAPTER 6
CHAIRMAN MAO

The C-47 circled above Xian for twenty minutes in a cloudless blue sky, awaiting U.S. fighter escorts for the final leg of the flight. The pilot, Capt. Jack Champion, ordered his passengers to put on their parachute packs in case the Japanese decided to attack. Service alone held no military rank, but he carried an official document stating that, if taken prisoner by the Japanese, he was to be afforded the same privileges as a U.S. Army colonel.

The aircraft now descended swiftly into a rugged and winding river canyon that cut through the loess hills that characterize this remote region. People emerged from their hillside caves to wave at the plane passing through the narrow valley. When the pilot sighted the landmark pagoda perched on the hill at the juncture of two forks of the Yen River, he banked the aircraft into a steep left turn for the final approach onto the old dirt runway built for Standard Oil's prewar operations.

Attracted by the loud drone of the aircraft's engines, people on the ground flocked to watch the landing. With its escort fighters circling overhead, the first American military transport touched down in Yenan. The flight had lasted a little more than three hours, but the Americans would soon discover a very different China.

As the aircraft started to taxi toward the excited crowd, there was a loud thud. The left landing wheel had punched through the ground over a long-forgotten grave, and the plane suddenly lurched and then settled awkwardly. The impact sheared off part of a propeller and sent it spinning into the left side of the pilot compartment. Luckily, the pilot was leaning forward to shut off the engines just as the blade slashed into the side of the aircraft, and he suffered only a slight bruise on his left hand; but the blade cut a gaping hole in the fuselage.[1] For several long minutes, everyone stood frozen in stunned and embarrassed confusion—the Communists' welcoming committee, their military honor guard, and the now-silent crowd of onlookers.

Only when Champion and Barrett jumped out to inspect the damage did the Communist delegation move forward, led by Zhou Enlai. Eighteen months had passed since John Service first suggested sending Americans to find out what the mysterious Communists were really like. The host delegation welcomed their American guests, and Col. David Barrett responded in perfect Mandarin: "We are mighty glad to be here—at last."[2]

After an informal lunch, Zhou Enlai sought out the pilot of the plane. "Captain, a hero has been wounded!" he exclaimed. "We consider your plane a hero," Colonel Barrett translated. "Fortunately, another hero, yourself, was not injured. Chairman Mao has asked me to convey to you his relief that you came to no harm." Within a few days, another American C-47 landed without mishap to deliver a new engine, propeller, and mechanics who stayed several weeks making repairs on the airplane that the Chinese had humorously dubbed "the Wounded Duck."[3]

The suave Communist leader had first issued an invitation for Americans to visit Yenan in 1942. Zhou Enlai still headed the Communists' Chungking office and served as a nominal member of the "national unity" war council that never met. Few members of the Dixie Mission understood that the Chinese Communist Party and the Nationalist Party had once been allies in the effort to unify the country in the 1920s. The Communists had supported Chiang Kai-shek's initial military expedition against regional warlords—before Chiang turned on them in the ruthless bloodletting of 1927. The Americans were well aware, however, that for the past few years, 300,000 of Chiang's best-equipped and most loyal troops had been stationed along the borders with Communist-controlled areas, not on the Japanese war front. Now, for a brief moment, the interests of the Americans and the Chinese Communists coincided: each sought an ally against the Japanese, and both sides were eager to achieve a reformed central government that could unify China for the war effort.

From the outset, the Americans' interaction with their Chinese hosts was characterized by good will and good humor. The Communists presented their guests with homespun high-collared Chinese suits and peaked caps much like their own uniforms. Years later, the photograph of the Dixie group adorned in those outfits would be seen as depicting a crew of Communist dupes and sympathizers. "Back in 1944, Communism was not the dirty word, involving accusations of folly or treason that it became in the McCarthy and Cold War days," John Service reflected. "The Soviet Union was our ally . . . and taking the great burden of losses." By 1950, when the clamorous search for Americans who "lost China" was in full swing, "membership in the Dixie Mission was not something one talked about."[4] Only after the historic handshake between President Nixon and Chairman Mao in 1972, signaling the restoration of Sino-American relations, did the group's secret wartime mission receive favorable recognition.

* * *

"The people alongside the road were robust, so were the horses, so were the mules, so were the dogs," noted one American on the bumpy, dusty ride from the landing strip along the banks of the river into Yenan. "Our officers exclaimed over the contrast to Chungking."[5] Japanese bombs had left few structures standing other than the hillside pagoda, the crumbling skeleton of ancient city walls, and an abandoned Catholic church. Most residents now lived in the caves carved into the cliffs: "Steep paths zigzag from one tier to the next, connecting the lowest with the highest tiers [of caves]. Before each cave opening is a tiny leveled patch notched into the cliff side for a chicken-coop, a pig-pen, a vegetable garden, or a children's playground, with perhaps a string of laundry flapping in the hot, dry sunshine."[6]

Sheltered against Japanese bomb raids, the local newspaper, *Liberation Daily*, was printed inside an ancient Buddhist temple cave adorned with ten thousand small, carved Buddha figures. It published an editorial (approved by Mao Zedong) hailing the Americans' arrival as "the most exciting event ever since the war against Japan started."[7] After that, the Americans were "treated with open arms and the red carpet treatment."[8]

Their celebrity sometimes caused problems. Within days of their arrival, the Communist leaders—embarrassed by the mishap at landing—mobilized a massive work party to make improvements at the old landing strip. Rocks and pebbles were painstakingly carried from the riverbed and pounded into the runway surface. "Everyone, from Mao Tse-tung on down to school children, was to contribute several days of labor," recalled Service. He suggested to Barrett that the American group join the effort. Their arrival at the worksite a few days later was so enthusiastically received that all work stopped. The curious locals crowded around to stare at the tall Americans with long noses, refusing to go back to work. "It was obviously the first time that the people assembled had ever seen foreigners doing coolie work. Our net contribution was certainly a minus and we did not return for a second day."[9]

Barrett and Service met officially with Zhou Enlai and Chu Teh, the commander-in-chief of Communist forces. Speaking in Mandarin, the Americans set forth their objectives: to learn as much as possible about the Communists' conduct of the war behind enemy lines; to gain intelligence on potential targets, landing strips, and location of enemy forces; to set up weather reporting stations; and to develop joint plans for rescuing any U.S. aircrews who might be downed in north China. Another part of their assignment, the Americans acknowledged, was to assess the fighting capability of Communist forces and determine what weapons and supplies might be usefully provided. But, they emphasized, they were there strictly as observers, with no authority to negotiate, offer aid or supplies, or make commitments of any kind.[10]

Chu Teh informed Service and Barrett that many of his guerrilla base leaders were arriving at headquarters for a party congress, and he offered to have them brief the American observers. Within a week, the visiting commanders began a series of sessions providing valuable up-to-date information about guerrilla bases and activities in enemy territory.[11]

In sharp contrast to the Nationalists, the Communist leaders were efficient in arranging for the Americans' independent radio communications, weather station, and other specialized needs. Service reflected that it had taken him a month to surmount the red tape in Chungking to get the Dixie Mission's travel permits. "It seemed to me that the Communists had decided that the best policy for dealing with we Americans was to be as much as possible unlike the [Nationalists]."[12]

The Americans had brought along some recreational materials provided by the Red Cross, to the delight of their hosts, who enjoyed dropping by in the evenings to play bridge. After watching a game of Monopoly, two Chinese officers showed up with a homemade version featuring Shanghai's streets, hotels, and famous landmarks. John Service wondered aloud whether such enthusiasm for the capitalist game would be encountered in Moscow.

Nestled in the hillsides on the far side of the muddy river were the central offices of the Chinese Communist Party and its military headquarters. The Communist nerve centers bustled with activity, dispatching orders, party directives, and personnel to remote bases: to Manchuria in the north and Canton in the south; to Hankou in the west and Shanghai in the east. The multitiered hillside cave dwellings of top officials and officers were furnished as simply as the Americans' spartan quarters. Nowhere in Yenan did Dixie members see anything resembling the ostentation of the Chungking officials. "Here was no such vast gulf," observed a visiting American reporter, "as separated a Chungking cabinet minister from his shivering, threadbare office clerk."[13]

At the official welcoming dinner held a few days after their arrival, John Service, as the group's only civilian and diplomat, had the place of honor on

Mao's right. Colonel Barrett sat on Mao's left, next to commander Chu Teh. Mao was then in his early fifties, a sturdy Hunanese who had once been a librarian. Chu was a short Sichuanese, with a personality as peppery as his province. The two men had fought as comrades since the dark days of 1927, when Chiang betrayed his Communist allies.

It would have been unthinkable for an American junior diplomat and a field grade military officer to be granted such access to such officials in Chungking. But here they sat between Yenan's top leaders, who claimed control of vast territory with nearly 90 million residents. For seventeen years, the Communists had been outlaws—and for the past six years, the Nationalist boycott had cut them off from contact with any outsiders. "Just going there was a form of recognition. This was tremendously important and welcome," John Service observed. "They were almost as interested to see us as we were to see them."[14] In fact, the Dixie group's own optimism about their mission perhaps magnified their importance in the eyes of the Communists.[15]

During the dinner, Mao asked Service if his inclusion in the mission meant that the United States planned to set up an official consulate. A permanent American diplomatic post would be helpful, Mao said, because it could help prevent open conflict between the two Chinese sides once the war against Japan was won—"the time of greatest danger of a Nationalist attack."[16] He then queried Service about "Tu-lu-man." It took a moment for the American diplomat to realize that Chairman Mao, in his thick Hunanese accent, was asking about Harry Truman, the Democrats' newly nominated vice presidential candidate. "They were astounded at Truman's nomination," Service said, "but then so were we all." The Communists worried that Wallace had been dumped because of his efforts on behalf of the Dixie Mission. Mao said he feared the United States was taking a terrible chance for the future. "The thought that one man's suggestion was sufficient to pluck out an almost unknown from the lower ranks and position him potentially to be the president of the United States and the leader of the great allied war coalition was staggering to them," Service recalled. Mao concluded the evening by suggesting that Service spend some time getting acquainted with Yenan life before they met again to exchange ideas.[17]

Mao's ascension to the role of party chairman in Yenan marked a sharp break with the hard-line policies of previous Soviet-trained party leaders. In a China that lacked any substantial industrial workers' base, the Leninist theory of revolution of the proletariat had led to disastrous results prior to the Long March. "Marxism must take on a national form before it can be applied," Mao insisted. "We must discard our dogmatism and replace it by a new and vital Chinese style and manner, pleasing to the eye and to the ear of the Chinese common people." As a result, Mao initiated a relentless "rectification" campaign—including harsh self-criticism sessions during party meetings—to strengthen party discipline. To further his revolutionary ideas, Mao imposed new party restrictions on the creative energy of artists and writers, harnessing it to fit his propaganda purposes.[18] By the time the Dixie Mission arrived, ideological consciousness and discipline had been well established—and was continually reinforced in meetings the Americans were never invited to attend.

After six days in Yenan, John Service reported on Dixie's impressions. He emphasized that the group had arrived with a healthy skepticism, determined not to be swept off their feet. But they all were thoroughly impressed. "We have come into a different country and are meeting a different people," he summarized. The contrast with Chungking was striking. There were no signs of desperate poverty, no beggars in the streets. "Bodyguards, gendarmes and the claptrap of Chungking officialdom are also completely lacking," he noted.[19] The Americans were struck also by Yenan's vigor, its apparent lack of war weariness. "Morale is very high," Service reported. "There is no defeatism, but rather confidence." Everyone appeared to have a job helping the war effort. Before classes, students could be seen spinning yarn. Instead of living off the peasantry (like the Nationalist soldiers he had observed in Honan), military work teams helped farmers to develop farmland and even harvested their own food. Self-reliance (*tzu-li geng-sheng*) was preached and practiced everywhere—even by the top Communist leaders, who tended their own vegetable gardens. Mao grew his own tobacco.

A pervasive spirit of confidence was the biggest surprise of all. "It was the same kind of optimism that motivated my father," Service explained in his unpublished memoirs. "[He] was a missionary convinced of the value and eventual success of his mission."[20] Service likened Yenan's atmosphere to that of an American religious summer conference, with the same tinge of "smugness, self-righteousness and conscious fellowship." And he looked forward to discovering how—despite its remoteness—Yenan had become "the most modern place in China."[21]

Under flickering candlelight, the chain-smoking John Service hunched over his portable typewriter late at night, pounding out a prodigious number of reports about his discoveries during three months in Yenan. These reports would give the American government (as even his critics later conceded) its most accurate picture of the rising Chinese Communist movement. As a result of his observations and experience in Yenan, Service developed a nuanced understanding of the Chinese Communists that went unheeded in Washington. He always eschewed the sympathetic term "so-called Communists," which was widely used at the time but obscured real ideological differences. At the same time, he learned not to assume that the strongly nationalistic Chinese Communists would submit to Moscow's direction.

Service's reports covered everything from the Communists' "new kind of people's war" to the Saturday evening dances in a pear orchard—where pretty young hospital nurses lined up to dance with Chairman Mao. (That some of them became his bedmates was kept confidential for many years.) The music was provided by a makeshift band of battered and improvised instruments, including a comb covered with paper. A local version of the conga, the *Yang-ko*, was a big hit with the Americans—and with Mao's young wife, Chiang Ching. A former actress, her trim figure and grace on the dance floor made her appear almost ravishing, even in the same unisex outfit worn by everyone else.[22]

On August 22, exactly one month after Dixie's arrival, Mao sent word to Service that it was time for a serious talk. The Chinese Communist Party Central Committee had just sent a secret directive to party members announcing an important policy shift. Dispatched to every Communist enclave (but declassified only in 1972), the directive "On Diplomatic Work" hailed the arrival of the American military observers as a significant event, bringing the hope of future "cultural and then political collaboration" with the United States.

Historians have long debated whether Mao's talk with Service was a truly remarkable conversation between the chairman and an American government official or simply an orchestrated part of the Chinese Communist Party's opportunistic efforts to deceive the Americans and gain an advantage over the Nationalists.[23] The conversation took place in Mao's cave dwelling and lasted eight hours, with a break for an informal dinner with Chiang Ching.[24] "America does not need to fear that we will not be cooperative. We must cooperate and we must have American help," Mao told Service. "That is why it is so important to us Communists to know what you Americans are thinking and planning. We cannot risk crossing you—and cannot risk any conflict with you." Service scribbled detailed notes during their session and afterward filed a long report, including translations of Mao's actual words. Critics would later claim that he naïvely accepted those words at face value.

Chairman Mao expressed great confidence that his party would either control China's government or play a significant role in it in the future. He spared no criticism of his Nationalist rivals. "Our support of Chiang does not mean support of despotism; we support him to fight Japan . . . [but he] was elected President by only ninety members of a single political party. . . . Hitler has a better claim to democratic power. He was elected by the people." And Mao made a strenuous bid for American cooperation with the Communists: "For America to insist that arms be given to all forces who fight Japan . . . is not interference. . . . To give arms only to the [Nationalists] will in its effect be interference. . . . Every American soldier in China should be a walking and talking advertisement for democracy. . . . There will have to be American cooperation with both Chinese forces. . . . The U.S. Army can see . . . that we have popular support and can fight."

Mao also talked about his dread of renewed civil war. "From bitter experience, we know it will mean long years of ruin and chaos for China . . . [and] a major international problem." The United States should take the lead in calling for a conference of all leading Chinese political groups, to work on creating a democratic constitution and to work out reforms for a reorganized, broader-based central government: half the conference seats should go to the Nationalist Party with the other half apportioned among all the other groups. Mao also spoke of his desire to rebuild China after the war with American assistance. Although the Soviet Union had been the only country to give Free China any aid before Pearl Harbor, he did not expect any further aid, noting that "the Russians have suffered greatly in the war, and will have their hands full with their own job of rebuilding." China's rapid redevelopment and industrialization, he asserted, could only be accomplished with free enterprise and the aid of foreign capital. Mao emphasized how well Chinese and American interests fit together, concluding: "We can and must work together."

Service was "almost taken off [his] feet by the warmth and fervor and earnestness" with which Mao argued for American support and sympathy.[25] His response, however, was astute. He jokingly remarked that American businessmen risking an investment in China might not consider a deal with Communists reassuring. "Mao laughed and said that they had thought of changing their name, but that if people knew them, they would not be frightened," he noted in his report. Mao ended their session by suggesting Service should take the next courier flight to Chungking and deliver his report personally to Ambassador Gauss, to expedite an official response to his questions and proposals. Service declined the suggestion, a decision he later regretted. "I didn't realize he was really putting himself down and asking, begging, pleading for a sort of American cooperation," Service told an interviewer twenty-seven years later—after Mao's historic handshake with Nixon. "[Mao] was right, I should have really gone down. I should have made it more clear what the Communists were asking, what they were proposing. . . . I think that was a mistake."[26]

John Service wasted no time, however, in filing a detailed report about his talk with Mao, with an introductory summary emphasizing that the Communists believed the actions and policies of the United States were extremely important for China's future. "These American policies will decide whether the Communists must play a lone hand and look out for themselves, or whether they can be assured of survival and participation in a democratic China, and so cooperate wholeheartedly in the war," Service wrote. "The Communists want our understanding and support; they are anxious to do nothing to alienate us or compromise that support."

In Chungking, however, the report was not treated with any sense of urgency at military headquarters, and the copy intended for Ambassador Gauss was not delivered promptly. Policymakers in Washington received the report a full two months later. By then, fateful decisions about China and the war had already been made, contributing to the deterioration of Sino-American relations over the next quarter of a century. Historians may continue to debate whether the Yenan conversation between Service and Mao was a watershed moment, representing a "lost chance in China."[27] One thing is certain: during the long years of bitter enmity, both sides kept silent about the cooperative spirit that flowered briefly in Yenan during the war.

* * *

Buoyed by the successful D-day landing in France and by the Allies' advance toward occupied Paris, Washington was now focusing on the alarming battlefield losses in China and Burma. The Generalissimo had set new preconditions for handing over command to General Stilwell, insisting that Chinese Communists could not serve under the American general until they first submitted to Chiang's authority. These preconditions were now bluntly rejected by the American president. "When the enemy is pressing us toward possible disaster, it appears unsound to refuse the aid of anyone who will kill Japanese," Roosevelt wrote in a top secret cable to Chiang. "With further delay, it may be too late to avert a military catastrophe tragic both to China and our Allied plans for the early overthrow of Japan."[28]

The men of the Dixie Mission were keenly aware of the worsening military situation, and they believed Yenan offered a gold mine of information about the Japanese. "The Communists were all we had hoped they would be, and even more," Barrett reported.[29] The OSS agents embedded within Dixie were especially enthusiastic about the prospect of working with the Communists. "Because of continuing skirmishing with the Japanese, they are an excellent source of POWs and captured documents," cabled Maj. Ray Cromley, a covert OSS expert on Japanese warfare. He was eager to exploit the potential for working behind enemy lines with Mao's guerrillas, just as OSS units were doing with Tito's Communist partisans in Yugoslavia. "People here are anxious to learn new intelligence methods, eager to supply information wanted, [and] quick to radio front line troops to secure missing details," Cromley told his superiors.[30] The

Communists had furnished him with an office and staff to translate captured Japanese documents, and they were willing to relay any American requests for intelligence to their forward guerilla positions, including specific questions for interrogation of POWs.

"We have an opportunity for doing a bigger job than you realize," Crowley enthused, "with men actually behind the Japanese lines in North China, Manchuria, Korea and Japan—if we work like blazes." He requested urgent delivery of supplies, including a hundred medical kits to be distributed as goodwill gifts to guerrilla units in the war zones. Colonel Barrett, who cleared all cables transmitted, added his own endorsement to the OSS message: "Possibilities of an Order of Battle Office in Yenan are limited only by the amount of trained personnel which can be assigned to it."[31]

Two other OSS agents were equally enthusiastic about their new Yenan connection. Capt. Charles Stelle, a bombing target analyst, and Capt. John Colling, a demolition and sabotage expert fresh from Burma's jungle warfare, considered it imperative to start gathering intelligence and begin special operations. "The Communists will agree to our establishing an independent communications and agent network and be glad to provide Chinese personnel for training in our methods," they cabled headquarters. They requested radio equipment and instructors to train the Communists. "We cannot too highly stress the potentialities of this center."[32]

Soon, Colling began giving lecture-demonstration classes on the use of powerful American demolition explosives and small arms to attentive audiences, numbering at times more than a thousand Chinese guerrillas, whose primitive but effective method for sabotaging Japanese-held rail lines involved pulling apart train tracks with their bare hands.

The OSS chief in Kunming enthusiastically endorsed a plan, code-named "Apple," to train and send Communist secret agents to Manchuria, Korea, and Japan. Apple's success would depend upon the cooperation of Susumu Okano. He was the top Japanese Communist residing in Yenan, one of many Asian revolutionaries trained (along with Ho Chi Minh) at a secret Yenan intelligence school that operated in cooperation with Soviet agents until 1943. For $400,000, Susumu agreed to provide operatives to penetrate Japanese territory. The OSS men voiced no objection to the amount and eagerly pushed the plan forward.

"This is just the kind of project Oboe Sugar Sugar [OSS] was created to do," Col. Robert Hall responded. "I am hoping we will be allowed to undertake it, even if it means a slight exposure of the neck . . . if the necessary courage and imagination can be mustered to put it through." Hall then warned Washington about a competing SACO-based OSS unit that was secretly training Tai Li's secret commandos near the Communist border region. "We are treading in somewhat dangerous waters, but the potential gains are enormous. . . . Any mixing of these two elements would cause a complete explosion."[33]

* * *

Five days after his talks with Mao, John Service sent a dispatch to Stilwell's headquarters with a controversial policy recommendation. Acknowledging that initiating active cooperation with the Communists would involve serious questions of military and political policy, he nevertheless strongly advocated giving basic military supplies and training directly to the Chinese Communist forces. "We must decide whether the gains we can reasonably expect from aiding the Communists will justify the overcoming—or disregarding—of this Kuomintang [Nationalist] opposition." He believed such aid would effectively contribute to the war effort—and would pressure the central government to institute long overdue political reforms. It would also "almost certainly make it impossible for the Kuomintang [Nationalists] to start a civil war." Service then posed a challenge: "If the Kuomintang [Nationalist government] is actually what it claims to be—democratic and sincerely anxious to defeat the Japanese as quickly as possible—it should not oppose our insistence on giving at least proportional aid to the Communists."[34]

Privately, Zhou Enlai had already assured Service that the Communists were willing to serve under an American allied supreme commander if the central government gave its approval. "We are convinced these people mean business," Service cabled to Davies in New Delhi. At the time, Stilwell's new command of all Chinese forces appeared imminent, and Service felt that work with the Communist forces needed to begin immediately. He urged Davies to make sure the long list of supplies requested by Barrett and the OSS agents—including rifles, bazookas, light artillery, ammunition, demolition supplies, radio equipment, and the gift medical kits—"doesn't get lost in the shuffle."[35]

Patrick Hurley, the president's new envoy, arrived in New Delhi on September 4 accompanied by Donald Nelson, the former head of the War Production Board. Stilwell, newly promoted to four-star general, had welcomed Hurley's appointment, telling General Marshall that "it takes oil as well as vinegar to make good French dressing."[36] After a private send-off meeting with Roosevelt, Hurley had informed State Department officials that his presidential orders were limited to improving relations between Chiang and Stilwell and facilitating the American general's command of Chinese armies. He was to keep Ambassador Gauss fully updated on his progress but would report directly to the president.

Hurley's first stop had been Moscow. The United States was still courting the Russians to join the war against Japan, and Hurley wanted to ascertain Kremlin reaction to his China mission. Soviet foreign minister Vyacheslav Molotov said his country had no objection to U.S. plans to put an American in command of Chinese forces, but he questioned whether they would ever be militarily effective. As for Mao's followers, they were "not true Communists at all," and he assured Hurley that the Kremlin had no intention of giving support to "the so-called Communists."[37] Hurley concluded that, if the Russians refused to offer support, the Chinese Communists would ultimately be forced to come to a political agreement with Chiang.

"I wish I had more men like Pat," Roosevelt told his son Elliot. "If anybody can straighten out the mess of internal Chinese politics, he's the man."[38] But he was wrong: Hurley and Roosevelt's strategy was based on the faulty assumption that the Soviets held decisive influence in Yenan.

Washington still did not recognize the potential strength of Mao's movement of national liberation. In 1944 only a handful of foreigners had actually observed the growing influence and popular support of the Chinese Communist Party, or witnessed Mao's innovative program that rejected many Soviet tenets of Communism. "We Chinese Communists . . . are convinced that the capitalistic world and the USSR can and will learn to cooperate closely in peace as in war," Mao told a visiting Western journalist. "China can and must be one of the bridges between the two camps instead of hoping to win foreign support as one of the zones of friction."[39]

On September 6, as General Stilwell accompanied Hurley and Nelson to Chungking to begin talks with Chiang, his trusted aide, John Davies, traveled to Washington to help grease the political wheels. He met with Harry Hopkins, who acknowledged that the Japanese offensive had validated General Stilwell's ground strategy rather than Chennault's air strategy. Given the strong backing of the White House, Hopkins expressed confidence that Stilwell would now succeed—and seemed surprised by Davies' comment that Stilwell still expected to face "a hard battle against Chinese recalcitrance, lethargy, and indifference."[40]

The high hopes for the new American command of China's armies soon foundered on the shoals of Chinese cultural pride—and the resistance of a stubborn and desperate Chiang. "Even had [Stilwell] had the tongue of angels, the temperament of a saint and the professional charm of a Japanese geisha," historian Barbara Tuchman noted, "the Generalissimo would still have had no more intention of giving him command of his armed forces than of giving it to Mao Tse-tung."[41] Over the next few months, Patrick Hurley's efforts would bring to an end Gen. Joseph Stilwell's long career in China and would exacerbate America's dilemma over the two Chinas.

CHAPTER 7
OCTOBER CRISIS

Once settled in Yenan, Jack sent an embassy friend, Tony Freeman, to tell Val Chao of his whereabouts; he had deliberately kept her in the dark about the venture. Tony Freeman also delivered some money from Jack, for use in furnishing their room, which she refused to accept: "If we are going to buy anything, it will be when Jack comes back."[1] Over the next three months Val received only two letters from him, although some old school friends in Yenan wrote urging her to join him there. They no doubt gave glowing descriptions of the warm reception given the honored American guests and their informal, easy mingling with locals at the Saturday night dances in the pear orchard. Perhaps they even reported on their baseball games—one even played against a team of Japanese prisoners of war.

There were more than 150 Japanese prisoners in Yenan. It was a sharp contrast to Chungking, where the Americans had little access to the handful of Japanese POWs held by the Nationalists. Here there was no stockade—the prisoners were "re-educated" at the Japanese Workers' and Farmers' School in caves below the hillside pagoda. Upon graduation, many of them joined the Japanese People's Liberation League and engaged in propaganda work to persuade Japanese soldiers to become deserters.

The OSS agents in Dixie were astonished to find these POWs willing and eager to provide valuable information, and even to infiltrate Japan's inner zone for their proposed intelligence mission. "It is highly probable they had been thoroughly brainwashed," Colonel Barrett reflected years later, noting that the process was generally unknown at the time.[2]

Following the guerrilla commanders' briefings, Service was allowed to conduct his own interviews. He was impressed by the accessibility and openness of the

Communists he was getting to know. Often Mao would send him to meet with a party cadre or military officer knowledgeable in a particular topic. These Yenan officials were unlike any that Service had encountered in Washington or Chungking—where he could often tell a man's rank by whether he had a water carafe on his desk, a rug on the floor, or a name on the door. "Mao Tse-tung might drop by for a chat in the evening, or Chu Teh, or we could go over and see them almost at any time or on very short notice," he recalled. These informal chats often took place as they soaked their muddy feet in a tub of hot water after fording the river. Several top cadres were from Sichuan; they posed for a photograph with Service, as fellow provincials. And Chen Yi (who would become foreign minister) invariably referred to Service as "the son of my teacher" because he once belonged to Bob Service's YMCA.

Service found these conversations with party stalwarts intellectually stimulating. The self-reliant Communists appeared in no rush to obtain American assistance; they realized that Roosevelt was too busy running for reelection to focus on China policy. Their frankness was very different from the traditional Chinese politeness that prized correct form over content. The American missionary's son felt very much at home in this rustic place, with its can-do spirit and pragmatism that in many ways mirrored his own family's values. And he felt the same sense "of acceptance, of hospitality, of not being guarded, of not holding people off" that he had first experienced on the long trip to the oilfield.[3]

After six weeks in Yenan, Service wrote a report detailing his positive impressions of the Communist leaders and their physical and intellectual vigor. He concluded that the Chinese Communist Party's growing power and influence could not be ignored. "They seem to know that they have been through hard times and have accomplished creditable things, and they are confident that they are now on the winning tide." He concluded that "the Communists will compromise, if it is decided to be for the best long-term interest of the Party; that they will fight when the need arises; and that they can be hard and ruthless if that becomes necessary."

He found it difficult to get them to engage in what they regarded as "useless" discussions of pure theory. The most ideological cadres were apparently now in disgrace; the current leaders insisted that "the test of everything was whether it works—in China." His report also highlighted the leadership group's uniformity of thinking and expressions, their effacement of individuality, and their relative lack of a sense of humor. In general, however, "their manners, habits of thought, and direct handling of problems seem more American than Oriental."[4]

Several senior State Department officials were extremely critical of Service's glowing reports from Yenan. Even John Carter Vincent, his friend and former embassy colleague, worried that the young diplomat might be unduly influenced by the Communists' openness and wondered if his interpretations lacked balance and objectivity. And during the Cold War—with the desperate wartime context long forgotten—Service's favorable assessments of the Communists would become highly suspect.[5]

Less attention was paid, however, to his comments about their ruthlessness. And several more decades would pass before the Chinese Communists' internal documents were released, revealing the rigid Leninist framework of party control underlying their pragmatism—and their deadly earnest plan to seize power.

* * *

In early September, missing American pilot 1st Lt. Joseph P. Baglio walked into Yenan after safely trekking across a thousand miles of enemy territory under Chinese Communist escort. He had been on a strafing mission over railroad lines in Shanxi Province on June 9 when his aircraft was hit by ground fire. He bailed out, and a peasant farmer gave him water and put him in contact with a guerrilla band. The astonishing account of his experiences provided the first independent confirmation of the Communists' claims to control extensive territory behind enemy lines.

Baglio was deeply impressed with the courage of villagers along the escape route: they kept a keen eye on the movement of Japanese units, served as scouts, and readily provided his rescue party with food and shelter, helping them evade the Japanese troops who were scouring the area for the downed flyer. After a week of cat-and-mouse maneuvers, sleeping in safe houses during the day and traveling at night, the band met up with a regular 8th Route Army unit. The tall American was outfitted in ill-fitting peasant clothes and a big conical straw hat for the long trek to the soldiers' headquarters. Before departing with the soldiers, Baglio's guerrilla guide returned his gun.

After a much-needed rest, Baglio traveled under armed escort through Japanese-controlled territory, sometimes within five hundred yards of enemy troops. The unit engaged in a few skirmishes, but they always prevailed and often returned to camp with captured Japanese weapons and ammunition. In the self-governing "liberated" territories, he could move safely in daylight, accompanied by a single guard, an interpreter, and two orderlies. He saw large areas devastated by the Japanese. Baglio, on what he called an embarrassing "march of triumph" was paraded through village streets decorated with signs of welcome and lined with smiling, curious people. Such celebrations made the security-conscious American pilot uncomfortable, but his guides remained unconcerned. "These people have no fear of the Japs," Baglio reported. "The people would rather die than give up secrets of the *Ba Lu Jun*—the 8th Route Army—and although security seems to be compromised, actually it is kept within this large, family circle and away from the Japanese."[6]

"Baglio spent no money—NOT ONE CENT," noted 1st Lt. Henry Whittlesey in his official report. Even more surprising, the Communist authorities gave no indication that they expected any compensation for the food, clothing, bedding, and cigarettes Baglio had been given during his eighty-five-day sojourn. "They feel it is part of their contribution to the war," the astonished Whittlesey reported. "This is a pleasant contrast to some of the ridiculous and high demands by certain [Nationalist] generals for expenses in connection with the saving of our fliers." Once he was safely in Yenan, the grateful Baglio sent his pistol back to the guerrilla leader who first helped him. "This is the only recognition that has been given," his debriefer reported, suggesting that if the U.S. Army wanted to express its appreciation, a gift of medicines or radios would be most appreciated by the guerrillas.[7]

A story about Baglio's rescue was filed by an American correspondent visiting Yenan but was quickly killed by American military censors in Chungking on the grounds that publication could jeopardize the safety and continued rescue of pilots from behind enemy lines. John Service considered this decision misguided and lodged a complaint. Even though American maps showed all north China as enemy territory, his memo explained, most of the region Baglio traveled through was *not* occupied by the enemy. He described China's territory as a checkerboard controlled by a variety of forces, including the Communists. Baglio's rescue vividly depicted the actual conditions of the north China war front, which, he felt, needed to be better understood back home. "This encouraging picture of active resistance and Chinese-American cooperation is all the more desirable," Service pointed out, "because of the gloomy news the American public is now receiving from the rest of China."[8]

News from other Chinese warfronts was indeed grim. In east and southeast China, the second phase of the Japanese Ichigo offensive was gathering steam. From recently captured Hengyang, enemy divisions were driving southward along a key railroad line. Other forces were moving north from Canton, clearly intending to link up for a joint assault on the major American air bases at Kweilin and Liuchow. Nationalist resistance was reported light, with many troops in retreat. And the battle front in Burma was heating up. Lacking the long-promised replacements from China for his American-trained forces, General Stilwell was worried that the Japanese might repel his planned offensive against their key position in north Burma and counterattack.

People in Chungking were beginning to panic. Some top officials were offering bribes to airlift their own families out over the Hump. Madame Chiang had already left, along with her sister, for a South American sanctuary. The Generalissimo was pressuring the White House and War Department for more supplies to Chennault's air force—but Chennault himself was now urging Washington to expedite supplies for Chinese ground forces, for defense of his threatened air bases.[9]

Dixie Mission observers, meanwhile, reported mounting evidence that Mao's guerrilla forces had mobilized effective popular resistance behind enemy lines in north China. John Colling, the OSS agent, took off on a six-week field trip with a small 8th Route Army unit to observe front line action, carrying cameras and a cache of powerful explosives. During their arduous tour of guerrilla areas, Maj. Melvin Casberg, the Dixie Mission's doctor, helped treat the wounded, including enemy soldiers. "There have been numerous accusations by the Kuomintang [Nationalists] that the 8th Route Army is not fighting the Japanese," he reported upon his return to Yenan. "From my observations, I am convinced that nothing could be farther from the truth." He also confirmed Lieutenant Baglio's observations of solidarity with the civilians. "I have seen villagers walk up to the soldiers passing through and give them gifts of food such as ears of corn, fruit and bread." Casberg likened the volunteer local militia to American Revolutionary Minutemen, marveling at their skill in evacuating villages in advance of Japanese patrols, their elaborate defensive cave networks, and, above all, their intelligence network: "When we attacked a blockhouse we knew not only the exact number of the soldiers, both the Japanese and puppet, but also in many cases even the names of the soldiers."[10]

Such eyewitness reports motivated John Service to dig deeper for answers to the big question: How had the Communists, unlike the Nationalists, been able to successfully expand their armies, increase territory, and improve life for a growing population during seven long years of the brutal Sino-Japanese War? The Communists' success, Service recognized, was causing a significant shift in the balance of Chinese political power. He now feared that an eruption of open civil war would be catastrophic.

"Even though such a civil war would be immensely harmful to our own interests," he cautioned, "we must consider that we would be accused—with much justification—of having contributed to it by our present arming of the military forces of the Kuomintang [Nationalists]." At a time when the situation was still fluid and the future alignment of the Chinese Communists was not yet firmly fixed, Service urged the United States to reassess how best to try to influence China's troubled affairs.[11] He expressed the hope that the United States could serve as an honest broker between the two Chinas.

The Communist idea of active personal resistance represented a radical shift for the traditionally apathetic peasantry. Throughout the ages, Chinese peasants had feared soldiers and dreaded government officials. Service had seen them flee from the rival warlord armies fighting around his hometown, Chengdu. As a Foreign Service officer he had observed long lines of half-starved conscripts roped together along the roadsides and witnessed how the Nationalist army's officers and officials—with their demands for exorbitant taxes and scarce food—helped turn Honan's drought into a famine. But in north China, the peasants enthusiastically supported and even fought alongside the Communist armies.

"Their whole program of political indoctrination and organization of the people, and of institution of economic policies to unite all classes and yet improve the condition of the poorer groups, is essential to support their warfare," reported Service. "Understanding of this interrelation of military, political and economic phases of Communist policies is of the utmost importance in any study of the present situation of the Chinese Communists because it is the key to their success."[12]

Service reported extensively on specific methods of Communist political indoctrination, and on the organization of various self-reliant cooperatives and volunteer militias. He wrote about the election of local government councils in the pacified areas where the Communists strictly limited themselves to one-third of the council seats. Once order and security were established, they reduced rents and interest rates to relieve burdens on the peasantry—but not so much as to drive away the landlord class. The peasants, he observed, had become genuine stakeholders in a movement that appeared to be moderate and relatively democratic. Later, however, critics would fault Service's claim that the Communist program involved "a tendency toward democracy" and an "apparent strong orientation of the Chinese Communists toward the United States."[13]

By early October the compelling evidence of growing Communist strength and confidence made a key conclusion inescapable: the Japanese were being actively opposed in north China. The enemy could temporarily crush opposition by concentrating overwhelming force in a limited area, but it could not subdue the vast territories the Communists had successfully organized in resistance. "This total mobilization is based upon and has been made possible by what amounts to an economic, political, and social revolution," Service reported in an October 9, 1944, memo.[14] Mao's "New Democracy" had evolved out of the character of Chinese feudal society and not from Marx's prescription for proletarian revolution in Western industrial society.

"The Japanese are being fought now not merely because they are foreign invaders," Service astutely pointed out, "but because they deny this revolution." Once the war ended, he warned, the people would fight any government that tried to limit or take away these newly won gains. "Unless the Kuomintang goes as far as the Communists in political and economic reform," he predicted, "the Communists will be the dominant force in China within a comparatively few years."[15]

* * *

Greeted by a buzz of optimism, Patrick Hurley arrived in Chungking in early September, accompanied by Stilwell, to begin secret negotiations with the Generalissimo. As the Americans drafted an agenda for their upcoming talks and the proposed directive for Stilwell's command responsibilities, "Vinegar Joe" made it clear that he planned to use the "Reds" in his plan to turn around the current military crisis. "There must be no misunderstanding on this point," he instructed Hurley. "They must be accepted as part of the team during the crisis." To avoid possible conflict with Chiang's forces, he would deploy Communist forces in separate sectors. "This was not exactly a conspirator's undercover plot to use the Communists to overthrow Chiang Kai-shek as was later, in the hysterical days of American anti-Communism, suggested," observed historian Barbara Tuchman.[16] Hurley voiced no objection at the time—although he would play a role later in orchestrating the hysteria.

Stilwell hoped finally to gain enough power to accomplish the military reforms he had been urging on the Chinese since 1942. As supreme commander, he told Hurley, he must have the right to reorganize and relocate Chinese forces as he saw fit.[17] Hurley exuded the confidence of a man who could put through a quick deal, and he clearly had Roosevelt's strong backing. Stilwell now saw the chance to realize his dream—although he must have recognized that these changes threatened to undermine the Generalissimo's power.[18]

* * *

While Hurley was presenting their draft proposals to Chiang on September 13, Stilwell received two representatives of the Chinese Communist Party carrying an important message from Zhou Enlai. Encouraged by their friendly interaction with the Dixie Mission, the Communist Party leadership had decided to seize the opportunity to compete openly with the Nationalists for American support. Zhou's emissaries informed Stilwell that the Communist forces were preparing to reenter southwest China and were ready to serve under his command, but they expected to receive a fair share of Lend-Lease arms and supplies. They also relayed an invitation for Stilwell and Hurley to visit Yenan. Stilwell assured them that, as soon as he became allied commander, he would travel there to negotiate Communist acceptance of Chiang's central government authority.

Later that same day, Stilwell flew to Kweilin to assess the military situation of Chennault's forward airbases. He found them virtually undefended. "The jig is up in south China," Stilwell cabled General Marshall, "largely due to lack of proper command and the usual back-seat driving from Chungking." He was reluctantly ordering the evacuation of the American installations—and the demolition of their airfields and stockpiles of precious aviation fuel.[19]

Returning to Chungking, Stilwell found an agitated Chiang Kai-shek threatening to pull his U.S.-trained forces out of Burma even as victory was in sight. The Generalissimo insisted that those troops were needed in China to shore up his poorly equipped armies against the Japanese assault. Yet he stubbornly refused to redeploy any of his well-armed troops from the border with Communist regions—or to release the large cache of American weapons and ammunition hidden near Kweilin (and later discovered by OSS agents) out of distrust of the local warlord.

In a private meeting with T. V. Soong and Hurley, Stilwell bluntly insisted that once he took responsibility for all Chinese forces, "the Generalissimo must refrain from any interference in operations." Foreign Minister Soong expressed great shock at the general's plain talk. "T. V. let that cat out of the bag," Stilwell recorded in his personal papers. "What the Peanut wants is an overall stooge, apparently foisted on him by the U.S."[20] The negotiations over American command of Chinese forces were at a standstill almost before they began.

* * *

As the battlefront crises mounted during the summer and fall of 1944, Chiang grew increasingly resentful of American pressure for action. Secretary of State Hull blandly advised him that "factional differences can and should be merged and settled by intelligent conciliation and cooperation." Ambassador Gauss tried to reassure Chiang: "We are not interested in the Chinese Communist cause. However, we are interested in seeing a prompt solution of a Chinese internal problem which finds the armed forces of China facing one another instead of facing and making war upon Japan."[21] He suggested that Chiang resurrect the united front war council. Chiang refused, complaining that the Communists had grown more arrogant and unwilling to submit to his authority since the Dixie Mission went to Yenan.

The Americans, in fact, were seriously contemplating sending Lend-Lease aid directly to Mao's forces—and Chiang well understood the truth of Mao's dictum, "political power grows out of the barrel of a gun." He confided to his diary that he would never yield to the foreigners' pressure.

In mid-September, while China's warfront and command crises were coming to a climax, President Roosevelt and his closest advisers were in Quebec for an intense strategy conference with the British. The Anglo-American allies were bickering over a variety of policy issues, including the postwar treatment of Germany and the recovery of colonial territories. Churchill told Roosevelt to "leave his Indians alone," promising in return to "leave the President's Chinese alone."[22]

When General Marshall received Stilwell's distressing situation report on Kweilin and Burma, he quickly prepared a stern message to Chiang Kai-shek from Roosevelt. The top secret presidential cable arrived at Chungking the morning of September 19, and Stilwell judged it "hot as a firecracker" and ordered a translation prepared immediately. Late that afternoon the general hastened to Chiang's country villa, where Patrick Hurley was in conference with the Generalissimo, Foreign Minister Soong, and the top Chinese military advisers. Stilwell sent in a message for Hurley to meet him on the veranda, where he showed him the "bundle of paprika" from Roosevelt:

> I have urged time and again in recent months that you take drastic action to resist the disaster which has been moving closer to China and to you. Now, when you have not yet placed General Stilwell in command of all forces in China, we are faced with the loss of a critical area in east China with possible catastrophic consequences. . . . I am certain that the only thing you can now do in an attempt to prevent the Jap from achieving his objectives in China is to reinforce your Salween armies [in Burma] and press their offensive, while at once placing General Stilwell in unrestricted command of all your forces.[23]

Patrick Hurley feared that the blunt message might upset his delicate negotiations. He urged Stilwell to let him paraphrase it, assuring him that "You've won the ball game already." Chiang, he claimed, was about to give him the command and make him "the master of China's future."[24] The general insisted that his orders were to deliver the message personally. Together they walked into the conference room.

After polite greetings were exchanged and tea was served, General Stilwell rose and told Chiang Kai-shek he had a message from President Roosevelt, which he passed to Gen. Chu Shih-ming to read aloud. Stilwell must have understood how humiliating this message would be, delivered aloud in front of the Generalissimo's subordinates; one of Chiang's greatest political assets was his claim to strong American support. Hurley quickly intervened, grabbing the translated message from Chu and handing it directly to Chiang.

After slowly scanning the Chinese characters, Chiang quietly remarked, "I understand," and then replaced the cover on his teacup—the traditional gesture by which imperial mandarins dismissed unwanted callers. Stilwell recognized the signal but refused to play along. He asked, in fluent Chinese: "Does that still mean in polite Chinese that the party is over?"

The two antagonist allies had finally crossed their Rubicon. Stilwell expressed his relish at Chiang's chagrin in a letter to his wife written in doggerel verse:

I've waited long for vengeance—
At last I've had my chance.
I've looked the Peanut in the eye
And kicked him in the pants.

I know I've still to suffer
And run a weary race.
But oh! The blessed pleasure!
I've wrecked the Peanut's face.[25]

Vinegar Joe's celebration was a Pyrrhic victory. Within days, the irate and humiliated Generalissimo told Hurley he would demand Stilwell's recall, since by giving him the memo he had proven insubordinate. The suave, Harvard-educated T. V. Soong (now Chiang's foreign minister) persuaded Hurley that Stilwell himself must have drafted the insulting presidential cable—and that Hurley's promising negotiations had been frustrated only by the bitter personality conflict between Stilwell and Chiang Kai-shek. Hurley was flattered with these reassurances.

The Americans seemed unaware that the confrontation signaled a significant turning point. Stilwell felt confident that a deal was inevitable and that the cable proved he finally had the president's full support. To restore some of Chiang's lost face, he promised the minister of war that he would defer sending weapons or supplies to the Communists. His clash of personality with Chiang, after all, was nothing new. "It is not a choice between throwing me out or losing CKS [Chiang Kai-shek] and possibly China," he assured General Marshall, "[but of] losing China's potential effort if CKS makes the rules now. . . . If I considered that my removal would be the solution, I would be the first to suggest it."[26]

Marshall continued to back Stilwell strongly, despite strong opposition from other presidential advisers—Hopkins, Wallace, Currie, and Hurley. These advisers urged "logical persuasion" rather than tough bargaining pressure. "If you sustain Stilwell in this controversy you will lose Chiang Kai-shek and possibly you will lose China with him," Hurley cabled Roosevelt, raising for the first time the specter of the loss of China. "There is no other issue between you and Chiang Kai-shek. . . . [He] has agreed to every request, every suggestion made by you except the Stilwell appointment."[27]

In truth, President Roosevelt was not prepared to make any major policy decisions on China. His energies were exhausted by a grueling fourth-term election campaign, renewed German resistance in Europe, and battles with Winston Churchill over postwar strategy. He was also afflicted by horrific headaches, caused by the atherosclerotic disease that his doctors quietly feared might kill him within a few months. After investing so much prestige in building up China's image as a major power in the postwar world, FDR must have wanted desperately to believe Hurley's upbeat assessment.

Negotiations over Stilwell's command remained at a standstill for nearly three weeks as the presidential advisers debated Roosevelt's options. T. V. Soong appealed to Hopkins for assistance. Finally, at a Washington dinner party on October 1, Hopkins drew aside his friend H. H. Kung, who was the brother-in-law of Soong and Chiang (as well as Service's landlord). Roosevelt would accede to Chiang's wishes and remove Stilwell, he assured Kung; a formal reply was being withheld only until a replacement could be selected. Kung gleefully cabled this insider's news to Chungking. The following day, Chiang announced to a secret party council that he was willing to risk losing American aid by getting rid of Stilwell—knowing that he had already won in Washington.[28]

* * *

By early October, the cold winds from the Manchurian steppes were blowing sharply down through Shaanxi Province into Yenan. "It is cold as hell," Service warned a newcomer. "Bring bedding and plenty of warm clothes."[29] One cold remedy gratefully enjoyed by the American observers was a hot toddy of rum or scotch mixed with hot water. Their quarters were heated by charcoal braziers that gave off dangerous carbon monoxide fumes, and the outfit's doctor, Major Casberg, sometimes had to revive unconscious colleagues. Despite the freezing temperatures, he admonished them to keep their tiny rice paper windows ajar as the only way to prevent asphyxiation.

On October 9, the American supply plane arrived with a fresh case of liquor—and the startling news of Stilwell's possible recall. The bombshell landed heaviest on John Service. He alone knew about Roosevelt's top secret cables to Chiang in July. By now he had become convinced not only that the Communists could effectively contribute to the United States' war effort but also that they were destined to be important political players in China's future. "The Communists have built up support of a magnitude and depth which makes their elimination impossible," he had reported just hours earlier.[30]

That the key issue between Chungking and Washington had become General Stilwell himself, rather than the current military crisis, seemed "the height of folly" to Service. He immediately wrote a memo to the general—"and in my agitated state, fulminated!"[31] His memo minced no words. "Our dealings with Chiang Kai-shek apparently continue on the basis of the unrealistic assumption that he is China and that he is necessary to our cause. . . . The fact is that no one who knows anything about China and is concerned over American rather than Chiang's interests will satisfy Chiang." Service urged that the United States adopt a new more realistic policy and a tougher negotiating stance, since "Chiang's own dealings with us have been an opportunist combination of extravagant demands and unfulfilled promises, wheedling and bargaining, bluff and blackmail. . . . We should end the hollow pretense that China is unified and that we can talk only to Chiang. This puts the trump card in Chiang's hands."[32]

Before he ever received Service's memo, Stilwell was hustled home. But the U.S. Navy–trained radio operators at SACO headquarters intercepted the cable, and Tai Li's agents made sure to deliver a copy to Patrick Hurley. This dispatch would earn Service the undying animosity of Chiang and his supporters, who would stir up "so much hullabaloo later on."[33]

Col. David Barrett, the Dixie Mission commander who approved all communications, became increasingly concerned about Service's strongly worded reports and his highly favorable assessment of the Communists. "In all sincerity, I saw nothing in them which savored to me of disloyalty," Barrett later noted, but he cautioned his friend to be careful. "Dave, I'm a Foreign Service officer," Service replied. "What I have written . . . and the recommendations I have made are my observations and carefully considered opinions. If they don't like them in Washington, they can throw them out."[34]

* * *

Before his unceremonious exit, Stilwell briefed Davies on his recall and received his aide's report on his Washington consultations. They decided Davies should immediately go to Yenan to update Service and give him priority travel orders to return to Washington for expected discussions about the China crisis. Davies arrived in Yenan on October 22, two days after Stilwell left Chungking. He and Service discussed the fallout from the Stilwell downfall and began planning for their "extrication from the debris." Both men feared that the United States might be sucked into the looming civil war on Chiang's side, which would force Yenan to turn to the Soviet Union. "After Stilwell's recall, I really felt that we were headed down the wrong track," Service confided. "Both Davies and I felt we were making a serious mistake in tying ourselves to the KMT [Nationalists] and giving in to Chiang. So as time went on, I certainly became much more of an advocate of a policy position. After the Stilwell affair, most of us felt that it was worth sticking our necks out."[35]

As Stilwell's top political adviser, Davies was now a lame duck. Nevertheless, before leaving Chungking he sent a note to Hurley urging him to make the trip to Yenan and meet the Communist leaders. "If the Communist leaders are phonies and small-time operators, the president should know it; if they've got what it takes, he should know it. And you're the one to make the estimate for him. I'll have the welcome mat out."[36]

At the time, no one realized that Roosevelt had written off not only Stilwell but also Chiang—and the China theatre itself. The president had become increasingly disenchanted with Chiang and more interested in gaining Stalin's cooperation, both for the fight against Tokyo and for the preservation of peace once the war was won. By mid-October 1944, the Soviet entry into the war against Japan was being planned in secret meetings held in Moscow by Stalin, Churchill, and the American ambassador, Averell Harriman. The Russians tentatively agreed to launch a counteroffensive against Japanese land forces in Manchuria and north China within three months of Germany's defeat. Americans would fly air operations against the Japanese islands from Siberia and would provide air support for the Russians following a U.S. ground offensive limited to capturing airfields along China's east coast. But in the north, it would be Soviet boots on the ground.[37]

These productive Moscow talks prompted FDR to shift gears on China. With the Russian entry into the war so near, he decided not to continue the fruitless command negotiations with the Generalissimo. Rather, the awkward China-Burma-India Theatre was restructured into two separate commands: Burma-India and China. Lt. Gen. Albert Wedemeyer was tapped to head the U.S. headquarters in China and to serve only as Chiang's allied chief of staff; another general would be given the Burma-India command.

American war planners thus dismissed China as a significant warfront. Just before his departure, Stilwell was informed that China would serve merely as a military decoy. America's counteroffensive would focus on the increasingly successful island-hopping campaign in the Pacific and Gen. Douglas MacArthur's fight to regain the Philippines. A major landing of U.S. troops in China was no longer under consideration. Few American officials—and certainly none in the

China war zone—had any inkling of the top secret atomic bomb research under way at Los Alamos.

* * *

Gen. Chu Teh and Zhou Enlai hosted a welcome dinner for John Paton Davies in Yenan, inviting the entire Dixie Mission along with Communist party and army leaders and the handful of foreign correspondents, including the Tass (Soviet news agency) representatives. Among the guests was an American doctor named George Hatem, known locally as "Dr. Ma," who had accompanied journalist Edgar Snow as an interpreter and remained in Yenan. Married to a Chinese woman, he worked in the Yenan field hospital and occasionally served as one of Dixie's interpreters.

After the meal, Zhou invited the American diplomats—Davies and Service, along with John Emmerson (Dixie's Japanese specialist, debriefing Japanese POWs)—to his private cave to continue the conversation. They were soon joined by Mao and Chu Teh.

"It was an inconclusive talk in that no definite decisions resulted," Davies recalled. "I tested Mao on his August statement that American forces should land on the North China coast. What support would the Communists give to such a landing? He replied that they would collaborate fully—provided that the American effort was a major one and included supplying them." Davies was asked to meet with Chu and his chief of staff to discuss the specific details.

Davies had already drafted a general plan for Stilwell calling for joint operations with the Communists, and it seems likely that he discussed the plan in his talks with the Communist leaders. His plan aimed to forestall a Soviet takeover of north China (though that was never one of Washington's major considerations). Chinese Communist units and U.S. paratroopers would seize Shanghai, the strategically important occupied port city, and its surrounding areas in an operation that was to be kept secret from Chiang until its successful completion.[38] Davies was no doubt aware that Dixie's OSS agents were negotiating to go into Japanese territory and establish a radio intelligence network throughout north China.

The following morning Service left Yenan, bound for Washington and an anticipated major review of China policy following Stilwell's recall. The general had tasked him to brief policymakers about their allies in Yenan. Once again, John Service was breaking the mold of a low-ranking diplomat, and he relished his extraordinary role.

Before departing, Chu Teh's deputy presented Service with a hand-drawn, three-foot-by-five-foot map of China's occupied territory and coastline showing the major Japanese troop concentrations and bunkers, the Communist guerrilla areas, and their politico-military base regions behind enemy lines. It also showed several airfields—disguised as village playing fields—under construction by the Communists in anticipation of a major American deployment. Service was encouraged to show this vital intelligence to top military and political leaders in Washington. "When I asked General Yeh whether it should be treated as having any security classification, he replied with a laugh: 'None at all; the Japanese know very well where we are.'"[39]

CHAPTER 8
WASHINGTON'S DARLING

Yenan's skies were cold and clear as John Service's plane lifted off, but a chilly, damp autumn fog was creeping into Chungking as he landed on October 23, 1944. After three months in Yenan, he was startled to see the throngs of street beggars, the inflated prices in the food stalls, and the sandbagged machine gun emplacements at Chungking's major intersections.

Staff officers at U.S. Army headquarters warmly welcomed him back, eager to hear the latest news from the other China. The G-2 intelligence chief was impressed with the map of occupied China and surprised by the news that Communist guerrilla units were already going north to infiltrate Manchuria. After typing up a report about this significant troop movement, Service sent a note to Gen. Patrick Hurley offering to brief him on Yenan, explaining he was only in town overnight. He spent most of the day rushing to say goodbye to Chinese friends and key contacts, buy a few Christmas gifts for his children, and pack his civilian clothes.

* * *

Later that day, Service raced down the steep ladder steps to the Chungking riverfront—crowded as always, and filled with the pungent aromas he had known since childhood—where he boarded a ferry. At the embassy, he found the ambassador in a particularly sour mood. Gauss had been unsuccessful in persuading Chiang to form a new national war council as a first step toward creating a coalition government with the Communists (and other anti-Japanese factions). Despite strong backing from the White House and State Department, his initiative had been dismissed without serious consideration. He was also frustrated at being kept in the dark about the Stilwell-Hurley conversations with Chiang. After nearly thirty-five years as a member of the United States' diplomatic corps, he wanted out. It is customary for all ambassadors to submit resignations after a presidential election, but Gauss insisted that his would not be pro forma. "I was to tell this to the highest person I had a chance to talk to in the Department."[1]

* * *

Service ferried back to the city to meet Patrick Hurley for dinner. Despite his recent failure, Hurley had confidently promised President Roosevelt that he would soon settle the dispute between the Nationalists and Communists and bring them together in the fight against the Japanese. Hurley had been diligently wooed by Chiang and his inner circle, with elaborate banquets and attentive flattery. Politely, but unwisely, he had asked Chiang's permission to talk with Communist representatives based in Chungking—thus inviting the Generalissimo to assume veto power over U.S. dealings with the other China. Soon Hurley would be acting more like Chiang's representative than Roosevelt's.

An embarrassing incident early in Hurley's mission raised serious concern about his capabilities. In hosting a formal banquet for Chiang's cabinet and important generals, he had asked for help from *Life* correspondent Annalee Jacoby. At the event, they took their seats at opposite ends of Hurley's long dining table, flanked by twenty Chinese officials and dignitaries. At the end of the meal, Hurley proposed a final toast to "my tall, blonde goddess of a bride." Everyone smiled indulgently, but Jacoby realized with a shock that he was looking down the table directly at her. "I was at my prime five feet three and a dark brunette and about as far from a goddess as it's possible to get," Jacoby related. "But he went on talking about our children, the joy I'd given him in our long life together." As Hurley reminisced publicly about their wedding night, "everyone in the room realized that this man did not know where he was, did not know who any of us were, and the next morning he alone was going to represent the United States in negotiations with many of the people in that room, that would affect the future of the civil war [and] United States-Chinese relationships."[2]

* * *

John Service intended to brief Hurley about the Communists' new and tougher negotiating stance as conveyed to him by Mao and Zhou. After Chiang's reactionary speech on October 10 commemorating overthrow of the Qing Empire in 1911, the Communists abandoned hope of an early agreement on unification. But they still expressed a desire for a coalition government and a new national war council as well as a fair share of U.S. Lend-Lease supplies. However, they realized there could be no serious U.S. pressure on Chiang Kai-shek until after the American presidential elections. Communist forces would continue to follow the Japanese advance into new territories, filling the political vacuum while avoiding direct confrontation with Nationalist forces. If civil war broke out, they assured Service, it would not be provoked by their forces.

John Service never got a chance to share the Communists' views with Patrick Hurley. "It was not much of a conversation," Service recalled, "because Hurley simply held forth and kept saying that he was going to get the Communists arms, he knew what they wanted, he knew all about them."[3] Hurley had never bothered to be briefed on China's complicated political-military situation or read Service's Yenan dispatches, and he had never sought Ambassador Gauss' advice. Hurley was so ignorant of Chinese customs that he referred to Madame Chiang Kai-shek as "Madame Shek," unaware that in China the family name comes first.

"While I tried to tell him that the Communists were going to be very tough and hard-boiled and were not going to yield on what they thought were the essentials, I never really got a chance to get through," Service lamented much later. "He went on saying, 'Don't worry, I'll bring these two sides together. [The Communists] are going to get American arms. That's what I'm here for. . . . I've had experience with this sort of thing.'"[4]

Patrick Hurley simplistically compared the bitter rivalry between Chinese Nationalists and Communists to the partisan squabbling he was familiar with in his home state. He had no understanding of the long, violent competition to control China's path toward a modern unified state after more than a century of foreign interference and thousands of years of imperial rule. He likened Mao's party to out-of-power Republicans and quipped, "The only difference between Oklahoma Republicans and the Chinese Communists was that the Oklahoma Republicans were not armed."[5] Hurley's ignorance about China, his unwillingness to hear professional advice, and his episodes of what Jacoby called "premature senility" would help shape disastrous developments in Sino-American relations—and would wreak havoc on John Service's career.

* * *

After Val Chao's theater performance, she met Jack at his embassy living quarters. "She came down and we spent the night together," John Service recalled many years later. "I was expecting when I got [home] to insist upon a divorce, so I told Val I'd come back a free man."[6] It was the last night they would spend together.

The next morning, on the first leg of his long journey back to Washington, D.C., Service discovered that a fellow passenger was his good friend, *New York Times* correspondent Brooks Atkinson. Stilwell had called Atkinson in to talk about his recall just before the War Department barred the general from talking to the press and had given him a preview of the unvarnished views he would deliver in his final report to Washington. Vinegar Joe's conclusion: "Americans would have done well to avoid committing themselves unalterably to Chiang, and adopted a more realistic attitude toward China itself."[7]

Atkinson was now heading home because the only way to avoid Chinese censorship of his story about Stilwell's recall was to carry it out of the country. The reporter and the diplomat flew over the Hump to India and across the Middle East and North Africa but were stranded in Algiers. Service's diplomatic status granted him higher priority for a rescheduled flight, and—like a runner handing off a baton—Atkinson passed his story to Service. Jack arrived in New York late at night and took a taxi directly to the *Times* office. The unshaven diplomat met with the night duty foreign news editor. "I told him what I had, and said that he had to get it cleared which, of course, he agreed with," Service recalled. "They published it as he wrote it, and it caused a terrific sensation."[8]

Atkinson's story appeared on the front page on October 31, 1944, under a startling headline: "Stilwell Recall Bares Rift with Chiang: Long Schism Seen—Stilwell Break Stems from Chiang Refusal to Press War Fully—Peace with Reds Barred—Generalissimo Regards Their Armies Fighting Japanese as Threat to His Rule."[9] Americans learned for the first time that Chiang Kai-shek had insisted on Stilwell's removal, demanded control of Lend-Lease supply distribution, and—despite much prodding from American allies—refused to reconcile with the Communists for the sake of the war effort. Atkinson reported that the recall was seen inside China as "the political triumph of a moribund anti-democratic regime that is more concerned with maintaining its political supremacy than in driving the Japanese out of China." Readers discovered that the Chinese Communists were actively fighting the Japanese in north China yet were regarded by the Generalissimo as "the chief threat to his supremacy."

The story portrayed the deposed American general sympathetically: "Amid the intrigue and corruption of China's political and military administration, General Stilwell has been a lone man trying to follow orders, improve the combat efficiency of the Chinese army, force open the Burma Road, and get China back into the war." Atkinson reported that Chiang's attitude toward America had become increasingly resentful and intolerant of criticism. He concluded that Stilwell's recall "has the effect of making us acquiesce in an unenlightened, cold-hearted autocratic political regime. . . . America is now committed at least passively to supporting a regime that has become increasingly unpopular and distrusted in China, that maintains three secret police services and concentration camps for political prisoners, that stifles free speech, and resists democratic forces."[10]

The *Times* article sent shockwaves throughout the world. China-based correspondents flew to New Delhi to file follow-up stories free of Chinese censorship. One Associated Press report revealed the confidential exchange of information between Harry Hopkins and Chiang's relatives about Roosevelt's decision to remove Stilwell. Chiang's brothers-in-law, T. V. Soong and H. H. Kung, immediately sent Hopkins apologetic letters about the story, "probably inspired by General Stilwell." Kung lamented "misrepresentations which will only create ill-feelings between the allies," adding, "I am glad that there are people such as the President and your good self who see bigger issues."[11] Roosevelt tried to pass off the controversy as merely a "case of personalities," but the idea of an American general being recalled to appease a corrupt regime did not sit well with the American public.

The Chinese Nationalists were surprised by the overwhelmingly sympathetic reaction to Stilwell, widely acclaimed as a genuine American hero, and they moved to contain the damage. "Almost simultaneously all over the world," Service recalled, "wherever there was a Chinese embassy or a bureau of the Chinese Central News Agency, the same story popped out that Stilwell was a fine person, the Generalissimo had the highest regard for him . . . but that Stilwell had been misled by the young pro-Communist advisers, Davies and Service." The Nationalist version of Stilwell's recall became "a sort of a litmus test" on where people stood regarding the two Chinas, one that would have serious repercussions for Service's future. "To anyone who knew Stilwell, it's laughable," Service pointed out years later. "Stilwell was a man of very strong mind, and he'd been in China since I was a kid. The idea that Stilwell . . . was being led around by the nose by these young advisers is for the birds."[12]

* * *

As the first diplomat with extensive experience of the mysterious so-called Communists, John Service found himself in great demand in Washington, with its insatiable appetite for information—and scandal. As he briefed interested groups at the departments of State and War, Donovan's OSS, and the Office of War Information, he developed a heightened sense of the importance of his own views. His listeners were amazed to hear of the Communists' organized underground resistance, their effective rescues of downed American air crews, and their enthusiastic willingness to cooperate with the United States in the war effort—as well as their desire for U.S. economic aid in rebuilding China after the war. Service described in detail the Communists' firm demands for political reform and inclusion in a new national coalition government. He also reported their fears that Chiang's forces, with American-supplied weapons, would instigate a renewal of civil war. Few in Washington had heard such views before.

Some listeners thought Service sounded more like an advocate than an observer. But those who had seen his widely circulated brief for Vice President Wallace were both impressed and apprehensive on his account. "More people said to me: 'Jesus, Service! I read that thing of yours, and I certainly agree with you, but it is going to get you in a lot of trouble.'"[13] Over the next three decades, leaked excerpts from John Service's memos would be used as ammunition by Chiang supporters and ardent anti-Communists to blame Service for undermining the Nationalist leader and helping to bring the Communists to power.

Presidential aide Lauchlin Currie invited John Service and John Carter Vincent—now director of China Affairs at State—for a quiet dinner at his home. It was crucial, they agreed, for top policy makers and the public to understand the reality of the two Chinas. If the United States remained tied exclusively to Chiang's regime, they feared serious long-term consequences. The United States would wind up on the losing side of the coming civil war, diminishing its influence in the world's most populous nation—and putting America at a serious disadvantage in the competition to fill the power vacuum in Asia after Japan's defeat.[14] Currie and Vincent encouraged Service to share his Yenan experiences with politicians, officials, and journalists, and they offered to help make those contacts.

Just as he had done in early 1943, Lauchlin Currie arranged an interview for Service with columnist Drew Pearson. The resulting article praised the "so-called Communists" for their fight behind enemy lines, noting that dynamite was "too precious to use in blowing up railroads, so the guerrillas rip up railroad ties and rails by hand."[15]

Service also talked with Henry Luce, the powerful publisher of *Time* and *Life* magazines and a strong Chiang supporter, at a private lunch arranged by *Time*'s China correspondent Theodore White. But their meeting did not go well. "I made no effect on Luce at all," Service recalled. "He went ahead and published what the Chinese said and what Judd said."[16] Along with Walter Judd, a conservative Republican senator and former medical missionary in China, Henry Luce would become a founding member of the influential "China Lobby" supporting Chiang.

The State Department set up a series of press interviews and background briefings for Service, including a fateful briefing at the Institute of Pacific Relations. There, as it happened, Service was introduced to a naval intelligence officer named Andrew Roth, who in turn introduced him to a new circle of China-watchers. That connection would ultimately jeopardize both Service's career and his credibility.

Service's views received a hearing in the White House as well. Harry Hopkins had received a copy of his first Yenan report from John Davies and passed it to FDR with a note: "Here is Mr. Jack Service's preliminary report on the Communist situation in North China. . . . He certainly makes some arresting observations."[17] Now Davies provided Service with a personal letter of introduction to Hopkins.

"Hopkins' White House office," Service remembered, "was a plain, small [basement] room not much larger than the cluttered desk." He found just enough space on the floor between two chairs to unroll the map he had been given in Yenan. On hands and knees, Service pointed out Communist-controlled areas, guerrilla bases, key centers of Japanese troop concentration, and the designated escape routes for downed American flyers set up by a joint American-Communist rescue team. After nearly forty-five minutes, however, Hopkins' laconic comment was a dismissal: "Very interesting, I have no doubt that the picture you give is largely correct," he told Service, "but the only Chinese that most Americans have ever heard of is Chiang Kai-shek. And they call themselves Communists."

"I tried to say, yes, they're Communists, believe in Marx, but they're not Russian stooges. . . . I didn't seem to make any impression," Service recalled many years later. "[The Communists] were not considered a major factor. No one realized how much of a foothold they had, unless you were there or familiar with the Chinese situation."[18] Hopkins did ask Service what he thought of appointing Patrick Hurley as the new ambassador to China. "A disaster," Service immediately replied. "He's in the Kuomintang [Nationalist] pocket, working against Stilwell."[19]

Despite John Service's energetic efforts to inform policy makers—and despite the embarrassing press revelations about Stilwell's recall—there was never a serious reappraisal of U.S.–China policy. The United States never seized the fleeting opportunity to become a real mediator between the two Chinas. U.S. policy continued to be implemented in a disjointed and contradictory fashion by various government agencies, and it eventually foundered due to what one historian has called "Washington's refusal to trust its own observers in the field, and . . . its predisposition to resolve Chinese dilemmas with Oklahoma logic."[20]

* * *

On November 7, 1944, Franklin Delano Roosevelt was elected to an unprecedented fourth term, winning nearly 54 percent of the vote. And on the same day, his special envoy to China, Brig. Gen. Patrick Hurley, made a surprise visit to Yenan. As usual, a large crowd gathered as the plane taxied to a stop. When the hatch opened, Col. David Barrett remembered, "there appeared at the top of the steps a tall, gray haired, soldierly, extremely handsome man, wearing one of the most beautifully tailored uniforms I have ever seen, and with enough ribbons on his chest to represent every war, except possibly Shay's Rebellion."[21] A startled Zhou Enlai asked Barrett who this was. When he learned that the visitor was none other than General Hurley, Zhou asked Barrett to keep him occupied until he could alert Chairman Mao, who soon arrived with a quickly mustered honor guard and army unit.

After greeting the Communist leaders, clad in padded peasant jackets and baggy trousers, Hurley reviewed the troops, snapped a return salute to their commanding officer, and then "swelled up like a poisoned pup, and let out an Indian war whoop." Barrett would never forget the expressions on the faces of Mao and Zhou at this completely unexpected behavior. That evening, during a banquet commemorating the November revolution in Russia, Hurley again startled his hosts by bellowing out an occasional Choctaw Indian yell of "Yahoo!"[22]

The next morning, when actual negotiations opened, Hurley impressed Barrett with his skill as a mediator, "leaning over backwards" to be fair to both the National Government and the Communists. Barrett translated Hurley's five-point proposal, with its Lincolnian call for the unification of all military forces and for "the establishment in China of a government of the people, for the people, and by the people." Mao pointedly asked whether the Generalissimo had agreed to all these points, and he attacked Chiang's one-party rule and the mistreatment of his troops. Hurley vigorously defended the Generalissimo, but after they both calmed down, he suggested that Mao offer a counterproposal.

At their next meeting, on November 9, Mao handed over his own five-point proposal. "I distinctly recall," Colonel Barrett wrote, "that General Hurley read over the terms and then remarked, in effect: 'The proposals seem to me entirely fair. I think, however, that they do not go far enough.'" The American mediator then suggested adjourning so he could study the document, promising to offer his own suggestions the following day. At that point, Colonel Barrett felt Hurley "had definitely got off the rails."[23] Although a little taken aback at General Hurley's unusual offer, the Communists quickly agreed to let him revise their proposal.

Hurley presented his new version the next day. "If the Communists present at the meeting had never before heard of the Bill of Rights in the Constitution of the United States," Colonel Barrett later observed, "they had a good opportunity to learn about them on this occasion." Hurley accepted the Communists' call for the formation of a "Coalition National Government"; he retained his earlier rendition of Lincoln's Gettysburg address; and, in a final flourish, he added some of Franklin Roosevelt's rhetoric, "to make effective those two rights defined as freedom from fear and freedom from want." The American envoy also endorsed the Communists' language about a reorganized "United National Military Council," including representatives of "all anti-Japanese armies."

"The Chinese traditionally do not show their feelings in their faces, but it was evident from their expressions that they were greatly pleased," Colonel Barrett observed. Their smiles widened even further when Hurley suggested that he and Mao should both sign the document "to indicate they considered it fair and just." In a cable to the secretary of state, Hurley described his negotiations with Mao: "We argued, agreed, disagreed, denied, and admitted in the most strenuous and most friendly fashion and pulled and hauled my five points until they were finally revised."[24] Soon after the document was signed, Hurley wrote Mao a note lauding his "splendid cooperation and leadership" and his "qualities of mind and heart." Mao in turn sent a letter to Roosevelt expressing his "high appreciation for the excellent talent of your personal representative and his deep sympathy towards the Chinese people."[25] The lovefest would not last long.

That same afternoon, accompanied by Colonel Barrett and Zhou Enlai, General Hurley flew back to Chungking suffering from a head cold; he spent the next two days in bed. Zhou had cautioned him to make sure the proposed agreement went directly to Chiang and was not first shown to Soong or other officials. Ignoring Zhou's advice, however, Hurley sent the proposal directly to Foreign Minister Soong for translation, bypassing the embassy translators. The following day, Soong appeared on Hurley's doorstep. "You've been sold a bill of goods," he informed Hurley. "The Nationalist Government will never grant what the Communists have requested."

Nevertheless, Hurley cabled Roosevelt that any defects in the proposal were trivial and would easily be corrected. He was confident that with shrewd bargaining—despite centuries of feudalism and foreign imperialism—he could settle any problems in China's emerging revolution. After all, both Mao and Chiang spoke eloquently of democracy, unity, and peace. Hurley took their words at face value, evidence that the reactionary and the revolutionary were close to an agreement.[26]

On November 12, the strategic town of Kweilin finally fell to Japanese troops, triggering real fear not only for the fate of Chungking but also for Chengdu and Kunming, important hubs for U.S. airlift operations and B-29 bases. The effort to forge a political settlement was more urgent than ever. The new American military commander, General Wedemeyer, shared Stilwell's eagerness to send arms to the Communists and to mobilize them under U.S. commanders for the defense of Free China.

Hurley continued meeting with Chiang Kai-shek and T. V. Soong, trying to convince them of the merits of the new Five-Point Proposal. If there were a breakdown in the negotiations, he confided to Davies, the blame would lie with Chiang, "not the so-called Communists."[27] The Nationalists nevertheless countered with a new Three-Point Proposal that made no mention of either a coalition government or a united national war council. Chiang's proposal retained Hurley's eloquent bill of rights language, but those rights were subordinated "to the specific needs of security in the effective prosecution of the war against Japan." The Communists were expected to submit to Chiang's authority without a guaranteed power-sharing arrangement or a voice in military decision-making. Rather, they would get a seat on the existing military council, which merely rubber-stamped the Generalissimo's decisions. Somehow, the unbridgeable gap between the Nationalist three points and the Communist five points was never apparent to the earnest American negotiator, who now praised the new Nationalist proposal for giving the Communists "a foot in the door."

* * *

"Things in Chungking look a little better," Roosevelt wrote to a friend upon receiving another optimistic report from his China envoy, "and I am hoping and praying for a real working out of the situation with the so-called Communists."[28] On November 17, 1944, Hurley was officially offered the ambassadorship and immediately accepted. The following day, Roosevelt lunched with Averell Harriman, his handpicked ambassador to Moscow. Harriman reported that Stalin was anxious for the Chinese to settle their differences before Soviet troops entered the war against Japan. He would pressure the Chinese Communists to accept any reasonable deal. But without a genuine settlement, Harriman was "very fearful" that, when the Russians moved into China and Manchuria, "they would back the so-called Communist leadership." In that case, their terms "would be very much stiffer," creating a serious new problem for U.S. efforts to end the war and negotiate the peace.[29]

Ever since Stalin dismissed the Chinese Communists as "margarine Communists" and "agrarian reformers," many Americans—including Roosevelt, Harriman, and Hurley—had begun to refer to Mao's group as the "so-called Communists." By November 1944, the president and his envoys were operating on two strongly held but contradictory false assumptions: that the Chinese Communists were not orthodox Communists and that they could be strongly influenced by the Soviets.

Soon after his meeting with Harriman, FDR cabled Hurley to press for a political settlement and unification of Chinese fighting forces. He hinted that the Russians also favored such a settlement. "I cannot tell you more at this time, but [Chiang] will have to take my word for it. You can emphasize the word 'Russians' to him."[30]

The Allies had already decided not to use China as their main launching pad against Japan, but the Ichigo offensive now made unification of China's armies an urgent priority. Military unification was inseparably linked to the critical task of political reconciliation. Without a settlement between the Nationalists and Communists, the Soviet Union might seize control in Manchuria and parts of North China, dooming Roosevelt's vision of postwar peace and cooperation.

* * *

Zhou Enlai was invited to a meeting with Hurley and top American military officers—General Wedemeyer, his chief of staff Maj. Gen. Robert McClure, and Colonel Barrett—to discuss the Nationalists' counterproposal. Hurley pointed to the recent reshuffling of Chiang's cabinet ministers as real reform. General Wedemeyer offered assurances that the Communists would receive munitions, training, and American officers to lead their forces against Japan. Zhou nevertheless refused to accept Chiang's impossible terms.

Even without a settlement, Wedemeyer had begun working on secret contingency plans for using Communist forces. One plan (outlined in a memo by Colonel Barrett) would airlift five thousand Communist fighters to southwest China under American command.[31] Wedemeyer was also supportive of the secret OSS operations. The Dixie Mission OSS agents cabled to headquarters: "If the negotiations break down and an official O.K. is lacking for supplies being brought up here, there may still be the possibility of a fairly large scale clandestine SO [Special Operations] operation. General Wedemeyer has mentioned this as a possibility, and specifically referred to OSS as the organization which might carry out a 'disownable' operation."[32] These clandestine American war plans involving the Chinese Communists remained strictly classified for decades—and some still remain clouded in secrecy.

* * *

John Service's next assignment was the topic of high-level discussion in Washington. A key question was whether General Wedemeyer would decide to retain Stilwell's Foreign Service advisers. "If Service . . . is not to return to Yenan, [acting Secretary of State] Stettinius indicates he would like to have him released for reassignment in the Foreign Service," General Marshall cabled Wedemeyer, who quickly agreed that "military activities will be hampered" without these advisers' assistance. The secretary of war then sent a formal request to the secretary of state asking that John Service return to China for continued duty with the Army.[33] State Department plans to send him to a new post in Moscow were accordingly shelved. There was not the slightest suggestion by anyone involved that John Service was too sympathetic to the Communists.

Ambassador-designate Hurley remained doggedly hopeful for his mission as mediator. On December 8, as Colonel Barrett was preparing to fly back to Yenan with Zhou Enlai, Hurley implored him to persuade Mao to consider the Nationalists' counterproposal favorably—apparently oblivious to the damage he had done by abandoning their Five-Point Proposal that he himself had helped draft!

"We did not expect General Hurley to come back and press us to agree to a counter-proposal which requires us to sacrifice ourselves," Mao told Barrett. The party's central committee decided there was no point in continuing negotiations. Mao and Zhou pointedly reminded Barrett that Hurley had judged their Five-Point Proposal "eminently fair, and in fact a large part of the proposal was suggested by him." The Communists found the attitude of the United States "somewhat puzzling."

Mao rejected Chiang's proposal outright, pointing out that although Communists would get no voice in his government, their troops were to submit to Chiang's absolute authority. "The foot in the door means nothing," Mao declared, "if the hands are tied behind the back." They welcomed Wedemeyer's offer of U.S. military assistance "with all our hearts, but we cannot be expected to pay the price which the Generalissimo demands for his permission for us to receive this help." Mao affirmed, "[Even] if the United States does not give us one rifle or one round of ammunition, we shall still continue to fight the Japanese, and we shall still be friends of the United States." The conversation with the Communist leader was an uncomfortable experience that David Barrett would never forget.[34]

Before the session ended, Mao hinted that he might release to the press the Five-Point Proposal document signed by General Hurley. A few days afterward, in Chungking, Barrett delivered that message to Hurley. "I was afraid for a moment he might burst a blood vessel," Barrett recalled. "'The mother-f——' he yelled, '. . . he tricked me!' At this point, I ventured to remind the General, I was not Mao Tse-tung."[35] Outraged at Mao's implied threat, Hurley increasingly turned to Chiang and Soong as his allies; he began to view with suspicion anyone speaking favorably of the Communists.

* * *

John Carter Vincent alerted Caroline Service that her husband was on his way home. There had been no letters between them since Service wrote asking for a divorce, and they had not seen each other in nearly two years. If there were any chance of reconciliation, they would need some time alone together. Leaving the children with her parents, Caroline traveled east to Washington, D.C.

After another long day of briefings at various agencies, Jack Service went to Union Station to meet Caroline's train only to learn that it would be delayed until morning. He returned to his hotel. At two o'clock in the morning, someone knocked on the door. "When he sleepily opened the door, he was naked as a jay bird," Caroline recalled with amusement many years later. Without much conversation, and despite their strained relations, they went to bed. "You know, every marriage has its ups and downs," Caroline observed, "but Jack and I have never had any problem of reverting to a very intimate, easy relationship."[36]

After ten days in Washington, Jack and Caroline traveled to California by train and car. Seeing his children again—ages nine and seven—Jack realized he could not forsake his family obligations to marry Val Chao. But he never managed to write to her about his decision. The Chinese actress continued to believe he would soon return "a free man"—and she looked forward to giving him the joyful news that she was pregnant with their "love child."

CHAPTER 9
THE AMBASSADOR'S PARANOIA

A few days after Christmas, the phone rang in the Berkeley home of Caroline's parents. It was long distance from Washington, D.C., calling for John Service, who was just then doing magic tricks for the children. He picked up the phone to hear John Carter Vincent's voice: "Davies has gotten in a row with Hurley. We've got to get him out. Will you go back?" "Sure." "Wedemeyer has asked for you," Vincent explained. "We're going to insist that you be allowed to continue contact with the Communists. This is our main reason in agreeing to your going back." Since Davies was being immediately reassigned to Moscow, Service was needed in Chungking as soon as possible. On New Year's Eve, Jack took a late night flight back to Washington, D.C., leaving Caroline with their two young children—and the third on the way.[1]

Val Chao—also expecting Jack's child—only recently had learned from Tony Freeman of his reconciliation with his wife. "I was furious . . . angry and hurt." She very much wanted the baby that she knew would be "very good, very clever and intelligent." But her situation was untenable. "Right now he's going to have another child with his wife at the same time I'm going to have his child? That I can't accept." Freeman arranged to take her outside Chungking for the abortion.[2]

* * *

By early December 1944, the Japanese offensive had begun to threaten both Chungking and Kunming. Defenses around key air bases were being strengthened, and preparations for possible evacuations were under way. Chiang Kai-shek continued to veto any U.S. plan to use Communist forces. The new American commander was worried. "The fighting effectiveness of available Chinese units is so unpredictable that no American officer can state categorically when, where, and how such resistance can be definitely provided," General Wedemeyer cabled Washington after his first inspection tour of the war zone. Echoing his predecessor, Wedemeyer complained: "What I require is men who will fight."[3]

Ambassador Hurley's optimism, however, remained intact. He assured Washington that the only hurdle standing in the way of a political settlement was semantic: Chiang and his advisers were looking for ways to avoid the use of the word "coalition." "There is very little difference, if any," Hurley proclaimed, "between the avowed principles of the National government . . . and the avowed principles of the Chinese Communist Party."[4]

However, like many Americans in China, John Davies was increasingly exasperated. "We can ill afford to continue denying ourselves positive assistance and strategically valuable positions," he advised Wedemeyer in a memo written on December 12. The Communists had already proven to Dixie Mission observers that they were willing fighters, eager to cooperate with America against the Japanese. Convinced that Hurley's negotiations between Chiang and Mao had failed, Davies minced no words: "It is time that we unequivocally told Chiang Kai-shek that we will work with and, within our discretion, supply whatever Chinese forces we believe can contribute most to the war against Japan."[5]

* * *

On December 16, Davies headed back to Yenan, in the company of Colonel Barrett and Lt. Col. Willis Bird, the new deputy chief of the OSS in China. Barrett was carrying another letter from Ambassador Hurley, urging the Communists to return to the negotiating table. And Bird was carrying an ambitious secret OSS proposal.

Davies later claimed he simply wanted to meet with top Communist leaders to get their views on current rumors of a possible peace deal between Chiang and the Japanese. However, on his October visit to Yenan, he had already begun to explore what assistance the Eighth Route Army might be able to provide to a U.S. landing force—and what types of American arms and supplies they could use.[6]

Barrett now had orders from Wedemeyer's chief of staff, Gen. Robert McClure, to get the Communists' reaction to a new contingency plan to drop thousands of American paratroopers into north China.[7] The U.S. Army needed to know whether the Communists were capable of supplying food and other essential supplies to such a large force.

The ambitious purpose of Lieutenant Colonel Bird's secret mission was to discuss a major joint intelligence operation for cooperation between the OSS and Mao's guerrilla forces. It would involve inserting seventeen secret OSS sabotage teams into north China on missions to "generally raise hell and run." Under the "Apple" plan, Communist guerrillas would be given powerful American explosives to target Japanese communications, airfields, and blockhouses; and reformed Japanese POWs would be sent on spy missions all the way to Tokyo. During their three-day stay and with Barrett acting as interpreter, the OSS officer also promised to provide training in the use of modern weapons, demolition explosives, and radio communications plus equipment to outfit 25,000 Communist guerrillas. In return, the Communists pledged their 650,000 armed troops as well as their militia of 2.5 million for any "strategic use required by General Wedemeyer."[8]

Davies would later claim that all he knew of Barrett's and Bird's missions was that they had "some sort of plan for using Communist guerrillas."[9] But, like Service, he was undoubtedly aware that the OSS was developing plans to work with Yenan to set up a radio intelligence network, conduct joint sabotage operations, and send American-trained spies deep into enemy territory. Davies' claim of ignorance would be disputed not only by Hurley but also by some later historians. "In essence," commented one critic, "it looked as though OSS had become the private army of a few partisan State Department officials in the China Theater." The comment was hyperbole; but clearly, there were Foreign Service officers, Dixie Mission observers, and OSS officials eager to cooperate with the Communists against Japan.[10]

* * *

Lieutenant Colonel Bird, a newcomer in the China theater, assured the Communist leaders that he was "very hopeful" Chiang Kai-shek would approve the Apple plan. They pressed him to say what the Americans would do if Chiang's government refused. "Everyone laughed at the question," Bird later recalled. "I said something to the effect that army personnel obeyed orders and we would do whatever our government instructed us to do."[11] This was the first time any U.S. military official had openly suggested that the Nationalists might be ignored by the United States' secret espionage service.[12] Bird's off-the-cuff response would have serious consequences.

These new American overtures might well have undermined Hurley's negotiations, if he ever had any serious prospect of success. Moreover, Mao had recently received a letter from President Roosevelt himself expressing his willingness "to cooperate with *all* anti-Japanese forces in China."[13] The Communists began to believe they could safely reject Hurley's appeals for more unproductive negotiations with their archenemy and still enjoy clandestine American military support in a war that was expected to last at least another year. Confident of their growing strength, the Communists could afford to be patient about getting political recognition: the worsening wartime situation, they calculated, would eventually force the Nationalists to accede to widespread demands for a coalition government. "Our sole task is to cooperate with the Allies to overthrow the Japanese invaders," Mao proclaimed in a speech to his followers on December 16, as the secret military talks with the American officers continued.[14]

Accordingly, when the Americans returned to Chungking, Barrett delivered the Communists' flat rejection of Hurley's latest bid for further negotiations. Zhou now insisted the Nationalists must end their one-party rule and agree to establish a democratic coalition government—and he sent his polite reassurance that the Communists would not at that time publicize Hurley's co-authorship of the Communists' coalition proposal.[15] Hurley sent several further appeals that month, all of them rejected. "Only renewed confidence in the prospect of American military support," observed historian Michael Schaller, "would have led Yenan to so completely slam the door in Hurley's face."[16]

The Communists now focused on preparing their forces for an anticipated American landing—and designing a barrage of anti-Chiang propaganda. In late December, they issued an ultimatum: unless their Five-Point Proposal was accepted, they intended to establish an independent administrative council in the territories they controlled to create the basis of a separate, representative postwar north China government. On December 27, Wedemeyer's chief of staff, General McClure—apparently unaware of the political implications—sent Bird and Barrett back to Yenan to hammer out the details of the OSS plan for cooperation.

* * *

Hurley was at a loss to explain the Communists' intransigence—until he learned of the secret Barrett-Bird approach to Yenan. T. V. Soong had learned of the Yenan visits from Tai Li's secret agents, and he immediately demanded an explanation from Hurley. The ambassador insisted he knew nothing about the mission and exploded in rage. "If he *had* been cut into the picture," Barrett later noted, "he had failed to take much cognizance of it." Greatly embarrassed, Hurley claimed he had been sabotaged. "He took the stand we had tried to work behind his back against the interests of the National Government," wrote Barrett.[17] Hurley nearly came to blows with General McClure when he met him at an official Chinese function—and he made sure he lost his job as Wedemeyer's chief of staff.

Hurley was equally outraged at Davies and Barrett, demanding Davies' transfer and the cancellation of Barrett's promotion to brigadier general. He blamed their secret machinations in Yenan for his stalled negotiations and accused them of personal disloyalty. His housemate, General Wedemeyer, was on another tour of the war zone, but upon his return, the ambassador refused to speak with him for several days. Wedemeyer, for his part, claimed to know nothing about the military plans discussed at Yenan—although this may have been an exercise in "plausible deniability."

Wedemeyer's visit to the front had been eye opening. By December 1944, the Japanese had linked up their forces in south China with those in Indochina. This would prove to be the high-water mark of their effort to conquer the mainland of Asia. (Japanese troops were soon siphoned off to meet the allied counteroffensive in the Philippines and the Pacific.) Wedemeyer, determined to preserve the Hump airlift, was focusing on the defense of Kunming and its air bases. Chiang Kai-shek had stubbornly resisted this obvious priority—and on his visit, Wedemeyer quickly discovered why. "There are so many political implications in everything we do here," he reported to the War Department. "If [Chiang Kai-shek] goes to the Kunming area, the Governor of Yunnan may kidnap him or at least place him under protective custody." Chiang also feared that, if Kunming were strongly defended, Chungking itself would become the more vulnerable target—and his shaky political base would likely crumble under a Japanese attack. In a cable to Marshall, Wedemeyer again echoed Stilwell's unblinking diagnosis. The Generalissimo's staff was "actually afraid to report accurately conditions for two reasons: their stupidity and inefficiency are revealed, and further, the Generalissimo might order them to take positive action and they are incompetent to issue directives, make plans, and fail completely in obtaining execution by field commanders."[18]

* * *

By the time John Service returned to Chungking in January 1945, the situation had soured further. Chiang Kai-shek's top spymaster, Tai Li, had fed the ambassador's suspicions with stories of intrigue about disloyal American embassy staff, military officers, and journalists—all allegedly in cahoots with the Communists. Hurley refused to allow the embassy staff to submit reports critical of Chiang and his one-party government. When the embassy's political section chief gave the ambassador a copy of an unsavory report on the Nationalists that he had sent out prior to the ban, the ambassador exploded. "You mean to say you sent them *that*?" he shouted, drawing a pistol. "Why, I've *killed* a man for less than that." The thoroughly rattled embassy official, Arthur Ringwalt, said he never knew for sure whether the gun was loaded.[19]

Having learned his lesson, Ringwalt submitted his next report for General Hurley's approval. When summoned to the ambassador's office, he was astonished to find Foreign Minister Soong reading the confidential document—a report that Nationalist officials were allegedly profiting from trading American arms and dollars to the Communists. "There's nothing to it, General," the irritated Chinese official assured the ambassador. "See, Arthur, there's nothing to it," Hurley admonished, and he refused to forward the report to Washington.[20]

To many Americans in China, it was clear that Hurley had abandoned his role as an impartial mediator between the two Chinas—and even as an emissary serving the best interests of his own country. "The Embassy staff's cup of bitterness has been filled to overflowing," Sol Adler, the Treasury representative, reported to his boss in Washington. "Someone in the embassy suggested if Hurley remains ambassador, T. V. [Soong] could fulfill the role of Chargé d'Affaires." Adler considered Hurley "a stuffed shirt playing at being a great man"—a man who had to be stopped from showing confidential messages to Soong. The ambassador's continuing blunders, Adler warned, would lead to civil war and the complete alienation of the Communists from the United States.[21]

Hurley worried, too, that the British were engaged in clandestine activities aimed at restoring their Asian colonial empire, at China's—and America's—expense. British intelligence operatives in China were in fact preparing to seize Hong Kong and other valuable colonial territories during the final push against Japan. Hurley and Wedemeyer feared such moves would undermine the United States' attempt to unify China, a goal shared, ironically, with both Chiang Kai-shek and Mao Zedong.

Astonishingly, Patrick Hurley had never received specific written instructions when he assumed the post of ambassador. Neither the White House nor the State Department ever provided him with an explicit statement regarding how far the United States was willing to go in support of Chiang's regime, and Hurley was left to interpret and execute policy toward the two Chinas according to his own instincts. "In all my negotiations" he wrote the secretary of state, in a Christmas Eve 1944 memo, "it has been my understanding that the policy of the United States in China is: (1) to prevent the collapse of the National Government; (2) to sustain Chiang Kai-shek as President of the Republic and Generalissimo of the Armies." No one directly responded to this statement of his priorities.

By then the terminally ill American president had decided to resolve the two Chinas dilemma by playing the Soviet card at his upcoming secret summit with Stalin and Churchill—despite a warning from his ambassador in Moscow about Russia's traditional interests in the region. Roosevelt chose to believe that his own powers of persuasion would convince Stalin to accede in his vision for the world.

John Davies, like Vincent, Service, and others, was convinced that the United States was missing a strategic opportunity. If the United States remains indifferent to Yenan's overtures, he warned, "the present nationalistic feeling among the Communists . . . will be superseded by a sense of persecution, isolation and dependence upon the Soviet Union. . . . We stand to lose that which we seek—the quickest possible defeat of Japan and a united, strong and independent China. The Kremlin is not likely to be unaware of what is at stake in this situation—the future balance of power in Asia and the Western Pacific."[22] It is one of history's ironies that these diplomats, later vilified by McCarthy for allowing "Soviet aggression" to turn China into a Communist state, were in fact those most focused on countering Russian influence in China.[23]

* * *

Emboldened by their secret talks with Bird and Barrett, the Chinese Communists attempted to bypass Hurley and contact top American officials directly. On January 9, 1945, Zhou Enlai asked the senior OSS agent in Yenan to transmit a special message: Mao and Zhou wanted to travel to the United States for direct talks with President Roosevelt. But this extraordinary request, radioed to Wedemeyer's army headquarters for relay to the United States, never reached Washington. Few people in the United States or China were aware of this extraordinary overture until 1972, when *Foreign Affairs* published Barbara Tuchman's article, "If Mao Had Come to Washington."[24] That account suggested how differently the postwar world might have developed if Roosevelt, rather than Nixon, had become the first American president to shake hands with Mao.

The Communists' message was never in fact relayed. It was secretly intercepted and decoded by U.S. Navy technicians at SACO. (When OSS files were declassified decades later, it became clear that Dixie Mission transmissions were in fact routinely monitored by SACO in cooperation with Chiang's secret police.) Tai Li and Captain Miles—SACO's director and deputy director, respectively—presented Chiang and Hurley with their own doctored version of Zhou's intercepted message: it described secret Communist efforts to discredit the ambassador with Roosevelt, complete with embellished details of a covert OSS operation sending agents and supplies into Communist-held territory.[25]

"The Communists are not yet aware that I know of their efforts to bypass me and go directly to you," Ambassador Hurley reported to President Roosevelt in an expansive, thirteen-page "eyes of the president alone" cable on January 14. He blamed the impasse in his negotiations on a plot hatched by "some of our own diplomatic and military officials" that offered Communist leaders "exactly what they wanted, recognition and lend lease supplies for themselves." If the Communists had succeeded in making such an arrangement through the U.S. Army, Hurley told the president, "it would be futile for us to try to save the

National Government of China." Assuring the president that he was "clearing up the situation with Wedemeyer's able assistance," the ambassador said he would convince the Communists that "they cannot use the United States in their effort to supplant the National Government of China."

Hurley's cable insisted that Chiang and Soong were "now favorable to unification . . . and agreement with the Communists." He urged FDR to get Stalin and Churchill's approval for "your plan for . . . a unified democratic China." At that point, he suggested, Roosevelt could meet with both Chiang and Mao to promulgate the political and military merger of the two Chinas.[26] "Hurley's optimism survived," one historian later noted, "on what others might think a thin diet of belief."[27]

* * *

After reading Hurley's surprising cable about a nefarious conspiracy of American officials and the Communists, an angry Roosevelt asked General Marshall to investigate and to determine whether he needed to send an official apology to Chiang. The Army chief of staff immediately fired off a copy of Hurley's memo to Wedemeyer demanding an explanation. Wedemeyer was highly embarrassed but also furious that Hurley would send such a red-hot cable without prior consultation, in violation of their pact to show each other any dispatches intended for Washington.

At first, General Wedemeyer tried to cover up the OSS connection. But after Lieutenant Colonel Bird submitted a full explanation of OSS involvement, he acknowledged that the OSS had indeed explored "the feasibility of using a Special Unit for operations in areas under the control of Communist forces." He stressed his support of Chiang's government and denied any conspiracy to bypass the Nationalists. "Needless to say I am extremely sorry that my people became involved in such a delicate situation . . . [and] that unauthorized loose discussions by my officers employed in good faith by General Hurley could have strongly contributed to the latter's difficulties in bringing about a solution to the problem."[28] To make amends, Wedemeyer fired his chief of staff and refused to approve Colonel Barrett's promotion.

* * *

On a layover in New Delhi, on his way back to Chungking, John Service stayed at the home of the American representative to the British colonial government. Another houseguest happened to be "Wild Bill" Donovan, the OSS director who had tried to recruit him in early 1943. With the war in Europe winding down, Donovan was also on his way to China, both to push his plans for north China and to work out a deal with Tai Li that would extricate his field agents from the constricting SACO agreement. The flamboyant OSS chief believed his outfit had "a unique opportunity" to organize, train, and lead Chinese commandos, "just like Lawrence of Arabia had done" with Arab tribes fighting the Turks in World War I.[29]

Donovan invited Service to fly to Chungking in his private plane. During the flight, the two men undoubtedly talked about Service's Yenan experiences and Donovan's OSS plans. It was another instance of the extraordinary access the low-ranking diplomat had to high-level officials. "Tai Li had turned out to meet Donovan," Service recalled with a chuckle. "The look on Tai Li's face, when I walked out of the plane beside Donovan, helped to make the whole occasion a little more happy."[30]

Tai Li had been giving Hurley fabricated accounts of Service's involvement in plots to undermine both the Nationalist government and the ambassador's authority. He had also provided an intercepted copy of Service's final memo to Stilwell, which bluntly recommended the United States "end the hollow pretense that China is unified and that we can talk only to Chiang." Hurley would later describe this memo as "outward evidence of a plan not to uphold, but to *cause* the collapse of the government of the Republic of China."[31] John Service had long been considered unfriendly—and would never be forgiven for delivering Roosevelt's humiliating messages to the Generalissimo.

Under General Wedemeyer, army headquarters operated within a more formal structure. Service was assigned additional duties beyond his political reporting—drafting communiqués on policy matters, attending regular briefing sessions, and playing a larger role in G-2 intelligence operations. Best of all, a jeep was put at his disposal, which made getting around town much easier.

Within days of his return, Ambassador Hurley sent for Service and issued a sharp warning. "If I interfered with him," Service remembered being told, "he would break me." Startled, Service replied that he had no intention of interfering with the ambassador, and that he was assigned to provide political intelligence to the army commander and his staff. General Wedemeyer assured him "not to pay too much attention to Hurley's blustering." But Hurley never accepted the fact that Service was assigned to Wedemeyer's staff rather than his own; as Service later noted, the ambassador "felt he was coordinating all American activity in China, including the army."[32]

Hoping to avoid future imbroglios, General Wedemeyer issued a blanket order on January 30. Everyone under his command was forbidden to "assist, negotiate, or collaborate in any way with Chinese political parties, activities, or persons not specifically authorized by the Commanding General." He insisted upon support for the Chinese Nationalist government and barred his staff from "discussing hypothetical aid or employment of U.S. resources to assist any effort of an unapproved political party, activity, or persons."[33] The edict made John Service's mission as special liaison with the Communists much more dangerous and difficult. Wedemeyer asked him to keep a low profile, hoping that the controversy over the Bird-Barrett mission would soon fade and he could authorize Service's return to Yenan.

In Washington, meanwhile, the War Department asked the State Department for clarification of its China policy and received top secret guidance recommending greater flexibility in the fluid Chinese wartime situation. The policy document, prepared by John Carter Vincent for the secretary of state, was circulated among top government officials and sent to the White House. A copy of the confidential policy document eventually arrived on General Wedemeyer's desk—on the very day he committed his command to support Chiang's Nationalist one-party government rule.[34]

* * *

John Service got a chilly reception from his heartbroken mistress, still recovering from her abortion. She refused to allow him into their room in Sol Adler's apartment. "He wants to stay with me," Val Chao remembered, "but I will never stay with him again. . . . I can't bear it."[35] Service said he had been "talked out of a divorce," although he later admitted he was also motivated by a revived sense of obligation to his children—and by fear of ruining his promising career.

Service's love life had come to the attention of the Foreign Service personnel chief, Nathaniel Davies, who raised the topic with him before he returned to China. "A friend of his . . . told me if he went back to China and there was another family separation, it would mean the breakup of his family," Davies wrote in a memo for Service's personnel file. "I didn't want the Department to contribute to such an event because of any mistaken idea of duty on his part. He seemed to know just what I was talking about and said he had been all over that ground with his family. . . . For the present, he wants to go to China and it will not cause any ruptures." The personnel chief reported he told Service that "if things didn't work out well, not to hesitate to drop me a line personally."[36]

In later years, Service would claim that his passion for Val Chao had started to cool even before he left for Yenan in the summer of 1944: "By that time, I was already out of ferocious love."[37] But it was Val Chao who sadly closed the door on their relationship when he returned to Chungking in January 1945. Service found temporary housing in an army billet before moving across the river to share an embassy house with Foreign Service colleagues.

* * *

January 20, 1945—a bitterly cold day—marked the first American inauguration of a wartime president since Lincoln. Franklin D. Roosevelt's fourth inaugural address, lasting barely five minutes, was delivered from the White House balcony on the South Portico to a shivering group of family, friends, officials, and disabled veterans. "The President was pale and drawn, his hands trembled constantly, his voice appeared weak," General Marshall's wife remembered. But FDR's remarks about the catastrophic war—challenging America's courage, resolve, wisdom, and belief in democracy—left a strong impression.

Then, after retiring to the Green Room before the luncheon reception, FDR felt stabbing pains in his chest. "Jimmy," he told his son, "I can't take this unless you get me a stiff drink. You'd better make it straight." After a half glass of whiskey, he briefly joined the reception.[38]

Just two days afterward, Roosevelt slipped out of Washington to begin an arduous journey to Yalta, on the Black Sea, for a secret strategy summit with Churchill and Stalin at the summer retreat of the czars. The Yalta conference (February 8–11, 1945) resulted in agreement on several thorny issues: Russia's proposed borders for Poland; Allied occupation zones in Germany; war reparations; and the establishment of a new postwar international security organization, to be known simply as the United Nations. "We really believed in our hearts that this was the dawn of the new day we had all been praying for and talking about for so many years," Hopkins told an aide. "There wasn't any doubt in the minds of the President or any of us that we could live with them (Russians) and get along with them peacefully for as far into the future as any of us could imagine."[39]

Roosevelt also worked to get a firm Soviet commitment to join the war against Japan. His top military advisers had told him it might take another year to defeat Japan—and cost many American lives—unless the Soviets joined the fight to shorten the war. No one put much faith in China's war-fighting potential. U.S. Marines were about to land on Iwo Jima and Okinawa, where massive casualties were expected; and Roosevelt knew that an invasion of Japan's home islands might cost a million more American lives. The secret atomic bomb had yet to be successfully tested.

Roosevelt was determined to secure Stalin's cooperation at almost any cost—and the result was a secret protocol that granted the Soviet demands: return of all territory seized by Japan (from Czarist Russia); Soviet domination of Outer Mongolia; a long-term lease of the Port Arthur naval base; the internationalization of the port city of Dalian, guaranteeing the "preeminent interests of the Soviet Union"; and shared Sino-Soviet control of Manchurian railroad operations.[40]

In return Stalin agreed to break his nonaggression pact with Japan and enter the Pacific war within three months of Germany's surrender. He also agreed to negotiate a friendship treaty with Chiang's government, which was interpreted (mistakenly) as a pledge to control the "so-called Chinese Communists" and not to provide them any support.

The official communiqué marking the end of the Yalta Conference made no mention of this secret protocol and was hailed as "a landmark in human history." Only years later, after Russia had reneged on many of its promises and the provisions of the secret protocol became known, did critics begin to view Yalta as "a symbol of failure in foreign policy, a series of surrenders to Russia that led inexorably to the Cold War."[41]

* * *

For many critical months, in order to prevent leaks that could tip off Japan, neither Chiang Kai-shek nor State Department specialists were told about the complete Yalta protocol. Stalin had notified the Chinese Communists that a secret Allied summit was going to take place at Yalta, but he never revealed the secret provisions that infringed upon traditional Chinese sovereignty. The Chinese Communists could not have imagined that their socialist big brother would impose such humiliating demands regarding Mongolia and Manchuria—the highly industrialized region so crucial to the recovery of their war-ravaged country. "The days of Russian imperialism are over," Mao had confidently assured John Service.[42]

Stalin had such disdain for Mao's ragtag self-reliant revolutionaries and unorthodox Chinese-style Communism that he did not yet recognize the CCP movement's dynamism. (Only later would he fear Mao as a serious political and ideological rival—much like Chiang did.) Roosevelt and Hurley similarly assumed that a Russian friendship treaty with the Nationalists would force the Chinese Communists to fall into line. The secret deal struck at Yalta proved a major miscalculation, both of Soviet intentions and of Chinese Communist capabilities.

"Roosevelt and Stalin strangely found that their mutually unrealistic views on China coincided," wrote John Service in an opinion piece nearly thirty years later. "That made inevitable a Chinese civil war in which the U.S. was hopelessly tied to the side of Chiang Kai-shek's Kuomintang [Nationalists], and thus was needlessly sealed the unhappy course of American-Chinese relations for the next 27 years."[43]

CHAPTER 10
FAREWELL TO CHINA

A small group of Dixie Mission observers returned to Yenan from a grueling, four-month trek deep into enemy territory. Traveling by foot and mule alongside Communist guerrillas, they had gone twelve hundred miles in the dead of winter—all the way to the outskirts of Japanese-occupied Beijing.

Around the same time, Roosevelt was making a trek of his own, heading to Yalta to broker a deal with the Soviet dictator. The president's journey would take him thousands of miles across the ocean, ending with a punishing eighty-mile ride along bumpy dirt roads, past the charred tanks, burnt-out houses, and rotting animal carcasses that remained from the fight against the Germans.

Ray Ludden, the lone U.S. diplomat on the trek to Beijing, was eager to report his extraordinary findings and asked Service to arrange a meeting with General Wedemeyer in Chungking.[1] "Popular support of the Communist armies and civil administration is a reality which must be considered in future planning," Ludden informed the general. Such widespread popular support for the Communists could not have been manufactured as "a stage-setting for the deception of foreign visitors."[2] Wedemeyer asked Ludden and Service to prepare a written report he could take with him to Washington, where he was headed for consultations with Hurley.[3] "Ludden and Service I like very much," Wedemeyer wrote to John Davies, "and believe that they are going to follow your precedent exactly in giving us loyal and effective support. . . . No one knows better than do you the complexities, machinations, and imponderables which combine to make our job difficult."[4]

Ludden's detailed account of the trip in enemy territory (actually written up by Service) reinforced the assessment first provided by 1st Lt. Joseph Baglio, the rescued American pilot, and confirmed by many others. In late 1944, John

Colling, the OSS sabotage specialist, had returned from a six-week trip behind enemy lines with film and photographs documenting successful Communist efforts to protect the population and sabotage the enemy. The Communists had organized popular resistance; they could be very useful allies against the Japanese. There was growing impatience in the Dixie mission to begin military cooperation with Yenan's forces.

* * *

By early 1945, Ambassador Hurley was adamantly insisting that American policy was to support and sustain Chiang's government. There would be no recognition of the Communists until they accepted Chiang's authority. But the Chinese Communist Party continued to insist on being given a significant share in the government that would control the unified forces. There was little hope of compromise on either side, and talks with Yenan on military assistance and contingency planning had come to a halt.

Conditions in Nationalist-controlled China were going from bad to worse. Inflation kept rising and the Japanese army kept marching toward Kunming. It was time to reassess the United States' options. In their report to Wedemeyer, Service and Ludden boldly offered their own recommendations. "We could not abandon China because we had a mission and special responsibility there," Service later explained, "or so it seemed to almost everyone."[5]

The Ludden-Service report would become well known for suggesting "the Tito option": the United States should follow Churchill's example in Yugoslavia by providing arms and supplies to any partisan group willing and able to fight the enemy. They quoted liberally from Churchill's pragmatic policy statement and its blunt conclusion: "This is not a time for ideological preferences for one side or the other."

Ludden and Service hoped a similar public statement by Roosevelt would serve as a rallying point for Chinese who desired government reform and national unity but who kept silent out of fear of the Nationalists' secret police. "By our very presence here we have become a force in the internal politics of China and that force should be used to accomplish our primary mission": the defeat of Japan in the shortest time, with the least cost in American lives. Without mentioning the ambassador by name, they suggested that his unconditional support had only made Chiang more unwilling to compromise. Echoing General Stilwell, they urged that American support should be based upon Chiang's actions, not his promises. "Support of the Generalissimo is but one means to an end; it is not an end in itself, but by present statements of policy we show a tendency to confuse the means with the end."[6]

After receiving their report, Wedemeyer ordered Ludden to Washington to assist at the planned policy consultations. "Al [Wedemeyer] says he agrees heartily with our general view of things," Service wrote to Davies in Moscow. "He is going to try and do something about it—within the limits of action of a soldier—and that he wants both of us to stay with him."[7]

At Stalin's urging, Zhou Enlai returned to Chungking in late January so the Communists would not be blamed for the stalled negotiations. He left a few weeks later with no progress toward an agreement. Chiang still refused any real power sharing and had appointed several new hard-line anti-Communists to important posts. Hurley nevertheless reported to Roosevelt that his negotiations were making progress.

"It is essential that we get PH [Pat Hurley] out of the chair he now holds," Service wrote privately to Vincent at the State Department. "He is an excellent bull in a China shop . . . the antithesis in this delicate situation of what a good servant of the American Government should be." Service bitterly complained about Hurley's ignorance of China's history: he had no inkling of the deep distrust between the two rival armed political parties. Hurley had refused to be briefed about the complex situation from his experienced staff, confident that his own experience as a mediator was sufficient preparation. "Most people believe him a psychopathic case, suffering from delusions of grandeur and advanced senility," Service told Vincent. "He is an idiot playing with fire. I may sound strong. But I'm not alone in thinking these things."[8]

There were, however, other Americans in Chungking—far more rational than the ambassador—who disagreed with John Service's recommendations. General Chennault's aide, Joe Alsop, argued forcefully that any attempts to arrange national reconciliation or to use Communist military forces would be "dangerous and idiotic." He believed the Americans were "childish to assume that the Chinese Communists are anything but an appendage of the Soviet Union." Alsop (who was close to T. V. Soong) advocated giving even more aid to help Chiang's regime, to "create a strong army, and then assisting (by our own forces if necessary) in unifying the country, liquidating the Communists, and establishing a strong government." Those with firsthand experience in north China countered that direct intervention against the Communists would hardly be an easy task—and it would jeopardize the goal of a united China. Most concerned Americans in both China and Washington clung to the hope that Chiang could still somehow be persuaded to reform. Only a few exasperated observers considered China "such a mess" that the United States should simply disentangle and get out.[9]

Open civil war, which Service first warned about in early 1943, looked ever more likely. "Things are worse than when you were here. Much worse and everybody now thinks we Americans are crazy," Service confided in a letter to John Davies. "The biggest problem is whether the 'small whiskers' (also known as 'paper tiger,' 'Major Blimp,' and various other less complimentary names) is to come back."[10] Such nicknames for Hurley were current among Chinese and Americans alike, but Hurley also contributed to the atmosphere of name-calling: "Moose Dung" was the name he used to refer to Mao Zedong.

Reports of clashes between Nationalists and Communist troops reached Chungking on February 19, 1945, the same day Wedemeyer and Hurley departed for consultations in Washington, leaving George Atcheson in charge of the embassy and Brig. Gen. Mervin Gross in charge at army headquarters. Atcheson was well aware that Washington had not been given a realistic view of the increasingly unstable China situation. After reading the Ludden-Service memo, he decided to send a cable expressing the honest views of the embassy's muzzled political reporting staff—hoping to spark a serious policy debate about how to handle the two Chinas. "One didn't expect him to suggest anything as bold and daring as this," Service recalled. "It was suggested that I do the first draft, because I had been writing a good deal along this line."[11] The final message bore Service's strong imprint, even though he was officially assigned to the general's staff rather than the embassy. To give the message more impact, staff members took the extraordinary step of sharing responsibility for the cable with this addendum: "This telegram has been drafted with the assistance and agreement of all the political officers of the staff of this embassy and has been shown to General Wedemeyer's Chief of Staff, General Gross."

The cable, sent on February 28, began with a diplomatic observation: "The situation in China appears to be developing in some ways that are not conducive to effective prosecution of the war, nor to China's future peace and unity." Noting that the consultations with Hurley and Wedemeyer offered an opportunity to discuss the situation, the message briefly outlined the circumstances that had fostered Chiang Kai-shek's presumption of unquestioning American backing—and his unwillingness to compromise.

The cable then described the Communists' response. Excluded from political participation, the Communists were convinced the United States was "committed to the support of Chiang alone." After Colonel Barrett's removal, the friendly atmosphere toward the Dixie Mission had turned frosty. Communist forces were now moving back into the area south of the Yangtze, officially off-limits to them ever since Chiang's decree of 1941 and the New Fourth Army incident, when Nationalist troops slaughtered thousands of retreating Communists.

Japan's capture of the Canton-Hankow railway had cut off east China from the rest of Free China, and the Communist guerrillas seized the opportunity to expand their influence into that strategically important region and win support of the now "liberated" peasantry. If American forces were to land anywhere on China's eastern coast, Mao's forces would present the United States with the uncomfortable choice of either accepting or refusing their aid.

While acknowledging the diplomatic correctness of dealing only with Chiang's regime—still recognized, even by the Communists, as the central government—the embassy staff's message boldly proposed that President Roosevelt confidentially inform the Generalissimo that "military necessity requires that we supply and cooperate with the Communists and other suitable groups who can assist the war against Japan."

The cable argued that the Communists should be "helped by us rather than seeking Russian aid or intervention." Chiang's government, they proposed, would continue to receive the bulk of U.S. supplies and would be kept informed about the extent and types of aid given to the Communist forces and other groups. But American military officers should take operational command of all Chinese fighting forces, including the Communists—just as Stilwell had urged. This new modus operandi would signal that the United States was neither unconditionally committed to support Chiang nor subject to his veto.

The embassy staff also recommended that the Nationalist leader be strongly encouraged to form a united front war council with his rivals, as a first step toward national reunification. If Chiang refused these American proposals, President Roosevelt should take the "much more drastic step . . . of a public statement of policy such as that by Churchill in regard to Yugoslavia."[12] This embassy cable was the climax of a long effort to influence Chinese policy, and Service knew it was risky.

"The fight that John D. and most of my younger friends in the China Service have been waging for the past 3 years has been in some ways a dangerous one," Service confided to his mother soon after the embassy telegram was sent. "We may become heroes—or we may be hung."[13]

* * *

A week or so later, in early March, the Communists alerted Service that their oft-postponed party congress—the first in a decade—was finally about to begin. Top party members had already begun gathering in Yenan at the time of the Dixie Mission's arrival. Service now requested authority to travel to Yenan, offering assurance that "my visit is only to listen and observe." Both Atcheson and Gross agreed it was vitally important for Service to attend the meeting. In approving the trip, General Gross gave explicit orders that he was "not to indulge in political conversations" or do anything that "might not be in conformity with Gen. Hurley's policies." He was to be an observer with "no official status whatsoever."[14]

Characteristically, Service did not worry whether this assignment might prove personally risky. He flew to Yenan on the same day—March 9—that hundreds of B-29s took off from Pacific island bases for a massive night attack on Tokyo. Their bombing raid touched off a firestorm that killed an estimated 100,000 residents in the most devastating conventional air raid ever carried out.

Although he was warmly welcomed back to Yenan after his four-month absence, Service immediately felt the changed atmosphere. There were new suspicions about the Dixie Mission, now under OSS control. Tons of U.S. Army radio equipment and other supplies earmarked for joint intelligence operations had been stockpiled and were now held hostage to the deadlocked political decisions in Chungking. Morale among the frustrated Americans was low. Service discovered a new air of "defiant determination" among the Communists, with younger cadre more belligerent and argumentative than their elders. They vowed to "seek friends wherever they can find them"—clearly indicating the Soviet Union. Some young radicals even suggested to Service that they would "become an active revolutionary force in all the countries (like India) which were close to China," if the world isolated them as it had revolutionary Russia in 1917.[15] At the time, Service reported, there were only three Soviets residing in Yenan, and they appeared to receive no special treatment. One was a surgeon and the other two were ostensibly Tass News Agency representatives, actually former agents of the Comintern (officially disbanded in 1943). Service concluded that there was almost certainly some contact between the Chinese Communists and Moscow, "probably through Chinese Communists in Moscow and radio," but he saw no evidence of any Russian aid or weapons in Yenan.[16]

The Communist political and military leaders peppered Service with questions regarding American official and public opinion toward the war, the China situation, and the Communists. Angry at Hurley—and puzzled by his rejection of the proposal for a coalition government that he himself had helped to write—the Communists told Service they felt the ambassador "had gone back on his word and had become in effect a spokesman for the Kuomintang."[17] Within two days of his arrival, Service sent out his first dispatch describing the current Communist attitudes.

On March 1 Chiang had given a hard-hitting speech, rejecting calls for a wartime coalition government and dismissing the idea of creating a political advisory committee (with Communists and other groups) to consider government reforms. "The Communists regard the Generalissimo's March 1 statement as a virtual declaration of war," Service reported. They were again postponing their long-awaited Seventh Party Congress in order to reassess their options.

Back in November Chiang had unveiled a plan to convene a "National Congress" to prepare for constitutional government. But most delegates were to be party loyalists, members of the Nationalist Party Assembly selected in 1936 during the civil war and before the Japanese invasion. "Those delegates cannot pretend to represent the people who have been fighting the Japanese and governing themselves in the liberated areas for the past seven years," Mao Zedong told Service, when they met for their first formal talk. "They cannot even pretend to represent the people of Chungking-controlled China." It would be a "farce," Mao protested, if these delegates elected Chiang president of a new "democratic" government. The real danger would come when Chiang insisted that the Communists lay down their arms and submit to the authority of this "assembly of stooges." If the Communists refused this demand, they would be labeled rebels and then, Mao told Service, "the stage for open civil war will be laid."[18]

During the month of March, John Service spent many hours in conversations with Yenan's top political and military officials. The chain-smoking American observer rarely slept more than a few hours, tirelessly recording his observations and analyses in cables to headquarters. The Communists held out little hope for reconciliation, he heard again and again. They did not seek civil war but were not afraid of it and were now openly preparing for it.

Despite the ominous developments, Communist morale remained high; they were still surprisingly self-confidant and self-reliant, Service reported. Gen. Chu Teh, the army's commander-in-chief, teasingly assured him, "We don't really expect any arms from you." Chuckling, he patted Jack's knee. "Ultimately, we'll get them from the Kuomintang [Nationalists] anyway."[19] (Decades later, however, declassified war records would show that during OSS chief Donovan's visit to China earlier that year, General Chu had submitted a secret proposal asking for a $20-million loan for "strengthening subversive activities among [Japanese-controlled] puppet troops."[20])

Late one night, Mao made a surprise visit to the Dixie Mission compound to talk with Service. "For me, it was a foreign movie without subtitles," recalled Service's roommate, who sat spellbound inside the small cave watching their conversation unfold over the next several hours. "Mao was doing most of the talking. . . . He spoke with intensity, gesturing for emphasis. But most of the action was in his mobile face . . . alive with thought and emotion; the political theorist was in full command of the actor's arts; smiles, nods, frowns, a roll of the eyes, a grimace with eyes narrowed, a gape of disbelief, a twitch of indecision, a cleverly inserted pause." When Mao finally ended his dramatic presentation, Service's roommate later admitted he "felt like applauding."[21]

Mao told Service he still hoped the United States would realize that giving support only to Chiang's government was "not the best way to fight the war, to speed China's progress toward democracy, or to ensure post-war stability in the Far East." He proudly claimed his forces had won popular support—and had inspired resistance against Japan—by offering a moderate reform program of rent and interest reduction, progressive taxation, and other measures. "Like fish swimming in the sea," Mao explained, their successful guerrilla warfare was tied to their revolutionary efforts to free the peasantry from the feudal oppression of landlords, bandits, and corrupt military forces. This formula had built up Mao's political power, even in the face of ruthless Japanese efforts to suppress resistance.

Service listened intently, occasionally asking for clarification. He noted in his report that Japanese brutality had probably helped strengthen the Communists' appeal: the Eighth Route Army soldiers were considered liberators who freed the peasants from the cruelty of Japanese patrols. "By contrast, to a peasant in the Nationalist rear, the war meant little except the constant fear of the death sentence of conscription, steadily higher tax demands and the unending impositions of half-starved soldiery."[22] Without any outside support, Yenan's revolutionaries had come to control a population of nearly 90 million.

Because Chiang's party was so dependent upon the support of the landlords and warlords, Mao argued, it was "incapable of improving the condition of China's masses . . . [and] is forced to be fascistic." The only solution, he said, was to establish a genuine united front wartime coalition government. "We hope that America will use her influence to help achieve it," Mao told Service. "Without it, all that America has been working for will be lost."

Mao again emphasized that American help would be vital to China's postwar recovery. A "long period of free enterprise and democracy" would be needed to raise living standards and build a new industrial base in China's agricultural society. "To talk of immediate socialism is 'counterrevolutionary,' because it is impractical and attempts to carry it out would be self-defeating." The United States was the "most suitable country" to help rebuild China because the Soviet Union would have its hands full with its own economic recovery. In conclusion, Mao declared, "There must not and cannot be any conflict, estrangement or misunderstanding between the Chinese people and America."[23]

Today, following decades of distrust between "Red" China and the United States and wars in Korea and Vietnam, it may seem hard to believe that these were ever the thoughts of Chairman Mao. But during the Japanese war, the Chinese Communists were pragmatic—and opportunistic: they appealed to Chinese nationalism, not ideology, to mobilize the peasants. Their political agenda was limited to moderate land reforms under honest local administration, free of corruption. And the United States was viewed as a potential partner.

"I am as convinced as I was during my talks with Mao last year that American policy is a decisive factor in influencing the actions of the Chinese Communist Party—as well as those of the Kuomintang [Nationalist Party]," Service wrote in another dispatch. "Applied to bring about a true coalition government, the Communists will be cooperative. But [if American policy is] devoted to support of the Central Government and Chiang, to the exclusion of the Communists, disunity will be stimulated and the consequences will be disastrous."[24]

Was a "true coalition government" ever a real possibility? Realistically, Service understood that any wartime coalition government would be, as he later acknowledged, "little more than a loose mantle to preserve the fiction of unity between what would in effect be two Chinas." The Communists would insist on retaining control of their "liberated areas" in north China and control of their army—unless there were strong guarantees of power sharing. Perhaps a viable coalition government was merely the wishful thinking of a native son of China.

Undoubtedly Service cared deeply about the country and its people as well as about America's long-term strategic interests. He chose a pragmatic approach to the dilemma: "Two Chinas, neither an enemy, were at least better than a civil war, with one China an enemy and the U.S. committed to the losing side."[25] Such an arrangement would be in the United States' best interest because "we would be in a position to adjust to and move with, rather than be standing against the tidal development of events in China." Many years later, he defended his views: "Whether Mao's revolution would be successful, and the final shape that it would take, were still in the future. But at least we would not be foreclosing an opportunity to see whether the preview in Yenan was indicative, and whether Mao's statements and reiterated invitation to friendly cooperation could be taken seriously."[26]

In the twenty-first century, Yenan has become a travel destination for Chinese tourists, nostalgic for those early days when the Chinese Communist Party was filled with idealistic patriots and uncorrupted officials. The "spirit of Yenan" is evoked by propagandists for the People's Republic of China whenever the prevailing political winds favor cooperation with the United States. The town boasts several museums filled with artifacts and photographs of the heroic war era. Mao's wartime political and military headquarters and the remnants of the Dixie Mission compound are preserved, and tourists can see the humble cave dwellings where Service talked with Mao.

* * *

At the time of their Yenan talks, neither John Service nor the Chinese Communists knew of the secret Yalta protocol between Roosevelt and Stalin. Nonetheless, Mao's military commanders told him that they expected the Soviet Union to invade Manchuria before the end of the war. Party cadres had already organized an extensive underground network inside Manchuria, which (prior to Japan's occupation in 1931) had always recognized Chinese suzerainty. Service learned that large numbers of Chinese guerrillas were already heading north to establish bases near Manchuria's southern border. Once the Russian army began its advance, Service reported in a March 14 memo, these fighters would move quickly into Manchuria to link up with the underground resistance units and to begin "disrupting communications, creating disturbances, and assisting the Russian main front by tying down as many Japanese forces as possible in the rear."[27] At war's end, the Chinese Communists hoped to control Manchuria's prized manufacturing centers and infrastructure. They scoffed at the notion that the Soviets might make any territorial demands or insist on special rights in Manchuria. But after Stalin's troops entered the war in August, the Chinese Communists would learn how wrong they were.

* * *

On March 1, Franklin D. Roosevelt reported on the Yalta summit to a joint session of Congress. When the doors of the great chamber swung open to reveal the president seated in his wheelchair, there was a moment's shocked hush followed by the ritual applause. This was the first time the president had ever appeared in his wheelchair in public. For twelve years, he had always "walked" to the raised lectern, either using crutches or leaning on the arm of an aide.

"I hope you will pardon me for the unusual posture of sitting down during the presentation of what I want to say," Roosevelt began, after settling behind a small table on the floor in front of the dais, "but I know that you will realize that it makes it a lot easier for me in not having to carry about ten pounds of steel around on the bottom of my legs; and also because I have just completed a fourteen-thousand mile trip."

The applause now thundered through the Capitol. "I remember choking up to realize that he was actually saying, 'You see, I'm a crippled man,'" Labor Secretary Frances Perkins, sitting in the first row, later recalled. "It was one of the things that nobody ever said to him or mentioned in his presence. It wasn't done. It couldn't be done. He had to bring himself to full humility to say it before Congress."[28]

Occasionally, the president's voice seemed to give out as he reported on Yalta—never mentioning the promised Soviet entry into the war against Japan.

Roosevelt spoke positively about collaborative allied plans for Germany's unconditional surrender, and about cooperation in the design of the United Nations, whose organizing conference was scheduled to open in San Francisco on April 25. "This time we are not making the mistake of waiting until the end of the war to set up the machinery of peace," President Roosevelt declared, his hand trembling as he turned the pages of his speech. "This time, as we fight together to win the war finally, we work together to keep it from happening again."[29]

"I saw the President immediately after his speech," wrote Harry Truman in his diary. "Plainly, he was a very weary man." It was their first encounter since inauguration day. Roosevelt told his vice president he was leaving for a rest at Warm Springs, Georgia, just as soon as he could clear his desk of the work that had piled up during the month he was away.[30]

Many others also realized for the first time that their great leader was a mere mortal after all. "I had not seen the President for several months and was shocked at his physical appearance. His color was ashen, his face drawn, and his jaw drooping," General Wedemeyer recorded after a White House meeting that month. "I had difficulty in conveying information to him because he seemed in a daze. Several times I repeated the same idea because his mind did not seem to retain or register." Roosevelt's mental and physical powers were clearly failing, but he was still often capable of engaging in spirited conversation as he worked on the tremendous issues of war and peace. "He'll come out of it," an aide assured a visiting senator. "He always does."[31]

* * *

Soon after President Roosevelt's March 1 address, John Carter Vincent showed Ambassador Hurley the cable from his embassy staff that proposed direct military cooperation with the Communists. Hurley skimmed the message and exploded in rage. "I know who drafted that telegram: *Service!*" he shouted. "I'll get that son-of-a-bitch if it's the last thing I do."[32] The next day, Hurley lodged a formal protest with Vincent's boss, the head of the Far Eastern Division, over this "act of disloyalty" by his staff. State Department veterans defended the message as a courageous act by Foreign Service officers who had sworn an oath always to report their honest observations and views, regardless of the political atmosphere. Indeed, the cable had already been forwarded to the White House with a favorable cover note from Acting Secretary of State Joseph Grew.

State and War department analysts by then had accepted the idea that the United States needed "greater flexibility" in applying American policy toward China. "There should be no question of choosing between Chiang and the Communists; of withdrawal of support from Chiang," Vincent wrote in early

March. "But likewise there should be no question of an exercise of our prerogative, dictated by military necessity, to utilize all forces in China capable of cooperating with us in the fight against Japan. Chiang, having failed to effect military unity, should be told that he has forfeited any claim to exclusive support."[33]

Meanwhile, at a Washington news conference on March 8, Adm. Chester Nimitz broadly hinted that American landings along the China coast might precede an invasion of Japan. In that eventuality, secret orders instructed Wedemeyer to "arm any Chinese forces which they believe can be effectively employed against the Japanese."[34] Wedemeyer had also quietly approved the OSS's taking command of the Dixie Mission, which enabled operatives to begin preparations for "disownable" sabotage missions with the Communist guerrillas throughout north China.

At the same time, however, Ambassador Hurley was given a new responsibility that would reinforce his self-importance. At a high-level White House meeting on March 8, Hurley was informed about the secret Yalta protocol and Stalin's promised entry into the Pacific war. At the appropriate time, the ambassador would be expected to brief the Generalissimo on the sensitive protocols. (In contrast, when Roosevelt met with his new vice president earlier in the day, Truman was told nothing about Yalta or anything else of consequence.)

At another private meeting a few days later, Hurley suggested stopping off in London and Moscow to obtain Churchill's and Stalin's endorsements of his negotiating efforts before returning to Chungking. He assured the president that he would deliver a deal within two months. He also suggested that Chiang Kai-shek be persuaded to include a Communist representative in the official delegation to the United Nation's founding conference. (Rather than the charismatic Zhou Enlai, the Nationalists eventually named an older, non-English-speaking Communist named Tung Pi-wu.)

Hurley emerged triumphant from his private meetings with FDR with a strategy based on the Yalta promises and on his own unquenchable optimism. The imminent danger of civil war in China, seen so clearly in Yenan, seemed a distant mirage. "It is not clear how thoroughly Roosevelt was briefed, and how clearly he understood the dispute over American policy in China as Hurley was representing it," Service mused many years later. "Nonetheless, Roosevelt was astute enough as a politician to be keenly aware that China policy was a sensitive subject, that Chiang Kai-shek had a large and fervent band of American supporters, and that 'Communist' was a dirty word to important segments of American opinion."[35]

There were some clues, however, that the president did not share his ambassador's commitment to unconditional support of Chiang. In a long conversation with his friend Ed Snow (the author of *Red Star over China*), FDR confessed his puzzlement over Chiang. "He was baffled, yet fascinated by the complexity of what was happening there, which nobody explained satisfactorily to him; myself included." Roosevelt expressed disappointment at the lack of progress toward a political settlement and allied military operations. "The president said Chiang Kai-shek had 'raised some perfectly absurd objections' to the Communists' requests for certain guarantees along lines of a bill of rights which appeared 'perfectly reasonable.'" Roosevelt even mentioned that the Chinese Communists had established effective government in the guerrilla areas, and he indicated that the United States intended to land supplies and liaison officers on the north China coast as the war drew closer to Japan. Snow then raised the issue of two Chinas. "I suppose the position is that as long as we recognize Chiang as the sole government we must go on sending all supplies exclusively through him? We can't support two governments, can we?" "Well, I've been working with two governments there," replied Roosevelt. "I intend to go on doing so until we can get them together."[36]

The record of American policy toward divided China provides abundant evidence of what one veteran diplomat politely termed "administrative confusion." The president's penchant for using private emissaries rather than official diplomatic channels contributed to the contradictory policy interpretations and actions of various American actors. "Roosevelt did give [Hurley] sets of instructions," Hurley's biographer points out. "[But] he did not at the same time hammer out with the State Department the basic points related to Hurley's instructions or, for that matter, all the elements of the U.S. position." And, as Hurley's biographer notes, three different men held the office of secretary of state during the war years—"one of them perhaps the most cautious in the annals of the Department and another perhaps one of the weakest and most ineffectual."[37]

A modern Chinese scholar, Tao Wenzhao, may have put his finger on the most important factor in the inconsistent American policy. At an extraordinary joint Sino-American academic conference on the war era, held in the 1980s, the Communist scholar commented that although career diplomats like Vincent repeatedly wrote policy papers, their positions were "never put into practice and never became effective," whereas "Roosevelt did not even write down his position, but his actions speak more eloquently than words." The American president "unquestionably clarified his policy through his support of Hurley."[38]

* * *

By March 22, information reached Washington that John Service was again in Yenan. General Wedemeyer, still in Washington, immediately cabled General

Chennault: "If found to be true, please indicate mission, who sent him, date of arrival and duration of stay. Gen. Hurley much disturbed."[39] A top secret cable from Wedemeyer's chief of staff quickly confirmed the news, insisting that "Service was not at fault in any respect": "Both this Headquarters and the Embassy concurred in sending John Service to Yenan as large gatherings of leaders and important discussions being held during this period. . . . Service was considered most discreet person because of his experience with matters of this kind. . . . This Headquarters accepted full responsibility for his presence."[40] Wedemeyer duly showed Hurley the explanatory cable as well as some of Service's recent dispatches, but this failed to defuse the ambassador's rage. Patrick Hurley saw yet another act of sabotage and personal betrayal. He stormed into the secretary of state's office demanding the recall of his disloyal, insubordinate Foreign Service officer. Politely, he was reminded that John Service was assigned to the Army, not the embassy—and he should take the matter up with Secretary of War Henry Stimson.

* * *

On March 30, John Service received orders to report as soon as possible to Chungking. At his final meeting with Mao two days later—the same day that 60,000 Marines and soldiers stormed the beaches of Okinawa—Service found Mao "in exceptionally good spirits, getting out of his chair to act out dramatic embellishments of his talk, and diverging to recall amusing anecdotes. [Zhou] occasionally explained or amplified Mao's points. Chu sat back, silent and smiling."[41]

Mao began by reviewing the "fruitless negotiations" with the Nationalists. Most foreigners did not understand that the issue was "far more than the usual bickering and jockeying between two ordinary political parties; the issues involved were "basic and vital to China's future." He reiterated his preference for political compromise based upon the five points for a coalition government and military command, as proposed by his party and "endorsed by Ambassador Hurley" during his Yenan visit. Mao was particularly incensed by Chiang's recent speech proposing a National Congress filled with party loyalists who would declare the Communists were rebels.

"When attacked, we will fight back. We are not afraid of the outcome, because the people are with us," Mao declared. "The Japanese haven't been able to wipe out the liberated areas; how can Chiang's conscripted, un-indoctrinated army of unwilling peasants? Chiang could not whip us during the civil war when we were a hundred times weaker." Mao again expressed his concern over the cost to China of another civil war. "China needs peace," he told Service. "But she needs democracy more, because it is fundamental to peace. And first she must drive out the Japanese. We think America, too, should be concerned, because her own interests are involved."[42]

Even if the Americans never provided his forces with "a single gun or bullet," Mao pledged that the Communists would continue to cooperate with Americans in any way possible. "If Americans land in or enter Communist territory, they will find an army and people thoroughly organized and eager to fight the enemy." The United States had to decide whether it wanted friendly relations with the Communists, but Mao could only see advantages for both sides: "in winning the war as rapidly as possible, in helping the cause of unity and democracy in China, in promoting healthy economic development in China through industrialization based on solution of the agrarian problem, and in winning the undying friendship of the overwhelming majority of China's people."[43]

As the son of YMCA missionaries, John Service had seen China's suffering firsthand since childhood. Now he could see only the slimmest of chances to avert a devastating civil war, but he deeply believed it was in his own country's own best interest to make that attempt. He left Yenan on April 4, unaware it would be his last visit—or that his extensive talks with Chinese Communist leaders would be their only substantive discussions with a U.S. official for the next twenty-seven years.

Service now felt he had an urgent mission. Like Mao, he assumed his recall meant that Washington was ready to adopt a more realistic approach. He would try to bridge the gap of misunderstanding and misinformation. To be swayed by Chiang would be to "let the tail wag the dog." If the United States did not take constructive action quickly, Service feared, it would wind up opposing the historic revolutionary tide he had seen, heard, and experienced in his travels throughout the war-torn country.

* * *

Reporting to army headquarters in Chungking, Service was shown the top secret cable sent by General Marshall: "Return Jack Service to states for consultation & reassignment by State Dept. Matter urgent and arrival here within two weeks is desired if feasible. Need not wait Wedemeyer's return."[44] The next day, Service flew out on a special flight that carried him all the way to Africa. He had no specific idea why he was being recalled, but at least he was traveling in style. For the trip across the Atlantic, Service was transferred to a C-54 flying back for an overhaul. "They had installed a special chair for me, right up behind the pilot's compartment," Service recalled. "I sat there like a goddam duck, in a special plane."[45]

Service no doubt anticipated a serious, high-level policy review, prompted by the embassy staff cable and the Ludden report he had co-authored. He had no idea he was heading into a hurricane—a stormy mix of personal vendetta, international intrigue, and political suspicion that would change his life forever. Nearly thirty years would pass before he returned to the land of his birth.

PART II
MAELSTROM

CHAPTER 11
THE FBI TRAP

Late on Sunday night, March 11, 1945, an undercover OSS team entered the New York offices of *Amerasia* magazine without a search warrant. Portions of a secret OSS report on Thailand had been published in the January issue of the Asian affairs journal, and the OSS wanted to know how the information had been leaked.

The illegal search turned up five copies of that report—plus much more. In testimony before a Senate subcommittee five years later, the agent in charge, Frank Bielaski, described their amazement at finding hundreds of government documents, along with a photocopy machine and a darkroom. "All over [the editor's] desk were documents that had been photocopied and that were drying."[1] Many were marked secret; a few were top secret. They carried seals and stamps not just of the OSS but also from Military Intelligence, Naval Intelligence, the Office of War Information, and the State Department. In the large library, the OSS undercover team found more documents strewn across a large table. The team's locksmith pried open the locks on file cabinets. Finally, a large suitcase was discovered in the editor's office, "stuffed so full of documents that we just dropped everything." Some documents bore the name of John Service, including "a secret document that dealt with the intimate relations between Chiang Kai-shek and Madame Chiang, and that document," Bielaski told the Senate subcommittee, "was very intimate . . . we didn't think that had any place in that office."[2]

Bielaski realized it would take too much time to inventory all this material. To back up his report, he took about a dozen documents with him, including some with markings and initials that might help trace the channels through which they had been obtained. Bielaski caught an early plane to Washington, D.C., and went directly to the office of Archibald Van Beuren, the OSS chief of security.

"He laid the documents on my desk one by one," Van Beuren recalled, "and I became more and more amazed as I heard him describe the circumstances under which he had found them and saw the documents themselves."[3] They decided to inform OSS director Bill Donovan. After reviewing the evidence, Donovan concluded that all the OSS documents bore a State Department intake stamp. At ten o'clock that evening, Donovan and Van Beuren went to the home of the secretary of state to meet secretly with Edward Stettinius and his assistant secretary for administration, Julius Holmes.

Only three days earlier, these officials had received a confidential FBI security survey report of State Department facilities. The survey reported a serious lack of security and accountability. Donovan's *Amerasia* cache dramatically confirmed that assessment. "The Secretary, after looking through the documents, turned to General Holmes, who was right beside his chair, and said, 'Good God, Julius, if we can get to the bottom of this we will stop a lot of things that have been plaguing us,'" Donovan later recalled.[4] Many of the papers from the OSS and other agencies had obviously been routed through the State Department. In some embarrassment, Secretary Stettinius thanked the OSS men for uncovering the breach.

It was also clear that a number of documents had been routed through the Office of Naval Intelligence (ONI). The FBI was now called in, and on March 15, FBI agents began round-the-clock surveillance of *Amerasia*'s editor, Phillip Jaffe. "Do not stop until we find out not only Jaffe's contacts here," Hoover ordered, "but also who he is working for and what he does with the material."[5]

* * *

Born in Ukraine, Phillip Jaffe had arrived in New York City with his mother in 1905 at the age of ten to be reunited with his father, who had immigrated a year earlier. Like many European immigrants, the family settled on the Lower East Side. As a young man, Jaffe worked as a messenger for a small advertisement office owned by Alexander Newmark, a prominent socialist. In 1918, he married Newmark's daughter and went back to college, working nights at the ad agency. After completing his master's degree in English literature and becoming an American citizen in 1923, Jaffe invested in a stationery distributor that he later acquired and diversified. And over the next ten years, despite the Depression, Jaffe became a wealthy man.

Troubled by the world's economic crisis, Jaffe began a serious study of Marxism. He enjoyed debating ideological issues with his cousin's husband, an exchange student from China named Chi Chao-ting who, years later, would become an adviser to the Nationalist Finance Minister H. H. Kung and a valuable mole of the Chinese Communist Party. Chi would also become John Service's upstairs neighbor in Chungking.

In 1933 Chi Chao-ting recruited Jaffe to help establish the American Friends of the Chinese People. Jaffe became editor of the association's pro-Communist paper, *China Today*. Although never a party member himself, Jaffe often contributed money to Communist-front causes. In 1936 Jaffe joined with several others from the association to found *Amerasia* with support from members of the respected Institute of Pacific Relations (IPR). And in 1937 he and his wife were among the first "blockade runners" to make the hazardous trip to Yenan, where they met with Mao and other Communist leaders.

Amerasia was well regarded by Asian specialists in academic and government circles and attracted such distinguished contributors as Stanley Hornbeck, chief of the State Department's Far Eastern Affairs Division. But after the Soviet Union signed a pact with Nazi Germany, the magazine began to parrot the new Soviet line about imperialist aggression, and subscriptions suffered. Later, when Germany invaded Russia, the magazine supported the Allies against the fascists, but it never recovered. The magazine became increasingly isolated, both financially and editorially. By 1945 Jaffe was paying for its publication out of his own pocket, and almost all the articles were authored by Jaffe or his deputy editor.

* * *

The FBI conducted a total of six illegal searches of the *Amerasia* offices. Agents inventoried and photographed documents, dusted for fingerprints, and took typewriter imprint samples.[6] Without seeking authorization, FBI Director Hoover ordered wiretaps on Phillip Jaffe's office and home telephones. Due to the wartime emergency, the bureau assumed that the vague federal laws on technical surveillance could be bent.[7]

The first night of FBI eavesdropping proved exceedingly fruitful. Agents listened in as the *Amerasia* editor telephoned two Washington contacts about plans to meet them the following day, March 21. The calls were traced, and the FBI had two new suspects: Emmanuel S. Larsen, a civilian employee at the State Department; and Lt. Andrew Roth, at ONI.[8]

Late that night, agents were dispatched to the State Department's Far East office to inventory documents in the desk drawers of officials such as John Carter Vincent, trying to identify items that might wind up at the magazine office. Other agents were assigned to stake out the homes of Roth and Larsen. Around midnight, an agent observed the naval officer and his wife gathering up papers from their dining room table and putting them into a manila envelope. The next morning (according to an FBI report) Roth left the house carrying the manila envelope.

The same morning, Phillip Jaffe took the train to Washington, D.C., and went directly to the Statler Hotel on 16th and K streets. There he met Larsen at the hotel restaurant. "At approximately 12:40 PM," an FBI agent reported, "Lt. Andrew Roth and a woman believed to be his wife enter[ed] the Colony room and [were] seated at the same table as Jaffe and Larsen." Throughout the meal, the group was "engaged in constant intense conversation." An hour later Mrs. Roth left, but the three men remained talking for another half hour.

When they finally departed, Lieutenant Roth was "carrying the manila envelope which he brought"; both Larsen and Jaffe carried briefcases. They all got into Roth's car and, after dropping Larsen off near his office downtown, took "a circuitous route to the parking area on the east side of the main Library of Congress Building." Roth and Jaffe sat in the car for twenty-five minutes, "engaged in discussion and examination of papers, certain of which were placed on the steering wheel of the car by Lt. Roth." The two men then entered the library and made a couple of calls at a pay phone booth, then got into Roth's car and drove to his apartment in Arlington.

At 5:40 PM, accompanied by Roth's wife, they drove back to Washington. Jaffe was dropped near the Statler, where he again met Larsen in the hotel lobby. The two men walked a few blocks to Larsen's bus stop. "During this walk," the FBI report noted, "Jaffe and Larsen were engaged in what appeared to be a confidential conversation." Returning to the hotel lobby, Jaffe was joined by the Roths and a well-known freelance journalist named Mark Gayn and his wife. The group walked to the Good Earth Restaurant nearby where, during dinner, they "engaged in intense conversation." Jaffe then caught a late train back to New York.[9]

Early the next morning, agents searched Larsen's office at State, where they found three documents that were "positively identified as having been in Phil Jaffe's office" just the week before. Later that day the lead investigator sent FBI Director Hoover a report identifying both Roth and Larsen as principal sources of government documents being furnished to Jaffe.[10]

By the time of the arrests in June, the FBI had assigned seventy-five agents and technicians to the *Amerasia* case and had conducted illegal searches involving the installation of wiretaps and listening devices in both New York and Washington. Only a few top officials were informed of the massive investigation. The *Amerasia* case files would continue to grow over several decades—eventually filling more than 17,000 pages—without anyone ever going to jail.

* * *

The Allied war machine was making costly headway in both Europe and the Pacific. After a bloody 36-day assault, American forces finally captured Iwo

Jima on March 26, 1945. The photograph of Marines raising the American flag immediately became an iconic symbol of the bravery and sacrifice of American fighting men. The captured island was valuable as a vital emergency base for bombers targeting Japan, but 6,800 American lives were lost. Nearly all the 20,000 Japanese island defenders were killed or committed suicide.[11]

Meanwhile, the end of the war in Europe was in sight. General Patton's Third Army had already crossed the Rhine River. Four days after getting the news about the rapid advance of the Soviet army into Austria, an exhausted President Roosevelt left Washington for Warm Springs, Georgia, on a train that traveled at slow speed to minimize his discomfort.

On April 1, U.S. Marines waded ashore on the beaches of Okinawa to face what would be the bloodiest battle of the Pacific war. The two-month land and sea battle would leave 12,000 Americans dead and 36,000 wounded, with more than 120,000 enemy fighters eliminated.[12] The Allied successes in the Pacific lessened China's importance as a theater of war, but its political divisions and rival fighting forces remained a significant strategic problem. Gen. Patrick Hurley was well pleased with his efforts in Washington, having won President Roosevelt's support against his State Department detractors. Along with General Wedemeyer and Capt. Mary Miles, Hurley had reassured the Joint Chiefs that, if necessary, a Communist "rebellion" in China could be put down "by comparatively small assistance to Chiang's central government."[13]

Yet at a farewell press conference on April 2—while John Service was holding his last meeting with Mao—Hurley emphasized the prospects for Chinese unity. "The Communist Party in China are [sic] not, in fact, real Communists," he proclaimed. They supported the "same principles" as the Nationalists and their demands were made "on a democratic basis." Both Chinese political parties wanted a government that will "conduct itself along democratic lines, employing democratic processes," and the only difficulty arose over "the procedure by which they can be achieved."[14]

The next day Hurley departed to seek the support of Churchill and Stalin for his ongoing negotiations. At Heathrow Airport, Hurley bumped into Bill Donovan, who passed along some State Department gossip: John Carter Vincent was suspected of leaking documents to a left-wing journalist in a case that might involve espionage for the Soviet Union.[15] This seemed to confirm the ambassador's long-standing suspicions that Vincent was one of several Foreign Service officers attempting to sabotage his efforts and undermine the United States' China policy. Hurley had already caused Davies' transfer to Moscow and Barrett's removal as head of the Dixie Mission. He had just engineered the recall of John Service, and soon he would purge from the embassy every disobedient staff member who had signed the cable criticizing his actions.

FBI investigators had learned that Vincent was one of thirteen officials who had received copies of the secret OSS report on Thailand that was plagiarized in *Amerasia.* He had first come under suspicion when the FBI's security survey at State uncovered leaks to columnist Drew Pearson. Suspicions were heightened on April 5 when Lieutenant Roth, Jaffe's contact at ONI, was observed passing a file of papers to Vincent's assistant during lunch. A few days later Roth was seen lunching with Chi Chao-ting, then in Washington seeking gold for China's treasury. The FBI's background check revealed that Chi was a former member of the American Communist Party—and that both he and Roth had worked with Jaffe. A few days later Chi was observed lunching with White House aide Lauchlin Currie, and he too was caught in the net of suspicion.

* * *

John Service arrived in Washington, D.C., on April 12 and immediately reported to John Carter Vincent's office. As he walked in the door, Vincent's telephone rang. "He picked it up and said, 'My God.' Roosevelt had just died."[16] The president had been going through his mail in Warm Springs when suddenly he moaned, "I have a terrific pain in the back of my head," and collapsed.[17] The president died of a massive cerebral hemorrhage at 3:45 PM. The public news announcement was made at 5:47 PM. Shortly past seven o'clock, a shaken Harry Truman took the oath of office and became the country's first new president in more than thirteen years.

News of Roosevelt's death shocked the nation and the world. Thousands upon thousands of weeping Americans lined the railroad tracks the next day as the presidential train carrying the president's casket slowly made the eight-hundred-mile journey from Georgia to the nation's capital. When Stalin was informed of the death by Ambassador Harriman, the dictator asked if an autopsy were being performed to determine if the great man had been poisoned. Then, as a gesture of respect for the dead president, Stalin finally agreed to send his foreign minister to the United Nations conference in San Francisco. Upon hearing of FDR's death, Winston Churchill said he "felt as if I had been struck a physical blow. . . . I was overpowered by a sense of deep and irreparable loss."[18] Among the thousands of condolence telegrams that arrived at the White House was a cable from Mao Zedong forwarded from Wedemeyer's headquarters.

On his first night as president, Harry Truman ate a late-night turkey sandwich and drank a glass of milk with his wife and daughter in their neighbor's kitchen. Then the family retired to their Connecticut Avenue apartment and went to sleep. Truman was back at the White House by nine o'clock the next morning for a series of briefings by Roosevelt's military chiefs and foreign policy advisers. Secretary of State Stettinius reported that since the Yalta Conference, the Soviet government had taken a firm and uncompromising position on nearly every major question. Soviet authorities in Poland were supporting their own provisional Polish government and refusing to exchange liberated prisoners, in violation of Yalta. Suspicion, distrust, and disillusionment were setting in. "We now have ample proof that the Soviet government views all matters from the standpoint of their own selfish interest," Ambassador Harriman cabled from Moscow. "We clearly must recognize that the Soviet program is the establishment of totalitarianism, ending personal liberty and democracy as we know and respect it."[19] The grand alliance had died with Roosevelt.

"To many it was not just that the greatest of men had fallen," wrote Truman's biographer David McCullough, "but that the least of men—or at any rate the least likely of men—had assumed his place." Harry Truman confided to his daughter, Margaret, that Roosevelt "never did talk to me confidentially about the war, or about foreign affairs or what he had in mind for peace after the war." According to his biographer, Truman "was unprepared, bewildered. And frightened."[20]

John Service stepped into this newly uncertain Washington with a firm sense of mission. The threat of a Chinese civil war was "like a time-bomb ticking steadily toward detonation," he told Vincent. Both sides were "actively and openly girding themselves for civil war," and the United States must find the means to prevent the conflict from starting.[21] Handing Vincent a carbon-copy set of his most recent Yenan reports, he argued passionately that there was no time to waste: the coming disaster would prolong suffering for the war-weary Chinese people, postpone economic recovery, wipe out the moderates on both sides, and keep the country bitterly divided for the foreseeable future. "Realism in foreign policy can probably be defined in various ways," Service later wrote, "but surely none of them included persisting, with eyes open, on a clear road to disaster by excessive (and unnecessary) commitment to a foreign political party whose decline is certain because it has lost the support of its own people."[22]

Vital American interests were at stake, he argued, both for winning the war against Japan and for maintaining American power and influence in postwar East Asia. Decisive action was needed immediately. The State Department's "careful diplomatic words" about maintaining flexibility in China meant "little more than passively standing by to award the prize of American recognition to whichever side proved the eventual winner." Service stressed that action was needed now, before the war ended, because "the starting signal for open civil war was likely to be the Japanese defeat itself." The Nationalists and Communists would race each other to accept the surrender of enemy troops.[23]

American military collaboration with the Communists, Service believed, could be used as leverage to get Chiang's agreement on a loose coalition government. This offered a way to avert civil war and make the Chinese Communists political stakeholders, which would encourage them to continue their moderate program of reforms rather than to seize power through revolution. Finally, American troops working with the Communist guerrillas in north China could as a counterweight to potential Russian efforts to gain territory and influence.

Over the next few weeks Vincent and Currie again encouraged Service to share his views with journalists, politicians, and opinion makers. With a new president in the White House, they hoped for another chance to get China policy back on a more realistic track. Foreign policy under Truman might become the domain of State Department professionals and interagency committees, rather than the White House. And they all hoped the ambassador would be recalled.

Hurley had offered his pro forma resignation to Truman in a cable following Roosevelt's death. From London, he cabled the new president about his recent meetings with Churchill before heading to Moscow to confer with Stalin about the Chinese situation. His message blamed "well meaning, but misguided Americans who seemed not to understand America's true policy in China" for nearly causing the collapse of the Nationalist government, and he claimed credit for saving the situation.[24] Truman decided to retain Roosevelt's man in China.

John Service eagerly accepted the task of sounding the alarm and even described himself as "Lauchlin Currie's designated leaker."[25] Currie again arranged for him to talk with columnist Drew Pearson and other journalists. Vincent and the State Department facilitated background briefings for foreign policy specialists at various government agencies, as well as academics. "In 1944 when I'd come home, everyone was interested in what I had to say and there was pretty general agreement. But this time, people were already beginning to divide a little bit," Service said. "Some people in the State Department were arguing . . . the Communists are in rebellion, we can't have any dealings with them."[26]

European and Soviet specialists were "bitterly anti-Communist" after years of experience of the Communist Party in the Soviet Union and its wartime manipulation of the Communist parties in Europe and the United States. And the Soviet "liberation" of Eastern European countries was beginning to cause severe strains in the alliance. "My suggestions that China might be different usually brought a knowing—and, it seemed to me, slightly condescending—smile, but no meeting of minds." Service's enthusiastic reports about the friendly relations between the Dixie Mission members and the Chinese Communists, as well as their freedom to explore the territory, seemed far-fetched to Soviet specialists accustomed to dealing with a closed society. "To me it seemed obvious—so much so that I hardly bothered to debate it—that China was not going to be a carbon copy of either the Soviet Union (if it turned toward Communism), or of the United States (if it turned, as we had hoped, toward liberal democracy)."[27] But many Soviet experts considered him merely naïve about the ruthless nature of Communism.

* * *

On the morning of April 18, John Service got a call from the freelance journalist Mark Gayn and agreed to have lunch with him. Gayn had gone to the same college as Service's younger brother, and he had sent Service a note expressing regret that he had been unable to attend Service's talk at the Institute of Pacific Relations (IPR) in the fall. Now back in Washington to write a series of articles for the *Saturday Evening Post*, Gayn was seeking Service's input. The diplomat had no inkling that Gayn was under FBI surveillance or that his apartment had recently been searched secretly—or that he was the son of a Russian political exile and had attended Soviet schools before his family emigrated.

Service knew that Gayn must have seen a copy of his secret report for Vice President Wallace; his piece in *Collier's* magazine contained nearly verbatim portions of his report. Far from being angry, Service had felt flattered. He now offered to let the journalist see other reports for background purposes. When they finished their lunch, Gayn told Service that if he ever needed a place to stay in New York, the extra bed in his apartment was available. It was an offer John Service would soon accept and later regret.

That was also the day that FBI agents informed Assistant Secretary of State Julius Holmes that the Bureau was ready to arrest its prime suspects—Jaffe, Roth, and Larsen. Holmes and his security officer urged that the probe be extended, both to find out if any others might be involved and to determine "whether Jaffe is obtaining this material for the use of the Russian Government."[28]

While the FBI agents were briefing Holmes upstairs at State, John Service was meeting with the chief of Foreign Service personnel. "He came in with a crooked grin to remind me that at our last meeting he had predicted that he would not last long in China and that's the way things have turned out," Nathaniel Davis noted in his file. "I told him he had nothing to worry about. Gen. Wedemeyer had personally stated that our officers with the Army in China had rendered useful service and were only being released because of certain personal situations with which Mr. Service was aware. His record had not suffered at all—on the contrary."[29]

After the isolation of Yenan, Service thoroughly enjoyed Washington's social whirl. "Everybody was interested in North China. I was being somewhat lionized," Service later told a security officer. "At least that is the way I regarded it at the moment."[30] When Lt. Andrew Roth invited him to a dinner party, Service cheerfully accepted, although they had only met once.

Roth had attended Service's talk at the IPR in November, and Service knew Roth worked in ONI on Asian matters, but he did not know that Roth once took classes from Chi Chao-ting, or that he had worked for Jaffe at *Amerasia*. Roth told him that Jaffe was coming to the party and hoped to meet Service for a serious talk beforehand. "As he was the editor of a well-known specialist magazine on the Far East," Service later told a Senate subcommittee, "I saw no reason why I should not meet and talk to him on a background basis as with any other reputable newspaperman."[31]

At 6:00 PM on April 19, 1945, John Service walked into Phillip Jaffe's room at the Statler Hotel—and directly into an FBI trap. A wiretapped phone conversation between Jaffe and Roth had alerted them that Jaffe would be in Washington again to return some "original documents." With the hotel management's consent, the FBI had placed a hidden microphone in Jaffe's room.

When John Service arrived, he was carrying a personal copy of his report on his recent conversation with Mao Zedong. "Jaffe was extremely interested and asked at once if I did not have other similar reports about Yenan which it would be possible to show him," Service later testified before a Senate subcommittee. "It was agreed that I would bring some of these with me the next day and that I would lunch with him at his hotel."[32] The FBI eavesdroppers listened with avid interest as the new acquaintances chatted like old friends about mutual acquaintances and interests. These illegal recordings were kept secret for five years until FBI Director Hoover decided to share their contents with McCarthy and others.

Jaffe told Service that Mark Gayn was not the only one who had seen his "brilliant report" for Vice President Wallace. An unsigned copy had circulated sub rosa at an IPR conference he had attended, and Jaffe said he immediately recognized it. "I said, 'Hell, that's Service's report.'" The editor was certain because an official State Department copy had already been leaked to him and he had loaned it to Mark Gayn for his *Collier's* piece.

Service then confided that his apartment-mate, Sol Adler, the Treasury representative in China, had actually collaborated on that memo. "One night we got chewing the fat how we ought to . . . write a report, sum up the whole situation, so we both sat down, we got all worked up, and that night, why, we each wrote out a base summary draft . . . then he took the two of them and hammered them into one and I took that and rewrote it and we kicked it back and forth." Service noted, "The final draft is mine." Jaffe commented, "Well, you must know Chi Chao-ting." Service acknowledged that Chi was their upstairs neighbor in the Chungking apartment house—and Jaffe disclosed that he was a cousin by marriage. "Is he?" replied Service in surprise. Chi and Adler were very good friends, he remarked, but he knew his neighbor only slightly.

Service then told Jaffe how Chi had once brought home a very sensitive manuscript on Chiang Kai-shek's latest economic theory. Adler asked Service to translate it so he could review it, producing a very critical twenty-six-page summary of Chiang's unabashed "mixture of feudalism and fascism" for his boss at the Treasury Department. Now, in Jaffe's hotel room, Service offered to let Jaffe see his personal copy of Adler's confidential report. When the editor asked to make his own copy, the young diplomat volunteered, "You can take it to New York for a while; I mean keep it for a week or so." But Service wanted Jaffe's assurance that he would use it for only background purposes, not publication, because the secret document had only been circulated "among very high Chinese officials."[33] Jaffe would later tell FBI agents he found Service "an immature and rather foolish man who 'chased after' newspaper people and magazine editors" to make the case that "the Chinese Nationalist government was wholly corrupt and that the taking over of China by the Reds was inevitable."[34]

"I had no particular reason to be on my guard," Service reflected years after his association with Jaffe had damaged his career. "Perhaps I should have."[35] Service always maintained that he was simply trying to provide background information to a respectable journalist, just as he had done in China. "Nobody warned me to avoid him on the grounds of Communism," he later told an official board of inquiry. "The general reaction was, 'well, he's a bit nosy.'"[36]

At 6:50 PM, Jaffe and Service—tailed by FBI agents—grabbed a taxi to cross the Potomac to Lt. Andrew Roth's apartment for a buffet supper with too many people in a small room. The other guests included Navy or government people with interests in Asia plus a few staffers from IPR. Roth's new book about Japan, still awaiting Navy approval for publication, was a main topic of conversation. At the end of the evening, Roth handed Jaffe a draft of the manuscript to review; FBI agents made a note of the thick manila envelope Jaffe carried when he and Service left the party and returned to Washington. The two were tailed to a café near the Statler, where they had coffee before calling it a night at 1:15 AM.

* * *

The following day, April 20, was Hitler's fifty-sixth birthday. It also marked the beginning of the Soviet Red Army's final assault on Berlin. President Truman met Averell Harriman, his ambassador to Russia, for the first time that morning. Although the USSR continually expressed a desire to cooperate with the United States and Britain, it was extending draconian control over neighboring states. The Soviets took American gestures of goodwill and generosity as signs of "softness." In short, Harriman told Truman, Europe was facing a totalitarian "barbarian invasion."[37]

Meanwhile, the Joint Chiefs of Staff gave final approval to General Wedemeyer's ambitious "Beta Plan" for training and supplying more Chinese Nationalist troops, which followed Stilwell's successful model. They also approved an offensive to cut Japanese supply lines in southeast China, and to capture Canton and the vital Hong Kong seaport. The plan authorized American officers and soldiers to act as advisers to the Nationalist Chinese troops. Wedemeyer was also given a new State Department policy directive that called for greater flexibility and suggested that military commanders be prepared to arm the Communists they encountered during operations along the China coast. The newly agreed upon policy guidelines stated that the eventual unification of China "did not necessarily mean" a government of Chiang Kai-shek.[38]

* * *

On April 20, John Service dropped off eight or ten more reports at Phillip Jaffe's hotel, intending to pick them up at their lunch meeting. He had carefully selected reports that were "purely descriptive and did not contain discussion of American military or political policy."[39] But at lunch with Roth in Jaffe's hotel room, the editor asked permission to take the reports with him to New York. Service hesitated, but knew he would be going to New York in a few days to address the IPR staff and could personally pick up the reports. On that basis, he agreed to let Jaffe take the documents—while the FBI technician in the next room recorded every word.

"I was conscious at the time that I was taking a risk," Service admitted to a State Department security officer many years later. "I regretted it immediately and I did not want him to use the material in a form that would be attributed to the person that furnished the source of the background. I was unwise to allow him to keep these in his possession."[40] According to FBI files, Service and Roth left the hotel together at 1:50 PM. The agents could not pick up their conversation as they walked, but Service recalled questioning the naval officer intently about whether or not Jaffe could be trusted or might have ulterior motives. "Unfortunately," John Service recounted, "the man of whom I made the inquiry was Lt. Roth, who assured me that Mr. Jaffe was not a Communist."[41]

Andrew Roth later said Service struck him as "a liberal crusader" who "wanted to use *Amerasia* as a megaphone." He was "*astonished* at the risks" Service was willing to take.[42] It is indeed puzzling that John Service, who moved so skillfully around the dangerous China landscape, could be so recklessly indiscreet in Washington. He may have indeed become too zealous in promoting his policy views. "By the time I left [China]," Service reflected more than fifty years later, "I had become very much involved . . . in what was going on there, and in the policy options for America, so that it had probably compromised my impartiality."[43]

As for Phillip Jaffe, according to the FBI's hotel telephone transcripts, he said he had "big plans for Service." Accordingly, on April 20, 1945, FBI agents conclusively identified John Service as "another individual furnishing Jaffe with classified information."[44]

CHAPTER 12
CONVERGENCE

John Service met Jaffe and his associates several times in the weeks before his arrest. When he traveled to New York City a few days after lending Jaffe his Yenan reports, FBI agents were watching Mark Gayn's apartment. On the evening of April 24, at about eight o'clock, Service showed up, overnight bag in hand. Several other dinner guests had already arrived, including Jaffe and his deputy editor, Kate Mitchell. Meanwhile, other FBI agents were searching the *Amerasia* offices for the second night in a row.

The next morning FBI agents tailed Service from Gayn's apartment to the Institute of Pacific Relations (IPR), where he had been invited to talk to the research staff. Afterward Service took a taxi to the *Amerasia* office. After picking up his Yenan reports from Jaffe, the Foreign Service officer spent the rest of the day visiting old friends—who instantly became new targets of the FBI investigation.[1]

"When I returned to Gayn's apartment that evening, I had the reports with me," Service told FBI agents on the night of his arrest. He was surprised to learn that Jaffe had already given Gayn copies of some of them. "I had known Gayn and Jaffe were close friends," Service told his interrogators, "but Gayn now told me that he and Jaffe worked very closely together and exchanged all their information."[2] Gayn had in fact previously been observed leaving Jaffe's office and pulling out a document with a Yenan dateline to read on the bus. FBI agents had already found—and photographed—other government documents, including some of Service's reports, during two early warrantless searches of Gayn's apartment.

* * *

Jack wrote to Caroline that he did not blame Hurley "for driving out his opposition" but that both the Army and the State Department had resisted, and Hurley "had to go very high to succeed." The talk around the office was that "Hurley won't last very long and then some of us will return to our jobs in China."[3]

The new team at the State Department was increasingly dissatisfied with Hurley's performance. "We have definite reason to believe that General Hurley has ordered that only political reports favorable to the Chinese National Government may be made to the Department," the deputy chief of the Far Eastern Division wrote in a memo to his superiors, "and it is apparent that we can no longer count on receiving factual and objective reports in regard to *all* aspects of the situation."[4] Most disturbingly, Hurley was refusing to allow any reporting on clashes between Nationalist and Communist units in southern China. From Moscow, Ambassador Harriman warned not to place much reliance on Hurley's enthusiastic report of the recent Moscow talks, or his claim that Stalin supported his efforts to unify the armed forces of China with "full recognition of the National Government under the leadership of Chiang Kai-shek."[5]

Finally, in early May, Acting Secretary of State Grew sent Hurley a stern message: "It is most important that we maintain complete flexibility, repeat flexibility, with regard to means of achieving [our objectives]." Grew instructed the ambassador to "make it clear to the Generalissimo" that U.S. support "is not of the 'Blank Check' variety."[6] The message failed to spell out, however, what steps Hurley should take to demonstrate American flexibility, and the irritated ambassador simply ignored the guidance. Hurley—supremely confident that he alone knew how to solve the bitter Chinese political crisis—paid little attention to the State Department.

By then the ambassador had replaced all staff who had signed the provocative February 26 cable with new officers—many who had no China experience or language skills. He had also made it virtually impossible for General Wedemeyer to provide arms and supplies to the Communists without Chiang's approval. Hurley took the position that anyone who opposed him either failed to understand the directives he had been given by the late president or else was disloyally plotting against him.

Even after John Service's recall, Hurley continued to single him out as a key saboteur. When a visiting State Department official prepared a memorandum titled the "Economic Policies and Views of the Chinese Communists" and referencing Service's Yenan reports, Hurley attacked Service personally in a cover memo: "My own directive was to prevent the collapse of the National Government of Republic of China, whereas Mr. Service was apparently attempting to bring about the downfall of that Government" and "could not be considered an impartial observer because of his feelings toward the Chinese Communists."[7]

(When Hoover later read his agents' report about Hurley's remarks, he scribbled a comment: "John Carter Vincent has thus far prevented the inclusion of Gen. Hurley's comments re: Service in Service's personnel file at Dept. of State."[8])

In the spring of 1945 Ambassador Hurley also engineered new restrictions on foreign correspondents. The U.S. Army was forbidden to fly reporters or other unofficial passengers to Yenan without the ambassador's approval, and Chiang's cooperative censor blocked transmission of any stories critical of the American ambassador. The Chinese government did not wish to disturb "the cordial relationship between the two countries," the censor politely explained to the incredulous foreign press corps, and "any attack by an American upon [Hurley] on Chinese soil is therefore not permitted to go out."[9]

* * *

On April 25, after twelve days as president, Truman was told about the super-secret atomic bomb project. "Within four months we shall, in all probability, have completed the most terrible weapon ever known in human history, one bomb of which could destroy a whole city," read the note that Secretary of War Henry Stimson handed to Truman at their private meeting.[10] Manhattan Project experts informed him that a test of the terrible new weapon would probably take place in early summer. If that test proved successful, the president would face the monumental decision of whether to merely demonstrate its destructive power or actually drop it on an enemy target.

On the same day, the United Nations organizing conference opened in San Francisco. On his way to the conference, Tung Pi-wu, the lone Chinese Communist delegate, stopped briefly in New York. The FBI spotted him entering Phillip Jaffe's apartment building in the company of Earl Browder, the American Communist Party leader. This gathering, according to FBI agents, presented "an ideal opportunity to pass on classified information about American policy to the Chinese Communists."[11] The agents apparently ignored the possibility that the magazine editor had no secrets to impart but was rather being briefed on the Communist position in advance of the United Nations meeting.

* * *

After five years, eight months, and seven days of the most devastating and costly war in history, Germany surrendered to the Allies in the early hours of May 7, 1945. The terms of unconditional surrender were signed at 2:40 AM by an officer of the German high command and Gen. Dwight Eisenhower's chief of staff. One week earlier Adolf Hitler had committed suicide by taking cyanide pills and shooting himself in his underground Berlin bunker as the Soviet army fought its way into the center of the city. Germany's capital was soon divided into sectors by the victorious allies, marking the beginning of an era of hostility between the wartime allies from the East and the West.

Fearful of Russian intentions, Churchill sent Truman a series of secret cables strongly urging him not to pull back the advancing American and British armies "until we are satisfied about Poland and also about the temporary character of the Russian occupation of Germany." These matters needed to be settled before "the western world folds up its war machines." Some U.S. troops and air force units had already been redeployed to the Pacific. "In a very short space of time," Winston Churchill warned, "our armed power on the continent will have vanished except for moderate forces to hold down Germany. Meanwhile what is to happen about Russia?" Those forces should not retreat to the occupation zones agreed upon at Yalta until the Soviet Union honored its other agreements. Churchill expressed his anxiety in vivid imagery: "An iron curtain is drawn down upon their front," he told Truman, "[and] we do not know what is going on behind."[12]

Despite the warning, the new president believed it important for the United States to honor its commitments to the Yalta agreements. He ordered the U.S. Army to pull back 150 miles from its forward positions, facing the Soviet army across the Elbe River. And he decided to try to reach an understanding with Churchill and Stalin as soon as possible at a face-to-face meeting.

* * *

May 7, 1945, was also the day Phillip Jaffe returned to Washington, D.C., sealing John Service's fate. Emmanuel "Jimmy" Larsen visited Jaffe's hotel room to drop off another batch of documents, including a copy of the Five-Point Proposal—the Chinese Communists' plan for coalition government that Hurley had signed. The two men met Andrew Roth for lunch in the hotel dining room, and afterward Roth returned with Jaffe to his bugged room. Their recorded conversation convinced FBI investigators that Jaffe intended to pass confidential information to Soviet intelligence.

"I shouldn't tell you this," Jaffe confided, "I shouldn't tell it to anybody." He then disclosed to Roth that he had been contacted by Joseph Bernstein, a former *Amerasia* employee, who claimed that an acquaintance—"an agent for the Soviet Union for many years"—was having "a problem" getting information out of Washington. According to the FBI transcript, Jaffe told Roth, "He says, 'I would like to ask you whether you are willing to give me the dope that you get on Chungking out of the Far East Division of the State Department.'" Jaffe admitted that this was the reason "why I'm so anxious to get some more contacts with the State Department." Jaffe's enthusiasm was nevertheless tempered with caution: "But I said, 'How do I know who you are . . . so far as I know, you and he may be OSS agents.'"

"Boy, you're getting yourself in deep," Roth told Jaffe. "I don't like it." Jaffe then boasted about a list of "all the White Russians in this country, their history, their addresses, everything," supplied by Larsen, that he thought the Soviet agent might like. Jaffe asserted he would be giving information not to spies but to Soviet intelligence agents. "There is a difference, you see if . . . you were at war with each other, that's wrong, see?"

"I wouldn't take any risks there unless you're very certain," Roth advised. "You and the magazine have a role in this country which is very important." Such clandestine work, he argued, was not necessary in America, where it was easy enough for a journalist to find out what was happening and to obtain leaked information. "I wouldn't meet him," Roth concluded. "Well, I think I'm going to meet him," replied the editor. Roth warned him to be "very, very, very careful" and "not put anything in writing." Bernstein was not positively identified by the FBI for nearly a year. However, intercepted Soviet cables would subsequently confirm Bernstein's prior activity as a Soviet agent.[13]

* * *

It was raining in Washington, D.C., the next morning when John Service met Jaffe for breakfast in the hotel coffee shop. They went up to his room where they listened to the radio broadcast of President Truman's historic "Victory in Europe" announcement. "This is a solemn but glorious hour," Truman declared. "I only wish that Franklin D. Roosevelt had lived to witness this day." The new president reminded his audience "our victory is but half-won," and he called upon "every American to stick to his post until the last battle is won."[14]

After the radio address, Service and Jaffe discussed the situation in China. Jaffe complained that Hurley "got us on the spot where we can't move any longer without openly defying Chungking." Service then cautioned him: "Well, what I said about the military plans is, of course, very secret." This comment apparently referred to something Service had said during breakfast, out of earshot of FBI agents sitting nearby. This incriminating comment would be cited many times over the next three decades as evidence that Service was a security risk.

The hidden hotel room microphone soon picked up another exchange that confirmed growing FBI suspicions. Service indicated how far the U.S. Army was prepared to go in cooperation with Communist forces, in spite of the potentially embarrassing political ramifications:

Service: That plan was made up by Wedemeyer's staff in his absence, they got orders to make some recommendations as to what we should do if we landed in Communist territory. They had some—

Jaffe: To cooperate with them?
Service: Well, yes, that's what we planned, and they showed me the plans they had drawn up.

Service proceeded to tell Jaffe that if American troops landed in "Chungking territory," they would cooperate with the Nationalist forces, but if they landed in territory "where the Communists were," the U.S. forces would cooperate with them. Chiang Kai-shek was now putting pressure on American authorities to bring along his government officials "wherever we land . . . [but] as far as we know, we had not been given any power to do that." The fact that Hurley had endorsed clandestine OSS plans to cooperate with the Communists was news to the FBI agents.[15]

Then the conversation turned to the United Nations conference under way in San Francisco. When Jaffe mentioned having recently met Tung Pi-wu, the Chinese Communist delegate, Service volunteered that he knew him and had sent a letter of introduction for Tung to a friend at the Office of War Information (OWI) in San Francisco. The friend was willing to invite the Chinese Communists out to dinner, but he "thought it too dangerous to be seen with them very much."

Even their idle gossip made its way into the FBI files. Both Service and Jaffe had been favorably impressed with Soviet foreign minister Molotov's first speech in San Francisco but very unimpressed with the activities of Edward Stettinius, the soon-to-retire U.S. secretary of state. The newsreel of the opening ceremonies showed Stettinius looking "right in the camera with that toothpaste ad smile of his, shaking hands all the time, patting people on the back . . . happy as a baboon," Service mocked. "That's the good old salesman way." And when Jaffe told Service that Drew Pearson would soon publish an embarrassing story about Ambassador Hurley, describing the extravagant $30,000-dollar necklace given to his wife by the Chinese ambassador, Service exclaimed, "You make my mouth water just to think about it."[16] The FBI took Service's disrespectful remark very seriously. It quickly became part of the burgeoning *Amerasia* case file as another indication that the Foreign Service officer represented a threat to national security.

Around 10:30 AM, the two men left the hotel and walked over to the State Department. In the China Affairs office—in view of the amazed FBI agents—Service obtained a document from a staff member and handed it to Jaffe, who promptly returned to his hotel. Late that afternoon Service was again observed entering the Statler lobby where Jaffe was talking to several people, including Roth and his wife. He delivered a manila envelope to Jaffe, the agents reported, and quickly left.

The FBI concluded that John Service was providing secret government documents to the leftist editor, who intended to aid Soviet espionage. But after his arrest Service offered a different explanation. Jaffe had asked him for help in obtaining a copy of Mao Zedong's recent speech to the 7th Party Congress in Yenan. "I suggested that Jaffe go with me to the State Department and if the FCC report was unrestricted and the Department had no objection," Service told his interrogators, "he could see it there." When they arrived at the China Affairs office, he was told there were no restrictions, and the duty officer "gave me an extra copy of the Mao speech which he had on his desk to give to Jaffe." Service later received a call from the same officer telling him that a more complete version of the speech was available, so before leaving work, he picked it up. "I took a chance of finding Jaffe in the hotel and walked over there," Service explained. "[I] met him in the lobby and handed it to him, but did not stay to talk."[17]

* * *

On May 10 General Wedemeyer sent a letter of commendation to the secretary of state in recognition of John Service's "outstanding performance of duty." Praising his thorough knowledge of Chinese customs and language and his ability to establish "cordial relations" with Communist leaders, the American commander extolled Service's "detailed reports on military, economic, and political conditions in areas under Communist control, a field in which the American Government had previously had almost no reliable information." Service's advice on political matters had had a "direct and important bearing on the military situation in China."[18]

* * *

Impatient with State Department admonitions, Ambassador Hurley chose to bypass the secretary of state and sent a top secret cable to President Truman telling him that President Roosevelt had secretly entrusted him with "two specific missions in addition to my duties as Ambassador to China." The first was to get Churchill and Stalin's agreement on the United States' policy in support of Chiang Kai-shek; the second involved the still secret Yalta agreements. "Both Roosevelt and Stalin advised me . . . that I would not open the subject of the Yalta decision with Chiang Kai-shek until the signal was given me by Stalin." He was confident Chiang would agree to Yalta's terms, despite the yet-unknown infringements on Chinese sovereignty, if it meant that the Soviets would refuse to back Mao's forces and would sign a treaty with the Nationalist government.

"Please continue your efforts to accomplish the purposes outlined to you by President Roosevelt," Truman cabled in reply. The ambassador was instructed not to reveal anything about Yalta to Chiang until Washington provided "all the available information on this subject that can be disclosed without damage to the overall prospect."[19]

This presidential endorsement closed the door on any chance that the erratic ambassador would soon be replaced. "The problem was—and it must have given Hurley considerable amusement—that no one on the operating levels in the State Department even knew of the existence of the Yalta agreement on China," Service observed years later. Hurley's knowledge of the secret protocols made him "seemingly indispensable."[20]

* * *

John Service again traveled to New York for the weekend of May 19 to visit a friend and to attend a picnic hosted by T. A. Bisson, an Asian scholar and member of IPR's board of directors whom he first met when a language student in Peking. Service was unaware that Bisson and Jaffe had worked together in the early 1930s on the pro-Communist magazine *China Today*, and even traveled to Yenan together in 1937. In fact Jaffe had orchestrated the picnic invitation to cement his relationship with John Service, his valuable new source of information. Jaffe even called to suggest that Service stay at Mark Gayn's apartment on Saturday night and offered to drive him out to Long Island for the picnic the next day.

FBI agents followed Jaffe's car, carrying Service, the Gayns, and Kate Mitchell to Bisson's home in Port Washington. The group took a walk along the beach after lunch and the agents reported that Kate Mitchell and Service had strolled off together, deep in conversation. According to Service's later testimony, Mitchell was writing a book about China and simply wanted information about the Nationalist Chinese morality campaign extolling Confucianism. "That was the only conversation with Miss Mitchell of which I have any specific recollection," Service told the Senate committee five years later.[21] He considered the afternoon a strictly social occasion, but to the FBI, his New York weekend was added proof of his close association with Jaffe and his circle. It served to reinforce the impression created when Jaffe, earlier that week, lunched with an unidentified Asian man and handed over a thick manila envelope with the remark, "Jack Service is in solid."[22]

"I began to feel that I was really being exploited by this group of people," John Service later recalled, "[but] I didn't have any feeling that I was under any cloud or threat or anything."[23] His self-confidence was presumably heightened by Wedemeyer's letter of commendation—and by the news that he was getting a rare two-grade promotion in the Foreign Service, from class VI to IV. Such favorable endorsements no doubt energized his crusade about the situation in China—and further inflated a sense of his own importance. In hindsight, however, it is hard to fathom how Service could have been so recklessly trusting with his new contacts.

* * *

Harry Truman and his top advisers were deep into a major policy review of the United States' relations with both Russia and China. With Germany now defeated, Truman was anxious for Russia to commit forces against Japan quickly to minimize American losses in the invasion of Japan, set to begin November 1.

Russia's entry into the war depended upon interlocking pieces in the Chinese puzzle. First and foremost was Chinese acceptance of Russian claims in Manchuria under the secret Yalta accords. Stalin also expected to see a settlement of the political dispute between the Nationalists and the Chinese Communists. Despite Hurley's optimism, this looked increasingly unlikely. American officials were worried about what would happen when Soviet troops met Communist guerrillas on the battlefront if Hurley's negotiating efforts failed.

On the U.S. side, American officials sought assurances that the Soviets would not aid Mao's forces. Without a substantial commitment of U.S. ground troops, of course, Truman would have little leverage to forestall collaboration between the two Communist entities. But some such agreement was viewed as essential not only to pressure Mao to return to the bargaining table but also to head off civil war and to enable a treaty of friendship between Russia and China.

"I have far more confidence in our people on the working level," Sen. Joe Ball wrote President Harry Truman, "than I do in the higher-ups who seem terrifically impressed by the T. V. Soong family, which as you know, has God only knows how many millions salted away in the U.S." The senator, an old colleague from Capitol Hill, suggested John Service as one of several government specialists that the new president should consult for a realistic picture of the situation in China.[24]

Truman decided to send Harry Hopkins to Moscow to seek assurances on these issues. America's hope for political stability in Asia would depend on achieving political unity in China—with Stalin's help. In view of the United States' decision not to send major forces to the Chinese mainland, as historian Tang Tsou observed, "the United States had no alternative but to rely on the good faith of the Soviet Union."[25]

Although gravely ill, Hopkins agreed to travel to Moscow for talks with Stalin on May 28. The Soviet dictator said his army would be ready to move against Japan by early August, but the exact timing depended on Chinese acceptance of the secret Yalta terms: a Russian naval base and commercial seaport in northeast China as well as joint management of Manchurian railroad lines. As John Davies would later observe, although Stalin would certainly have entered the war against Japan solely to promote Soviet territorial and economic interests in the region, "he preferred to bedeck [his plan] with trappings of legality and represent it as a favor done for others . . . with a shrewd understanding of both American and Chinese psychology."[26]

Stalin reassured Hopkins that Soviet troops would respect Chinese sovereignty in all areas they entered, and after the fighting ended they would cooperate with Chiang's representatives. He also indicated readiness to begin negotiations for a Sino-Russian Friendship Treaty and suggested that China's foreign minister should arrive for talks by early July. "Stalin made a categorical statement that he would do everything he could to promote unification of China under the leadership of Chiang," noted historian Tang Tsou. "He further stated that . . . no one else, and specifically, no Communist leader, was strong enough to unify China."[27]

* * *

On May 28 the United States' delicate diplomacy with China and Russia began to converge with the *Amerasia* case—and John Service was the nexus. While Harry Hopkins negotiated with Stalin, the lead *Amerasia* investigator, Myron Gurnea, held an urgent meeting with key contacts at the State and Navy departments. Phillip Jaffe was returning to Washington that day to pick up confidential government documents from Larsen and to meet with Lieutenant Roth. The FBI wanted to make the arrests before Roth's impending transfer to Hawaii. Thanks to a "reliable confidential source" (i.e., wiretapped phone conversations), the FBI knew that Roth planned to accompany Jaffe to New York on May 30. Agents wanted to arrest them as they boarded the train with Jaffe's suitcase—they hoped—stuffed with confidential government documents. Even though there was no evidence that Jaffe was actually delivering information to Soviet representatives, the FBI considered it sufficiently damning that the Soviets could glean confidential information from *Amerasia*.

Secretary of the Navy James Forrestal was disturbed to learn that a naval intelligence officer was about to be arrested on espionage charges involving the Soviet Union. "I pointed out that the inevitable consequences of such action [prosecution] now would be to greatly embarrass the President in his current conversations with Stalin," Forrestal recorded in his diary, "because of the anti-Russian play up the incident would receive out of all proportion to its importance, particularly in view of the fact that the people involved were members of the American Communist Party." He immediately called the White House naval attaché and told him to make sure Truman was informed. "I then called Mr.

Edgar Hoover," Forrestal wrote, "and suggested that he advise Mr. Tom Clark [attorney general designate] and have him also see that the President is in full information of all the facts in the matter, as well as their implications."[28]

* * *

Jimmy Larsen arrived at Phillip Jaffe's hotel room just before noon. He was carrying several documents, including two reports written by John Service. They lunched again in the hotel restaurant with Lieutenant Roth, who afterward returned with Jaffe to his room. Again they discussed Jaffe's efforts to confirm Bernstein's ties to Soviet intelligence. They also spoke about Roth's disappointment over the Navy's recent decision to bar publication of his book about Japan while he remained on active duty. Later that afternoon, Jaffe telephoned John Service, who was surprised to learn Jaffe was back in town, and they agreed to meet for a drink after work the next day before going together to a farewell party for Roth.

At the Statler Hotel on May 29, John Service's conversation with Jaffe was again recorded by the FBI. The editor started to relate how the *New York Times* broke the real story of Stilwell's recall, but Service interrupted to brag about his unique role as messenger for reporter Brooks Atkinson, using his diplomatic privileges to get the story out after military censors tried to confiscate Atkinson's materials at a stopover:

> I wrote a card and said that this material Mr. Atkinson had was of interest to the State Department and other departments of the government. . . . Well, then I said to Brooks, "For Christ Sakes, this may happen again. Give me that damned story." Well, he gave me the story and then when we got in Tunis and the plane broke down. . . . Well he had a No. 2 priority and I had a No. 1 priority, so he was held over. And I went on. So I get to New York and I walked to the Terminal and the news broadcast was announcing that the President at the press conference had recalled Stilwell. Well, I had it right there, so I grabbed a taxi and chased up [to] the *New York Times* office.

Another recorded exchange between the editor and the diplomat that afternoon appeared to indicate Service's willingness to share secret information in the future:

Jaffe: Jack, do you think we'll land on the shores of China?
Service: I don't believe it has been decided. I can tell you in a couple of weeks when Stilwell gets back. I rather think we will.

Jaffe: Well, if we land in China, it will probably be in Shanghai, then we would accept aid from anybody, Communists or not Communists.
Service: I think that's correct.[29]

Across town, the *Amerasia* case had set off a flurry of activity at the Justice Department. By ten o'clock that same morning, J. Edgar Hoover met with the head of the criminal division, Tom Clark (slated to become the new attorney general). They discussed Forrestal's concerns about Hopkins' sensitive talks in Moscow. Hoover then gave Clark a memo detailing the *Amerasia* investigation—the same memo that had been hand-delivered that morning to Forrestal and to Assistant Secretary of State Julius Holmes. The memo identified Jaffe as "a well known Communist in New York" with connections to "all of the leading Communists in that city." It disclosed that through "a highly confidential source" the Bureau knew *Amerasia*'s offices contained "a tremendous amount of originals and copies of highly confidential Government documents" which had been supplied to Jaffe during his visits to Washington by Larsen and Roth. "It is also known that John Stewart Service, a foreign service officer . . . is also submitting to Jaffe copies of his confidential reports prepared . . . in China." The FBI memo acknowledged that much of the evidence had been obtained through "highly confidential means and sources of information which can not be used in evidence."[30]

That afternoon, after receiving a detailed briefing from the FBI's chief investigator, Clark's top prosecutor authorized the arrest of the *Amerasia* suspects. However, James McInerney urged that all the suspects be picked up "simultaneously at their homes or offices." This would maximize the FBI's opportunity to search—legally—for the incriminating documents they already knew existed. He later told Tom Clark they expected the confiscated documents would provide "sufficient evidence to make the case against all the subjects."[31] The prosecutors then could expect one of the defendants to be persuaded to testify against his coconspirators.[32]

* * *

After returning to Washington on May 31, President Truman was briefed on the *Amerasia* spy case by Assistant Secretary of State Holmes. "These men should be vigorously prosecuted," Truman ordered. The case would serve as a powerful lesson to others in government service who considered leaking confidential information. Truman even gave Holmes the name of someone he thought would make an ideal prosecutor.[33] Armed with the president's approval, Holmes called Gurnea at the FBI, giving the green light for the arrests. The Secretary of the Navy also concurred but insisted that Lieutenant Roth be stripped of his active duty commission before any arraignment. Forrestal would have preferred a quiet court-martial proceeding, but he understood that Roth was needed to help prove conspiracy in the civil case.

Late that same afternoon, FBI special agent Gurnea got a very different message from McInerney: the White House had told Clark not to make any arrests until the United Nations conference ended in mid-June—two weeks away.[34] But no one at Justice had bothered to inform Navy and State Department officials of the delay. When the State Department liaison called Gurnea two days later, he was shocked to learn of the postponement. An indignant Assistant Secretary Holmes hastily arranged another meeting with the president, who then insisted on speaking directly to the FBI agent in charge of the case.

"The president's secretary called, advising that the President wished to speak with me," Gurnea reported to Hoover. "General Holmes then came on the line stating that he was in the President's office and the President had requested he get in contact with me. The President then came on the line and stated, 'I want you to go right ahead with it [the arrests] as quickly as possible.'"[35] Holmes recalled the president's no-nonsense orders when he testified before a Senate subcommittee five years later: "'I don't care who told you to stop this. You are not to do it . . . and if anybody suggests that you postpone, or anything else, you are not to do it without first personal approval from me.' And then he grinned and said 'Does that suit you?' And I said, 'Yes, sir.'"[36]

On June 6, 1945—the first anniversary of D-day—the six *Amerasia* suspects were arrested: Jaffe, Mitchell, and Gayn in New York; Larsen, Roth, and Service in Washington, D.C. The *Amerasia* case would soon capture the nation's attention—adding to the growing doubts about its Soviet ally and feeding public fears about the new Cold War with Communism.

CHAPTER 13
CASE CORKED

When Americans unfolded their morning newspapers on Thursday, June 7, 1945, they discovered a shocking front-page story about the arrest of the *Amerasia* suspects—including three U.S. government officials. News coverage included their mug shots or the grim photograph of Service, Larsen, and Roth awaiting their predawn arraignment. The most sensational headlines—nearly two inches high—bannered the front pages of the Hearst and Scripps-Howard newspapers, which had been tipped off by the FBI to Jaffe's Communist ties: "Spy Ring Linked to U.S. Reds: Secret War Data Leak Is Laid to Jaffe, High Communist, and 5 Others" (*New York World-Telegram*). The *New York Post* took a more factual approach, but its headline was also shocking: "FBI Seizes 6 as Spies, Two in State Dept; Secrets Stolen—Naval Officer and Two Editors of Magazine Here Arrested."

FBI Director J. Edgar Hoover provided a statement about the intense two-and-a-half-month FBI investigation instigated by the State Department and the Navy, which led to the recovery of confidential government documents ranging in classification from "Restricted" to "Top Secret." Acting Secretary of State Joseph C. Grew was quoted as saying his department had been giving "special attention" to security matters for months and had called in the FBI when they realized information "of a secret character was reaching unauthorized persons."

These prepared statements by Hoover and Grew had been carefully coordinated prior to the arrests. Assistant FBI Director Lou Nichols had met with representatives of Justice, State, and Navy—all eager to share credit for the arrest of "The Six"—to thrash out the press releases. But at his news conference later that day, Grew focused on the leak of information rather than the suspected espionage: the *Amerasia* investigation was part of "a comprehensive security program which is to be continued unrelentingly in order to stop completely the illegal and disloyal conveyance of confidential information to unauthorized persons."[1]

Grew's statement suggested that the case represented a new crackdown on journalists and government leakers rather than the Red espionage loudly touted by the conservative media. On his weekly radio program, the influential Drew Pearson predicted the case would "boomerang" on Secretary Grew, who would eventually be forced to resign as a result of fallout from "America's Dreyfus case." The chilling effect of the arrests, wrote the leftist columnist I. F. Stone, would be to "frighten into silence officials who disagree with the [State] Department's policies and to lay the basis for prosecuting newspapers and newspapermen who publish information which provokes criticism of the Department." In the margins of Stone's commentary included in his lead investigator's report, FBI Director Hoover scribbled a comment: "It is too bad that the State Dept is making a 'field day' of this. It may materially hurt the case and certainly lends credit to accusations of some that [the] case is result of State Department's sensitiveness to criticism."[2] Grew's remarks reinforced the defendants' suspicions that they had been targeted for criticizing Hurley's policy of unconditional support of Chiang Kai-shek—and Grew's conservative policy for postwar Japan.

From jail, John Service wrote a letter to his mother assuring her of his innocence. "I will be cleared, but a trial seems necessary." He hoped to find "the instigating force or forces behind this."[3] Service had been given a blanket, a mattress, and a cell to himself, but he did not get much sleep. His jailers were impressed by the news stories about their infamous inmate, but Service was deeply mortified to be lumped together with suspects accused of stealing documents. His sister-in-law Helen joined with some Foreign Service friends to raise one thousand dollars to release him late Thursday evening on a ten-thousand-dollar bail bond. "After the bail was posted, Jack went to Helen's apartment and I talked with him," recalled Caroline (then seven months pregnant and living at her parents' Berkeley home). "Just hearing his voice gave me courage."[4]

Service himself was in a state of "numbed shock, heightened by the FBI interrogation, the jail experience, and the publicity given to charges of 'espionage.'" By morning, his mood had changed to anger. "I felt that my career had been ruined. It just didn't seem to be possible that I could come back into the State Department disgraced."[5] He sought the advice of friends—especially Vincent and Currie, who had encouraged his background briefings for journalists. "They urged me to calm down and to fight the thing out, since I was innocent of anything beyond indiscretion."[6] They also said he needed to find a good lawyer, and they promised to help.

Currie consulted his friend Ben Cohen, top legal counsel of the State Department. A veteran New Dealer who had helped draft much of the landmark legislation of Roosevelt's early administration, Cohen was now actively involved in the effort to get congressional approval of the United Nations charter. He immediately understood the larger ramifications: a big "spy" trial could prove highly embarrassing on many fronts. President Truman would soon travel to Potsdam for his first summit with Churchill and Stalin where he hoped to restore the frayed alliance and to obtain Russia's commitment to military action against Japan. In China, Hurley's talks had been suspended amid stirrings of civil conflict.

Cohen contacted Thomas Corcoran, the ultimate Washington insider. The two attorneys, formerly roommates, had worked together for Roosevelt as early as 1933. Corcoran had begun a lucrative private practice in 1940, building a reputation as "the fixer." The burly, blue-eyed Irishman combined an insider's knowledge and contacts with charm, energy, and strong-arm political tactics. A favorite mode of operation was the "triple play"—manipulating two separate clients to exchange favors while he himself was compensated in a way that was both tax-free and untraceable.[7] Corcoran would later be remembered as Washington's first modern lobbyist. "Tommy the Cork" immediately got busy checking out possible lawyers for "Ben's friend," John Service.

On Sunday morning Jack breakfasted with General Stilwell, just back from talks with General MacArthur about the planned invasion of Japan. Stilwell was very upset that Service was "being caught up in the same political mess that had caused his recall," according to a long-time aide. Stilwell was still under orders from the Army chief of staff not to talk publicly about China and Chiang, but if called as a witness in a legal proceeding, "he would have welcomed a chance to 'unload'. . . and was anxious to do anything he could to help."[8]

* * *

As legal proceedings got under way, newspapers and radio broadcasters increasingly reflected a deep left–right split over the *Amerasia* case and its domestic and international implications. The liberal press questioned its legitimacy. A *New York Post* editorial, "Spies or Victims," demanded to know if Secretary Grew's statement meant that a foreign power was receiving confidential material—or merely that journalists were getting leaks from government officials. "The first is espionage. The latter is an old Washington custom practiced . . . by just about every Washington correspondent worth his salt to his newspaper. . . . If Mr. Grew is able to throttle the editors of left wing *Amerasia* because they expose his policy, any decent American newspaper which similarly opposes his policies may be next on the list of Grew's State Dept. Gestapo—maybe even one of the papers now gleefully belaboring the indictees."[9]

The same day, Scripps-Howard newspapers across the country carried the headline "Reds Caused Stilwell and Chiang Break." The story charged that John Service's secret mission in Yenan was "partly responsible for the Stilwell–Chiang Kai-shek split." Moreover, "secret military and police data stolen from State Department and other Government files was used to help turn this country against Generalissimo Chiang Kai-shek and in favor of the Chinese Communists."[10]

Only experienced China watchers recognized that these outlandish charges reflected Nationalist propaganda. Soon stories from the Chinese Central News Agency began appearing in newspapers around the world that, as Service said, "cheerfully and loudly" called him a Japanese spy.[11] Assiduously, the FBI clipped *Amerasia* newspaper stories and transcribed radio commentaries for its files.

* * *

FBI Director Hoover was greatly perturbed by the initial skepticism regarding the legitimacy of the case. Even staunchly anti-Communist news organizations were having second thoughts about the issue of press freedom and the time-honored tradition of government leaks to journalists. An editorial in the moderate *New York Herald Tribune* went further: "The necessity of living in peace and amity in the same world with Soviet Russia [made] the Red baiting now in progress disturbing and dangerous."[12]

Hoover met with Lee Woods, an executive of the Scripps-Howard newspaper chain, to offer his personal assurance. An FBI memo declassified decades later revealed: "The Director actually showed him some of the exhibits in the case and told him that the case was 'air tight.'"[13] Perhaps Hoover even showed Woods a summary of the taped hotel room conversation, with Service cautioning Jaffe that what he had said about military plans was "very secret." After the meeting, the journalist prepared an editorial that appeared in all Scripps-Howard papers across the country: "Isn't it just a little silly for critics of the prosecution to cry 'freedom of the press' merely because three of the defendants are engaged in magazine publishing and writing and espouse political views contrary to those of the State Department? It is pertinent that the government's charge at the time of the arrest was that the defendants were trafficking in military secrets. If evidence supporting that charge is produced at the trial, a plea of 'freedom of the press' will be no defense."[14]

* * *

Bolstered by his talk with Stilwell and others, and by the favorable reporting of some prominent journalists, John Service's mood turned defiantly combative.

Big-name attorneys were being recruited on behalf of other defendants, and Service was urged to hire a famous civil liberties lawyer. A Foreign Service friend established a defense fund. Service considered resigning to fight "a crusade" and to write about the case. He was also very tempted by a job offer from the *New York Post* to return to China as its war correspondent.

"If you heard [Drew] Pearson and [Walter] Winchell last night and if you remember certain things from my letters and our conversations," Service wrote to his mother, "you will realize some of the broad and basic issues involved." Admitting that he had shown personal copies of some of his reports to "reputable writers and researchers specializing in China," he assured her that it was done "with the knowledge and approval of certain higher officials," who were now helping him find "the best lawyer available." None of the reports he lent Jaffe pertained to American policy or military plans, but he admitted the prosecutors might be able "to hang a technical charge" on him. "It will not convince me, nor any of the people who know what has been going on, that I have done wrong or committed a crime against my country." In closing, he confided, "Pearson is not alone in thinking that this may rock the present Grew [gang] in which case, even though I may have to be the sacrificial goat, some good will come of it all . . . it may be fun—and certainly exciting." Thanking her for offering help, he then asked for a loan of two thousand dollars to help with his legal expenses.[15] Grace Service immediately fired off a letter to relatives, soliciting their financial support and telling them, "we want publicity and no hole-in-the-corner-hush-hush of the affair."[16]

* * *

Tom Corcoran was already looking into the case and figuring the angles. Assisting Tom Clark in his confirmation as attorney general was one possible angle: A recent news story about an old Texas oil deal had raised concerns about Clark's Senate hearing. Over the weekend, Corcoran gleaned reassurances that Republicans would not block Clark's appointment. He called Clark to tell him there was "nothing at all to worry about." "Well, I do thank you," Clark responded. Tommy the Cork was now in a position to trade favors.

The FBI became well aware of Corcoran's conversations, thanks to a wiretap they had put on his phone at the behest of the White House. The insecure new administration was worried about possible sabotage by former Roosevelt aides. Over the next five years, summaries of Corcoran's phone conversations were routinely delivered to Harry Vaughan, Truman's trusted military aide.

The secret FBI phone taps reveal that Corcoran also called E. Barrett Prettyman, a prominent attorney who would soon be named to the federal appellate court by Truman. "Who is Godfrey Munter?" he asked Prettyman. Munter had been retained to handle the preliminary hearing, just a few days away, while Service continued his search for a trial lawyer.

Corcoran: "Is he a Red?"

Prettyman: No, heavens no. He's on the conservative side. He's a gentle sort of fellow, not a rough and tumble fellow. . . . He's adequate . . . very reliable character, entirely good.

Corcoran: Well with any kind of handling at all he can win this one. (Both men laughed) . . .

Prettyman: I think he is in adequate hands. . . .

Corcoran: My strategy on playing his game would be to let the other fellows do the jumping up and down and let him slip out.

Prettyman: Might very well be. And Godfrey Munter might manipulate a thing like that.

Corcoran: I'm not the slightest interested in the principle of the thing. I want to get my fellow and my friend out.[17]

That afternoon Corcoran spoke with Currie to confirm Munter's qualifications. He assured Currie he would "back-stop this thing." "I am not going to let them push this kid [Service] around. If we have to get to the ulcer in the stomach stage, I will be very tempted to step in." Both men understood, however, that Corcoran preferred "to work around the edges of this thing" rather than be out in front leading the charge. "It may be embarrassing for you for a client," Currie cautioned. Corcoran served as legal counsel for T. V. Soong's company, China Defense Supplies, which handled China's Lend-Lease program. He readily agreed that he must be "awfully careful"—and confided: "I don't believe this case is ever going to be tried."[18]

Currie mentioned the names of several high-profile trial attorneys, to which Corcoran strongly objected. "What I want to do is to get the guy out. These other fellows want to make a Dreyfus case out of it." Both men had their own reasons for not wanting the case to become a cause célèbre.

On the following morning, a complete transcription of this strategy discussion was sent to Hoover.[19] The only player unaware of these behind-the-scenes machinations was the defendant himself. John Service had no idea that Corcoran was in effect taking charge of the case. But when Service first met his temporary lawyer, Godfrey Munter, he was not impressed. "He knew nothing about the State Department," Service recalled, "and appeared confused by the complications of [my] work for Stilwell." Munter found it hard to understand key elements: Service's relations with the State Department and other officials in the government, the intramural policy debate regarding China, and the always ticklish issue of giving background information to the press.[20] Service informed Munter that friends were looking to make other arrangements for his defense counsel, and he agreed to handle legal proceedings only for as long as needed.

* * *

From its illegal wiretaps, the FBI learned that Phillip Jaffe had hired the law partner of Emmanuel Cellar, an influential congressman from Brooklyn who had taken an interest in the highly publicized case. Mark Gayn would be represented by the *Chicago Tribune*'s legal counsel. He was overheard telling his father that the notion of a conspiracy was "ridiculous" and that the arrests were "probably due to the Chinese trying to get rid of Service whom they detest."

On Tuesday, June 12, Hoover met with Assistant Attorney General James McGranery. To handle the *Amerasia* case, he favored an assistant U.S. attorney, Robert Hitchcock, who had successfully prosecuted members of the German American Bund in New York. Hoover wanted an early trial, but government prosecutors still needed evidence to support charges of conspiracy to commit espionage; their most damaging evidence had been gathered illegally and could not be introduced in court. In a "strictly confidential" memo for Clyde Tolson, his top deputy and closest companion, Hoover revealed his own misgivings. "If it is not necessary to prove the intent, we have a foolproof case," the FBI director wrote, "but should it be necessary to prove the intent, we do not have any case."[21]

The FBI had a serious problem. None of the suspects had either confessed or volunteered to testify against the other alleged conspirators. Agents had confiscated stacks of documents and other materials in conjunction with the arrests, but they had yet to find any clear evidence of a conspiracy to commit espionage—and certainly nothing that pointed to passing information to Soviet intelligence. Agents were compiling detailed inventories of the huge cache of documents, filling fifteen file drawers in the bureau's evidence room. Others were trying to track the paper trail from government files to the suspects while field agents around the country were detailed to interview the defendants' friends and acquaintances. Analysts conducted lab tests for fingerprints, compared handwriting samples, and even examined typewriter ribbons and paper stock found on the premises where suspects were arrested. Of the 1,722 papers collected, 928 were identifiable as stolen government documents. Many of these turned out to be unclassified or "were found to be of so little importance," according to historians

Harvey Klehr and Ronald Radosh, "that their classification was a technicality."[22] And the small percentage of documents relating to national security or military affairs dealt with issues from the early war years and might be considered merely historical documents. The snippets of John Service's hotel talk about secret military plans and anticipated American troop landings had aroused great interest, but the FBI could not turn over such illegally obtained evidence to prosecutors.

Service had readily admitted lending Jaffe eight or ten reports about the Communists, but when the FBI inventoried the entire cache of reports, they found dozens. Forty-two were located in *Amerasia* offices, including eight official State Department copies of recent Yenan reports found in Jaffe's suitcase, and fourteen typed copies of Service reports (which Jaffe's typist identified as her own work). Gayn's apartment contained a typed copy of Service's report about rumored domestic trouble in Chiang's household, and Larsen's apartment yielded several more official copies of Service's reports. FBI lab tests revealed that many of the documents seized at the *Amerasia* offices bore Larsen's fingerprints or notations in his handwriting. During his interrogation, Larsen (a civil service employee in State's Far Eastern Division) had admitted taking home official copies of Service's reports and showing many of them to Jaffe.[23] Nevertheless, the FBI agents assumed that Service had not told them the whole truth about the documents, and he remained a prime suspect.

As soon as Service was taken into custody, FBI agents spent more than an hour rifling through his desk in Room 145 of the State Department. A suspicious looking list—with code names for U.S. intelligence agencies, people, and places—had already been found in his borrowed apartment. Now they confiscated the contents of his office drawers: personal letters, a few notes in Chinese characters, a manila folder marked "Yenan Materials," and a thick file of typed carbon copies of eighty-three field reports written between 1944 and that very day. The last memo, addressed to John Carter Vincent, discussed the current political line being taken by the American Communist Political Association.[24] To FBI investigators, the mere topic looked suspicious.

* * *

John Service was overwhelmed by an outpouring of letters and telegrams of support from friends and colleagues, including a letter from retired Amb. Clarence Gauss, who enclosed a five-hundred-dollar check for Service's defense fund. From China came heartening news from Service's younger brother, who had followed his example and joined the Foreign Service. "Chinese friends here are putting straight the lousy angle which [Nationalist] Central News put on the affair in all of its statements," Dick Service wrote from Kunming. "Your reputation is too good to suffer by this sort of thing with those who know you . . . [and] you would be surprised at the number of persons who have never met you, but who know of you, who have come to me to say what they think of this." Dick Service also relayed a vote of confidence from General Wedemeyer. "He is anxious and ready to do anything that he can to assist you. . . . Also said he spoke with General Hurley a few days ago about your case, making clear his views." Wedemeyer had affirmed that his entire headquarters staff had complete confidence in John Service "and will not believe you have done anything that could be considered disloyal or underhanded."[25]

By the middle of June, press reaction across the nation began to be decidedly critical of the arrests. The FBI was warned by a friendly Scripps-Howard reporter that their case was turning into a public relations disaster. With great fanfare, *Collier's* magazine published Mark Gayn's article criticizing both American policy on Japan and ex-ambassador Joseph Grew; the magazine boasted that the article was based upon classified information obtained from confidential government sources. The New York Newspaper Guild denounced the arrests as an effort to stifle government sources that were crucial for the conduct of responsible journalism and intelligent public policy discussion. In a national survey, 67 percent of newspaper editors said the *Amerasia* prosecution threatened the First Amendment and that the government's system of classifying documents was "rigid and unreasonable."[26]

On June 14, the date set for the preliminary hearing of the three *Amerasia* defendants in Washington, the newly appointed federal prosecutor asked for a delay, explaining to the U.S. commissioner that he needed more time to become familiar with the case. Defense attorneys argued that the defendants had a right to hear the government's evidence that had led to the arrests. At least the Justice Department should furnish the defendants with the information provided to the State Department in preparation of its press release about the arrests. The attorneys feared federal prosecutors might sidestep the preliminary hearing altogether by obtaining quick indictments from a secret federal grand jury as a way of avoiding embarrassing public revelations.

* * *

Before traveling to Moscow to begin negotiations on a Sino-Russian friendship treaty, T. V. Soong stopped in Chungking to confer with the Generalissimo—flying in with his retinue from the San Francisco UN conference in a plane provided by the U.S. Army and overloaded with luxury cargo. Stopping in Washington, D.C., Soong met with Truman and Hopkins shortly after Hopkins' return from Moscow. Now he was told about the secret Yalta agreement, and Truman finally cabled Ambassador Hurley the green light to tell Chiang as well. As long as Stalin would sign a treaty with the Nationalist government and refuse to support Mao's forces, the Chinese would be willing to swallow Yalta's humiliating concessions. "Without the support of the Soviet," Hurley reported to the president, "the Chinese Communist Party will eventually participate as a political party in the National Government."[27]

* * *

On June 15 Acting Secretary of State Joseph Grew held another press conference where he again defended the controversial *Amerasia* arrests: "We heard somebody in the chicken-coop and went to see who was there." Grew insisted he never knew the names of the suspects or that *Amerasia* was the magazine implicated until "long after the inquiry had been turned over for investigation by FBI." He ridiculed allegations he had been motivated by "any personal animus" in the case of Lieutenant Roth, claiming he only learned about Roth's book and its criticism of his alleged "appeasement policy" toward Japan by listening to the radio after the arrests.[28]

When John Service heard Secretary Grew's comment about catching foxes in the chicken coop, he quickly lodged a protest. "I saw somebody in the Secretary's office," he later recounted. "I said, 'Look, I object to this sort of statement. It's prejudging the case.' The man looked as though he'd seen a ghost. He said, 'You mean you're not guilty?' I said, 'Of course I'm not guilty. I'm going to be cleared, and it is very foolish of the State Department to make this kind of statement.'"[29] This was the beginning of John Service's forty-year fight to restore his tarnished reputation.

Several days later, Grew announced his retirement from public service. With Secretary of State Stettinius also due to retire, this meant a major changing of the guard at State. Truman chose a trusted former Senate colleague, James Byrnes, as secretary and Dean Acheson, a polished diplomat, as undersecretary. Acheson soon promoted John Carter Vincent to head the Far Eastern Division, and Grew's loyalists were quietly moved out.

* * *

On June 18 Service arrived at Union Station early to meet the train carrying his wife, Caroline, and their two children, nine-year-old Virginia and eight-year-old Robert. Caroline told him about watching fellow passengers read about the *Amerasia* case. "It went through my head, 'Wouldn't they be surprised if they knew who was sitting opposite them?'" she recalled with bemusement many years later.[30] Jack happily drove his family to a newly rented three-bedroom house in Chevy Chase, Maryland, where they would try to begin life again as a family.

In June President Truman met with his top military advisers to review plans for the invasion of Japan, scheduled to begin November 1 with an assault on the southern island of Kyūshū. General Marshall assessed the operation to be as difficult as the storming of Normandy beach, one year earlier. The invasion of Honshū—the main island, where Tokyo is located—set for March 1946, promised to be just as difficult. The war against Japan might last another year, cost half a million lives on both sides, and leave more than a million injured or maimed. Their alternative strategy was a carpet-bombing campaign coupled with a naval blockade to starve Japan into surrender. Truman confided in his diary that deciding whether to invade or to bomb and blockade "is my hardest decision to date."[31] That terrible choice added to the urgency of getting Russia to declare war against Japan by early August, as Stalin had promised Hopkins, to lessen American casualties and shorten the conflict.

The July summit in Potsdam with Churchill and Stalin would be crucial. Truman ordered a full review of American policy options in postwar Europe and in the Pacific war zone, to address all the important decisions he might have to make at Potsdam. He told his advisers he was not sure unconditional surrender was necessary, but this was no time to try to change public opinion.[32] Although insecure about his lack of experience in foreign affairs, Truman was an astute politician who knew how to read the political winds. He certainly was aware of the public debate over China—and the controversy swirling around the *Amerasia* "spy case."

* * *

The defense attorneys' fears were confirmed when the *Amerasia* case was presented to the District of Columbia Grand Jury four days in advance of the rescheduled court hearing. The FBI Director had instructed Myron Gurnea to ensure "a vigorous conclusion" in the case.[33] Gurnea had in turn supplied prosecutor Robert Hitchcock with a detailed report, including information from "highly confidential sources."[34] Fourteen FBI agents, Jaffe's typist, and three government officials were called to testify.

Late that evening, Gurnea telephoned Hitchcock for a report on the secret grand jury proceedings and was surprised to learn that the Justice Department had decided to seek indictments on reduced charges. Instead of conspiracy to commit espionage, the government had gone with the far less serious charge of embezzling government property. "I inquired why we were not proceeding on Section 31 [conspiracy to commit espionage] as charged in the complaints and as was originally planned," Gurnea wrote Hoover the next day. "[Hitchcock] stated they wanted to get quick indictments before the grand jury to preclude the necessity of discussing the case at commissioner's hearings." Confident of getting quick indictments on lesser charges, Hitchcock claimed that this would pressure the defendants enough to gain "the expected cooperation of at least one of the six." With a friendly witness, Hitchcock could then resurrect the more serious charge of conspiracy to commit espionage.[35]

This change of strategy served to increase the FBI's growing suspicions. The secret wiretaps had uncovered political pressure being applied on the new attorney general and his deputies by several defense attorneys—not just Tom Corcoran.

When Service's temporary lawyer learned that the case had gone to the secret grand jury, he advised him to settle on a lawyer quickly because indictments and a trial date could be expected soon. By then Service had decided not to "make a stink" or seek out "crusader lawyers" to handle his case. Currie and Vincent had persuaded Service that a low-key approach was the best way to save his career and achieve vindication. Currie now steered him to consult Corcoran about an appropriate attorney and legal strategy.

"This seemed like going into the enemy's lair," Service argued, well aware of Corcoran's close ties to Soong and Nationalist interests. Currie told him, somewhat disingenuously, that it was "absurd" to be afraid to approach Corcoran "merely because he had a reputation for influence—which we did not intend to use," and that it was "ridiculous" to think that Corcoran's friendly advice would be affected in any way by his entirely separate business relations with the Chinese.[36]

* * *

Thanks to the tap on Corcoran's office phone, the FBI knew in advance about his 3:30 PM meeting with Service scheduled for Friday, June 29. Taken by surprise at Corcoran's seemingly "unfriendly, hard-boiled attack," Service soon recognized the value of Corcoran's "brusque and penetrating grilling" and his "quick and thorough grasp" of the case. Corcoran promised to find him another attorney; meanwhile, Munter should try to learn as much as possible from the prosecutors.

Two days after the *Amerasia* case was presented to the grand jury, Jaffe's attorney—accompanied by his law partner, Rep. Emmanuel Cellar, as well as lawyers for Gayn and Mitchell—sat down with Attorney General Clark and his lead prosecutors, McInerney and Hitchcock. The defense attorneys made it clear that they would push the freedom of the press issues if the case went to trial and emphasized the embarrassment for the government to lose such a high-profile case. The prosecutors indicated that no indictments had been announced and that the grand jury's term was about to end. Mitchell's lawyer suggested that they let it expire to give them time to continue informal talks about possible plea bargains before the case was presented to the next grand jury later that summer.

"This is most unfortunate," wrote an irritated Hoover on the bottom of a confidential memo reporting these developments. "Case should go to present Grand Jury, indictments obtained and case set for trial. I don't like all the manipulation which is going on."[37] Although Hoover himself remained unconcerned that his information came from spying on confidential attorney–client phone conversations, some of his lieutenants now began to worry that if their wiretaps were discovered, "we might find ourselves embarrassed."[38]

Late in June the tap on Kate Mitchell's phone revealed that her attorney had indicated to the attorney general that if the current grand jury's term were allowed to expire without handing down indictments, his client might testify voluntarily before the next grand jury. It was exactly the break the FBI had been hoping for. Mitchell could shed light on Jaffe's other government leakers and perhaps even talk about the attempt of a Soviet agent to recruit Jaffe.[39] If she became a government witness against the others, the burden of proof problem could be resolved and the inadmissible evidence would become superfluous.

* * *

Even before John Service first met Tom Corcoran, Munter met informally with Justice Department officials and convinced them that the FBI had no legal right to seize materials from Service's office desk without a warrant. A judge concurred. Eventually, the FBI returned Service's private papers, along with a detailed fifteen-page inventory of seized items—but only after secretly making copies of all the documents for its files. These materials would resurface as ammunition against Service in the years to come.

By early July the efforts to find a different lawyer to handle Service's case had fallen through. As an alternative, Corcoran proposed keeping Godfrey Munter as the counsel of record while he continued to give friendly—and confidential—advice. "It ended up with Corcoran actually as my lawyer, unofficially," Service later admitted, "with Munter the front man."[40] When Service expressed concern about his ghost attorney's fee, "Corcoran immediately stated that he would accept no fee, that his assistance was offered as a matter of friendship." He said he believed Service had been doing a good job for the government and "although he had blundered into a jam, was innocent of any crime." John Service had already been forced to rely on family and friends to pay his bail bond and could not afford to refuse Corcoran's offer.[41] Only years later would Service realize the high price of Tommy the Cork's advice and counsel.

CHAPTER 14
FBI PERSON OF INTEREST

"I am getting ready to go see Stalin & Churchill," Harry Truman wrote to his mother and sister before departing for the Potsdam Conference, on July 7, 1945. "I have to take my tuxedo, tails, Negro preacher coat, high hat, low hat and hard hat." His briefcase was packed with background material and "suggestions on what to do and say." The man from Missouri confessed, "Wish I didn't have to go."[1] Truman had been president of the United States for fewer than three months. How would he measure up against Roosevelt's historic accomplishments and his special relationship with Winston Churchill? What could he do to convince Josef Stalin to abide by Yalta's agreements for the liberation of Europe, and to pin down a definite date for Russia's entry into the war against Japan?

Accompanying Truman on the USS *Augusta* were fifty-three top officials and advisers. Among them were James Byrnes, his newly appointed secretary of state, and John Carter Vincent, State's recently appointed chief of East Asian Affairs, who had prepared a set of briefing papers on China and Japan. One day at sea, Secretary Byrnes paid an unexpected visit to Vincent's stateroom. Tossing the policy papers onto the berth, Byrnes pronounced them "all out of date." Vincent then learned for the first time about the top secret Yalta protocol. The secretary himself had only recently learned of the special concessions granted a full five months earlier to the Soviets in China.[2] The State Department's top China policy specialist felt as if he'd been broadsided.

General Wedemeyer had cabled his recommendations for Potsdam. He urged the allied leaders to use their influence to force the two rival Chinese parties to make "realistic concessions" and stated—in a clear rebuke to Ambassador Hurley: "Continuing appeals to both sides couched in polite diplomatic terms will not accomplish unification. There must be teeth in the Big Three approach."[3] But

China never became a top priority at Potsdam. The agenda was driven by more immediate concerns: the Soviets' brutal occupation of Poland and other East European countries; and the growing tension over Allied occupation zones inside Germany.

* * *

"A few minutes before twelve I looked up from the desk and there stood Stalin in the doorway," Truman noted in his diary for July 17. The Russian dictator, standing only five feet five inches, wore a khaki uniform with red epaulets and red-seamed trousers, with a red-ribboned gold medal pinned above his left breast pocket. "I told Stalin I am no diplomat but usually said yes or no to questions after hearing all the arguments," Truman recorded in his diary. "It pleased him." Truman made no mention of the momentous news he had just received about the first successful test of the atom bomb in the New Mexico desert. Stalin—surprisingly soft-spoken—talked about his recent treaty talks with T. V. Soong, claiming that most of the major issues had been settled. He had given assurances to the Nationalist Chinese delegation that the Soviet Union would not interfere in Manchuria's internal political affairs, and had accepted its special relationship with China. Much to Truman's surprise and relief, Stalin then announced he would be ready to declare war on Japan and attack Manchuria by August 15. "I got what I came for," Truman happily told his diary that night.[4]

The first formal summit meeting of the Big Three took place later that afternoon in the cavernous oak-paneled reception hall of the Cecilienhof Palace in Potsdam. There were five chairs for each of the three delegations at the round conference table. Additional seats for supporting members of the delegations lined the walls of the room. One of the U.S. seats was occupied by Ben Cohen, legal counsel for the State Department, who had asked Tom Corcoran to take care of John Service while he was away.

President Truman presented an agenda detailing the most sensitive issues facing the leaders. The only agreement reached that first day, however, had to do with the organization of the conference itself. The foreign ministers, accompanied by staff, would meet each morning to thrash out the agenda for the Big Three session in the afternoon. "As all the questions are to be discussed by the foreign ministers, we shall have nothing to do," commented Stalin, and laughter broke the tension in the huge hall. "All the same," he added, "we will not escape the disagreeable." Truman bluntly responded, "I don't want to *discuss*. I want to *decide*." Over the next two weeks he would work tirelessly to reach agreements on a staggering range of postwar issues. As he remarked in a letter to Bess Truman, Potsdam made presiding over the Senate look tame.[5]

* * *

The FBI's hoped-for quick trial of the *Amerasia* case did not materialize. The sitting grand jury, having served already for several months, allowed the case to be withdrawn from its caseload. Prosecutors were to present the case to a new panel at the end of July. In the meantime, they continued to meet informally with defense attorneys, hoping to pressure a defendant into cooperating with the government. From tapped phone conversations, however, shocked FBI investigators learned that deputy editor Kate Mitchell was being offered a very different arrangement. If she agreed to appear voluntarily before the new grand jury, she and her attorney would be allowed to see the prosecutors' evidence and the list of questions they planned to pose. "It looks to me as if it is hard to tell whether government [prosecutor] is representing the government or the defendants," was Hoover's exasperated notation.[6]

John Service's legal advisers were divided on whether he should risk appearing voluntarily. When Munter met with prosecutors, they indicated they were inclined to believe Service's story. They had been impressed by the statement he gave FBI agents on the night of his arrest—and especially by his frank admission of lending personal copies of Yenan reports to Jaffe. His explanation of his contacts with Jaffe and the other defendants checked out with the FBI's chronology. Telling his story to the grand jury, the Justice attorneys suggested, might be a good way to clear his name. They wanted Munter to bring Service in to discuss the possibility.

Corcoran feared a trap. He cautioned that prosecutors might be holding back evidence to spring on Service during the secret grand jury session, with no lawyers allowed. The suspicion lingered that Hurley and Tai Li might actually be behind his arrest; otherwise, the evidence seemed far too slim for the charges. They knew nothing, of course, about the nature of Jaffe's operation, or the enormous quantity of confidential material collected. Corcoran informed Service that he was talking with the new attorney general and hoped to get him quietly "cut out" of the case before it ever reached the grand jury. "The important question," Service later recalled, "was whether or not positive steps should be taken in an effort to forestall indictment."[7]

Jack Service pondered the conflicting advice of his legal advisers while he continued adjusting to life as a family man. His decision about a grand jury appearance could determine whether he would be able to continue the career he loved and provide for his expanding family. Caroline Service was due to deliver in just a few weeks.

* * *

A few days later, the FBI's tap on Corcoran's telephone picked up more provocative intelligence. "I did want you to know I'd gone right up to the top on the damn thing," Corcoran boasted to Service, in recounting a conversation with the attorney general. "He said he'd try to give me an answer on the whole damn thing—a final answer—this afternoon."[8]

Later Corcoran called James McGranery, the chief deputy at Justice. "If what I understand from everybody is the truth, [Service] is just involved in a little tag end of nothing here." He told McGranery that Justice Department prosecutors wanted Service to testify but that he had told Attorney General Clark "the smart thing to do" would be to remove Service as a defendant before the case ever got to the grand jury. "I certainly never had a client that I was willing to let go before a Grand Jury," McGranery commented. He promised his old friend he would "check it out."[9]

* * *

President Truman and his advisers were surprised at Joseph Stalin's mild reaction to the revelation that "a powerful new weapon" had successfully been tested. "All he said was that he was glad to hear it," Truman remembered, "and hoped we would make 'good use of it against the Japanese.'" Earlier that morning, July 24, 1945, the president had given his approval to drop "the most terrible bomb in the history of the world" as soon as it was ready. "Let there be no mistake about it. I regarded the bomb as a military weapon and never had any doubt that it should be used," Truman noted in his memoirs.[10]

A political bombshell exploded the next day with news that Churchill had been defeated in the British elections. His Conservative Party captured only 213 of 640 seats in Parliament, and his seat at Potsdam's conference table was quickly taken by Clement Attlee, described by Truman as a "sourpuss." Attlee, not Churchill, joined Truman and Stalin on July 26 in signing the Potsdam Declaration, which called for Japan's unconditional surrender and threatened "prompt and utter destruction" if the enemy refused.[11]

* * *

Meanwhile, Corcoran intensified his lobbying campaign to get Service excused as a defendant in the *Amerasia* case. He phoned McGranery on July 26 to ask whether his old pal had learned anything yet "on that thing that Ben Cohen told me to watch." McGranery had no news but assured Corcoran that he would take care of it. "Your man is Service. I got it." He called back the same afternoon to say that Service should *not* appear before the grand jury. "Munter is very anxious to have me go," Jack later protested. "Personally, I would just as soon appear." He told Corcoran that Munter had arranged for him to meet with prosecutors to discuss a possible appearance. "Let me put another call in," Corcoran responded, with slight irritation. "Only thing is, when I have a flat deal like that you are going to be cleared . . . I don't like anyone to have to talk before a grand jury."[12]

The attorney general finally returned Corcoran's calls. "According to the boys over here, [Service] is supposed to be a pretty good man," Clark remarked. "The way they put it, he is the only good guy in the outfit." He surprised Corcoran by saying his prosecutors did indeed want Service to appear. "Aren't you always afraid of Grand Juries and inexperienced people in front of them?" asked Corcoran. "If these boys were antagonistic, I'd say yes," replied the Attorney General, "but from what I understand this morning from these people, they don't have any such idea." Corcoran was more confused than ever. Seeking clarification, he left a message for McGranery to call him as soon as possible.[13]

Meanwhile, Service and Munter met with the team of prosecutors. The diplomat explained why he was authorized to keep carbon copies of certain informal reports, and described his assignment to provide background information to journalists in China. He patiently answered all their questions, and by the time the meeting was over, prosecutors seemed convinced that Service had never stolen any official documents from State Department files. More importantly, Jack and his attorney got "the definite impression" that there was nothing more to the case against him beyond his association with Jaffe and his group.

His lawyer, pointing out that the government really had no case, urged that the charges be dropped. The supervising prosecutor replied that it would be better "if the case was put up to and the question of indictment decided by the Grand Jury."[14] After the cordial meeting, Service walked over to Corcoran's office to report the good news. Still uneasily awaiting a call from McGranery, Corcoran again expressed strong reservations about anyone ever volunteering to testify before a federal grand jury.

On that hot, hazy day, one thing seemed clear: neither John Service nor his lawyers expected the diplomat would actually have to stand trial. In a letter to General Stilwell written that same day, John Service confided that although "a knock-down, drag-out court fight" might be fun and would bring certain China issues out into the open, he realized such a trial would inevitably "pull in a great many people who now hold important jobs"—and might destroy his own career.[15]

* * *

On Monday, July 30, the new grand jury began hearing testimony in the *Amerasia* case. That evening Corcoran dined with Attorney General Clark, and early the next morning John Service received a phone call. "Tell Munter that you don't want to go before the Grand Jury," Corcoran ordered.

Jack's appearance before the grand jury had been tentatively scheduled for Friday. He told Corcoran that Hitchcock, the lead prosecutor, had insisted—in his last conversation with Munter—that they needed him to be "cleared by a legal body." The deal-maker interrupted impatiently. "The signals have gone down that you are not to be in the thing. Up at the top the advice still is they don't want you to go in there. Why it hasn't gotten to Hitchcock, I don't know."[16] Hanging up, Corcoran immediately dialed first the attorney general's office, leaving a message with Clark's secretary, and then his friend McGranery, asking him to find out what the hell was happening.

The following day Corcoran informed Service that his insiders now agreed he should not appear before the Grand Jury as scheduled, now just two days away. But Service had again spoken with the lead prosecutor. "Well, the way Hitchcock talked," he told Corcoran, "there wasn't much chance of clearing myself unless I made an appearance as Exhibit A." Corcoran responded, "The orders are not to agree to go before that jury until you hear further from me."[17]

Late that afternoon McGranery called Corcoran back with surprising news: after hearing Service's story, the department's prosecutors did in fact want Service to testify and were convinced he would be cleared by the grand jury. McGranery had finally spoken with the supervising prosecutor, James McInerney, who had been impressed when his team met with Service and his lawyer. "He said if he was his lawyer he would have him in there every day . . . so let him go," McGranery told Corcoran. "I'll keep my bargain and I'll make [McInerney] keeps his." McGranery went on to explain that some of the litigators still hoped "to kick [Service] around a little" to pressure him into becoming a friendly government trial witness. This was precisely the trap Corcoran wanted to avoid. "If that guy ever is a witness in this thing, he is through with the State Department. That's the trouble with this thing," Corcoran insisted. "See, this is Ben [Cohen]'s problem, not mine. Ben said, 'I want to use this guy in the State Department and if he ever has to get tied in where he has to peach on fellows in the Department or if he ever has to appear in it, the publicity on this'—he says that although the guy may get cleared, he is in a mess as far as his future career is concerned." "All right," McGranery promised, "I'll take care of that for you."[18]

In fact, Ben Cohen had never met John Service, and Corcoran knew it. Corcoran was undoubtedly concerned for his other influential friends, Currie, and Vincent—as well as for his Chinese business associates—who all stood to be embarrassed by a public airing of dirty diplomatic linen.

* * *

The transcription of this conversation between the two Washington insiders gave Hoover valuable new ammunition about influence peddling in high places, and increased his suspicions about John Service. Corcoran apparently had a deal with top Justice Department officials to prevent Service from standing trial, or even testifying against the others. Hoover's indignation grew—despite the lack of incriminating evidence.

Throughout the muggy summer, FBI agents ran down numerous leads, interviewed dozens of the defendants' contacts, conducted a variety of lab tests, and painstakingly analyzed the recovered government papers. "Of the 928 documents obtained," an FBI memo recounted, "one was classified as top secret, one very secret, a substantial number were secret, and the balance were stamped confidential, restricted, or bore no designation whatever."[19] Agents reviewed back issues of *Amerasia* but found no more examples of plagiarism from the pilfered documents beyond that originally discovered by the OSS.

The FBI's evidence remained either circumstantial or inadmissible. The evidence was limited to the physical surveillance of defendants, information gathered from technical surveillance of telephones and hotel rooms, and the unlawful searches of defendants' homes and offices. While some of the suspects had been observed carrying thick manila envelopes, no one had actually been seen passing any official documents. "Since both Jaffe and Roth were writing books at the time and all of the persons were interested in a common subject," John Service would later observe, "no significant or guilty connotations could be drawn from such conduct without some admissible evidence of identification of the papers as official documents."[20]

By following the document trail from Jaffe's office back to the State Department files, the FBI hoped to identify the culprits who stole the confidential materials found in Jaffe's office. To investigators, the eight official copies of reports written by Service and found in Jaffe's briefcase offered the best possibility of a positive identification link. The FBI agents considered the diplomat "the logical and probably only individual who could have furnished these particular documents to Jaffe." They chose to ignore the statement of a China Affairs official who explained that such copies of Service's field reports were routinely distributed to the research office where Larsen worked. Lab tests turned up Larsen's fingerprints on the documents—and Jaffe's attorney admitted that Larsen had supplied them to his client, who had paid seventy-five dollars a month to Larsen for typing copies of selected materials. Nevertheless, FBI agents and officials clung tenaciously to their hypothesis incriminating Service himself.[21]

The many favorable interviews with Service's close associates did not budge the FBI's blinders. Retired ambassador Gauss told agents in California that he considered the Foreign Service officer "best informed on the Chinese Communist situation" and that he had "the highest regard and respect for Service's ability, loyalty and trustworthiness." At the War Department, a naval intelligence officer explained that Service was so careful about classified information, he never shared what he knew with anyone "unless they were both entitled to it and in need of it." After praising Service's intelligence, loyalty, and devotion to duty, the officer added, "I am sure this is not an admiration merely out of friendship, because high American government officials who have supervised his work or have been associated with him officially have remarked to me on their admiration of Service's work."[22]

Such glowing testimonials, however, were easily trumped by Ambassador Hurley's critical remarks about Service. And it is very likely that the FBI's assessment of Service was influenced by negative reports from its operatives in China and from Tai Li's secret police. Many pages from the FBI's *Amerasia* file obtained under the Freedom of Information Act still retained redactions for the stated reason that the material originated with a foreign government—presumably Chiang's Republic of China—and thus remained confidential, even more than sixty years later.

Nothing would shake Hoover's firm belief that John Service divulged military secrets to Jaffe during their May meetings at the Statler Hotel. Moreover, the visit to Jaffe's home by the American Communist Party leader and the Communist Chinese U.N. delegate compounded the suspicions of FBI officials, who were convinced that *Amerasia*'s editor intended to pass information to Soviet spies.

FBI officials believed that the *Amerasia* case was floundering solely because of political pressures on Justice officials, not because of the bureau's narrowly focused approach. They appeared not to understand that in an American courtroom, where a presumption of innocence prevailed, prosecutors had to prove guilt "beyond a reasonable doubt."

* * *

On the morning of August 2, the day before Service's scheduled grand jury appearance, the FBI recorded another Corcoran phone call to Service. "I spent last night on this thing and I finally know what the score is," Corcoran cheerfully told him. "I find out that these fellows down below hope to use you as a witness against the others." Service replied that prosecutors had indeed suggested it and had scheduled another meeting with him for later that morning. Corcoran told him not to worry: "This is double riveted from top to bottom. I also have a deal that you are not going to be used as a witness. . . . Just don't talk any more about anyone else than you can help." "That is my idea," Service replied. Corcoran announced he was on his way to a breakfast meeting to get "this thing triple-riveted" and would call him later. "You are okay, as far as charges are concerned,"

Corcoran reassured the diplomat. "As far as your future in the Department is concerned, don't talk too much and this witness deal is off anyway."[23]

Within a half hour, Corcoran was again on the phone to Service to let him know the attorney general "still tells me to tell you not to worry." The two men talked once more after Service's meeting at the Justice Department. Service reported that the prosecutor "wants to clear me, but that it would be very hard for him to do it" and that it was best to appear before the grand jury "and make as good an impression as possible." At the end of their conversation, Corcoran asked for Service's home address so he could pick him up in the morning and drive him to the courthouse for his session with the grand jury.

Just before midnight, the FBI recorded another significant conversation between Corcoran and McGranery. The Justice official provided feedback about the prosecutors' morning meeting with Service and his lawyer. "[McInerny] told me that Service puts up a hell of a fine appearance," McGranery reported, "[and] that he has a very pleasing personality and a very convincing manner." Since the federal attorneys had no evidence linking Service to any stolen documents, McInerney now considered it completely safe for Service to appear before the grand jury and "the best way of cleaning it up." He had even promised to take personal responsibility "to see that nothing happened" to Service, whom he called "a very convincing fella."[24]

* * *

In China, meanwhile, the cooperative spirit of Yenan had completely evaporated. American promises to train and equip Communist guerrillas and to set up a radio network were being held hostage to Hurley's stalemated negotiations. And a shooting incident involving the OSS had developed into a serious crisis. In late May an OSS/SACO outfit secretly parachuted a five-man team into a Communist-held area for a reconnaissance and intelligence gathering operation (code-named "Spaniel")—without notifying Yenan. Gunfire was exchanged, and a local Communist army unit quickly captured the intruders, including a Chinese interpreter from Tai Li's spy network. When news of the incident reached Yenan, the Communist leaders concluded the team was trying to recruit the locals for "fighting the Communists and not the Japs."[25] The "Spaniel incident" soon heightened tensions on all sides.

"The disarming of the OSS demolitions team makes it fairly evident that [the Communists] will take whatever measures they deem necessary to carry out what they consider self-defense," cabled Capt. Charles Stelle to his OSS chief in Kunming. "[The Communists] can only regard OSS operations . . . in their areas, particularly which have any [Nationalist] Chinese personnel . . . as being directed against themselves as much as against the Japanese [and] as being spearheads for the KMT [Nationalists]."[26]

The Communists were also upset over reports of the *Amerasia* arrests. On June 25—the same day that Service was advised to contact Corcoran—Yenan's *Liberation Daily* published an angry editorial about the *Amerasia* case arrests. The Communist newspaper interpreted Service's arrest as a turning point in American policy toward China. It accused Hurley and his "ilk" of destroying the United States' ability to act as an honest broker between the two Chinas and warned that Americans would inevitably be drawn into a civil war if they supported only the Nationalist Party and "the despot Chiang Kai-shek." Unless the imperialists like Hurley "withdraw their hands," the *Liberation Daily* proclaimed, "the Chinese people will teach them a lesson they deserve."[27]

* * *

As the *Amerasia* case neared its climax, the situation in China was growing more complicated—and more dangerous. The ending of war in Europe allowed for the rapid transfer of troops and supplies to Pacific war zones. Supplies were pouring into China over the Hump and along the recently reopened Burma Road, now renamed in honor of General Stilwell. Hard-won Allied victories had established new airbases in the Philippine Islands and on Iwo Jima and Okinawa. B-29 bombing raids were now crippling the Japanese war machine. In anticipation of an Allied assault on the homeland, Japanese troops in China had been ordered to abandon the forward American air bases and important towns they had captured less than a year earlier and to prepare for redeployment home. Nationalist propaganda naturally recast this systematic withdrawal as the heroic achievement of Chiang Kai-shek's brave forces, battling to reclaim Chinese territory.

By then General Wedemeyer had greatly expanded Stilwell's training program for Nationalist Chinese troops. Thirty-six Chinese divisions were receiving U.S. training, equipment, logistical support—and a decent diet. But American efforts to reform Chiang's warlord armies were often stymied by the regime's venal military commanders and its draconian system of peasant conscription. The lack of combat-ready soldiers threatened Wedemeyer's plans to capture strategic seaports in preparation for the November invasion of Japan.

Nearly 2 million Japanese soldiers remained in China in the summer of 1945, along with their Chinese puppet troops numbering another 900,000. Chinese mercenary armies and Chinese Communist forces, totaling more than 1 million men, were on the move. "The Nationalist regime was barely dominant in southern China, Sichuan, and Yunnan, while the Japanese and the Communists ruled nearly everywhere else," noted historian Gary May.[28]

"Frankly, if peace should come within the next few weeks we will be woefully unprepared in China," General Wedemeyer cabled General Marshall on August 1. "On the American side we could handle our own unilateral personnel and property interests, but many of our activities are inextricably tied in with the Chinese, and, if peace comes suddenly, it is reasonable to expect widespread confusion and disorder."[29]

Wedemeyer also worried about the rising number of clashes between Nationalist and Communist units, racing to recover territory from retreating Japanese forces. Chinese Communist forces were infiltrating the Manchurian border—just as Gen. Chu Teh had advised John Service that they would if reunification efforts failed. Meanwhile, a secret Nationalist guerrilla army under Tai Li was moving just as aggressively toward Shanghai, Nanjing, and other key eastern cities. Conflict between these forces was inevitable, and General Wedemeyer knew it. In the absence of a political compromise between the two Chinas, civil war now threatened to complicate the United States' defeat of Japan, as John Service had foreseen.

Most disturbing was the evolution of the relationship between the Nationalist guerrillas and SACO, the unorthodox Sino-American Cooperative Assistance Organization run by Tai Li and the U.S. Navy's Capt. Mary Miles. Wedemeyer knew that Tai Li's paramilitary units and secret police had been clandestinely trained and armed by SACO, and he knew of their unsavory undercover activities —including torture, poisonings, mass trials, and live burials of political prisoners. But when the Army commanders complained to the War Department, the Navy Department always backed up Miles. Once, when Wedemeyer heard rumors of SACO-American trainers (including recruits from the FBI) participating in the assassination of suspected Communist sympathizers, he confronted China's spy chief. "Americans would not be asked to do that," Tai Li assured him. "Their job was to train the Chinese to do it."[30]

Wedemeyer was now receiving alarming reports that Americans were not just providing weapons to Tai Li's secret army but were also actively joining in open skirmishes against Communist forces. He confided in a letter to a friend at the War Department: "If the American public ever learned that we poured supplies to a questionable organization such as Tai Li operates, without any accounting, it would be unfortunate indeed. . . . Miles has been Santa Claus out here for a long time."[31] The Communists, increasingly fearful of full-scale U.S. intervention, complained loudly about the secret American support of Tai Li's forces. Top officials in Washington never recognized that the actions of these American operators had encouraged the Nationalists' uncompromising pursuit of a military solution against their domestic rivals—and contributed to Mao's growing bitterness toward "the American imperialists."[32]

* * *

Relations between Americans and the Chinese Communists had been deteriorating ever since Hurley's turnabout on the proposal for a coalition government. By the summer of 1945, all OSS operations with Mao's forces were in limbo due to Hurley's stalled negotiations. Chiang and Tai Li had convinced the ambassador that secret OSS talks with Yenan, aided by a disloyal group of U.S. military officers and diplomats, had undermined his peace effort. A downsized and demoralized Dixie Mission remained in Yenan only to operate weather stations, gather enemy target information, and assist in rescuing downed American airmen. The Communists no longer expected to see the promised American weapons, training, and radios. By July the only contact between American and Communist officers in Yenan revolved around pheasant hunts in the hills. Although the Chinese enjoyed riding in American jeeps and shooting the birds with modern American rifles, they made clear they would prefer using such equipment in the fight against the common enemy.

During the long, hot summer, Communist suspicions about the United States' real intentions were fueled by the report of John Service's arrest in the *Amerasia* case, by escalating clashes with Tai Li's guerrillas, and by escalating clashes with independent OSS units or SACO affiliates secretly infiltrating into territory claimed by Mao's forces. On the American side, the Communists' failure to release the "Spaniel" commandos provoked resentment. By the end of July, the Spaniel team was still being held incommunicado. When Wedemeyer sent Mao a cable demanding their release and an explanation of the incident, he received no reply—and took it as a grave insult. In fact, the Communist leader never received the general's message. Fearing that Wedemeyer's strongly worded cable might endanger their working relationship, the OSS radio man in Yenan simply failed to deliver the message.[33] This small but significant act of insubordination—and the "Spaniel Incident" itself—exemplified the freewheeling style of the semiautonomous U.S. intelligence agencies in China that contributed to mounting suspicion, distrust, and misunderstanding between Mao's supporters and the Americans as the war against Japan moved toward its sudden finale.

On July 28 General Wedemeyer issued orders further restricting relations with Yenan. Distribution of any American supplies without his specific approval was forbidden. If Americans were present when skirmishes broke out between Communists "and any forces other than Japanese," U.S. personnel were ordered "to withdraw immediately and report facts." And OSS units were instructed "to steer clear of any possible contact with the Communists for the time being."[34] His orders were the final blow ending any possibility of cooperation between the United States and Chinese Communists.

By August 2, when President Truman was returning from Europe and Tom Corcoran was vowing to "triple rivet" John Service's grand jury appearance, General Wedemeyer went a step further in trying to inoculate U.S. military personnel from the spreading virus of Chinese political violence. The general placed a ban on all OSS and SACO secret operations within Communist areas north of the Yellow River. Every American field officer was now ordered "to insure his equipment and supplies are not used in Chinese civil strife."[35] On paper, the orders appeared clear-cut—but they proved impossible to enforce in China's patchwork war zone, where the American army commander could never completely control the undercover activities of OSS or SACO units. Still less could he expect to control the Nationalists' use of American-supplied arms.

Wedemeyer—and the United States—faced a terrible dilemma arising from the contradictions of American policy. Officially, Washington still wanted to forge a united war effort with all Chinese forces against the Japanese, and accordingly emphasized the need for flexibility in forging a coalition government of China's rival political parties. But the policy was subverted by uncoordinated operations in China undertaken by outfits like OSS and SACO—and by actions of the American ambassador. Patrick Hurley had transformed U.S. policy into unconditional support of Chiang's China, and the Generalissimo was determined to use his American support to destroy his domestic rivals. Far from accepting defeat, Mao's forces were all the more determined to pursue his program of revolutionary change.

* * *

On a steamy morning in the nation's capital, John Service made his first appearance before the grand jury in the U.S. federal courthouse on Pennsylvania Avenue. It was Friday, August 3, 1945—his thirty-sixth birthday. "I have asked to appear," Service told the twenty grand jurors, "because I am innocent and because I want to clear this matter up. My career is at stake and a lot more than my career."[36] The jury had been hearing testimony all week and had already heard Service's statement to the FBI on the night of his arrest. The lead prosecutor, Robert Hitchcock, proposed that Service begin by describing his background and how he had become acquainted with the other defendants. "I have never been in this sort of situation. If I am nervous I hope you will excuse me," Service began. When he mentioned it was his birthday, Hitchcock interrupted to offer congratulations. "I hope you can make it a happy one," Service replied.

After briefly telling the jury about his two children and his wife, who was due to deliver their third child the following Sunday, Service launched into a chronological account of his association with the other defendants. Jimmy Larsen, the other State Department defendant, had mentioned in his testimony a long-ago family connection: Service's parents had briefly provided a refuge for Larsen's family after a flood evacuated their town. Service—who was too young at the time to remember that event—said he had rarely seen Larsen except in the hallways of the State Department, and once at a lunch with other staff.

Service then recounted his brother's college connection to Mark Gayn, and Navy lieutenant Andrew Roth's invitation to a dinner party—the occasion of his introduction to Jaffe. He told jurors that "out of Chinese politeness that I was the host in Washington," he had insisted on picking up the check for a meal with Jaffe in his hotel. The prosecutor interjected humorously, "Be careful or you will be getting invitations to lunch from some of us."

The atmosphere was far from adversarial as Service detailed his encounters with the other defendants. There was "nothing underhanded or secret or conspiratorial" about his activity; he noted that he was "meeting people for lunch and dinner practically every day for the same sort of talk about China." Service explained that his two trips to New York City were prompted by, first, a formal invitation to speak at the Institute of Pacific Relations (IPR) that had been approved by his supervisor, and then an informal invitation to attend a weekend picnic hosted by another China specialist. One juror asked if people interested in Asian affairs liked to get together "just like a bunch of lodge members." "There is a good deal to that," Service responded. "There are not very many experts on China. To me, it is my bread and butter and pretty much what I think of most of the time. . . . Most of my meetings, most of my friends, are people who have the same interests, and I see a good deal of them."

After the diplomat laid out his account of interaction with other *Amerasia* defendants, the prosecutor politely but persistently raised questions about several key issues. Hitchcock was particularly interested to know about the official copies of Service's reports found in Jaffe's briefcase by FBI agents. The diplomat said that when he left China, he had permission to carry his most recent reports with him to Washington, and he had delivered copies for the State Department directly to the China Affairs office, which was responsible for official reproduction and distribution of such field reports.

Hitchcock: You never gave those to Mr. Jaffe or to anybody else?
Service: That is right.

Hitchcock: You never saw them until you saw them in my office last week?
Service: That is right.
Hitchcock: Would you have given them to Mr. Jaffe or anybody else if they would ask you for them?
Service: I would not, because they are obviously part of the files of the State Department.
Hitchcock: Have you any idea at all as to how Jaffe got them?
Service: Obviously, I wish very much I could tell you, it would help my case.

The diplomat acknowledged having access to China Affairs files but pointed out that he kept his own personal copies of the "briefcase memos" in his office desk drawer file—a fact confirmed by Hitchcock, who reminded the grand jury that FBI agents had found carbons of the briefcase reports in the office desk files seized on the night of his arrest. "It would be very foolish of me to take the risk of going up and removing them from the C.A. files," Service explained. "I would be extremely foolish to steal from the State Department my own reports and thereby prevent officers . . . from reading my reports and prevent recognition which is the basic factor in my getting promotions."

"I want to have it clear on the record, Mr. Service," the prosecutor interposed. "You certainly would not have gone to the State Department and taken one of their copies that were filed there?" "Absolutely not," Service replied. Hitchcock continued helpfully, "If you had wanted to give him anything, you would have given him one of your own carbon copies?" "That is right," the defendant responded, noting that "a good many people" had access to the official files, and it was "quite customary" for returning field officers to visit the file room. He testified that official copies of field reports were routinely sent to the research unit where defendant Larsen worked, but quickly added, "I don't know whether he ever received these."

Next the prosecutor asked why Service was allowed to keep his own personal copies of his reports. This gave the Foreign Service officer an opportunity to discuss what he called the "very special and unusual character" of his job in China for the Army, a post that was "not even well understood by most people in the State Department." He described his freewheeling political reporting assignment, writing up informal memos of his observations and information gathered from his network of Chinese contacts. By contrast, an embassy staff officer normally "writes nothing on his own initiative unless he is assigned to it by his superiors." The typed originals of these memos were always submitted to army headquarters, which sent carbon copies to the embassy and to his New Delhi–

based supervisor, John Davies, but he never knew what further distribution was made of them. He told the grand jurors he was authorized to keep copies of such reports for his frequent background briefings of American personnel and foreign correspondents; and when he returned to Washington, he was allowed to bring reports for similar briefings he expected to give. "I asked permission of the Army Chief of Intelligence in Chungking, and I went through and culled out of them anything which might be considered confidential in that it discussed American policy or was highly critical of the Central government of China."

"Were they classified at all?" asked the prosecutor. Because of China's "peculiar political situation," Service explained, he always put his own arbitrary "Confidential" or "Secret" classification on the reports, "since some of them are critical or would be considered by the Chinese Government to be critical of it." He never knew what official classification the Army or the embassy put on any of his reports before further distribution. The grand jury had already heard testimony from an official from the Office of War Information that it often allowed journalists to see confidential reports, and that a "main reason for what may seem to be a high classification of such a document is that we want to get the stuff out of the country without getting it into the hands either of the enemy or of the Chinese."[37]

The prosecutor asked about Service's admission that he showed some personal copies of his reports to the *Amerasia* editor. "The State Department had shown it had no objection to the making of this type of information known to writers and correspondents," Service replied. He pointed out that the department even arranged a press conference for Ray Ludden to talk about his impressions of the Communists after he returned from his long trek behind enemy lines. Knowing that Jaffe was interested in information about the area controlled by the Communists, Service had "simply picked out a number of recent [reports] which were purely descriptive, which in my opinion would be perfectly permissible for him to see," and took them along to their first meeting.

In conclusion, the prosecutor asked Service if he wanted to say anything else. The diplomat talked about the letters of support he had received from the two retired ambassadors for whom he had worked during twelve years of service in China. He also described a recent experience at the War Department when he was in the "rather unusual position" of being asked to read secret War Department reports and to brief an officer assigned to General Wedemeyer's staff—even though he was out on bail as a criminal defendant in a case involving the theft of confidential government documents. "I think my actions have not been those of a guilty man. I have not made charges of persecution or anything else, even though my friends have told me . . . people assumed I was guilty because I wouldn't talk. But I have assumed all the way through that I was a loyal servant of the Government and I wanted to go on."[38]

John Service's testimony ended at 3:45 PM on August 6, 1945—the same day that Truman announced that a B-29 bomber called "Enola Gay" had dropped the first atomic bomb on Hiroshima, instantly incinerating 80,000 people. It was also the day that Philip Service was born into the new atomic age.

"Let there be no mistake; we shall completely destroy Japan's power to make war," President Harry Truman said in a prerecorded message broadcast to a worldwide radio audience while he was aboard ship returning from Europe. "If they do not now accept our terms, they may expect a rain of ruin from the air, the like of which has never been seen on this earth."[39]

Three days later Stalin declared war on Japan, and Soviet troops stormed into Manchuria. On that day—August 9, 1945—a second atomic bomb, named "Fat Boy," obliterated Nagasaki, instantly killing 70,000 people. Thousands more in the two Japanese cities would die horrible deaths from thermal burns and radiation poisoning over the coming months and decades.

* * *

On August 10 the secret federal grand jury issued its judgment in the *Amerasia* case. After more than a week of testimony from twenty-four FBI agents and other government witnesses, the panel voted to issue indictments against three of the defendants. With twelve votes needed to indict, the jury determined that Phillip Jaffe, Jimmy Larsen, and Andrew Roth should stand trial, facing maximum penalties of two years in jail and ten thousand dollars in fines. The grand jury voted not to indict the three others: *Amerasia* deputy editor Kate Mitchell; freelance journalist Mark Gayn; and diplomat John Service—the only defendant cleared by the unanimous vote of all twenty jurors.

* * *

"Certain aspects of this matter 'smell,'" scribbled a disgusted J. Edgar Hoover at the bottom of a memo reporting the latest developments in the *Amerasia* case. Hoover had sent his boss, Attorney General Clark, a warning about "rumors that the prosecution of this case being 'fixed' through the efforts of influential persons having connections with the Department of Justice."[40] After the verdicts were announced, Hoover's lead investigator pointedly asked prosecutors if "any pressure had been brought to bear on this case." McInerney replied that he had heard something about such rumors but "there was absolutely no pressure on the case."

Prosecutors also informed Myron Gurnea that, after hearing the voluntary testimony of some defendants, they had decided not to call any of those cleared as witnesses in the forthcoming trials, claiming they would not make good prosecution witnesses. "Obviously it was not indicated to McInerney and Hitchcock in any way that this Bureau had been kept fully informed on the negotiations between the attorneys and other interested parties," Gurnea noted primly in his report to Hoover. "It is interesting to observe that the three who were not indicted were well represented by very influential groups."[41] In the end, Tommy Corcoran's assistance, solicited by Lauchlin Currie and John Carter Vincent, only served to enmesh Service more deeply in the FBI's web of suspicion.

* * *

Newspapers across the country carried front-page banners announcing the Russian invasion of Manchuria as well as the first gruesome details of nuclear holocaust in two Japanese cities. The *New York Times* pushed its story about the *Amerasia* case to the back pages of its sports section. Many conservative newspapers that had originally sensationalized the arrests, failed to carry any news of the grand jury's decisions. And the press release from the Justice Department only gave the names of the three indicted defendants. Grace Service only learned of the outcome when a Western Union operator called her to read a brief telegram from her son: "Grand Jury has cleared me, signed Jack."[42]

The legal case against John Service was now closed, but he would remain "a person of interest" to the FBI over the next quarter of a century.

CHAPTER 15
CLEAN AS A WHISTLE

The day after the grand jury verdicts, John Service was called before a special meeting of the Foreign Service Personnel Board to be chastised—and congratulated. The unusual Saturday session took place around the coffee table in the high-ceilinged office of Assistant Secretary Julius Holmes. Service had "gone too far" in discussing American policy in China, and he was put on six months' probation for criticizing officials of friendly governments to news media, in violation of regulations. But he was roundly congratulated on his "complete vindication" by the grand jury.[1]

Service was being reinstated to active duty, but he objected strongly to the suggestion to assign him to a post outside Asia. That might appear to confirm suspicions that his clearance reflected political pressure. "If the Department sent me elsewhere it would cast doubt on my exoneration, [which was] won legally and at the expense of world-wide publicity and smearing," Jack wrote to his mother. "I said I wanted to go back to China, where I could be most useful." The special panel concurred but stipulated he could not return to China while Patrick Hurley was ambassador. In the interim (which was expected to be brief), Service would be assigned to General MacArthur's new Allied Control Commission in Tokyo.[2]

Temporarily, Service reported to work in the China Affairs office, preparing to reopen consulates after the war. The chief of personnel, Nathaniel Davis, reassured him that the department knew him to be an accomplished officer, as shown by the rare double promotion he was awarded even while under investigation. "The only advice I could give him," commented Davis, "is to use discretion and not be a crusader."[3]

After the American atomic bomb attacks on Japan, the two Chinas accelerated their race to control surrendered territory. The commander of Communist forces, Gen. Chu Teh, ordered his troops to begin seizing cities, towns, and communication centers and to reestablish order under Communist-appointed administrators. This was immediately countermanded by Chiang Kai-shek's order that Communist troops were to remain in their quarters until further notice and were specifically forbidden to disarm Japanese forces. "You have issued the wrong order, very wrong indeed," responded General Chu, who had already ordered units to Manchuria to link up with the Soviet Red Army.[4]

A few days later, Chiang issued a proclamation directing all Chinese collaborators to switch allegiance from Tokyo to Chungking. Mao immediately denounced Chiang as a "fascist ringleader, autocrat, and traitor" who preferred to "cooperate with the enemy rather than with his own countrymen." He insisted his armies had earned the right to accept the surrender of enemy troops, after their five-year war of resistance.[5] Civil war looked inevitable—even to Ambassador Hurley and General Wedemeyer, who now sent warnings to Washington.

Most of Chiang's warlord armies, equipped with modern American weapons, were still based in the remote southwest region. The Communist forces were better positioned, inside occupied China, to seize control of enemy territory and to capture the huge stocks of Japanese weapons. Chiang now issued urgent orders to Tai Li's underground guerrilla army to block any Communist takeover of Japanese-held territory. SACO's Miles ordered American trainers to assist General Tai's guerrillas—flouting Wedemeyer's orders forbidding American involvement in any operations in Communist areas. "Carry with you complete radio equipment and go fully armed," Miles secretly instructed SACO's Americans, promising to provide logistic support and armaments for the guerrilla units. In his top secret cable, Miles acknowledged that his instructions were "probably going to get me a general court martial for disobedience to orders," and he directed his officers "to burn this after swearing your units to secrecy."[6]

* * *

In Lafayette Square, across from the White House, the crowd had been growing for several days, waiting for official notice that the war was over. On August 14, 1945, at seven o'clock in the evening, President Truman stepped before the microphones in the Oval Office to make the historic announcement: "I have received this afternoon a message from the Japanese government. . . . I deem this reply a full acceptance of the Potsdam Declaration which specifies the unconditional surrender of Japan." Gen. Douglas MacArthur was now named Supreme Allied Commander and designated to preside at the official surrender ceremonies. The Japanese would be allowed to keep their emperor, but, as Truman noted in his diary, "We'd tell 'em how to keep him."[7]

"V-J day left me cold," John Service confided to his mother. His glum mood was due in part to "a state of nervous semi-exhaustion" caused by the *Amerasia* ordeal and in part to his concern that the decision to retain the Emperor would impede democracy in Japan. "But most of all, I was unable to feel joyful because of the situation in China. Civil war is already a fact and I fear it will be long and bloody and bitter," he told Grace. "It is no joy to see one's gloomy predictions come true. And one's personal triumph in an affair like my arrest seems dwarfed into insignificance by the complete failure of what one has been working for."[8]

* * *

The same day Japan surrendered, the Sino-Soviet Friendship Treaty was signed in Moscow. Nationalist China had to concede even greater concessions in Outer Mongolia and Manchuria than the secret Yalta accords had presented. "The United States was not in a position to take military measures to back up her diplomatic support," observed historian Tang Tsou.[9] Nevertheless, the Nationalists believed the treaty would give them protection against their hated rivals. Stalin pledged not to give aid or support to the Chinese Communists or to interfere in the internal affairs of China, and he agreed to turn over the administration of recovered territory to the Nationalist government. Under those circumstances, the Nationalists assumed, the Communists would be forced to reach a political settlement recognizing Chiang's authority.

In Washington, John Service disagreed with that rosy assessment. The treaty would be "catastrophic" and "lead the [Nationalist] government and ourselves into the trap of assuming that the Chinese Communists could be easily liquidated." It would make civil war inevitable, engendering "chaos which would lead to eventual total victory by the Communists."[10] Very few other Americans recognized the strength of the revolutionary movement among China's peasantry, or the Chinese Communist Party's determination to remain self-reliant and independent of Moscow's control.

* * *

In his first order as the new Supreme Allied Commander, Gen. Douglas MacArthur issued instructions for the surrender of Japanese troops throughout Asia, with special attention to divided China. The Soviet army would accept surrender of Japanese forces within Manchuria and in Korea north of the thirty-eighth parallel. But in China, Formosa, and northern French Indo-China, Japanese soldiers were ordered to surrender exclusively to Chiang Kai-shek's representatives, even though the situation on the ground made compliance exceedingly difficult.

Chiang soon issued his own extraordinary directive to enemy troops: resist the Chinese Communists until his Nationalist troops could arrive to accept their surrender!

At war's end, Americans in China's chaotic war zone found themselves trapped in bizarre circumstances. SACO's Americans fought against the Communists while independent OSS units trying to avoid involvement found unlikely allies. One OSS outfit, having taken over Nanjing's airport, found Communist forces closing in behind them. "The Japs have offered us assistance," radioed the perplexed major in command, "and I refused their help, waiting instructions." He told headquarters they would avoid fighting the Communists "at all costs" and hoped to "talk our way out."[11]

In hindsight, it seems clear that the chaotic close of the war against Japan might have been avoided if the American embassy staff's cable, six months earlier, had been heeded. American trainers, intelligence officers, demolition experts, and radio teams would have been working together with the Communist military units during the summer. "There would have been no basis or arguable need for ordering that the Japanese surrender . . . be made only to Chiang's forces," John Service observed many years later, "nor would it have been necessary for the U.S. to land . . . Marines to hold North China ports as proxy for the Nationalists."[12]

* * *

"My dear Mr. Service," wrote Secretary of State Byrnes on V-J Day, "I congratulate you on this happy termination of your ordeal and predict for you a continuance of the splendid record I am advised you have maintained since first you entered the Foreign Service." Service even received a warm letter from Joseph Grew, who was retiring as undersecretary of state. "When I learned a few days before your arrest that your name had been coupled with thefts of official documents, I was inexpressibly shocked, having known you for some time and of the high caliber of your work I could not believe that you could be implicated in such an affair." Grew said he was "particularly pleased" that Service would soon be returning to duty in Asia, where he "already had established an enviable record for integrity and ability."[13]

The letters provided great comfort, particularly to Caroline Service. She was distressed that, after all the notoriety of his arrest, his clearance had been so completely eclipsed by momentous world events. "But, the main thing was that Jack was a free and innocent man," she recalled, "and we could put our lives, so long separated and then so violently jarred, back together." When she learned he was soon leaving for Japan, she could "hardly bear this idea that Jack was going to go away again."[14]

"I am definitely cleared and okay as far as the department is concerned," Service proudly informed his mother. "As far as I am concerned the whole affair is history and the sooner forgotten the better. However, there may still be a few tag ends."[15]

* * *

One "tag end" that would haunt John Service over the next three decades grew out of Hoover's continuing feud with the Justice Department and his suspicions about the diplomat. On August 21, Hoover sent a highly confidential memo to Attorney General Clark aimed at discrediting Service, despite his clearance in legal proceedings.

The memo, finally declassified fifty years later, claimed that inadmissible evidence (obtained from FBI's hidden microphone) revealed that Service had "orally commented upon military, political and policy matters" to Jaffe and cautioned him that some of the information "was 'top secret' and should not be disclosed by him to anyone else because of possible repercussions against Service and some of his friends in China." Hoover's memo also noted that Ambassador Hurley considered Service "not an impartial observer." Because he had tried to disrupt his effort "to prevent the collapse of the National Government of the Republic of China," Hoover claimed, Hurley had demanded his recall.

Hoover also cast doubt on the reliability of John Carter Vincent (the chief of State's Far Eastern Division), who had "thus far prevented" Hurley's critical comments from being added to Service's personnel file. And he repeated the Nationalist Chinese insinuation that John Service's field reports had led to the removal of General Stilwell and Ambassador Gauss. Finally, he reminded the attorney general of the "persistent rumors" that political pressure was the real reason for dropping the charges against Service.[16]

Within days of receiving Hoover's memo, Attorney General Clark sent a note to Secretary of State Byrnes assuring him that John Service was completely cleared and that "no surveillance or investigation of his activities is being conducted."[17] The top Justice official was apparently unaware that his FBI chief was still keeping tabs on the suspect diplomat.

* * *

The same day Hoover sent his memo to Attorney General Clark, the *Washington Post* ran an editorial about the recent *Amerasia* grand jury verdicts. Noting that the allegations of espionage had been debunked, the editorial stated that "as a matter of elementary justice," reparations were due to the three defendants found innocent on all charges. It chided Joseph Grew for creating "the appearance of persecution" with his claim that the *Amerasia* arrests were part of a widespread investigation of leaks at the State Department—an investigation that had never materialized. "The morale of the entire department, as well as the integrity of the public service is involved in the clearing up of the atmosphere in which this case is wrapped." The *Post* editorial then suggested the secretary of state should swiftly reinstate John Service and issue an apology.

Service's college town newspaper was one of the few to trumpet his victory with a front-page headline: "Jack Service Is Exonerated: Oberlin's Confidence in Him Is Proved Justified But Where Are the Newspaper Headlines?" The article lamented the fact that the Oberlin grad had been accused with maximum publicity, but that many newspapers either ignored or played down his exoneration, giving "the average, careless newspaper reader . . . an entirely mistaken impression."[18]

Service attached this item, along with other news clippings, to a letter to his mother about meeting with Ben Cohen, "one of [Secretary] Byrnes' closest advisors." When Service asked for permission to publicize Byrnes' congratulatory letter, Service was told by Cohen simply to "sit tight." At his press conference the next day, Secretary Byrnes released the letters he and Grew had written to Service.

"So now," Jack told Grace Service, "I've had all the publicity I could reasonably expect on the exoneration."[19] He then wrote to Secretary Byrnes to express his gratitude "for the very fair treatment" he had received from the department.[20] After the degrading experience of spending a night in jail and the notoriety of the *Amerasia* case, John Service finally felt "clean as a whistle."[21]

* * *

"The devastation beggars description," Service wrote his mother, soon after arriving in Tokyo at the end of September. "I think I have yet to see a smile or hear a laugh." What little remained of the city she once knew was now drab and shabby.[22] Service and his old friend, George Atcheson, had traveled across the Pacific as VIPs, lunching in Honolulu with the army commander and dining in Guam with the Navy admiral. Atcheson was the new U.S. political adviser to MacArthur's Allied Control Commission, and Service was his executive officer. When Service's new assignment became public, it made headlines: "Byrnes Hires Diplomat Once Held as Spy."

Soon after their arrival, General MacArthur demanded to know why his new staffers were considered persona non grata in China. He had received a heads-up report of a top secret cable to the White House from Chiang (drafted by Hurley) urging the State Department not to reassign the two diplomats to China because their views were "definitely unfriendly" to the Nationalist government and "supported the Communists and favored the overthrow of China's government."[23]

"MacArthur called us in and he says, 'Jeeze, who the hell are you guys and what's all this about?'" Service recalled with a chuckle. "He thought that it was a big joke."[24] Truman, however, took it seriously enough to send a top secret reply on September 25, reassuring the Generalissimo that "neither Mr. Atcheson nor his assistants will go to China." They would remain in Tokyo "dealing with problems directly connected with the surrender and occupation of Japan."[25]

After securing office space in the Mitsui bank building, an imposing granite structure that had survived the bombing, Service set to work organizing the understaffed office and setting up its filing system. Working past midnight if necessary, and on weekends, he also prepared the political-economic news digest cabled each week to the State Department. Atcheson's staff included a Foreign Service officer named Max Bishop, recruited by the FBI to report on Service's activities. Bishop considered Service "either a Communist dupe or Communist sympathizer," and he secretly photographed Service's paperwork for FBI headquarters.[26] He also reported on meetings Service held with released political prisoners and representatives of Japan's newly legalized political parties—including the Communists. Such standard diplomatic activities served to confirm the FBI's suspicions of John Service.

* * *

New developments in the *Amerasia* case reinforced the FBI's suspicions. When Larsen discovered that his building superintendent had allowed FBI agents into his apartment, he filed a motion to quash the indictment. Prosecutors then moved swiftly to negotiate a plea bargain with Jaffe, before he could learn of Larsen's motion. The editor admitted purloining and receiving government documents and was fined $2,500, half the maximum penalty recommended by the Justice Department—thereby avoiding a possible two-year jail sentence. "I regret that in your zeal to carry out your work," the judge pronounced, "you were misled to do those things which, of course, did tend to break down the fidelity of government employees and officials in the performance of their work."[27] Prosecutors never informed the judge of Jaffe's Communist ties.

The FBI was disgusted by the legal maneuvering. Investigators had assured Hoover that the "documentary, fingerprint, and eyewitness evidence against Larsen and Jaffe presents the Government with a very strong case." While the evidence against Roth was "not as strong," chief inspector Gurnea considered him "unquestionably the brain behind Jaffe's operations in Washington" and "closely connected with the Communist Party" during his college days.[28] As part of any plea bargain, Hoover had urged the attorney general to pressure both Jaffe and Larsen to testify against Roth; otherwise, "justice would not be properly served."[29] Now, with Jaffe off the hook and Larsen expecting charges to be dismissed, the *Amerasia* case was in serious jeopardy. Of the original six defendants, only Roth remained, and he vowed to fight the charges that (he proclaimed to the press) were politically motivated by Joseph Grew's pro-Japanese coterie. Already convinced that Corcoran had "fixed" the case for John Service, Hoover's FBI saw a "further gross miscarriage of justice."[30]

* * *

Other new developments involving real spies soon came to the FBI's attention. In late August 1945 a thirty-seven-year old woman walked into the FBI's New Haven office. Elizabeth Bentley claimed to have led a secret life as a courier for Soviet spy rings operating in official Washington; FBI agents diagnosed her as neurotic and declined to follow-up. Then, on September 5, a cipher clerk named Igor Gouzenko defected from the Soviet Embassy in Ottawa. Canadian authorities at first refused to believe him or to provide protective custody for fear of offending their Soviet allies. But after a series of in-depth debriefings with Gouzenko, who turned over coded telegrams and pages smuggled from his superior's diary, Canada expelled nearly two dozen Soviet nationals as spies.

This was the first convincing evidence of a Russian espionage network that had breached the national security of Canada, Great Britain, and the United States. Gouzenko's documents revealed that the KGB had even obtained vital information on the atomic bomb from a prominent British scientist, as well as significant military and political intelligence. The defector described an elaborate system used by Soviet spies to exchange coded information with Soviet embassies and consulates in North America and Great Britain. When FBI agents interviewed Gouzenko, he repeated a Soviet military attaché's boast about an unnamed spy who worked as an assistant to former secretary of state Stettinius.[31] Hoover immediately ordered agents to track down that woman from New Haven, Elizabeth Bentley.

These defections gave Hoover live ammunition for his hunt for Communist spies within the government, and he soon recruited willing allies in Congress. Rep. George Dondero was quick to link the *Amerasia* case to Gouzenko's shocking revelations about Soviet spies. "[The *Amerasia*] whitewash . . . means that from now on Soviet agents can carry on espionage with impunity." Five of the suspects, he railed, "have public records which show convincingly their sympathy and cooperation with the foreign policy of the Soviet Union and the cause of international Communism."

The Michigan congressman demanded a Congressional investigation to know why the case had fallen apart. "Who is responsible for its liquidation? What is behind it?" He noted that Joseph Grew, the State Department official who had pressed for prosecution of the case, "for some reason issued a public apology to John Stewart Service, who was immediately reinstated and is now part of a group supervising the work of General MacArthur in the Far East." Ominously, Dondero drew attention to the fact Grew had recently resigned. "This is an open invitation to subversive elements in our Government to continue, expand, and increase their activities and defy all consideration of national security."[32]

When Jimmy Larsen read about that speech, he immediately contacted Dondero. He was desperate to find work to support his family. The legal proceedings to quash his indictment were taking much longer than expected, and he felt betrayed by Jaffe, who had pleaded guilty and was urging him to do the same. Dondero persuaded Larsen to look to Congress for vindication and advised that once his legal problem was settled, his value as an informant in a congressional probe would be greatly increased. Larsen reluctantly agreed. On November 2 Larsen pled nolo contendere for leaking government documents, and Phillip Jaffe stepped in to pay his five-hundred-dollar fine and his legal fees, plus an amount equivalent to his lost wages.

At the bottom of the FBI report on Larsen's sentencing, Hoover commented, "Of all the wishy washy vacillations this takes the prize."[33] At the very least, he had expected the prosecutor to compel Jaffe to identify which documents had come from Larsen and which from other sources. Now, all hope of obtaining any information from these defendants was gone. Within a few months, the case against Roth himself would be dropped for lack of evidence.

* * *

For more than eight hours on November 7, Elizabeth Bentley gave a detailed account of code-named contacts, late-night telephone-booth phone calls, and clandestine meetings. She recounted frequent train trips between Washington, D.C., and New York carrying a knitting bag full of film canisters of photocopied government documents and other intelligence. As a graduate student at Columbia University in the early 1930s, Bentley had joined the Communist Party; later she had fallen in love with a Soviet agent named Jacob Golos, whom she described as "the ideal Communist." His cover job was running a travel agency bankrolled by Earl Browder, the head of the American Communist Party. After Germany attacked the USSR, Bentley became a courier for Golos' expanding network of Soviet agents and informants in Washington. After his death in 1943, the despondent and increasingly disillusioned Bentley continued to serve as a courier until January 1945. Then the KGB stopped using her—and later tried to liquidate her as a turncoat.[34]

Bentley met fourteen times with FBI agents that November, laying out a complex web of current and former federal employees who were Soviet agents or sources of information. A "one-woman encyclopedia of espionage," she gave the FBI more than eighty names, including four associates of John Service with access to sensitive information: Laughlin Currie, Sol Adler, Assistant Treasury Secretary Harry Dexter White, and Duncan Lee of the OSS.[35] On the very day of John Service's arrest, FBI agents had tailed him to an appointment with Lee at OSS headquarters.

When Hoover received the seven-and-a-half-page summary of Bentley's staggering disclosures, he "could not contain his enthusiasm." He immediately sent a confidential preliminary report to presidential confidant Harry Vaughan, who had approved the tap on Tom Corcoran's phone. A few days later, Truman told Hoover to brief Secretary of State Byrnes. Many of the people mentioned by Bentley were, Hoover reported, still working for the government and were already in the FBI's files. Byrnes agreed on the importance of convincing the public of the existence of Soviet espionage.[36] In early December Hoover submitted a formal seventy-one-page confidential report—based almost entirely on Bentley's allegations—to President Truman, his cabinet officers, the attorney general, and other key officials.

FBI agents in New York and Washington, D.C., were ordered to begin intensive physical surveillance of all those Bentley had named—a move that had the effect of inadvertently "alerting the suspects and spurring them to cover their tracks," according to the FBI's own counterintelligence expert, Robert Lamphere. Nevertheless, as Lamphere conceded, "The FBI had to do something about them quickly."[37] Hoover now successfully lobbied Congress for a bigger budget, more agents, more field offices, and more independence of action to fight the new menace of Communism at home. In any case, Moscow had already learned of Bentley's disclosures from Kim Philby (the Soviet mole inside British intelligence) and had ordered a freeze on North American espionage activities.

* * *

In the wake of the Sino-Soviet Friendship Treaty, Ambassador Hurley convinced Chiang to invite Mao to Chungking for talks before their clashes turned into full-blown civil war. The Communist Party chairman initially refused, certain that Chiang would never compromise and that he planned to destroy the Communists with American help. "Relying on the forces we ourselves organize, we can defeat all Chinese and foreign reactionaries," Mao told his followers. "Chiang Kai-shek, on the contrary, relies on the aid of U.S. imperialism which he looks upon as his mainstay." The day would come, Mao prophesied, when the United States would find it impossible to back Chiang any longer.[38]

On August 20 Stalin sent Mao a secret radio message advising him to meet with Chiang in Chungking to avoid being blamed for the long, bloody civil war everyone feared. Still wary about the Soviets' intentions, Mao finally agreed. With the major allies—the USSR, the United States, and Britain—all urging a political settlement, there was a slim chance that a period of peaceful coexistence might be possible. If the Chinese Communist Party could extend its influence through participation in a reformed political process, then civil war might still be avoided.[39] To guarantee Mao's safety, Ambassador Hurley himself flew to Yenan and returned triumphantly to Chungking accompanied by Mao and Zhou Enlai.

The city received them with an outpouring of hope. "The outcry in the press and in private was a spontaneous welling up of public opinion such as had never been seen since the outbreak of war," reported Teddy White and Annalee Jacoby. "'Victory has come,' was the cry; 'let it bring peace.'"[40] But negotiations dragged on for more than a month, deadlocked on the basic issue of mutually assured security. The Communists asked Chiang to recognize the legitimacy of their regional governments established behind enemy lines in several north China provinces. They accordingly demanded a federal system for the republic while the Nationalists insisted upon a tightly controlled centralized state.

After the inconclusive peace talks, Mao returned to Yenan. Ambassador Hurley left for the United States for urgent dental treatment, confident that he would be hailed by historians as China's savior. But hostilities between the Nationalists and Communists almost immediately resumed—and intensified. A Communist victory was averted only by the U.S. airlift of Nationalist troops into central and eastern China, and by the deployment of U.S. Marines to protect railways and other strategic resources.[41] In the areas around Peking and Tientsin, U.S. troops were now ordered to treat as enemies the same Communist partisans who had previously risked their lives to rescue downed U.S. flyers.[42]

American newspaper editorials reflected a growing unease about U.S. policy in China. "The Chinese schism is old and deep," noted the *Milwaukee Journal*. "Surely it is not an American responsibility to furnish arms, transportation, or one American life to settle this civil war." The *Christian Science Monitor* editorialized, "We realize that the U.S. can hardly wash its hands of its responsibility in China overnight. But we do not believe the present position can be long supported. It involves a degree of intervention which American opinion will not support even in Latin America."[43]

It became increasingly evident that the Russians, having belatedly recognized the potential of Mao's movement, were secretly aiding the Chinese Communists.

Japanese weapons captured by Soviet troops were often turned over to Mao's forces. American ships transporting Nationalist troops to Manchuria were refused permission to land in Dalian. The Soviet commander directed the vessels to two smaller ports already in the hands of Communist partisans—who then refused them disembarkation. Chiang's dispirited and seasick forces had to return to a Chinese port and then march for several days to reach the Soviet-occupied territories.

Yet, in order to prevent a major American intervention, the Soviets were careful not to go too far. After the frustrating delays in its sealift, the United States requested permission to airlift Nationalists troops to Changchun and Shenyang, and the USSR politely agreed. "But secretly," historian Michael Sheng noted, "they encouraged the CCP to take over the area surrounding the airports [making] it impossible for U.S. airplanes to land there."[44]

China was effectively divided along the Yellow River: the northern provinces were controlled by the Communists with Soviet support; the south was controlled by Chiang Kai-shek and the Americans. Confrontation between the Soviet Union and the United States over China—as Service and Davies had foreseen—now appeared a real possibility.[45] Hurley's embassy reported the situation "almost hopeless."[46]

General Wedemeyer presented the Joint Chiefs with a stark choice. Chiang's Nationalists did not have the capability to disarm the Japanese or take control in north China. He reported that Chiang "lacked able, honest advisers" and was surrounded "by selfish and unscrupulous men"—officials and warlords "who had helped him in the past, but who were now exploiting their position to enrich themselves and their families."[47] If the United States continued aiding the Nationalists, it would become involved in China's civil war. Either Wedemeyer should be given a new directive to influence the outcome decisively in Chiang's favor or all American military personnel should be withdrawn from China as soon as possible.

No one in Washington was politically prepared to make that momentous decision. Instead, a bizarre stopgap measure was approved: the United States would continue to airlift Nationalist troops to the northern territories but would remove U.S. Marines from China as soon as the one million defeated Japanese troops were repatriated. American forces would try to observe neutrality in the civil strife. Meanwhile, a vigorous diplomatic effort was to be launched to bring about a truce and a political solution—a task described by historian Herbert Feis as the "pursuit of the unattainable."[48]

John Service lamented Washington's "ruthless, cold-blooded decision to use force to establish Chiang in power, regardless of the interests or wishes of the

Chinese people or what kind of government he stands for." To his mother he confided that America's current effort betrayed "the things we have always said we stand for" and was "criminally dangerous" because it would result in more "years of struggle and warfare in China."[49]

In the United States on home leave, Ambassador Hurley was seriously considering resigning. He was disillusioned by the reports of battles between Nationalists and Communists and deeply stung by criticism—in the press and in Washington—that blamed the United States' China dilemma on his own policy of supporting Chiang. Hurley thought he had done reasonably good work in China. "Like a pitcher with a five-run lead in the seventh inning," Hurley's biographer observed, "[he] had nothing to lose and everything to gain if he were relieved. He wanted out while he was ahead."[50]

Hurley met with Secretary Byrnes on the morning of November 26, 1945, to submit his letter of resignation. Byrnes refused to accept it and persuaded the ambassador that if he returned to China, he would have the full support of the State Department and President Truman. He was critically needed, Byrnes assured him, for the United States' new diplomatic offensive.

The following morning, Hurley and China's ambassador met briefly with President Truman. "We agreed it would be best if he returned to Chungking without delay," noted Truman in his memoirs. But Hurley once more changed his mind—and he took the extraordinary step of calling news organizations to announce his resignation.[51] He pointedly complained of career Foreign Service officers who "continuously advised the Communists that my efforts . . . did not represent the policy of the United States."

"See what a son-of-a-bitch did to me!" Truman exclaimed, storming into his weekly Cabinet lunch meeting and waving the wire story. To Truman, Hurley's resignation was "an utterly inexplicable about-face."[52] His agriculture secretary then made the inspired suggestion that General Marshall might be coaxed out of retirement to lead a special mission to China. The following day, Marshall accepted this thankless new assignment.

Hurley followed up his surprise announcement with an address at the National Press Club. He repeated his charges that American policy had been "subverted" by career diplomats who "openly advised" the Chinese Communist Party against unifying their forces with the Nationalist Army "unless the Chinese Communists were given control." Nevertheless, Hurley preened, he had been able to prevent civil war—"at least until after I had left China."

The ex-ambassador now went even further, charging that U.S. forces had been "used in support of ideologies foreign to our American democracy and ideals for which we fought in the war." Certain diplomats and military officers had even tried to give American arms and supplies to the Communists. And now, two "disloyal" diplomats that he had removed from China had been "assigned as advisors to the Supreme Commander in Asia."[53]

Newspapers on November 29 carried the sensational story on page one, reporting that the Senate Foreign Relations Committee would investigate Hurley's shocking charges. The *Los Angeles Examiner* story identified George Atcheson and John Service as the political aides charged by Hurley. The caption beneath their photos indicated that Service had been "recently exonerated of violating espionage laws." If Hurley's charges were true, Nebraska's senator and the Republican minority whip, Kenneth Wherry, told reporters, some State Department employees were guilty of "little short of treason." House members were also demanding a full inquiry into the Foreign Service.[54]

* * *

In Tokyo, John Service caught a news flash on the wire announcing Hurley's resignation. He broke out a precious bottle of bourbon and brought it into his boss' office. "The rest of the staff . . . assembled to join in the excitement," Service recalled. "We had some paper cups and were just having good slugs of whiskey when suddenly the press was at the door, because by this time, they had gotten more news about Service and Atcheson [as] the principal culprits accused by Hurley." To Service, this was "just a venomous kick from a senile old fool, . . . frustrated that I hadn't been fired in the *Amerasia* case—and of course he *had* failed in China."[55]

"I am not a Communist," John Service declared in a long letter to Secretary of State Byrnes. "I did not 'sabotage' American policy in China." He categorically denied all Hurley's charges, declaring that any review of his reports would show that he "consistently took the view that the Central Government could (and should) strengthen itself by liberalization which would promote unification of country on a democratic basis, and that American influence should be exerted to that end."[56]

Service also pointed out that (as several high State Department officials could confirm) certain Nationalists had for years spread stories that he was a Communist because they resented his officially mandated activities: contacts with Communists and other opposition groups, independent travel throughout China, his Dixie Mission role, and his close relationship to Stilwell. "Unfortunately when Hurley arrived in China," Service wrote Byrnes, "he was willing to give credence to these unjustified attacks . . . [and] refused to accept factual reports if contrary to what he apparently wished to believe." Hurley had mistaken differences of opinion for "opposition" and "disloyalty."[57]

* * *

After Hurley's first day of testimony before the Senate Foreign Relations Committee, the *New York Times* ran a front-page headline: "Hurley Accuses Five Officials of Sabotaging China Policy; Says Two Sought Chiang's Ruin." In his testimony Hurley alleged that a "pro-Communist, pro-imperialist" conspiracy flourished inside the State Department, and that Service and Atcheson had tried to destroy Chiang Kai-shek's government. As proof he mentioned their authorship of the confidential embassy staff memo as well as Service's final memo to Stilwell. The news story reported that after examining the confidential dispatches in a special closed-door session, the committee had found no support for Hurley's allegations.

Hurley did succeed in reviving suspicions about Service's role in the *Amerasia* case, telling the committee that some of his own reports were among the leaked documents discovered by FBI agents. One Republican senator expressed amazement that Service had been exonerated and welcomed back to work with a congratulatory letter from Secretary Byrnes. He insinuated that a high official had influenced the State Department not to press charges against Service. "If this in itself, combined with the testimony of General Hurley, does not warrant a thorough and complete investigation of the State Department," thundered Senator Styles Bridges of New Hampshire, "I do not know what does."[58]

Hurley also described conspiracies among European powers, intent on reclaiming their colonies, to keep China divided and weak. But he insisted that Russia was "still together" with the United States on its China policy and "does not recognize the Chinese armed Communist Party as Communists at all." There was "no evidence" the Soviet Union had transgressed on China's territory or sovereign rights in Manchuria. "[Hurley] blamed everyone for the failure in China but the one party largely responsible for the changed situation in November, the Soviet Union," noted his biographer, Russell Buhite.[59] And he never admitted—or perhaps even understood—his own role in the China tangle.

Secretary of State James Byrnes was next to testify. "There was no excuse, in my opinion, for me to refuse to reinstate [Service]," Byrnes told the Foreign Relations Committee. Considering the grand jury's decision, the prosecutor's statement to his State Department representative, and the commendation of General Wedemeyer, the secretary decided that "we owed it to him to do what was proper under the circumstances to remedy the wrong that had been done to him."[60] And he forcefully defended the appropriateness of Service officers' expressing their views: "I should be profoundly unhappy to learn that an officer of the Department of State . . . might feel bound to refrain from submitting through proper channels an honest report or recommendation for fear of offending me or anyone else in the Department. If that day should arrive, I will have lost the very essence of the assistance and guidance I require for the successful discharge of the heavy responsibilities of my office."[61]

Caroline Service was gratified to hear Secretary Byrnes' strong defense of her husband. During a break in the proceedings, she introduced herself to the official Senate committee recorder. When the hearings ended a few days later, he gave her a copy of the transcript, which she promptly entrusted to a diplomat bound for Tokyo to give to her husband.

The Senate Foreign Relations Committee inquiry ended without recommendations for any action. His credibility in tatters, Hurley thus ended his public service career in bitterness, frustration, and failure. But although he had made no headway in the hearings, Hurley's vendetta had political coattails. As the *New Republic* reported, "The Republicans are seizing upon it as propaganda to discredit President Truman and the Democratic Party, but far more serious, the Hurley statement is being used by the conservatives of both parties as the excuse for a witch-hunting 'investigation' of liberals in the State Dept. and an attempted purge."[62]

* * *

Behind the scenes, the FBI's feud with the Justice Department over the *Amerasia* case was heating up. Justice Department attorneys met with Representative Dondero to dissuade him from calling for a congressional investigation. Such a highly publicized probe, they argued, might divulge confidential FBI methods of investigation and might "jeopardize other Communist cases that were pending." When Dondero suggested that prosecutors might have been given instructions from "someone higher up" to be lenient with certain defendants, the Justice Department officials flatly denied the charge.

After learning from Dondero of this unusual visit from Justice, Hoover fired off an angry memo to Attorney General Clark. He disclaimed any concern about "divulging any confidential methods used by this Bureau" and insisted that "all the documents obtained in this case were obtained as an incident to a lawful arrest upon a duly issued warrant." Hoover sternly lectured Tom Clark, his official superior: "I think it is essential in our dealings with Congress, first, that we are accurate as to facts and, secondly, that the Dept present a unified front based upon a properly correlated exchange of facts and ideas."[63] Thanks to Hurley, Hoover's support for his anti-Communist crusade was growing—and he had no intention of letting Justice off the hook on the *Amerasia* case.

And, in Tokyo, John Service remained unaware of the political undercurrents swirling just below the surface at the end of 1945.

CHAPTER 16
THE STORM GATHERS

Val Chao arrived in Seattle aboard an army transport ship on March 20, 1946. She was three months pregnant. More than a year had passed since her break-up with John Service. "I wanted to forget Service, to forget him at all cost," Chao admitted, "but I could not forget him." In the fall of 1945, she met William Hanen, a handsome American Army major. After the Japanese surrender, when wartime refugees were scrambling to leave Chungking, Major Hanen helped Val secure passage to Shanghai for her mother and herself. "At that time, I had a fantasy that perhaps he will help me forget about Service," the actress confessed. "But, after being together for several times, I knew it was impossible."[1]

Through friends at the U.S. Embassy, Chao obtained a student visa and an invitation from Yale University to study drama and to teach Chinese. Jack Service sometimes wondered if her desire to go to the United States had any bearing on her interest in him. "It would be unfair of me to say so," Service later remarked, "but I sometimes had my doubts."[2] As she waited to depart for the States, Val discovered she was carrying Hanen's baby. "I didn't want to get rid of this child," the actress explained sixty years later. "I had already lost Service's child so I wanted this one to be born," she said, adding, astonishingly, "to bring it up as Service's."[3] But upon reaching the United States, she was again heartbroken: Jack, she learned, had been posted to Japan. She had hoped to see him again and ask "why the wonderful love between us met with such an inexplicable ending."[4]

* * *

Meanwhile, John Service was in a Tokyo hospital suffering from hepatitis. He would remain there for more than four months—and during that time the *Amerasia* case sprang to life again. The Justice Department had quietly dropped the case against Andrew Roth—the sole remaining defendant—due to "insufficient evidence." His dismissal, according to a *Washington Post* editorial, made it "impossible to avoid the conclusion that the State Department or the FBI or both went off half-cocked." The case amounted to "nothing more than an attempt to punish left-wing leakers."[5]

Again the thin-skinned FBI director fumed. He promptly sent a scolding memo to the prosecutors, reminding them that he had urged them to compel Jaffe and Larsen to testify against Roth as part of their plea deals. Again he insisted that the incriminating stolen documents had been seized properly, "incident to a lawful arrest upon a duly issued warrant." He ignored the problematic secret FBI break-ins, without search warrants, that showed his agents what to look for when the arrests took place.[6]

Hoover also sent an angry memo to Attorney General Clark warning that it would be risky to try to blame the FBI for the failure of department lawyers to break any of the *Amerasia* defendants.[7] Reinvigorated by the recent revelations of Elizabeth Bentley and Igor Gouzenko, the FBI chief now actively recruited Capitol Hill allies and began leaking confidential *Amerasia* information to friends in the press.

In early spring, Rep. George Dondero made headlines with another floor speech on *Amerasia* that charged the case was a "good illustration of the power and influence of the Communists in the government." Armed with ammunition supplied by Hoover and the embittered Larsen, he successfully demanded a congressional investigation of the "undercover influences at work inside our government to destroy the republic"—including the *Amerasia* "whitewash." The special inquiry was chaired by Sam Hobbs of Alabama, considered "always very friendly to the Bureau." The FBI furnished Hobbs' committee with confidential exhibits, investigative reports, and a suggested list of potential witnesses.[8]

The State Department's new security office was itself now headed by an ex-FBI agent, who recommended removing John Service from duty in Asia "because of his Communist associations, connections, and leftist beliefs." In a memo dated March 22, 1946, the security office urged that Service be transferred to "some post where the Communist movement is negligible and where his opportunities to commit overt acts on behalf of the Communist movement would be reduced to a minimum." While admitting there were insufficient grounds to call for Service's dismissal, the memo claimed his reporting was "of limited value" and "predicated in favor of the Communist movement."[9] (This first internal department effort to paint John Service as a Communist sympathizer came to light only when his confidential State Department security file was released in 2003, under a Freedom of Information Act appeal.)

Just three weeks earlier, Service had been completely cleared of all Ambassador Hurley's accusations by the Senate Foreign Relations Committee. "I have found nothing that leads me to feel that the charges were warranted," concluded the State Department's top legal adviser in a March 1 report to Secretary Byrnes. Although Service "minced no words in describing conditions within the National Government and its failure to improve the lot of the Chinese soldier and the Chinese people," the review found no evidence he ever suggested "the ousting or non-recognition" of Chiang Kai-shek's government. After examining Service's reports from Yenan, State's top Soviet expert, George Kennan, declared they were "eminently fair statement[s] of Communist views as evident at that time [and] his conclusions [presented] a reasoned choice between the lesser of two evils." Service's conclusions were "what might be expected from one judging on the basis of Chinese experience only, not with reference to experience with Communist seizures of power elsewhere."[10] Kennan further noted that Service's field reports "advocated the same thing that Gen. Hurley was advocating which was political accomodation."[11]

* * *

In May Representative Hobbs' committee began closed-door sessions in his office. The first confidential witness was Frank Bielaski, the former OSS security agent who had led the initial break-in at the *Amerasia* offices and discovered the treasure trove of government documents. Next was James McGranery of the Justice Department, who told the committee that evidence obtained by the FBI in the *Amerasia* case was "clumsily handled" and consisted mostly of insignificant gossip about Chinese officials. To counter McGranery's contentions, the FBI's lead *Amerasia* investigator, Myron Gurnea, arrived with fifteen large file boxes of seized documents. Newspapers competed fiercely for the inside scoop on the secret sessions, where the parade of government witnesses became "a round-robin game of shunting the blame for the Amerasia fiasco onto the next guy in line."[12]

The star witness turned out to be Jimmy Larsen, who was still trying to find a job. "It was a very friendly little party," Larsen later recalled. "We sat around a small table all in easy chairs . . . and just chatted." Larsen's chatter was filled with damaging new allegations against John Service, who, Larsen now claimed, had sent confidential reports to Jaffe from China. Although never substantiated, this charge became one of several damaging *Amerasia* myths that dogged Service for many years. Larsen also told the Hobbs Committee he had once heard Service and Vincent talk openly against Hurley and his allies, during lunch in the spring of 1945. "They sabotaged Hurley," Larsen asserted. "You may take my word for that."[13]

* * *

Caroline Service and her three children left Washington, D.C., while the Hobbs committee was still hearing testimony. They planned to stay with her parents in California only a month or two before joining Jack in Tokyo. But his medical condition worsened: complete bed rest was ordered. After nearly five months in the army hospital, he sailed into San Francisco Bay in mid-September.

This home leave was to be short-lived. The State Department ordered him to report as soon as possible as the new deputy chief of mission in New Zealand. Caroline was delighted. Their new post would be a healthy place, "not only for his physical health, but for his professional health." And within two weeks of his return home—after a quick car trip to southern California to see his mother—the newly reunited family set sail on the SS *Monterey*, the same ship that had evacuated Caroline and their oldest children from the China war zone six years earlier. "Just the idea of being together, of having Jack back again, of having a family life," Caroline recalled, "it was a simply wonderful feeling."[14]

* * *

While Service was in California, Val Chao delivered a baby girl in New York City. With blue eyes and blond hair, the infant resembled her American father more than her Chinese mother. Val had attempted unsuccessfully to locate Major Hanen, hoping he might lend financial support for his child. After leaving the hospital, Val's old friend, journalist Annalee Jacoby Fadiman, arranged for her Japanese gardener's wife to care for Val's new baby while she went to Yale.

* * *

By the time the Services arrived in Auckland in mid-October, the world had changed significantly. General Stilwell had died of cancer; General Marshall's mission to halt the Chinese civil war was failing; the Soviet grip on Eastern Europe was tightening; and President Truman's popularity had plummeted to a 40 percent approval rating. The revitalized Republican Party was campaigning for the midterm congressional elections on the slogan, "Had enough?"[15] But for John Service and his family, the next two years in New Zealand would turn out to be "an idyllic interlude."[16]

As the Service family settled into their new home, the Hobbs Committee released a public report on its *Amerasia* inquiry that found "no evidence or hint, justifying adverse criticism" of the FBI, the prosecutors, or the grand jury. However, "an astonishing lack of 'security'" in government agencies had come to light.[17] This assessment reinforced the American public's deepening fears over the developments in Europe and China—and deteriorating relations with the USSR.

On October 21, 1946, a secret FBI report on "Underground Soviet Espionage Organization in Agencies of the United States Government" was hand-delivered to carefully selected government officials. Based upon the revelations of "Gregory" (the code name for Elizabeth Bentley) and another self-confessed ex-Soviet agent named Whittaker Chambers, the report exposed surprising details about two Soviet spy rings that operated in Washington during the war. Current and retired federal employees were suspected of involvement, including several of John Service's professional associates: Currie, Adler, and White of the Treasury Department and Duncan Lee at OSS. Among several State Department officials named was Alger Hiss, a veteran diplomat already suspected of being a leaker.[18]

That same month, *Plain Talk*, a new conservative political magazine, was launched with a provocative cover story, "The State Department Espionage Case." Jimmy Larsen was credited as its author. He had been approached by two ex-FBI agents (now employed by *Plain Talk*'s publisher) to write the *Amerasia* insider's story. Publisher Alfred Kohlberg, a wealthy textile magnate who imported silk from China, was a zealous Chiang supporter and crusaded against Communist influence in the United States. When Larsen's story proved too tame, editor Isaac Don Levine embellished it with juicy new charges to create a sensational exposé. John Service now became the "real pipeline" for the pilfered *Amerasia* documents—and a member of a Communist clique inside the State Department. Their alleged aim was to discredit Patrick Hurley and Joseph Grew, and to tilt the United States' Asia policy toward the Soviet line. Galley proofs of the article went directly to the FBI and were placed in the bulging *Amerasia* case files.[19]

* * *

The U.S. mission in New Zealand was so small that its chief ranked as a minister, not an ambassador. Minister Avra Warren was an energetic man who loved hunting and fishing. Once John Service arrived, he was quite content to let Service run the office. Trade was a key issue between the two countries after the war, and the United States was interested in weaning New Zealand away from the United Kingdom. John Service spent much time laying the groundwork for what became ANZUS, the Australia-New Zealand-U.S. security alliance. He thoroughly enjoyed "getting back into the groove" of conventional foreign service work.[20] "Wellington was a wonderfully happy post for us," Caroline Service recalled. "The *Amerasia* case, we thought, was forever behind us."[21]

* * *

The Republican Party won a landslide victory in the congressional elections on November 5, 1946. For the first time since 1928, the GOP captured control of Congress, picking up fifty-five seats in the House of Representatives and twelve seats in the Senate. (One of the few Republicans defeated that day was Patrick Hurley, who lost narrowly to an incumbent senator.) President Truman was widely blamed for a long list of postwar problems, including lax handling of national security matters. By Election Day, his approval rating had plummeted to 32 percent, and he was increasingly the butt of sarcasm. When Truman first assumed office, a standard question had been, "What would Roosevelt do, if he were alive?" Now Republicans asked, "What would Truman do, if he were alive?" and joked, "To err is Truman."[22]

* * *

By January 1947 George Marshall's mission to China had ended in failure. "The greatest obstacle to peace," he reported, "has been the complete, almost overwhelming suspicion with which the Chinese Communist Party and the KMT [Nationalist Party] regard each other."[23] When he arrived in China a year earlier, he had engineered a truce and a tentative agreement, establishing tripartite teams to monitor the tense equilibrium among the rival forces. But when Soviet troops finally withdrew after packing up most of Manchuria's rich industrial and manufacturing assets, fighting again broke out between the competing Chinese armies vying for control of the vacated territory.

Marshall's efforts to broker a second truce were soon stymied by Chiang's actions. "I can foresee no permanence in what he [Marshall] has accomplished so far, for both sides will be at each other's throats again," Wedemeyer wrote to retired Ambassador Hurley. And in fact, the second truce only lasted until the end of June.[24] Communist troops had captured the Manchurian capital in April, and while Marshall attempted to negotiate their withdrawal, Chiang's forces launched an all-out attack against the city.

Chiang himself flew to Manchuria, ostensibly to stop the assault, but then took no action to rein in his commanders. "On the contrary, his presence . . . made it appear that his journey was timed to coincide with a previously planned military triumph," wrote historian Tang Tsou. "[Chiang's] use of Marshall's official plane for his flight to Manchuria conveyed the impression of Marshall's close connection with the trip."[25]

In Yenan the situation seemed clear: American-trained and -equipped Nationalist troops had been transported by American aircraft into Manchuria to prevent the Communists from taking the Japanese surrender—and now the Generalissimo was flying to the front in the American envoy's personal plane. Distrust and anger killed any lingering hope for the United States' role as honest broker. Communist propaganda attacked America for its alleged role in the Nationalists' campaign, and skirmishes with U.S. Marines resulted in casualties on both sides. The hard-line faction of the Chinese Communist Party gained the upper hand and began to portray the United States as a major obstacle to the realization of the Chinese revolution.[26]

Nevertheless, Marshall soldiered on. He put intense pressure on the Nationalists by suspending their deliveries of military supplies, but his efforts to achieve a fair settlement were continually frustrated by what the general called "extremist elements of both sides."[27] And by the time he prepared to return home, he suspected Chiang of "a definite policy of force under cover of the protracted negotiations."[28] Nevertheless—like Wedemeyer, Hurley, and the president—Marshall still considered Chiang Kai-shek indispensable. "No one ever suggested anyone [who] could take his place," he once complained. The American peacemaker was also frustrated by his lack of information about "attitudes in the innermost Chinese Communist circles."[29] Since Service's abrupt departure from Yenan in early 1945, no American official had been assigned to ascertain the views of Communist leaders or assess the power of their growing revolutionary movement.[30]

General Marshall returned to Washington to become Truman's new secretary of state, convinced that the China problem was insoluble. More than 113,000 American soldiers, sailors, and Marines had been dispatched to China. They helped with the surrender of Japanese troops and managed the repatriation of 3 million Japanese. By the time Marshall's mission ended, in early 1947, only 12,000 U.S. military personnel remained. Without a huge commitment of American troops, General Marshall knew that the Nationalists could never defeat "the millions of people and an army of more than a million men" that had rallied to the Communist side. Even the administration's harshest critics never urged a major American military intervention to settle the dilemma of the two Chinas. Instead, they continued to lobby for more aid to Chiang's lost cause, and to look for scapegoats.

* * *

The postwar world presented the Truman administration a host of pressing issues. In February 1947, the British government announced that it could no longer continue giving financial aid to Greece and Turkey—two new critical Cold War flashpoints—and asked for U.S. help. Greece was under attack from Communist-led guerrillas based in Soviet-controlled areas across the border, and Turkey was resisting Soviet demands to share control of the strategic Dardanelle Straits. President Truman addressed a special joint session of the Republican-controlled Congress and asked for $400 million in emergency military and economic aid for the two beleaguered nations, whose fall to Communist domination would endanger countries from Iran to India. "It must be the policy of the United States to support free peoples who are resisting attempted subjugation by armed minorities or by outside pressures," the president declared.[31] The Truman

Doctrine would become the cornerstone of a bipartisan American foreign policy commitment to counter threats from the Soviet Union that lasted four decades.

To the China Lobby, it seemed obvious that the Truman Doctrine should apply equally to China policy. "With all its weaknesses [China] has steadfastly refused to yield to such internal and external pressures as today threaten Greece and Turkey," declared Rep. Walter Judd, the Republican from Minnesota.[32] Like other Chiang supporters, Judd insisted that the Chinese conflict must be seen not as a civil war but as part of Stalin's push for Communist world domination. Former ambassador Hurley, who originally supported the Yalta deal, now denounced it as a sellout of China's interests. The American public was by now greatly disturbed and bewildered by the growing power of the Soviet Union—the nation's new enemy.

In exchange for supporting aid for Greece and Turkey, pro-Nationalist politicians in Congress demanded more economic aid for Chiang and an end to Marshall's embargo on delivery of military supplies. Soon appropriations for Marshall's expanding economic recovery program for Western Europe became hostage to an alliance of Chiang supporters and social conservatives. Over the next few tumultuous years, the Truman administration would be forced into a delicate balancing act on its politically charged China policy. George Kennan, the State Department's new top policy planner, defined the administration's policy as extending "the minimum aid necessary to satisfy American public opinion, and, if possible, to prevent any sudden and total collapse of the Chinese government."[33]

* * *

In the spring of 1947 John Service completed his probation for his admitted *Amerasia* indiscretions, and he received a long-delayed promotion. In mid-July, when Avra Warren was appointed U.S. minister to Norway, Service became the acting chief of the United States mission in Auckland. It seemed that his career was finally back on the fast track, and the young couple enjoyed their new status in Wellington's diplomatic community.

One of the first duties Service performed in his new role was to circulate a memo to his staff about President Truman's Executive Order 9835, which established a new loyalty-security program for all federal employees. The loyalty program represented the Truman administration's counteroffensive against Republicans, who continued to attack Democrats as "soft on Communism"[34] and were now demanding that nominees for important federal jobs must swear under oath that they were not—and had never been—a Communist. The announcement of Truman's new program "pulled the rug" from under his political detractors, according to *Time* magazine, and made Republicans realize the president "was no pushover."[35] According to his trusted aide, Clark Clifford, Truman never attached "fundamental importance to the so-called Communist scare," and really thought "it was a lot of baloney."[36] Nevertheless, Truman was determined to eliminate real security risks while protecting the nation's civil rights. "If I can prevent [it] there'll be no NKVD or Gestapo in this country," Truman confided in a letter to his wife. "Edgar Hoover's organization would make a good start toward a citizen spy system. Not for me."[37]

When Caroline Service first read about Truman's new loyalty program in *Time* magazine, it gave her an uneasy feeling. "I said to Jack, 'What do you think of this?' He said he didn't think anything of it," she recalled. "He said, 'I've been cleared. The *Amerasia* case is over.'" He had no idea that as soon as Truman's loyalty program went into effect, the FBI had alerted the State Department's newly expanded security office about his role in the *Amerasia* case. Within a few months, a man claiming to be a missionary turned up at the U.S. mission in Wellington asking a lot of questions about Service. Warned by a colleague that "this is no real missionary," Caroline was convinced the stranger must be working for "the CIA or the FBI or somebody."[38]

* * *

Chiang Kai-shek had boasted that his troops moving into Manchuria would annihilate the Communists by August 1947. Instead, his overextended forces were completely isolated and overwhelmed by Mao's fighters. The victorious Communist forces moved down into central China for the first time early that autumn. The expanding civil war brought even greater hardship to the war-weary Chinese people. Economic conditions deteriorated; with inflation spiraling out of control, prices jumped 100 percent. Despite the Nationalists' ruthless repression of demonstrations and labor strikes, political and social unrest mounted. Even docile Nationalist legislators now began calling for resumption of peace talks with the Communists.[39]

Pressured by the worsening situation in China and the clamor of Republican critics, Secretary Marshall sent General Wedemeyer on a fact-finding mission to China. After spending a month surveying the situation, the general blamed recent military reversals squarely on government failures, criticizing the regime for its corruption, nepotism, incompetence, inefficiency, and repression of political critics.[40] "In China today, I find apathy and lethargy in many quarters," Wedemeyer admonished a stunned audience of top civilian and military officials in Nanjing. "Instead of seeking solutions of problems presented, considerable time and effort are spent in blaming outside influences and seeking outside assistance."[41] Wedemeyer hoped to convince the government it must urgently implement "far-reaching political and economic reforms" to prove that additional American aid would not be wasted. Reaction from Nationalist officials was predictable: Wedemeyer had "failed to understand the Chinese situation and had not sought his information impartially."[42] Returning to Washington, Wedemeyer recommended more U.S. military and economic assistance for China, but only if strictly supervised by American economic and military advisers, and if necessary reforms were enacted. This was the same formula originally suggested by Gen. "Vinegar Joe" Stilwell in 1942.

Wedemeyer's report also expressed his concern that the Communists might soon carve out an independent Communist state in Manchuria and north China. To block such a move, he suggested establishing a UN "guardianship" over Manchuria under the joint administration of China, the United States, Great Britain, France, and the Soviet Union. Secretary Marshall rejected the idea as impractical and dismissed Wedemeyer's recommendations for more American aid.[43] Wedemeyer's trip report, like Wallace's 1944 report, remained highly confidential, and he was ordered to remain silent.

* * *

By 1948 the success of Communist military campaigns in Manchuria, north China, and central China was stunning. Mao Zedong proclaimed that China had now reached "a turning point in history." Chiang Kai-shek would never crush the growing popular revolution by relying solely on his American-equipped and trained armed forces, which would flee rather than fight. The commander of the American military adviser group blamed the collapse on "the world's worst leadership and many other morale-destroying factors that lead to a complete loss of will to fight."[44]

Chiang's supporters in Congress again pushed for more aid to the Nationalists, ignoring the fact that an estimated 75 percent of American weapons and military supplies ended up in Communist hands. The China Aid Act, totaling $570 million—with no requirements or incentives for political reform—was eventually passed in late 1948 to obtain bipartisan support of the Marshall Plan aid package. A special $125-million grant was allocated to Chiang's government for military supplies. The irony of its timing was well noted by one historian: "The policy of limited assistance thus reached its climax at a juncture when it had even less chance of success than at any time since V-J Day, and when its only political effect in China was to identify the U.S. further with an admittedly hopeless cause."[45] Watching the deteriorating situation in China from Wellington, John Service found that many officials there shared his view that a Communist victory in the civil war was "perhaps not a foredoomed disaster"—and that, in any case, there was nothing that the United States or anyone else could do to prevent it.[46]

* * *

Service's work continued to garner outstanding performance review ratings. One reviewer lauded his "flair for the administration of a happy and efficient office" and his network of "wide and useful contacts." His reports were judged "very well prepared, concise, and timely." In awarding an outstanding rating, the State Department's inspector general noted that "both he and his wife are popular and well-liked by both the American community and by a wide and diverse group of New Zealand acquaintances."[47] With his promotion to minister in April 1948, John Service became the youngest man "both in age and in years of service" to enter the ranks of senior Foreign Service officers—with a salary of ten thousand dollars a year. "The promotion seemed to seal it all [and] wipe out the past."[48]

As soon as Service's promotion became known, the FBI notified the State Department that if he were assigned to a sensitive position, the bureau would provide a comprehensive summary of the information in its files. Under Truman's new loyalty program, FBI and State security agents were already interviewing Service's former colleagues and acquaintances. Most, like the distinguished diplomat Paul Nitze (who knew Service in Tokyo), told investigators they had no reason to doubt Service's loyalty. No one voiced any suspicion of Communist sympathies. Investigators were told by the former G-2 chief in Chungking that Service "disliked the Nationalists" but did not believe in Communism.[49] Even retired General Chennault said that although he would not want Service to hold a policy-making position, he refused to judge him "a Communist or having Communistic leanings."[50]

* * *

In the summer of 1948, the House Un-American Activities Committee (HUAC) began holding public hearings featuring the shocking testimony of Elizabeth Bentley, dubbed "the blond spy queen" in one newspaper account. When the former Soviet agent first appeared on Capitol Hill, she shocked the nation by naming prominent citizens and government officials who, she claimed, had been involved in Soviet espionage during the war. Although she had never met Lauchlin Currie, Bentley charged that the former White House aide had often been helpful to a Soviet spy ring headed by Nathan Silvermaster. On one occasion, Currie had even warned that army cryptanalysts were close to breaking the Soviet diplomatic code. She alleged that he had also passed along sensitive information from Sol Adler about Vice President Wallace's mission to China in 1944. Denouncing Bentley's accusations as "fantastic," Currie testified voluntarily in his own defense.

Adler's former boss, Harry Dexter White—the former assistant Treasury secretary and architect of the Truman administration's postwar international economic policies—was also named as a wartime Soviet spy. He was accused of recruiting Communist agents for government work and providing sensitive information to the Soviet Union. Three days after testifying in his own defense, White suffered a fatal heart attack. Liberals were appalled by the HUAC's rough treatment of such respected retired public servants, and its unquestioning acceptance of Bentley's hearsay evidence. The *New York Times* ran a scathing editorial implying that the HUAC ordeal had caused White's heart attack, although in fact he had long suffered from serious heart disease.[51]

A key focus of indignation—from both ends of the political spectrum—was Bentley's accusation of respected diplomat Alger Hiss, a veteran of Yalta and a key organizer of the United Nations conference. Bentley's accusation of espionage was backed up by another repentant ex-Communist agent, *Time* editor Whittaker Chambers. Neither offered any tangible evidence, but Chambers testified that he warned a State Department official nearly a decade earlier that a group of federal employees—including Hiss, Currie, White, and Adler—were engaged in Soviet espionage, but his tip was ignored.[52]

By 1948 the Soviet Union was an implacable enemy, no longer the United States' valuable wartime ally. In June the first major crisis of the Cold War had erupted when Stalin's army, demanding the right to inspect cargo bound for Berlin, blockaded all road, river, and rail traffic through East Germany to the allied sectors of the city. In response, President Truman launched the extraordinary "Berlin Airlift"—an armada of aircraft that supplied the marooned citizens with everything from coal to candy bars for more than a year.

Truman proved equally firm in protecting the rights of accused government officials, refusing to provide the HUAC with loyalty files and calling its proceedings "a red herring." In fact, it later became known that the GOP national chairman had urged Republicans to "set up spy hearings" as a way to "keep the heat on Harry Truman" before the start of the fall presidential campaign.[53]

Nevertheless, some of Bentley's and Chambers' shocking accusations were supported by evidence that could not be made public. By 1948 the five-year effort to decode Soviet wartime cable traffic was beginning to pay off. The Army's top secret counterintelligence project, code-named "Venona," uncovered startling information about Soviet efforts to steal some of the United States' most sensitive wartime secrets—including plans for the atomic bomb. Coupled with information from defectors such as Gouzenko and Bentley, these intercepted Soviet cables eventually corroborated the identity of secret Soviet agents such as

Bentley herself, who was identified as agent "clever girl." The activities of "Ales," another agent identified in Venona cables, appeared to mirror those of Alger Hiss. But those secrets could not be publicized without jeopardizing the Venona effort. Moreover, establishing the matches took time: only in 1951 did Truman learn that Harry Dexter White had indeed been identified as mentioned in the Venona cables.[54]

Amazingly, President Truman may never have been fully briefed about the Venona project. The head of the supersecret Army counterintelligence program, Gen. Omar Bradley, had decreed that he alone would "personally advise the president or anyone else in authority, if the contents of any of this material so demanded."[55] Truman, like many citizens, remained dubious about the accusations against Alger Hiss. And the GOP continued to stick the "soft on Communism" label on liberal Democrats, even though government counterintelligence agents were fully engaged in tracking down subversives by 1948. "We were inside the enemy's house," the FBI's Lamphere reflected. "I could look ahead and see us coming closer and closer, not only to Russian agents whose trails the intervening years had muddied, but also to spies who were actually still at work among us."[56]

* * *

In early January 1949 John Service was reassigned to Washington, D.C., to serve on a Foreign Service promotion selection board—an honor and a responsibility the Services deeply appreciated. Caroline embraced his temporary appointment as solid confirmation that the shadow of *Amerasia* had really passed, and "nobody would be attacking us or be after us."[57] However, as soon as news of this prestigious assignment was leaked to the press, he again became a lightning rod for controversy. The Scripps-Howard newspapers fulminated about the *Amerasia* defendant sitting on a panel deciding all Foreign Service promotions and assignments. Members of the House Appropriations Committee went on record expressing their disapproval, and the letters of fearful constituents were forwarded to the State Department.[58] To spare the department further embarrassment, Service offered to resign from the board.[59] His offer was refused, but Service's intended next assignment was canceled. The high-profile position in the Division of Foreign Service Planning would have involved frequent trips to Capitol Hill, hardly friendly territory.[60] Instead, Service was given what he called "an invisible job" as special assistant to the chief of Foreign Service personnel, assigned the thankless task of reorganizing personnel files and reforming the arcane job performance rating system.[61] Arriving in Washington, D.C., Caroline was shocked to find her husband again under bitter attack and the capital gripped by fear and anxiety.[62]

CHAPTER 17
THE HURRICANE STRIKES

On January 20, 1949, Harry Truman was inaugurated to his own term as the thirty-third president of the United States. The following day, Chiang Kai-shek "retired" as head of the Nationalist Chinese government. A general named Li Tsung-jen became the new acting president of the Republic of China, but the reins of power remained firmly in the Generalissimo's grasp. Chiang maintained control of the navy, the air force, and two key army groups. He made sure that all military supplies remaining in the U.S. military aid grant pipeline were shipped to the offshore island of Taiwan (then known by its Portuguese name, Formosa). And he secretly arranged the transfer of $300 million of the Chinese government's gold, silver, and foreign exchange holdings to Taiwan. After nearly fifty years of Japanese colonization, the island territory was once again in Chinese hands.[1]

By the end of January, Mao's forces were marching victoriously into Peking, the seat of imperial power for six hundred years. They captured Tianjin in March and by the end of April had swept across the Yangtze to occupy Nanjing and Shanghai without a fight.[2] Chiang refused to commit his best and most loyal forces to halt the Red armies at the Yangtze. General Wedemeyer complained that the river could have been defended "with broomsticks if they had the will to do so."[3] Instead, Nationalist soldiers often disappeared, leaving behind their modern American weapons and ammunition, while the Nationalist government retreated farther south to Canton. An American official observing the continuing disintegration of the Nationalists cabled Washington that it would be "useless to extend further aid" and advised that the United States should not feel obliged to "support a hopelessly inefficient and corrupt government which has lost the support of its people."[4]

When Chiang's mainland troops took over Taiwan after the Japanese surrender, they were greeted as liberators. But less than two years later, on February 27, 1947, the people of Taiwan erupted in protest against Nationalist misrule and corruption. In the ensuing crackdown, 28,000 prominent Taiwanese were reportedly slaughtered in the "228 Incident," the beginning of a brutal martial law regime that would last for decades. The murderous Nationalist repression was a taboo topic for all those years—and it remains a potent symbol of the political divide between the Taiwanese majority and the Nationalist (mainland Chinese) minority.[5]

"By the spring of 1949, the collapse of the [Nationalist] Government on mainland China was irreversible and nearly complete," John Service recalled. "But the partisan attacks on the administration's China policy showed no signs of abatement; on the contrary, they were steadily more frequent and more violent."[6] To counter the continuing criticism, White House and State Department officials decided to publish a documentary record of U.S. relations with China, with special emphasis on the years 1944–49. The aim was to present strong evidence of American efforts to assist Nationalist China and to demonstrate the blunders of a repressive regime that refused to reform.

After wrapping up his work on the promotions selection board, John Service was vacationing with his family in California when he got a long-distance call from John Paton Davies, now on the State Department's policy planning staff. Davies told his friend that the record would include an annex with an extensive summary of the views of some China field officers who had predicted what was going to happen. "Apparently, the State Department wanted to have it both ways: first, it hadn't done anything to push Chiang Kai-shek, and also it wasn't so stupid that it didn't know what was going on," Service recalled, "so they decided to put in some of our field reports." Service cut the family vacation short and hurried back to Washington, D.C., to begin work on the project. "Of course we were pleased," he said. "We even thought it was good to have it on the record, to prove we were right."[7] He compiled twelve pages of selected excerpts from his own memos and several authored by Davies and Ray Ludden for the annex. These selections warned of the coming civil war, analyzed the causes and effects of the Nationalist regime's rapid economic and political disintegration, and urged that the United States provide military supplies to any Chinese forces willing to fight the common enemy. With hundreds of pages of selected documents and excerpts, many items were nevertheless omitted, such as reports on various wartime cooperative ventures with the Chinese Communists.[8]

Officially titled "United States Relations with China, with Special Reference to the Period 1944–1949," the 1,054-page volume was delivered to President

Truman at the end of July and released to the public on August 5, 1949. Secretary of State Dean Acheson wrote a seventeen-page introductory "Letter of Transmittal" that generated impassioned reaction at home and abroad. He wrote:

> The only alternative open to the United States was full-scale intervention in behalf of a Government which had lost the confidence of its own troops and its own people. . . . The unfortunate but inescapable fact is that the ominous result of the civil war in China was beyond the control of the government of the United States. Nothing that this country did or could have done within the reasonable limits of its capabilities could have changed that result; nothing that was left undone by this country has contributed to it. . . . It was the product of internal Chinese forces, forces which this country tried to influence but could not. . . . We will not help the Chinese or ourselves by basing our policy on wishful thinking.[9]

Acheson's words inflamed the China Lobby and reinvigorated the attack upon the administration's China policy. The China "White Paper" quickly boomeranged, becoming the Truman Administration's "self-inflicted wound."[10] A *New York Times* editorial noted: "This inquest on China is not the work of a serene and detached coroner but of a vitally interested party to the catastrophe."[11]

Patrick Hurley denounced the volume as "a smooth alibi for the pro-Communists in the State Department who have engineered the overthrow of our ally."[12] On Capitol Hill, Chiang supporters loudly attacked State Department officials and "pro-Communist foreign service officers," who, having done in the Nationalist government, were now fabricating history. They were convinced the State Department had withheld secret documents that would show conclusively that China was betrayed—and that those who had "lost" China were guilty of indictable offenses.[13]

For the first time, outrage over the impending defeat of Chiang's forces was linked to that old bugaboo, the *Amerasia* case. Hurley and his allies demanded that Acheson provide "an explanation of the reasons why the officials arrested by the FBI in the *Amerasia* case were released and white-washed by the State Department."[14] In contrast, Nationalist Chinese reaction was remarkably restrained. Officials stressed that the United States had finally acknowledged that the Chinese Communists were "thorough Marxists and tools of Moscow," and the fight against Communism remained a common cause. Nevertheless, some now realized that the United States was no longer going to prop up the regime. "The White Paper has awakened us," the authoritarian governor of Taiwan declared; "we must now start on the road to self-help."[15]

For the Chinese Communists, the White Paper became the focus of a major campaign to erase the reservoir of good feeling that was the legacy of decades of American philanthropic, medical, and educational activity in China. They focused on Acheson's revelations about the huge amount of American aid given to the Nationalists; his flat assertion that the United States had done all it could to support Chiang; and his claim that Communist leaders had "forsworn their Chinese heritage and publicly announced their subservience to a foreign power, Russia." Acheson's statement that China would eventually "throw off the foreign yoke" was seen as a sign that, even after the anticipated Communist takeover, the United States intended to support Mao's enemies.[16]

All the more infuriating was the timing of the White Paper. Two months earlier, the Communists had made overtures to improve relations with America after several ugly antiforeign incidents, including the house arrest of an American diplomat in Mukden and the beating of another U.S. official in Shanghai. Zhou Enlai sent an unusual message to the American consul general in Peking. He recalled the cordial relations with Americans in the bygone Yenan era. Hinting at an internal political struggle between hardliners and moderates, he pleaded for U.S. economic aid and continued contacts. But Zhou's secret initiative received no response.[17]

Also that June the U.S. ambassador to China, Leighton Stuart, expressed the hope to visit Peking's Yenching University, where he had been president for many years. Mao and Zhou responded that his visit to Peking would be welcomed. "This was the first time since the Marshall mission that the CCP [Chinese Communist Party] had responded positively to a proposal for high level contacts—a response that caught American policymakers totally by surprise," noted Yuan Ming, a Chinese mainland scholar, at a joint U.S.-PRC conference more than thirty-five years later.[18] However, when Ambassador Stuart sought official approval, President Truman personally vetoed the trip, overruling the advice of Acheson and others. Such confidential overtures (like the 1945 request by Mao and Zhou to meet with FDR) would remain secret for decades.[19]

To celebrate the twenty-eighth anniversary of the Chinese Communist Party's founding, on July 1, 1949, Mao Zedong issued a major foreign policy decision that sealed the tragic fate of Sino-American relations. "On People's Democratic Dictatorship" set forth his decision to ally China with the Soviet Union: "In order to attain victory and consolidate it, we must lean to one side. . . . Not only in China, but throughout the world, one must lean either to imperialism or to socialism. There is no exception. Neutrality is merely a camouflage; a third road does not exist."[20] Following Mao's pronouncement, *Life* magazine observed that his new policy "shattered the illusion cherished by many an American . . . that China's Communists are 'different.'" Mao's words had a sobering effect on Washington policy makers, who now began to work in earnest on ways to contain the spread of Communism in Asia while moving ahead with the release of the White Paper discrediting Chiang Kai-shek, Asia's staunchest anti-Communist. Mao's "lean to one side" pronouncement helped ignite criticism of the White Paper.

In late August an even more ominous event occurred. The Soviet Union successfully tested its own atomic bomb, taking American military strategists by surprise. The United States no longer held a monopoly on nuclear power. The American public was shocked and its confidence shaken. The Soviet bomb increased fears about the rising threat of worldwide Communism and gave added significance to what many saw as America's abandonment of Nationalist China, its loyal ally in the war against Japan.

* * *

A few days after the White Paper was published, John Service ran into Clarence Gauss, his former boss at the Chungking embassy. With the controversy over the two Chinas again in the headlines, Gauss said it was a "terrible mistake" for the State Department to have included the names of Service and other Foreign Service officers who authored the reports cited. "I was really amazed. It just hadn't occurred to me," Service reflected later. Having his work recognized had seemed to him "a pat on the back," and he had even felt vindicated. "But the old man was right. This gave information and ammunition for the attacks on us. This was all used later on. It proved to a lot of people that we were the villains."[21]

* * *

On September 7, Val Chao left the United States on a ship bound for Europe. She would perform in a charity benefit show in London to help China's children and then go home to China to be reunited with her three-year-old daughter and her mother. Unsuccessful in her effort to obtain a resident visa and knowing she might be unable to return to the United States, she determined to see Service again. "This time I must see him for myself, because all I know of him had been through others," Chao explained more than fifty years later. "I want to hear the truth from him. Our feelings cannot be destroyed by any outsider, only we ourselves can ruin it."

In late August, after more than four years, the former lovers finally met again in Washington, D.C. They had a long private conversation at the home of a Foreign Service friend from Chungking. Val told Jack how angry and confused she had felt on learning of his wife's pregnancy after he had promised to return and marry her; how difficult it had been to abort their child; and how, after learning of his arrest by the FBI, she had grown deeply remorseful about the abortion. She explained that her brief affair with Major Hanen was a desperate effort to forget him and that she wanted to raise her illegitimate daughter as Jack's child. "When I talked about our lost child," the actress recalled dramatically, "we cannot help but weep in each other's arms. . . . It seemed we were back in the old days, with no distance between us."

Val Chao's memory of their reunion remained vivid. "As we talked about our mutual experience, the old Service returned." Recounting his experience of being arrested, handcuffed, thrown into jail, and forced to wear torn prison garb, he "wept like a child." He told her, "After I got into trouble, I was worried if the KMT [Nationalists] would harm you, but after I heard that you were acting all along, I was relieved." And then as they sat together, Service added, "You have survived. I have survived, too."

"As I got ready to leave, Service said to me: 'I will go to China yet, please wait for me even if it takes ten years,'" Val Chao recalled. "In my heart, I thought, I would wait for you not just ten years or even twenty years, if you are still the man I knew before, but I didn't say it. I said, 'You have your trouble now, and I have my work, and I hope that you can concentrate your energy in solving your predicament.' But my heart was bleeding."

The diplomat's recollection of their rendezvous was less detailed, and much less romantic. Many years later, he claimed that the "ferocious love" he initially felt for Chao had already begun to cool by the time he departed for Yenan in the summer of 1944. "Maybe it's just men," Service said, "but most love affairs cool off soon after they reach the peak." Of their 1949 reunion, he remembered only that Val Chao asked his advice about returning to China. Since the civil war was winding down, he encouraged her to go: it would be easy for such a well-known actress to find theater work there.

Years later Chao claimed their brief reunion confirmed "his love for me, his kindness, his consideration and longing." The diplomat and the actress would not meet again for more than thirty years, yet their conversation in Washington remained for her a treasured memory: "We had never parted, although we were oceans apart."[22]

* * *

Standing above the Forbidden City's main gate on October 1, 1949, addressing 300,000 cheering supporters in Tiananmen Square, Mao Zedong proclaimed the establishment of the People's Republic of China (PRC). After a century of humiliation by foreign powers, decadent emperors, and feuding warlords, China would "never again be an insulted nation" now that the people had "stood up."[23]

The new government was quickly recognized by the Soviet Union. Within a few months, even Great Britain established normal diplomatic relations with the new regime. But recognition had become such a sensitive political issue for America, it would be delayed another thirty years.

* * *

As soon as "Red" China was proclaimed, Chiang's supporters on Capitol Hill went on the warpath. Fearing that the Communists might soon invade Taiwan, where Chiang and his loyalists had taken refuge, they demanded that Truman pledge to defend the island retreat. Infuriated by the White Paper's treatment of the Nationalist government, Rep. Walter Judd of Minnesota, the former medical missionary in China, went after John Service. Railing against "the conniving against the highest officials of the Government of China," Judd inserted into the *Congressional Record* Service's blunt confidential October 1944 memo to General Stilwell as proof of the treachery: "We need feel no ties of gratitude to Chiang. The men he has kept around him have proved selfish and corrupt, incapable and obstructive. Chiang's own dealings with us have been an opportunist's combination of extravagant demands and unfilled promises, wheedling and bargaining, bluff and blackmail. . . . We should end the hollow pretense that China is unified and that we can talk only to Chiang." In his relentless effort to portray Service as part of a dangerous anti-Chiang conspiracy, the congressman linked his betrayal of Chiang to the *Amerasia* case, amplifying the misinformation and myths surrounding Service's role: "Suitcases of documents from [Service's] office were found by the FBI in the office of a notoriously pro-Communist magazine. The case was hushed up under circumstances never yet disclosed or explained. Since then he has been promoted several times and is now chairman of the committee within the State Department which makes recommendations for all promotions."[24]

In fact, John Service had recently been the subject of a lengthy loyalty investigation; in January 1949 the new Loyalty Security Board of the State Department reported "no reasonable grounds to believe that Service is disloyal to the Government of United States or a security risk to the Department."[25] The board's findings were sent to the FBI director, who remained unconvinced.[26] Hoover had enlisted U.S. Army intelligence officers in Asia to conduct further background checks and interview Service's former acquaintances, but the investigators found no proof of disloyalty or subversion. "Hardworking, loyal, [and] level-headed" were the terms used by Service's former colleagues in Tokyo to describe him. "In fact," one official told investigators, "if I were running the security affairs for the nation, I would give Service a job." Another acquaintance from the early days of the U.S. occupation spoke admiringly of Service's "conscientious and tenacious efforts to bring order out of the existing administrative chaos." General Wedemeyer called John Service one of "the strongest supporters of the Chinese Communists" on his staff in China—but he insisted that he "didn't believe Service was disloyal."[27] Even Gen. Claire Chennault reported "no reason to question Service's loyalty." But such responses apparently were never shown to Representative Judd or other critics, and they were declassified by the Pentagon only in 2004.[28]

Most sources, according to investigators, said Service's "character, integrity and discretion were unblemished." But one former naval intelligence officer informed them of Service's "reprehensible" wartime affair with Val Chao, saying it was common knowledge that he sought a divorce and wanted to marry her. He reported rumors that she "may have been an agent for Nationalist Government," and speculated that the Nationalists might have made trouble for Service "in order to keep him from influencing the U.S. Government to increase aid to the Communists." The investigators reported, "Service was becoming more Chinese than American and was apparently losing his American perspective and his sense of moral responsibility to his wife and children."[29] During 1949 the FBI churned out seven separate investigative reports on the suspect diplomat. Each included misinformation about his role in the controversial *Amerasia* case, but not one contained any hard evidence of disloyalty.

* * *

In the last weeks of 1949, Alger Hiss was convicted of perjury in his second libel trial. His antagonist, ex-Communist spy Whittaker Chambers, had produced bizarre evidence: incriminating film, hidden inside a pumpkin found at Chambers' farm. The controversial Hiss conviction heightened public fears of espionage, deepening the schism between conservatives and liberals over the seriousness of the Communist threat.

Early in 1950, President Truman set off new shockwaves. The United States was cutting off all military aid to the Chinese Nationalist government on Taiwan. Limited economic aid would continue, but the president refused to spend the seventy-five million dollars of military aid allocated by Congress. "I've still got [the money] locked up in the drawer of my desk," he told reporters, "and it is going to stay there." Rather than prop up the defeated Nationalists, the Truman administration planned to focus government resources on the Marshall Plan for Europe and on programs to improve American health, housing, and education. In his no-nonsense style, President Truman made it clear that the United States would not interfere in the Chinese situation. America, he declared, had "no desire to obtain special rights or privileges or to establish military bases on Formosa . . . at this time."[30]

White House press aide Eben Ayers was startled to hear the words "at this time," which he knew had not been in the president's prepared remarks. Adm. Sidney Souers, head of the National Security Council, enlightened him: after a last-minute conversation with the secretary of defense, Truman decided to add that phrase. "It's a hell of a way to run a railroad, isn't it?" remarked the admiral.[31] Those three little words would later provide the basis for a defense treaty with Taiwan.

At his own press conference the same day, Secretary of State Acheson told reporters that once "the dust settles in Peking," the United States would consider granting official diplomatic recognition to the People's Republic of China. A few weeks earlier Acheson had sent a confidential cable to all American embassies advising that Taiwan was expected to fall soon to the Communists, and emphasizing that such an event should not be considered disastrous to American national security interests. Leaked to the press, the cable instantly became ammunition for the China Lobby.

On the Senate floor that afternoon, Senator Knowland of California (also known as the "Senator from Formosa"), together with the relatively unknown junior senator from Wisconsin, Joseph McCarthy, pounced on those statements by the president and secretary of state as further proof that the administration was abandoning a faithful ally. Knowland demanded to know whether John Service had drafted Acheson's recent cable, reminding his Senate colleagues that this was the same John Service who had been arrested in the *Amerasia* spy case. McCarthy then falsely quoted Service as saying, "the only hope of Asia was Communism."[32] For the first time, John Service's name was directly linked to the fate of Chiang's defeated forces.

* * *

On New Year's Day 1950, Jack and Caroline Service were packing for a cross-country trip to California to visit family before traveling to their new post in India. Jack's appointment as consul general in Calcutta still required Senate confirmation, but they were optimistic—and glad to be leaving Washington, D.C. The new decade, they told themselves, was bound to be better than the war-torn and fearful 1940s.

But the renewed political uproar about Taiwan worried the State Department's congressional liaison office. The notion of Service's authorship of the leaked cable was absurd, but it might nevertheless create trouble for his confirmation vote. So, before leaving Washington, Jack was asked to pay a call on Capitol Hill.

Senator Knowland kept John Service waiting for nearly an hour before he was ushered in to a chilly reception. The diplomat immediately assured Knowland he did not write the leaked communiqué about Taiwan. He pointed out that he had not worked on any China matters since 1945, and he was not the dangerous character described in the Scripps-Howard newspaper stories. But Knowland merely insisted that it was wrong for the United States to abandon the Nationalists.

Service argued that the effort to bring about a loose coalition government of Nationalists and Communists during the war was "simply trying to prevent a disaster in China"—the very disaster that had now come about. Grudgingly, Knowland admitted that coalition governments "hadn't meant the end of the world" in postwar Western Europe. At the end of the meeting, they even shared a chuckle: Service thanked the Senator for the gold pocket watch he had received in 1932, for winning the foot race sponsored by the *Oakland Tribune*—when the senator was the newspaper's publisher. "At least I was no longer a punching bag," Service remembered. "He never attacked me after that."[33]

Nevertheless, the State Department decided to delay the request for Senate confirmation, hoping that the furor over Taiwan would abate. "The State Department is now solidly behind Jack and is fed up to the teeth with his being pushed around so unmercifully for political reasons," Caroline reported to her parents. But she suggested that her staunchly Republican parents reconsider their vote for Knowland the next time he came up for reelection.[34]

* * *

In the meantime, the *Saturday Evening Post* published the first of three explosive articles about wartime China written by Joseph Alsop, the influential journalist who had been Claire Chennault's trusted aide. Alsop had assiduously lobbied his cousin, President Roosevelt, to favor the Chennault-Chiang air power plan over General Stilwell's ground forces strategy. Now, as Chiang faced defeat in the civil war, Alsop's articles blamed Stilwell and his political advisers, John Service and John Paton Davies, for Chiang's predicament. "In the end, they came close to offering China up to the Communists like a trussed-up bird on a platter over four years before the eventual Commie triumph."[35] Alsop's articles failed to describe the confused and complex context of the war in the two Chinas. "The tragedy is," John Service would later observe, "that neither view, his nor ours, was consistently followed."[36]

* * *

In mid-January, after the American consular office in Peking was taken over by the Chinese Communists, President Truman ordered all Americans out of China. The expropriation inflamed the American public and ended the behind-the-scenes effort to normalize relations with the People's Republic of China. Americans continued the Nationalists' practice of calling the Communists' capital Peiping rather than Peking; around the world, the choice of name became an ideological litmus test of the Cold War.

Americans were soon startled by other disquieting headlines. Judith Coplon, a former Justice Department official, was sentenced to fifteen years in prison for passing government documents to a Soviet agent on a New York street corner. And Alger Hiss was sentenced to five years in jail for perjury.

The Hiss case had deeply polarized the American public: the veteran diplomat was seen either as the victim of a witch hunt or as a traitor. "Whatever the outcome of any appeal which Mr. Hiss or his lawyers may take in this case," Secretary of State Acheson told reporters, "I do not intend to turn my back on Alger Hiss." Sen. Joseph McCarthy asked sarcastically whether his statement meant the Secretary "would not turn his back on any other Communists in the State Department."[37] Acheson offered to resign over the issue, but Truman refused the offer. Hiss would serve several years in prison, always insisting on his innocence. But when the Venona files of decoded Soviet cables were declassified forty years later, Hiss was identified by some analysts as the Soviet contact code-named "Ales."[38]

After the Hiss sentencing, even Jack Service had a premonition of trouble. "I said to Caroline at the time that this could be very bad news. It seemed very threatening."[39] As Caroline remembered, people were beginning to feel that "the country was simply crawling with Communists, subversives, and whatnot."[40] Richard Nixon, campaigning to become California's junior senator, attacked Truman for soft-pedaling the Communist threat. "Because President Truman treated Communist infiltration like any ordinary political scandal," Nixon thundered, "he is responsible for this failure to act against the Communist conspiracy and has rendered the greatest possible disservice to the people of this nation."[41] Truman ignored the accusation and dismissed McCarthy as "a ballyhoo artist who has to cover up his shortcomings by wild charges." But his trusted aide, George Elsey, began keeping a file on McCarthy's remarks. Elsey sent Truman a memo proposing a major presidential speech to argue that "anti-Communism is not the sole or principle test of American patriotism."[42]

* * *

The Cold War arms race officially began in room 215 of the State Department at a meeting of Truman's top secret Z Committee. There, on January 31, the president gave the green light for development of a hydrogen bomb. Other developments soon heightened the tension and fear between the former allies.

On February 2 the British announced the arrest of a physicist, Klaus Fuchs, who confessed to stealing atomic bomb secrets during the war for the Soviet Union. His arrest resulted from clues in a decoded Venona cable. Coming less than two weeks after the sentencing of Judith Coplon and Alger Hiss, the Fuchs case was "political dynamite."[43]

One week later, on February 9, 1950, Sen. Joe McCarthy delivered a Lincoln's Day address in Wheeling, West Virginia, that would launch his career as the chief anti-Communist crusader. The GOP had directed all elected Republicans to focus their remarks that day on "subversion in government." McCarthy now targeted Dean Acheson and his State Department, where, McCarthy claimed, "the bright young men who are born with silver spoons in their mouths are the ones who have been most traitorous." McCarthy focused on four cases, giving John Service top billing:

> [Service] sent official reports back to the State Department urging that we torpedo our ally Chiang Kai-shek and stating in unqualified terms (and I quote) that "Communism was the only hope of China." Later this man—John Service—and please remember that name, ladies and gentlemen, was picked up by the Federal Bureau of Investigation for turning over to the Communists secret State Department information. Strangely, however, he was never prosecuted. . . . Today, ladies and gentlemen, this man Service is on his way to represent the State Department and Acheson in Calcutta, by far and away the most important listening post in the Far East.[44]

McCarthy assured his audience, "I have in my hand a list of 205 . . . names that were made known to the Secretary of State as being members of the Communist Party and who nevertheless are still working and shaping policy in the State Department."[45] When the senator repeated his diatribe two days later, his list included only "fifty-seven card-carrying Communists."

After giving the electrifying speech in a few other towns, McCarthy began to draw national media attention, attracted by local news headlines such as, "McCarthy Charges Reds Hold United States Jobs: Truman Blasted for Reluctance to Press Probe."[46] The administration was troubled and the country was rattled. McCarthy's biographer, David Oshinsky, captured their anxieties: "Would a United States senator go this far out on a limb without hard evidence? Would he dare to make fraudulent charges that could so easily be unmasked?"[47]

* * *

On February 14, soon after the Service family arrived in California, the nation's newspapers reported another world-shaking event: Chairman Mao and Joseph

Stalin had signed a Valentine's Day friendship treaty in Moscow. The Soviets pledged credits worth $300 million in a five-year plan to assist China's economic redevelopment. Stalin also promised to return two strategic Manchurian ports, Port Arthur and Dairen, within two years. (They were returned only after the Soviet dictator's death in 1953).[48]

The perception of a menacing Communist alliance fed American feelings of vulnerability and fear. Caroline Service later recalled the atmosphere of the era: "Why did we 'lose China?' We'd been so good to China. . . . How could China turn on us like this? How could the Russians do what they were doing and we couldn't save the people in Eastern Europe? So, there must be something wrong at home."[49] The growing outcry over these disturbing developments would soon engulf her own family.

* * *

Although delighted with the media attention, Joseph McCarthy knew he was on shaky ground: when he returned to Washington from his wildly successful speech-making tour, Democrats and the press were clamoring for proof of his sensational charges. McCarthy turned to his old friend, J. Edgar Hoover, admitting he had simply made up the numbers of subversives. The FBI director advised him to stop mentioning numbers, and he promised to provide some ammunition. Hoover quickly fired off a memo ordering his staff to "review the files and get anything you can for him." His support for McCarthy involved not only confidential information but also speechwriters, clerical staff, informers, and his acknowledged master of public relations, Assistant FBI Director Lou Nichols. According to one Hoover critic, Nichols "personally took McCarthy in hand and instructed him in how to release a story just before press deadlines, so that reporters wouldn't have time to ask for rebuttals."[50]

On Monday afternoon, February 20, Senator McCarthy was ready to fire back at his critics from the Senate floor. For nearly eight hours, McCarthy indulged in falsification, innuendo, and manipulation of rumors in presenting an amended list of eighty-one "loyalty risk" cases. The Democrats tried to respond to the outrageous charges but never mounted an effective counterattack. Close to midnight, the Senate finally adjourned—confused, exhausted, and unable to grasp the political significance of what had just happened.[51]

* * *

Sitting alone in a local Berkeley public library, John Service read the *New York Times* to keep up with the Washington firestorm. The Senate had appointed a special committee to investigate McCarthy's charges, to be chaired by Sen. Millard E. Tydings of Maryland. On the first day of hearings, the jammed Senate Caucus

Room "humm[ed] with the electricity that often precedes a bloodletting."[52] The first witness was McCarthy. His testimony was shaped not only by the FBI but also by a network of right-wing journalists and Chiang supporters, including Alfred Kohlberg, the publisher of *Plain Talk*. For years they had targeted John Service; now they eagerly signed on to help fan the fires of anti-Communism, reignited by McCarthy's speechmaking.

Before the Wisconsin senator finished reading his prepared statement, Chairman Tydings interrupted. Eager to challenge McCarthy's outrageous accusations, he demanded to know specific details about just one of the eighty-one alleged security risk cases. Dodging and feinting like the boxer he had once been, the senator from Wisconsin evaded the question. As one journalist reported, "McCarthy's verbiage outran his evidence." Even *Time* magazine admitted that McCarthy "has probably damaged no reputation permanently except his own." Sen. Robert Taft, an influential and respected Republican, was stunned by McCarthy's testimony and called it "a perfectly reckless performance."[53] FBI counterespionage agent Robert Lamphere would later lament that "McCarthy's approach and tactics hurt the anti-Communist cause and turned many liberals against legitimate efforts to curtail Communist activities in the United States."[54]

From his vantage point in the Berkeley library reading room, John Service was cautiously optimistic. Nothing about McCarthy's list of security risk cases, as reported by the *New York Times*, seemed to apply to him. To make certain he was clear of any danger, he placed a long-distance phone call to the Foreign Service chief of personnel. "I said, 'Well, what do I do? Here I am. Do I go to India or not?' He says, 'You're not on the list. Go! Take off!' . . . the intimation being the sooner the better."[55]

* * *

On his second day of testimony before the Tydings Committee, McCarthy fingered John Service as "a known associate and collaborator with Communists and pro-Communists, a man high in the State Department, [who] consorted with admitted espionage agents."[56] Alleging a conspiracy of Soviet spies in the government, he resurrected the "whitewash" of the 1945 *Amerasia* case. He then informed the packed hearing room that the "untouchable" John Stewart Service was in Calcutta, "one of the most strategically important listening posts . . . since the fall of China the most important new front of the cold war."[57] McCarthy repeated, nearly verbatim, misstatements and hearsay evidence contained in the confidential files of the FBI and the State Department security office; the plagiarism became evident when those files were declassified more than fifty years later.

The attack on John Service included McCarthy's announcement that a new investigation of his record was being undertaken by President Truman's new Loyalty Review Board (LRB). The revelation rocked the hearing room. The State Department vigorously denied the senator's claim. A few days later, however, State received a letter from the LRB requesting the diplomat personally appear before the department's own loyalty board. The letter had evidently been leaked to McCarthy, who had exaggerated its contents.

"State Department Recalls India Aide for Loyalty Check—J. S. Service, Accused of Red Ties by McCarthy, to Return for Review of His Record." This was the *New York Times* headline on Wednesday, March 15, four days after the Service family had sailed for India. "State Dept informants emphasized that Mr. Service's papers had gone up to the LRB more than one year ago," the story reported, "and only now were being returned for further action." The statement hardly mattered. McCarthy had already succeeded in damaging Service's reputation in the public perception.

"Congratulations on your effort to get the Communists out of the State Department," a former Army intelligence officer who had served in China during the war wrote to McCarthy. "We discovered Service to be, in our opinion, a Communist propagandist and were delighted very shortly thereafter when the State Department took action against him. May I suggest that the Republican Party attack this mad subversive foreign policy every day from now until the time that we have a Republican president in the White House?"[58]

* * *

On Saturday, March 11, Service and his family had embarked aboard the *Island Mail* from Seattle. The freighter carried only twelve passengers, including the five Services. The passage to Yokohama usually took eight days, but foul weather struck. Only thirteen-year-old Bob Service enjoyed the rollercoaster ride in the churning seas. Caroline stayed in her cabin, nursing a sore tooth and taking penicillin. Jack spent his time studying about India. It would be two weeks before the ship finally docked in Yokohama.

"Is your name John Stewart Service?" asked the ship's radio room operator, politely interrupting the captain's table conversation one night at sea. Service replied that he was. The crewman told him excitedly, "Well, you had better come up to the radio room, because there's some senator talking about you."[59] Jack and Caroline rushed to the radio room to listen to the static-filled shortwave radio news broadcast. "I feel as though I were living in some weird melodramatic dream that cannot possibly exist," Caroline wrote to her parents. "We have listened to news every day and there has always been some mention of Jack."

From the broadcasts they learned he was being recalled to appear before the State Department's Loyalty Security Board (LSB). On March 17, Service finally received an official radiogram from the State Department ordering him to leave the ship in Yokohama and return to Washington for "urgent consultations." It also informed the diplomat that he was being reassigned as first secretary at the New Delhi embassy—a post that would eliminate the need for Senate confirmation. Jack and Caroline decided it would be best for the family to continue on to India. The two teenage children could get settled into their boarding school for the new semester, and Caroline and four-year old Philip would set up house and wait for Jack to arrive. The ship would take another month to reach India from Japan, and by then, Caroline wrote her parents, "Jack should be on his way back by air and perhaps will be there to meet us."

* * *

"As a result of Sen. McCarthy's resuscitation of these dead, discredited, disproven charges against him," the State Department press release declared, "Mr. Service finds his character once more called into question, his name once more blazoned in headlines of the whole country's press, and his brilliant career as a diplomat once more interrupted so that he can be defended, and can defend himself against such baseless allegations all over again." The statement from the Deputy Undersecretary of State called the seventeen-year veteran of the Foreign Service "an able, conscientious, demonstrably loyal foreign service officer . . . and one of our outstanding experts on Far Eastern affairs." John Peurifoy added, "It's a shame and a disgrace that he and his family should have to face, once again, such humiliation, embarrassment and inconvenience; and I'd like to say that the sympathy and good wishes of the entire department go out to them."[60] Senator McCarthy seized upon Peurifoy's statement as more evidence that the State Department was "soft on Communists."

* * *

"This should be the final foray for Jack's bitter enemies and everything should be at last cleared up, and the insinuations and lies and the cruel persecution and the terrible thing of accusing a man of something he did not do and then never giving him a chance to defend himself should be over," Caroline Service wrote her parents in a long, plaintive letter from Yokohama. "We have had five years of it and that is enough and too much. And all because he and others had the courage to report the truth from China." Wistfully she continued, "If only we were still in Washington . . . all of this should have been cleared up then. Here we sit in the Pacific Ocean able to do absolutely *nothing* . . . caught between the sea and the sky."[61]

CHAPTER 18
THE INQUISITION BEGINS

A swarm of news reporters and photographers crowded the Yokohama pier when the *Island Mail* docked on March 24, 1950. John Service was unprepared for this reception and limited his remarks to a statement that he was "not a Communist, never been a Communist nor a fellow traveler" and that he was "at the disposal of the State Department and investigating agencies and wished to clear up any charges conclusively."[1] An embassy car whisked the family to Tokyo for a relaxed dinner with some old friends and colleagues. Caroline and the children would spend a few days there while the freighter took on cargo, but Jack left late the same night for Washington, D.C.

"Every place the plane stopped, the press were after me," Service recalled. "I wasn't prepared for the tremendous hullabaloo." The reporters, while not hostile, annoyed him by asking "the same foolish questions." But his fellow passengers gave him "a friendly hand clap" when he deplaned in Seattle to catch his cross-country flight.[2]

Arriving in Washington, Jack was greeted at the airport by a large gathering of well-wishers from the State Department. He was even a guest of honor at the monthly luncheon of the American Foreign Service Association, where the chairman, Hervé L'Heureux, introduced him as a colleague "entitled to our affection, to our esteem, to our confidence, to our best wishes." A standing ovation erupted, lasting more than two minutes, before L'Heureux could continue: "He is entitled to our respect, to our support, to our assistance. Let us pray that his cause may be righteous . . . and that the cloud that tends to despoil his honor may soon be dissipated." Once again, the audience rose to give John Service a warm round of applause.[3] Jack sent an upbeat radiogram to Caroline: "fine reception solid support board hearing about two weeks not much til then relax love to all."

But even before Service returned to Washington, attacks by the media had begun. "The same forces for protection which closed in around the then unknown Alger Hiss are now closing in around John S. Service," proclaimed Henry J. Taylor, an ABC radio network commentator, on his March 20 program. "Why all this stir of defense, this bleeding because John Stewart Service is to be questioned? Who is he?" The broadcaster offered "some firsthand facts" he had learned from Ambassador Hurley (whom he erroneously identified as Service's former boss). Taylor recalled meeting Hurley in China: "I can see him now, pacing the floor of his Chungking house, a worried and frustrated patriot." Hurley had eleven diplomats recalled—including the notorious John Service. "Please listen carefully, if you fear America's position in a next war," Taylor told his audience, before repeating much of the old misinformation, adding some new twists of his own. "When Service reached America, he was *arrested* by the FBI. He wasn't just *questioned* by the FBI." The radio commentator then claimed Service had been "let off" by a grand jury—and "a State Department whitewash quickly followed." In conclusion, the broadcaster told his listeners, "Today we have John S. Service on the way to high official duties in India, a critical place in our problem of Communism. The question arises: what mysterious power has protected his record? . . . Certainly something has gone frightfully, tragically, terribly wrong with our security measures, even if our own officials will not admit it."[4]

The day after Taylor's broadcast McCarthy made headline-grabbing new allegations, promising to reveal to the Tydings Committee the identity of "the top Soviet espionage agent" in the United States. Speculation about this mysterious "Mr. X" swirled for several days. The senator then divulged the name to some favored reporters, announcing his testimony would "stand or fall" on this one loyalty case.

Columnist Drew Pearson soon revealed the identity of "Mr. X," McCarthy's alleged superspy, thus breaking the journalistic taboo on publishing an unsubstantiated and possibly libelous accusation. He named Owen Lattimore—the distinguished director of Johns Hopkins University's School of International Relations. Lattimore had briefly served as an adviser to Chiang Kai-shek with White House approval, had worked in the Office of War Information, and in 1944 had accompanied Vice President Henry Wallace to China. But he had previously been associated with the Institute of Pacific Relations and had once served on the infamous *Amerasia* magazine's editorial board.

Caroline Service was disgusted by the attack on Lattimore, whom she had met in Peking. "People will soon be afraid, if they aren't already, about voicing an honest opinion in contradiction to such bigots as McCarthy because someone will leap up and call them 'Communist' or 'Pro-Communist' when that is the last thing in the world that they are." In a letter to her parents, Caroline worried about the impact of the new witch-hunt: "Young men going into government these days will have to consider whether to give honest reports . . . or whether to play it safe and just never give any opinion at all. That is certainly not the type of thinking that made our country great—terrified yes-men."[5]

* * *

Lattimore himself was in Afghanistan on assignment for the United Nations when McCarthy's sensational charges exploded in the media. An Associated Press reporter cabled him for his reaction, and he fired off a combative reply: "McCARTHY'S OFF RECORD RANTINGS PURE MOONSHINE. DELIGHTED HIS WHOLE CASE RESTS ON ME AS THIS MEANS HE WILL FALL FLAT ON HIS FACE. EXACTLY WHAT HE HAS SAID ON RECORD UNKNOWN HERE SO CANNOT REPLY IN DETAIL BUT WILL BE HOME IN A FEW DAYS AND WILL CONTACT YOU THEN." Upon his return, Lattimore appeared on Capitol Hill and denounced the senator for "instituting a reign of terror among officials and employees of the United States Government." His remarks garnered loud applause from the packed public gallery. To blame the State Department for Chiang Kai-shek's defeat, the professor told the Tydings Committee, was nothing but mindless scapegoating: Chiang lost because his regime was hopelessly incompetent, brutal, and corrupt—and it was time for the United States to cut its losses. As for the senator from Wisconsin, he was nothing more than "the dupe of a bitter and implacable and fanatical group of people who will not tolerate any discussion of China which is not based upon absolute, total, and complete support of the Nationalist Government in Formosa."[6]

By the time of Professor Lattimore's blistering testimony in early April, the Tydings Committee knew there was no evidence to support McCarthy's outrageous charges against him. After reviewing Lattimore's FBI file (under the supervision of the attorney general and FBI Director Hoover), even the Republican members recognized the charges as bogus. The FBI file clearly indicated that Lattimore had never been a State Department employee and had only rarely served as a consultant. And former American Communist Party leader Earl Browder had assured the FBI that Lattimore had never been a party member.

But by now the facts hardly mattered. McCarthy had touched a nerve in the national psyche, triggering public paranoia. The *Washington Post* reported that he was "being 'snowed under' by more than 2,000 letters a day."[7] Far from being dismissed as irresponsible, the former Wisconsin chicken farmer and amateur prizefighter had become a national figure who commanded front-page attention whenever he spoke.

Again taking the floor of the U.S. Senate on March 29, 1950, McCarthy called Lattimore the "architect of our far eastern policy"; his followers inside the State Department were "more loyal to the ideals and designs of Communism than to those of the free, God-fearing half of the world."[8] In his usual mumbling monotone—and speaking on the very day that Service was being honored at the Foreign Service luncheon—McCarthy blamed Lattimore and his State Department allies for the "betrayal" of China. Linking Lattimore to John Service, McCarthy displayed letters from two "loyal Americans" who allegedly witnessed Lattimore, together with Service and Lt. Andrew Roth, declassifying documents shortly before the 1945 arrests. Waving papers in the air, McCarthy announced he was turning the letters over to the FBI.

McCarthy described *Amerasia* as "the case which Hoover says was a 100 percent airtight case" and John Service as "the man who stole the documents for *Amerasia*, an outfit which is clearly Communist-controlled." Mysteriously, Service, who never stood trial, "was not only reinstated but was placed in the position of controlling placements and promotions of personnel in the Far East. This may explain why men like Lattimore were assigned such important jobs in the East." Service, he went on, had submitted a wartime report that, "according to Ambassador Hurley, was a plan for the removal of support from the Chiang Kai-shek Government with the end result that the Communists would take over." Senator McCarthy then identified Service as "a ranking officer in the policy-making group of 'untouchables'" inside the State Department—recently assigned to duty in India "one of the most strategically important listening posts in the world today, and since the fall of China, the most important new front of the cold war." In conclusion, Senator McCarthy told his Senate colleagues and the packed public galleries that John Stewart Service had never been, and would never be, "a sound security risk."[9]

* * *

"You've got to have a lawyer," John Peurifoy, the undersecretary of state for administration, advised John Service on his first day back at the department. He had been gone from Washington for fewer than two months, but he felt like Rip Van Winkle. McCarthy's anti-Communist campaign had transformed the political atmosphere. In an already insecure and fearful nation, loyalty oaths were becoming routine. Reputations could be ruined by mere allegations. The nation was reeling from dramatic and troubling world events: Stalin's "Iron Curtain," Mao's takeover in China, a Soviet spy ring's theft of atomic secrets, and the sentencing of Alger Hiss. As one historian later observed, "McCarthy sensed the country's need for simple answers to the challenges of the cold war, and he provided them."[10]

* * *

The State Department's legal adviser recommended the law firm of Reilly, Rhetts, and Ruckelshaus. Gerard Reilly, a labor lawyer, was a good friend of Robert Taft and other respected conservative Republican senators. His partner, Charles Edward Rhetts, a Harvard Law School graduate, had served as assistant attorney general during the New Deal. "Ed and I liked each other as soon as we saw each other," Service recalled. During their first long session, the lawyers probed the diplomat's story in careful detail. The next day, Rhetts announced he would take the case if Service agreed never to take refuge in the Fifth Amendment. The law firm refused to accept a fee but asked that he cover their expenses.[11] Friends at the State Department set up a defense fund, and soon contributions were coming in from Foreign Service officers around the world who read about Service's plight in the American Foreign Service Association Journal.

"The first thing that we did was to go and talk to Currie," Service remembered. "He rather surprised us by saying that he was very sorry, but he felt that we just shouldn't call on him. He wouldn't be able to be of any help."[12] Currie's testimony that Service had sometimes acted on his instructions would have carried considerable weight, and his refusal to testify left Service in an unfavorable position. Service knew that Elizabeth Bentley had named Currie at the 1948 HUAC hearings "but the loyalty board hearings were to be confidential and Lauch's White House position would have given his testimony considerable importance."[13] Later that year, Currie accepted an assignment to do economic development in Colombia, where he lived for many years. John Service would only learn four decades later that the FBI's interest in Currie was in fact based on the Venona decryptions.

* * *

On April 6, Service attended the Tydings Committee's interrogation of Owen Lattimore. "He really got down and slugged it out with McCarthy," Service recalled. "He called McCarthy as many names as McCarthy called him. It wasn't a dignified way to act. We decided it would be better tactics to be low key, to admit some blame . . . some indiscretion."[14] Service's case revolved around the complexities of the conduct of war in China, and Rhetts feared that a vigorous defense might be interpreted as confirming Hurley's charge of politically motivated opposition.[15]

Service, with Rhetts, was now working full time on his defense while remaining on the State Department payroll. He analyzed the transcripts of Senator

McCarthy's remarks to the Senate and to the Tydings Committee. Next to each of McCarthy's false charges he wrote a bright red-penciled "NO," assigning each a number, written neatly inside a circle next to his red-lettered "NO." He tallied twenty false accusations—beginning with the charge that Undersecretary Grew had insisted upon Service's arrest and was therefore forced to resign and ending with the claim that some grand jurors had voted to indict Service on espionage.

The defense team then set about trying to locate government and court documents to disprove the allegations—and finding witnesses willing to testify amid the publicity of a witch hunt. With time and patience, they obtained an incomplete set of copies of his wartime dispatches. Unfortunately, most of Service's personal records—including his notebooks from Yenan—were on the freighter headed to India. Caroline, fearing that they might appear incriminating, had in fact tossed the notebooks overboard—although she never mentioned it to her husband in her letters.

When it leaked to the press that Service was now being given access to official documents, the *Washington Post* headlined its story: "State Department to Let Service See Secret Papers Senate Couldn't—Will Declassify Some Documents to Help Him Prepare Defense for Delayed Loyalty Hearing." The story seemed to confirm McCarthy's claim that Service was one of "the untouchables" still being protected.

The FBI quickly rebuffed Ed Rhetts when he requested a copy of Service's statement made on the night of his arrest. "FBI files are confidential and no information may be disclosed without the Attorney General's direction," he was primly informed.[16] On April 12, Service wrote directly to J. Edgar Hoover, politely asking him to confirm or deny McCarthy's claim that in 1945 he had said the *Amerasia* was a "100 percent airtight case." Promptly, the FBI director responded by saying he had "made no public statement on the *Amerasia* case." Service assumed that the story was merely another McCarthy distortion.[17]

Service sent a flurry of letters to former colleagues and associates who might agree to serve as character references. "I did not 'insist on your prosecution,'" retired Undersecretary of State Joseph Grew responded from Switzerland in reply to Service's query. Grew said he felt "great relief" when Service was cleared by the grand jury and "great satisfaction" when Service was reinstated "with no stigma whatever on your record." McCarthy's charge that Grew had been forced to resign was untrue; in fact he left the State Department "entirely on my own initiative" due to advanced age and ill health, "even though Secretary Byrnes strongly urged me to continue in service."[18]

From around the world came testimonials from friends, former war correspondents, and colleagues offering confirmation of his loyalty. "Mr. Service, though he helped me to understand the basic forces at work in China, never gave me any information secret in nature," CBS newsman Eric Sevareid wrote to the State Loyalty Security Board chairman, calling Service "one of the ablest diplomatic officers I have known in some thirteen years of professional work." Officials in New Zealand's foreign office wrote the State Department expressing concern that "the very men who had seen the China situation correctly were now hounded from positions of influence by those who still identified China with Chiang Kai-shek."[19] From London came a letter from a former Chungking embassy colleague who recalled numerous occasions when, "in his usual colorful language," General Hurley commented about Service. "I can even hear the ring of his voice," Arthur Ringwalt wrote, "when he stated on more than one occasion: 'I will get Service if it is the last thing I do.'"[20]

* * *

Caroline Service arrived in India with the children on April 14. Deeply disappointed that Jack had not yet arrived, she handled alone such practical issues as retrieving their trunks from the Madras docks and paying the children's private school tuition. The family's official travel funds were ending, and she worried about access to funds sent from the State Department while her husband remained in limbo. "Do you suppose the FBI is reading these letters?" she wrote him. "I keep having the oppressive feeling that I am being watched and tracked and that I mustn't talk to anyone." She marveled to her parents at her husband's calm while "trying to prove he is not something he never was." "Do you think," she wondered, "the children are going to be subjected to this kind of persecution when they grow up?"[21]

John Service was kept so busy during the month of April gathering information for his defense that there was little time to keep his family informed of developments. "Days drag on and no word at all from you," lamented his mother in one letter. "It is annoying to know nothing at all save the newspaper yarns. . . . My blood pressure is up—wish I could send doctor's bill to McCarthy!" She implored her son to jot her just a line, because "people ask me every day if I've heard from you." But Grace Service was, as ever, a pillar of strength: "In the end, truth will win; else we, and all we stand for, are lost."[22]

FBI documents, declassified decades later, show that the Bureau did intercept some communications sent to John Service. When William Sebald in Tokyo cabled Service that he had no doubt of his loyalty and was preparing an affidavit, an internal FBI memo reported on those reassurances.[23] The declassified documents also show that favored reporters were often given access to the FBI files. One declassified FBI memo indicates that Scripps-Howard newspaperman Fred Woltman "must have had access to stuff in [FBI] files" to have written his sensational series about the *Amerasia* case (lead article: "The Amerasia Case—Key to US Debacle in China").[24]

When syndicated journalist George Sokolsky broke the story about the secret 1945 OSS raid of the *Amerasia* offices, he actually bragged about his access to FBI files. The stolen materials, he claimed, were "more vital" than the Hiss-Chambers papers—and they included a document about the secret A-bomb project.[25] The story caused a sensation, triggering a flurry of requests to the FBI for more information from the State Department, State's Loyalty Security Board, the President's Loyalty Review Board, and the Justice Department. In May, Frank Bielaski—the OSS agent who led the break-in and told Solkosky he had seen an A-bomb document—appeared on "Meet the Press." When he was later subpoenaed by the Tydings Committee, Service and Rhetts were able to obtain his sworn affidavit about the illegal raid.

* * *

In New Delhi, the Service family was given a warm and sympathetic welcome by Amb. Loy Henderson and his embassy staff. Four-year-old Philip was happily enrolled at a small local kindergarten attended by Indira Gandhi's sons. His brother and sister were enrolled at Woodstock, a boarding school with a fine academic reputation about 170 miles away. They were initially homesick. "Apparently the school is really quite primitive when it comes to living conditions," Caroline wrote her parents. "The only way to get a bath is to lug the water up two flights of stairs in a pail and then sit in a tin tub to take the bath." However, at 7,000 feet elevation, the school had much more comfortable weather than stifling New Delhi. On the weekend, she told her parents, she planned to drive with another mother to Mussoorie to visit the children. "I hate to leave Delhi for even three days as I keep thinking that I should get a cable from Jack in the next few days. It is surely hard not to know what is going on."[26]

* * *

"It looks now as though there is little chance of my reaching India before the end of May," Jack wrote his wife on May 2. "I know you must be perplexed over the delays."[27] Contacting people and lining up affidavits and witnesses for his hearings was taking a tremendous amount of time. And he had decided to testify voluntarily before the Tydings Committee to answer McCarthy's slanderous attacks—so they were now preparing for two separate hearings. There was an "unbelievable delay" in getting documents from State Department files, and less cooperation from the Department of Justice and the FBI. But other efforts were paying off: Ambassador Grew had agreed to be a witness before the State Department's Loyalty Security Board, and Teddy White (now based in Paris) had just sent an affidavit. "This fight is not for you alone—it's for everything good," White declared in his cover letter.[28] Even Joseph Alsop had sent a letter to the Loyalty Board chairman—and had it printed in the *New York Herald Tribune*—saying that, although they had strongly disagreed over policy, he "never had the faintest doubt of the loyalty of any of the American officials or others whom McCarthy has attacked."[29]

McCarthy meanwhile produced an ex-Communist—and paid FBI informant—to testify to the Tydings Committee about Owen Lattimore. The former managing editor of the *Daily Worker*, Louis Budenz, claimed to remember hearing talk about Lattimore at high-level Communist Party meetings. This hearsay evidence supported McCarthy's pivotal contention that Lattimore was part of a Far Eastern conspiracy. "More than any single event," observed a McCarthy biographer, "the Budenz appearance was responsible for keeping Joe in business." Some in the press quickly dubbed the repentant ex-Communist "McCarthy's Whittaker Chambers."[30]

By mid-May, mounting public and political pressure forced Congress to release the transcript of the confidential 1946 Hobbs Committee probe into the alleged *Amerasia* "fix." Most damaging was the disclosure that a former *Amerasia* prosecutor, Robert Hitchcock, had later joined the same Buffalo law firm where Kate Mitchell's uncle was a partner. Newspapers also played up the testimony of James McInerney, now chief of Justice's criminal division (and former *Amerasia* prosecutor), saying that the *Amerasia* investigation was "clumsily handled" and proclaiming that most of the recovered documents were unimportant "teacup gossip." The implication that the FBI had bungled the case reignited the long-standing feud between the FBI and the Justice Department.

Hoover ordered his deputies to find the original case memos showing that Justice officials—including McInerney—had been fully informed about the investigation before giving the green light for the arrests. These documents were hand-delivered to the deputy attorney general—along with a sharp verbal reprimand—by Lou Nichols, the FBI's deputy director for public affairs. It was "pretty weak to try to pass the buck," Nichols told Peyton Ford. "If the taint was there, then why didn't somebody think about it before authorizing the arrests?" After reading Nichol's detailed report of the conversation, Hoover scribbled a note of praise: "At last for the *first* time to my knowledge we are fighting back. We most certainly shouldn't take the pushing around we have been getting."[31]

* * *

McCarthy's supposed list of subversives working for the State Department still had not been revealed. "Lay the evidence before us and sustain it," Senator Tydings repeatedly instructed. "Otherwise it's just a lot of hocus-pocus." The Wisconsin senator now insisted that the proof could be found in the loyalty files that President Truman was refusing to furnish. "I don't answer accusations," McCarthy explained to a Senate colleague, "I make them."[32]

In the face of continuing charges from Republicans of a partisan cover-up, Truman finally agreed to allow the Tydings Committee to look at the confidential files of about eighty State Department employees—but only at the White House and under the strict supervision of the State Department Loyalty Board's chairman. Tydings and his committee began a daily trek up Pennsylvania Avenue to review the stacks of sensitive files. If Truman's decision to open the files was intended to discredit McCarthy and take the heat off Tydings, it backfired badly. Instead, it appeared that the president was caving in to the senator from Wisconsin. McCarthy even managed to make headlines out of the lack of incriminating evidence by declaring the files must have been "raped" and telltale evidence removed.[33]

"There are so damned many investigations going on and so many people tramping around the woods that we have run into a sort of stall," Service wrote in frustration to his brother Dick.[34] And to Caroline he wrote: "I am sorry that this [delay] is going to mean that I will have to miss the children on their vacation, but there is no help for it." He and Rhetts were working "both night and day." He reassured her that soon she would be receiving four hundred dollars a month for family living expenses; he was economizing by staying with friends.[35]

Caroline felt as if she were living in "suspended animation": "almost every decision I make is dependent on your plans." To her parents she wrote: "Poor Jack. What a wretched time he must be having. I keep thinking of such insignificant items as what he is doing for clothes. All his warm weather things are here and Washington must be getting good and hot. . . . I wish I knew how the lawyers are to be paid. They can't work for nothing."[36]

* * *

Meanwhile, on orders from the embattled State Department, the FBI had opened a new loyalty investigation of Service. On May 10 he was interrogated by FBI agents—this time, following up on the tip about the weekend he and Roth spent as Lattimore's houseguests, just prior to their arrests. A Johns Hopkins professor and his wife had written McCarthy claiming to have seen Lattimore, Service, and Roth declassifying documents. Firmly denying their allegation, Service explained that the three men had gone upstairs to discuss Roth's unfinished book manuscript; otherwise, the weekend had been strictly a social get-together.[37] Service never forgot those FBI interrogations. "You're always alone, and there are two of them," he later reflected. "You don't know what they write down, what notes they take. . . . Then even that is probably selected again for writing up their report."[38]

Throughout the spring, FBI agents fanned out across the country searching for witnesses to provide damaging information against Service. Wedemeyer told agents that when he "inherited" Service from Stilwell, he found Service's reporting "uniformly favorable" to the Chinese Communists and "very critical" of the Nationalist Government. Nevertheless, the retired general did "not believe that Service was disloyal."[39]

In Boston, agents twice interviewed Milton "Mary" Miles. He was now a rear admiral, although removed from China and suffering from drug abuse and a mental breakdown in September 1945. He told agents about his SACO work with Chiang's secret police chief, who had died in a mysterious plane crash in 1947. The agents reported that Miles had seen Tai Li's files on Service and John Paton Davies, indicating that Service "consorted with representatives of Chinese Communist 'government' at Yenan; attempted to direct the services of OSS into developing a stronger Chinese Communist Army; [and] attempted to destroy the reputation of [Tai Li]." Miles also claimed that Service and his colleagues "contributed to the present attainment of power in China by the Chinese Communists." However, he refused their invitation to testify.[40]

Former ambassador Patrick Hurley was interviewed several times that spring, but he too declined to testify. One FBI agent prepared this "synopsis of facts": "[Hurley] considered Service sabotaging American policy and working for Chinese Communists against United States interest. He requested Service to be discharged . . . based on secret documents re: American policy to be followed in China found in the hands of the Chinese Communists and believed to have been furnished by Service."[41] Hoover sent confidential update reports with these unsubstantiated allegations to officials at various government agencies and shared them with selected anti-Communist politicians and journalists. Decades later, these declassified documents provide insight into the FBI mindset—and they reveal why Hoover believed John Service was a serious security risk, unfit for government service.

* * *

McCarthy continued to repeat Hoover's remark about *Amerasia* being "a 100 percent airtight case" so often that—following up on Hoover's assurance to Service that he had never made the remark publicly—the State Department finally sent an official query to the Justice Department. The assistant attorney general replied that Hoover never said it. A signed copy was routinely sent to Hoover, and he angrily objected—but it was too late. John Peurifoy at State had already received Justice's reassurance, and had promptly released it to the press.[42]

Outraged at the morning news headlines, Hoover sent his deputies to lodge a protest. The embarrassed Justice official claimed that his draft letter had been "signed thoughtlessly" and "inadvertently mailed" before he received Hoover's feedback. Hoover sent a scalding memo of his own: "In the event I had been asked at the time the arrests were made whether I thought we had an airtight case, I would have stated that I thought we had. Further, if I were asked today, I would have to so state." He also denounced Justice Department assertions that illegal FBI entries had spoiled the prosecution of *Amerasia* defendants: "[The issue] certainly has no bearing on the case of John Stewart Service, since at no time did Agents of the FBI ever enter his residence until June 6 when they entered with a warrant of address." As if scolding an errant child, Hoover added, "it is my considered opinion that you should realize the unfairness at this late date to try to place blame on the FBI."[43]

Nevertheless, a few days later, Justice's James McInerney testified at a closed-door Tydings Committee session that the FBI director had never made the "100 percent airtight" remark. Hoping to mollify Hoover by shifting blame to the defunct OSS (now supplanted by the CIA), he asserted that the case was "fatally vulnerable" because the illegal OSS raid "tainted" the FBI's investigation. McInerney also said that prosecutors were "well convinced" of Service's innocence even before the grand jury voted unanimously not to indict him. In fact, he testified, Larsen had admitted being the "main abstractor" of stolen documents, and his fingerprints were found on many of the official copies of Service's reports discovered in Jaffe's office. Again, McInerney characterized the vast majority of recovered documents as "very innocuous" and "little above the level of teacup gossip in the Far East"—using almost the same description he had given to the Hobbs Committee four years earlier.[44] When asked if he knew of anything that would "justify the use of the word 'fix'" in characterizing the case, McInerney replied, with his poker face in place, "No sir; and he has denied it."[45]

FBI officials quickly learned about his secret testimony, and—armed with their knowledge of the tapped phone calls between Corcoran and McGranery—they immediately escalated their war with the Justice Department. Two veteran FBI agents from the *Amerasia* investigation were preparing testimony for the Tydings Committee. Hoover sent his trusted deputy, Lou Nichols, to visit the assistant attorney general, Peyton Ford, with a warning: his agents might drop a bombshell about the Currie-Cohen-Corcoran efforts to influence the Justice Department. "I told him the highlights of the whole matter are these: Lauchlin

Currie of the White House was obviously interested in Service. Corcoran and Currie had several conversations, [and] as early as June 11, 1945, Corcoran was saying he didn't think the case would ever be tried," Nichols reported to Hoover.

Ford was also told of Corcoran's wiretapped phone conversations with Attorney General Tom Clark and his top assistant, James McGranery, regarding Service's grand jury appearance—and his boast that it was "triple riveted." Immediately Ford protested that such dirty linen could never be revealed. "I told him of course we didn't want to admit it, but if we were ever *forced* into a position the only thing we could do would be to tell the truth." Within days, Hoover himself followed up, telling Peyton Ford he was "outraged" over McInerney's suggestion "that the FBI was the only one at fault" in the *Amerasia* case. "I stated that if the documents were actually silly or 'teacup gossip' as he put it, then we should not have made the investigation, nor arrested people."[46]

The FBI reinforced its threat by alerting the friendly media. A *Washington Daily News* article by the crusading Fred Woltman now suggested names of possible witnesses for Tyding's hearings: "Call Supreme Court Justice Tom Clark (he was Attorney General when case disposed of) and ask him who talked with him about the case, what was said, what was agreed to." The reporter also suggested that McGranery, Clark's former top assistant—now a federal judge—should be asked who talked to him about the case. "In other words," railed Woltman, "find out about the fix."[47]

* * *

On May 26, 1950, newspapers around the country broke the startling news that a second Soviet spy had been arrested for stealing wartime atomic secrets. After a long investigation (aided by Venona project decrypts), Harry Gold, a chemist, had confessed to FBI agents in Philadelphia. Gold's identity had been confirmed by Klaus Fuchs, the spy now imprisoned in London. Within three weeks, the FBI would pick up another A-bomb spy, David Greenglass, who would lead agents to the arrest of several more—including the ringleader: his brother-in-law, Julius Rosenberg.

On the same day that Harry Gold's arrest was announced, John Service's State Department loyalty hearing finally got under way—more than two months after his return to Washington. Suspicions that had shadowed him for the past five years were now headline news. In the minds of many Americans, Gold's arrest became intertwined with news of other shocking revelations—such as John Service's comments about "secret military plans" and Bielaski's claim of seeing an A-bomb document at *Amerasia*'s office. By the time Service's loyalty hearing got under way, he had become a lightning rod for the United States' growing anti-Communist hysteria.

CHAPTER 19
THE HEARINGS

At ten o'clock on a Friday morning in late May 1950, the State Department's Loyalty Security Board hearing opened with a reading of the formal charges against John S. Service:

> That] you are a member or in sympathetic association with the Communist Party which has been designated by the Attorney General as an organization which seeks to alter the form of government of the United States by unconstitutional means; and further that . . . you are a person who has habitual or close association with persons known or believed to be in the category . . . to an extent which would justify the conclusion that you might, through such association, voluntarily or involuntarily divulge classified information without authority.[1]

For the next four weeks, John Service and his attorney, Ed Rhetts, participated in 15 grueling sessions, generating a 516-page transcript. Rhetts provided the three panel members a detailed "document book," including Service's 46-page personal statement, a chronology of events, an annotated list of Service's reports (with excerpts), and a tabulated list of all the charges made by politicians and pundits, as reported in the media. Additional documents included excerpts from the *Congressional Record*, the Hobbs Committee probe, the China White Paper, and selected news clips, all organized for easy reference.

The charges against his client, Rhetts told the panel, would be addressed in three phases: Service's duty in China, his involvement in the *Amerasia* case, and his Tokyo assignment. He identified General Hurley as "the grandfather" of all the China charges, parroted by many others and "most recently repeated over and over by Senator McCarthy."[2]

The defense faced significant problems. Currie had refused to testify about his role in encouraging Service's media contacts, and Stilwell and Atcheson had died. But the greatest difficulty they faced was the general atmosphere of fear and distrust. "Chiang Kai-shek was still a hero and we really couldn't get very far on the idea that Chiang Kai-shek was hopeless," Service later reflected. "It was an impossible basis for our arguments." It was equally hopeless to argue that, in 1944, "Mao Tse-tung was really more of a nationalist than a Communist and we were kind of winning them away from Moscow."[3] Moreover, Service and Rhetts did not know what (if any) evidence the FBI had collected, and the diplomat had none of the rights recognized in a court of law.

* * *

"You gentlemen, I am sure, already know a good deal about me," John Service told the loyalty board after being sworn in, "but perhaps you will allow me first to give a consecutive summary of my background and career." After describing his early life in China and his education, he turned to his diplomatic career. China was a weak and backward country, undergoing a revolution that was "one of the great changes of history." As a U.S. Foreign Service officer, he had tried to find solutions to China's problems that would "best serve the long-range interests of the United States . . . within American capabilities and willingness to act"—an effort that had "led to my present difficulties."[4]

Service then addressed several controversial episodes of his work in China—as an instigator of the Dixie Mission, and as the translator of Roosevelt's tough "eyes alone" telegrams to Chiang Kai-shek. "I have been sure since then my presence on these unpleasant occasions helped to contribute to [Nationalist] Chinese animosity toward me."

He defended his October 10, 1944, memo to General Stilwell, which Hurley and others claimed was a plan to bring about the collapse of the Nationalist government. "[The memo] was an attempt to refute the argument so commonly advanced that we were dependent on Chiang and that if he were to fall, Chinese resistance to Japan would collapse. I did not advocate the abandonment of Chiang but rather a more realistic policy toward him."[5]

In a clear, calm voice, Service methodically refuted other Hurley accusations. The board had invited Hurley to appear as a witness, but he declined. Nevertheless, Rhetts cited his public comments to score some points:

Rhetts: Am I correct that [Document] 35-18 is as extensive an expression of General Hurley's views that the Chinese Communists are not really Communist and the Russians are not really interested in them. Is that a fair statement?

Service: It is an extensive and repeated statement of that view.

Rhetts: I would like to ask you if you shared General Hurley's views that the Chinese Communists were not real Communists at all?

Service: [In] a memorandum I drafted at Yenan on March 23, 1945, I make it very clear that there is contact between the Chinese Communists and Moscow despite the Chinese Communists denials. . . . In Document 168 which I prepared on August 3, 1944, I state: "The Chinese Communist Party claims it is Marxist . . . to which all short-term considerations of temporary advantage or premature power are ruthlessly subordinated."

Rhetts: I take it then it was your view that the Chinese Communist Party was essentially Marxist?

Service: Certainly.[6]

Rhetts also provided Service the opportunity to respond on the record to McCarthy's widely publicized allegations:

Rhetts: Referring, Mr. Service, to charges by Senator McCarthy, . . . I would like to ask if you ever expressed the view that Communism represented the best hope of China or the best hope of Asia.

Service: I would say the best summary is contained in document 192, which I drafted on October 9, 1944 . . . "from the basic fact that the Communists built up popular support of a magnitude and depth which makes their elimination impossible, we must draw the conclusion that the Communists will have a certain and important share in China's future. . . . I suggest the further conclusion that unless the Kuomintang [Nationalist Party] goes as far as the Communists in political and economic reform, and otherwise proves itself able to contest this leadership of the people . . . the Communists will be the dominant force in China within a comparatively few years."

Rhetts: That, I take it was a political prediction based upon your observation of political facts?

Service: That is correct.

Rhetts: Was it in any sense a statement of your aspirations or hopes?

Service: It certainly was not.[7]

Next the board chairman asked about the Tydings testimony of OSS agent Bielaski: "Did you at that time [1944] have any knowledge of the Manhattan project?" Service patiently explained that, like most Americans, he learned of the secret atomic project only after the first bomb was dropped on Japan.[8]

Another member of the loyalty panel asked if the diplomat knew a Chinese actress named Val Chao and whether she had any Soviet associates. Service acknowledged knowing Chao but denied knowing of any Soviet acquaintances. "Did you ever by any chance," probed his interrogator, "disclose to her any classified information?" "Certainly not," replied Service, without mentioning their love affair.

The board, however, had undoubtedly seen an FBI report of a 1949 interview with a former naval intelligence officer who had heard that Service contemplated divorcing his wife to marry a Chinese actress. Moreover, the FBI's New York office had recently received a tip about a Chinese woman—"an ardent Communist"—who "influenced Service to be sympathetic toward Russia" and was now "teaching in New Haven."[9]

* * *

The next day Rhetts called Service's first two witnesses: ambassadors Nelson Johnson and Clarence Gauss. "Both were superb," Service wrote his mother. "Johnson, incidentally, mentioned knowing you and father in Chungking in the early twenties and spoke of your fine reputation."[10] In his thirty-nine years of service, Ambassador Gauss told the panel, he had never met a Foreign Service officer "who impressed me more favorably than Jack Service."[11] And Gauss had nothing but contempt for his own successor. "I am sorry General Hurley isn't here because I would call him a liar to his face. There was never at any time any suggestion of disloyalty on the part of Mr. Service . . . or any of the other members of my staff in Chungking with reference to American policy in China or any desire to bring about the collapse of the Chiang Kai-shek's government."[12]

The featured witness at the third session was George Kennan, one of the architects of America's containment policy toward the Soviet Union and the director of the State Department's influential Policy Planning Group. "I find no indication that [Service's] reports reported anything but his best judgment candidly stated to the Department," Kennan told the loyalty panel. "On the contrary, the general level of thoughtfulness and intellectual flexibility which pervades the reporting is such that it seems to me out of the question that it could be the work of a man with a closed mind or with ideological preconceptions."

Kennan found Service's Yenan reports and his interviews with Communist leaders "highly pertinent" to the war effort and likened them to his own efforts in Moscow "to tap the views of the Soviet leaders and to report them faithfully to this Government." Had Kennan found any suggestion in Service's reports, the board chairman asked, "to torpedo or sabotage" the official American policy in China? He had not. In fact, the dispatches consistently urged finding a political accommodation between Chiang's government and the Chinese Communists to avoid a civil war. "What bewilders me here is that they advocated . . . the same thing that General Hurley was advocating." Kennan reminded the panel of Hurley's statement that there was "no stronger advocate of negotiations between the Chinese Communists and the Chinese Government than himself."[13]

"Did you find any indication in Mr. Service's reports of a desire on his part for extension of Soviet domination into Asia?" asked the third member of the panel. On the contrary, Kennan said, Service warned about just such a possibility. He quoted from a report he found particularly perceptive: "Chiang unwittingly may be contributing to Russian dominance in eastern Asia by internal and external policies which, if pursued in their present form, will render China too weak to serve as a possible counterweight to Russia."[14]

Kennan also told the panel that Stalin had been "too preoccupied" resisting the German attack to bother much about Mao's guerrillas. "The [Chinese] Communists felt themselves on their own and were themselves uncertain how their relationship with the Soviet Government was going to shape up when the war was over. It is quite plausible that during those years they wandered further from the typical Comintern outlook of affiliation with the Soviet Government than perhaps any Communist Party in good standing has ever wandered." Service had recommended closer cooperation with Mao's forces as a way of keeping them out of the Soviet orbit, even after the war.

Kennan followed with a startling assessment: "I cannot be sure in my own mind that the view reflected in [Service's] reports might not have been accurate, and that if we had not supported the Central Government at all after the war, if we ourselves had taken a more or less equal attitude toward the two regimes, it is possible that these things would not have turned out in the way that they did."[15]

* * *

On the last day of May the defense began to address the *Amerasia* case. Emmanuel "Jimmy" Larsen—"the man who has done such harm by smearing the others in efforts to clear himself"—made a significant admission. His *Plain Talk* article had been written mainly by [Isaac] Don Levine, Kohlberg's associate, and Larsen now repudiated its litany of outrageous charges that had been so readily accepted by the China Lobby. Rhetts underscored Larsen's startling act of contrition:

Larsen: I did not write that at all, that Mr. Service was in communication with Mr. Jaffe. They [Levine and Kohlberg] told me about it and it is not in my original manuscript.

Rhetts: Did they give you the facts which supported that assertion?

Larsen: No, they did not.

Rhetts: Nonetheless you permitted it to be published under your name?
Larsen: Yes, on the grounds that my knowledge of the case was insufficient, and as Mr. Levine said, we were collaborating on the article.

Rhetts asked Larsen about the published assertion that John Service had sabotaged Hurley and been "a leader of the pro-Soviet group" at the State Department.

Rhetts: You are aware, are you not, Mr. Larsen, that this statement, like all the other statements in this article, have been repeated by Senator McCarthy as a part of the charges which have been made against Mr. Service?
Larsen: Yes, I am aware of that; very much so.
Rhetts: As I understand you, you repudiate the authorship of this and all other statements we have discussed.
Larsen: Yes I would.[16]

While Larsen was recanting his published story at Service's State Department hearing, across town the FBI was settling scores with the Justice Department in testimony at the Tydings Committee. To prove its investigation had not been botched, two of Hoover's top lieutenants provided damaging testimony against Service. They falsely claimed that Service "admitted removing classified documents from the State Department" and even implied that he had furnished confidential documents to Tung Pi-wu, the Chinese Communist representative who met with him in Washington after the UN conference. "As a further illustration of the operations of this group, Service met with Jaffe in his hotel room on May 8, 1945," Mickey Ladd testified. "Service discussed military, political, and policy matters with Jaffe and cautioned him by saying: 'Well, what I said about the military plans is, of course, very secret.'"[17] For the first time, the agents now disclosed the verbatim comments picked up during its illegal technical surveillance of Jaffe's hotel room—and their confidential testimony was quickly leaked to the press.

* * *

On the fifth day of his hearing, John Service testified about his encounters with Jaffe and the other *Amerasia* suspects. He admitted loaning Jaffe "eight or ten" personal carbon copies of some Yenan reports in 1945. "It was not unusual to allow writers to have access to this type of factual material for background purposes," Service told the board. "It was not, however, customary to loan such material and I have always regretted having turned it over to Jaffe, although at that time I had no reason to doubt his responsibility."[18]

However, Service was "at a loss" to explain how his other memos had ended up with *Amerasia.* To prove that none of his other reports seized by the FBI had been supplied by Service himself, Rhetts began a careful examination of employees from the State Department's printing office regarding the special reproduction process for official copies. He asked Service detailed questions about seized copies bearing official stamps from the State Department and the OSS. Rhetts also succeeded in getting into the record excerpts of Justice officials' testimony from the Hobbs and Tydings hearings, noting the "thin evidence" on Service as well as the discovery of Larsen's fingerprints on some of Service's purloined reports. He also introduced the exchange of letters between Service and Hoover regarding the oft-repeated "100 percent airtight" remark, emphasizing Hoover's reply: he had "made no public statement on the *Amerasia* case."

"It is a grueling business," John Service wrote his mother, after seven sessions in eight days. "Naturally I am tired—mentally and physically." There had been several valuable affidavits and favorable testimony by wartime associates, such as the former G-2 intelligence chief and John Davies. But, Jack cautioned his mother, "we are not yet out of the woods." He lamented that the *Amerasia* case had not been "better handled and completely solved" back in 1945 and that a "thorough investigation of me and my 'loyalty' wasn't made" at the outset.[19]

But by now, the *Amerasia* case had taken on a life of its own. Many Republicans up for reelection had joined forces with McCarthy, putting the administration on the defensive. The FBI was engaged in "a bitter intramural fight" with the Justice Department—and had leaked information from the taped hotel room conversations to selected politicians and journalists. Jack assured his mother that the information did not prove anything except that he had been indiscreet in his criticism of Hurley and the handling of China affairs. "It doesn't matter much in the present atmosphere that I was right, or that the background of the strength of my feelings was the certainty that we were going to lose China. If I do get dragged into a public investigation, be tough, because it is not going to be entirely pleasant." He advised her to share his letter "only with family or *very* close and trusted friends."[20]

* * *

On June 6, the Scripps-Howard newspapers ran another exposé by Fred Woltman based on new tips from the FBI. A "controversial 'eyes only' *Amerasia* document . . . revealed a top secret wartime plan of President Roosevelt and Chiang Kai-shek" to put Stilwell in charge of all of China's armies shortly before the general was recalled—and the president's top secret cables had been translated by John S. Service. "The fact is," Woltman wrote, "[the secret plan] found its way into the

Amerasia files. And the aim of *Amerasia* magazine was to mold American opinion in favor of a Communist China."[21]

The Woltman story forced Service and Rhetts to change their game plan. Instead of proceeding to the "Tokyo phase" of their case, Service responded directly to the new revelations, admitting that he had told journalist Mark Gayn about his role as translator of the president's "eyes alone" cables. Gayn was then writing about General Stilwell's controversial recall, and Service now recalled that his wife had taken notes during their breakfast chat. Those notes might have been shared with Jaffe—and a typed memo thus ended up in *Amerasia*'s files. But by the time of his conversation with Gayn, the aborted plan to put Stilwell in charge of Chinese forces had already been widely reported; his role as translator merely added a colorful detail for Gayn's story. The *New York Times*' former war correspondent Brooks Atkinson—the first reporter to publish a story about Stilwell's recall—rushed to Washington to appear as a defense witness. Atkinson assured the panel that Service, who was then stationed in Yenan, was not a source for his story. Their first conversation about it was when they shared an airplane on the way back to the States.[22]

* * *

Caroline Service rarely heard news from her preoccupied husband and often felt as if she were "living on another planet." Yet, as she confessed to her parents, being in India provided a kind of sanctuary for the family during his ordeal. And Caroline admitted enjoying her curious status, serving on occasion as Ambassador Henderson's hostess at diplomatic events. Had she been home, she knew she'd have been "nothing but a burden to Jack."[23] Her husband later agreed: "She would have driven everybody nuts."[24]

* * *

On June 15 the FBI office in New Haven cabled to Hoover that they now believed the Chinese mystery woman was Val Chao, "one of foremost actresses on the modern stage of China." She was no longer in New Haven, but she had attended Yale after the war. They reported finding "no indication of any Communist Party activity," but they had discovered the actress had given birth to an illegitimate baby girl in a New York hospital in September 1946. Hoover immediately wanted to know whether she "might have been the 'leak' through which information from General Hurley's office reached the Chinese Communists." He demanded a report by June 22, the day John Service was scheduled to begin testifying before the Senate's Tydings Committee.[25]

An urgent "personal & confidential" cable from New Haven soon arrived with a juicy new tidbit for the FBI director. "The suggestion is respectfully offered that the Bureau may desire to consider the possibility of Service's being the father of this [illegitimate] child." The New York birth certificate had listed a "John Hsieh" as the father; although the name had been crossed out, it was still visible. A Chinese informant told them "Hsieh" was Chinese name given to Service's family soon after his father's arrival in 1906.[26]

* * *

By 1950 Val Chao had disappeared behind the Bamboo Curtain. Alumni records at the Yale Drama School gave her address as The Academy of Dramatic Arts, 12 Cotton Lane, "Peiping." To the suspicious FBI agents, the mere fact of an address in "Red China" confirmed her Communist sympathies. In fact after leaving the United States when her student visa expired, Chao had spent several months seeking work in London and Paris before arriving in Hong Kong. In February 1950, after the civil war had subsided, she arrived back in China. "I wanted to take a look and see if it is good to stay," Chao explained many years later. "Otherwise, I want to come back to America with my daughter. That was my plan."

Chao had been welcomed in Shanghai as a respected artist and was reunited with her daughter, who had been in the care of her mother. She was invited to become a principal actor with the People's Theater and a teacher at the drama school in Peking. Her family was given good housing and she received special ration cards and other privileges, including a permit to shop at the store reserved for foreigners, where she could buy American cigarettes. Curiously, the Yale Drama School alumni magazine arrived regularly in the mail for nearly ten years, in spite of the American embargo. "I got them," Val Chao recalled more than forty years later, "but I can't reply."[27]

* * *

Service and his attorney quickly dispensed with allegations regarding his duty in Tokyo—the claim that he had met with a Japanese Communist Party leader (whom he first met in Yenan) and that he supported the party's political agenda. William Sebald had cabled from Tokyo that Service "took no part" in the interview of the Japanese Communist leader, and that he had "no reason whatsoever" to doubt Service's loyalty.[28] "We produced affidavits or had personal testimony from every man who was in the [Tokyo] office there with me—except the one person who is obviously the accuser, the unnamed 'confidential informant' of the FBI," Service reported to his mother. Max Bishop had refused Service's request to testify, apparently because he "didn't have the guts to face cross examination."[29]

On June 19—at Service's fourteenth appearance before the loyalty board—questions were asked about the personal items illegally seized from his office desk by the FBI on the night of his arrest. A judge had ordered the return of Service's personal property. Such evidence was inadmissible in a courtroom, but not in the loyalty hearing. Here, the FBI's illegal copies of its illegal discoveries became a major topic of inquiry.

Service was also asked about the list of code names seized at the time of his arrest. Who was "Snow White"? ("Madam Chiang Kai-shek.") Why was Washington known as "asylum"? ("It is sophomoric perhaps.") And what was the significance of designating "Harvard" as the code name for the Communists? ("None whatsoever.") Service explained that the codes were "simply a list of names that John Davies and Ray Ludden and John Emmerson and I arranged between ourselves for use in correspondence, since that correspondence might conceivably fall into enemy hands if a plane was lost over the Hump."[30]

* * *

Service was excused by the loyalty board for a couple of days to prepare for his voluntary appearance at the Tydings Committee hearing amid continuing attacks in the partisan press. New allegations from Hurley's most recent "confidential" FBI interview were leaked to the *Washington Evening Star*: Service had provided Mao with "secret information," and his State Department clique planned "to sabotage the American system of government and American policy in China."[31]

Rather than testify behind closed doors like other witnesses, John Service insisted on appearing in a public session before the Tydings Committee. "McCarthy was so unscrupulous and tricky about leaking stuff that had gone on in executive hearings," he later explained, "that we wanted to have it all out in public." Permission for the unprecedented public session was granted only at the last minute, and only a few of his friends managed to attend.[32] "Jack looked amazingly fresh and dapper," reported Helen Service, in a letter to family members.

"As an American citizen," Service stated, "there is nothing more important to me than my good name and reputation for loyalty. These charges, repeated in the face of all the evidence which refutes them, are as false today as they were when they were uttered in 1945 and when they were repeated by various persons, including Congressmen Judd, Dondero, *Plain Talk*, and McCarthy before your committee."[33]

As Service began reading his prepared statement, Senator McCarthy slipped into the chamber and seated himself behind Senator Tydings, directly opposite the witness table. "He sat there scowling the whole morning," Service recalled. Press photographers scrambled, angling for shots of the adversaries.[34]

"Much has also been said about my contacts with Chinese Communists," Service continued calmly. "Active cultivation of these contacts was a basic and vital part of my full-time assignment," and through such contacts he obtained "valuable first-hand information for which I have been commended by both the Department of State and the United States Army."[35]

Rhetts introduced into the record the 1945 letter of commendation from General Wedemeyer recognizing Service's "outstanding performance of duty" in providing advice on political matters. In sharp contrast to the recent news reports, Wedemeyer's letter praised Service's "thorough knowledge of Chinese customs and language" that enabled him to establish "cordial relations with Mao Tse-tung, Chu Teh and other Communist leaders."[36]

It was noon before Service finished reading his prepared statement and began answering questions. Finally, as they were leaving the caucus room for the lunch recess, a photographer asked Service if he could get a photo of him standing by the caucus room door. "To hell with it," he replied irritably. "You guys have been taking pictures all morning [and] I just want to go and have some lunch." Ed Rhetts intervened, and Service reluctantly agreed to pose. "And then right out from behind the door popped Joseph McCarthy. He'd put this photographer up to it. So, we got this picture of startled me."[37] That photo would be featured in newspapers across the country.

During the afternoon session, the minority counsel, Robert Morris, began a harsh cross-examination of the witness. (Morris had secretly coached Louis Budenz, the former Communist and paid FBI informant who had accused Service of being "Owen Lattimore's pupil.") He read aloud brief excerpts from some of Service's China reports regarding the "democratic character" of the Communists. Service refused to rise to the bait. "My use of the word 'democracy' requires a great deal of explanation, and that is why I do not think it fair to take brief excerpts. . . . I am reporting to people who have a very long and developed background concerning China." Those professionals would understand that "that word 'democracy' is used in a comparative sense, as compared to conditions, perhaps, in [Nationalist] areas, and not as compared to the United States."[38]

When Service referred to the favorable review by George Kennan, presented to the State Department's loyalty board, Morris dismissed its significance. Kennan, after all, was another employee of the tainted State Department—and he worked closely with Service's friend, John Paton Davies. Morris then demanded to know if John S. Service had ever been a member of the Communist Party, a suggestion the Foreign Service officer emphatically denied. It was nearly seven o'clock in the evening when the hearing adjourned, and Service's voice had grown hoarse. "All during this long hard day," a friend later reported to Service's family, "Jack's voice and manner was never anything but pleasant, dignified and helpful. . . . He never lost his composure."[39]

The next morning, fresh revelations from McCarthy again dominated the news headlines—and trumped the story about Service's public testimony. McCarthy disclosed that the FBI had given the Tydings Committee information gleaned from its hidden microphone about Service's hotel chat with Jaffe—including the quote: "Well, what I said about the military plans is, of course, very secret." A few publications took a firm stand against the senator. "Senator McCarthy's attacks on Mr. Service's performance as a political intelligence officer first to Gen. Stilwell and then to Gen. Wedemeyer, are simply contemptible," declared a *Washington Post* editorial. Service's only crime had been to be "prematurely right" about the outcome of the civil war in China.[40]

The Tydings Committee and the State Department's Loyalty Security Board now demanded access to the FBI hotel transcripts. Despite his initial shock, Jack now explained to Caroline that this development might work in his favor: "We feel that they may expose the thing publicly in a way which we would be unable to do, because the material is not available to us."[41] Justice officials, however, refused to release the transcripts, after its lawyers asserted the illegal recordings were inadmissible as evidence. "I don't agree," Hoover scrawled on the bottom of one memo. "I want all on Service given. This is a loyalty proceeding and the rule of evidence doesn't apply."[42]

That afternoon, Service's lawyer formally requested that the senators demand the FBI recording of the alleged 1945 hotel room conversation. Senator Tydings admitted that for two weeks he had been trying to get hold of the FBI's record of the Service-Jaffe conversations, but his request had been denied. "To take one sentence out of a purported telephone or surveillance conversation and utilize it for any purpose is not fair," Tydings complained. "It is not good Americanism, it is not good law, and it is not in the interest of serving the public, who want to know the truth about this matter."[43] The chairman told committee members to refrain from asking questions about the issue until he asked again for the controversial material.

Morris, the hostile minority counsel, peppered Service with questions about people in his address book. Did he know Sol Adler—the Treasury official recently grilled by the HUAC? Yes, they had shared living quarters in Chungking for about a year, but he had not seen him lately. "Did you during that period of time realize that Mr. Adler was a Communist?" asked Morris. "Certainly not," replied Service. Morris then inquired if Service knew Adler had been identified by Elizabeth Bentley in her HUAC testimony as "a full-fledged member of her espionage ring."[44] Service said he only heard of the accusations secondhand.

Rapid-fire questions followed about other names. Had he realized Mr. Jaffe was a Communist? "I had been specifically told that he was *not* a Communist."

What about Louis Budenz's charge that he had been "Lattimore's pupil"? "Mr. Budenz is entirely wrong": he first met Lattimore in Peking in 1936 while in language training, and had seen him infrequently during the war years. Morris rattled off the names of several others before commenting, "I say, it seems incomprehensible to me that you should have no inkling in every case that any one of these people was a Communist or Soviet espionage agent." "The charges against many of these people were made years later," Service observed, and "most of them have not been proved."[45]

Before the hearing adjourned for the weekend, the minority counsel turned to Hurley's allegations. "Is it your testimony you never disobeyed orders of General Hurley not to go to Yenan?" Morris asked. "I knew of no such orders, and General Hurley was not in a position to give me such orders," Service replied calmly. "I went there under orders of United States Army headquarters in China."[46]

* * *

On Saturday morning, Service appeared once again before the State Department's loyalty board for his fifteenth and final session. The taped hotel conversation with Jaffe was the first topic. The chairman, like Tydings, had attempted unsuccessfully to obtain the FBI's full transcript. He assured Service that the panel "will give you its best knowledge of what these statements consisted of."[47] Again Service explained that he had no specific recollection of their meeting or of the context for his alleged remarks. Perhaps he had generally discussed a contingency plan for American landing forces to cooperate with whatever Chinese forces they found but without knowing "when we were going to land, or where, or whether we would."[48]

For two and a half hours, Service answered follow-up questions on the entire range of accusations. Finally he was asked to summarize his thoughts about Communism and democracy. "We in the United States have been able to achieve a balance between the protection of the rights of the individual and the affording of the fullest opportunity for improvement and advancement with competition and encouragement and free enterprise, all of which I think are important," Service told the loyalty board. "I think it's obvious that I am not a Communist."[49] The month-long examination of John Service by State Department's Loyalty Security Board ended at 12:50 PM on June 24—with no indication of when they would make the fateful decision on his loyalty.

Service and Rhetts spent Sunday, June 25, trying to anticipate the unknown in the next Tydings' session—and the contents of the FBI's private files. "The strangest role of all in this has been that of the Bureau." Service remarked. "Against this sort of thing, one is defenseless."[50]

Late in the afternoon, their work was interrupted by a shocking radio news bulletin: North Korea had invaded South Korea with 90,000 troops equipped with Soviet tanks and artillery. The surprise assault fanned the United States' fears about the growing menace of Communism—and the threat of internal subversion.

* * *

"It is for the most part unintelligible," Ed Rhetts told the Tydings Committee after reading the FBI transcript. "It is internally inconsistent, and as I say, largely gibberish." Rather than read the "very poor transcription," he suggested they listen to the actual recording of the hotel conversation.[51] But after checking with the FBI, the Justice Department reported that the original recording had been destroyed. (More than thirty years later, declassified FBI documents indicated that the original May 8, 1945, recording was actually kept for several more years; the FBI was lying.[52])

* * *

No further revelations regarding secret military plans were revealed in the sketchy transcript. Yet the written transcript did reveal Service's friendly—even chummy—relationship with the editor. When Sen. Henry Cabot Lodge Jr. asked to question the witness, he focused on Service's comment about secret military plans:

Lodge: It gives the impression that you were telling him not to reveal what you said about military plans because they were secret.

Service: I chose my words in what I was saying very unwisely, because I was not revealing any military plans. I had no knowledge of the military plans.

Lodge: You think you misspoke?

Service: I think I misspoke. Yes.[53]

When asked for the names of Wedemeyer's staff who showed him the plan, Service said he could not recall. "You remember what was the plan and you don't remember who showed it to you?" asked Morris, the adversarial minority counsel. "It was simply a policy memorandum on what our policy would be, with several alternatives," retorted Service; he noted that he was "not a military man" and had "used these terms extremely loosely."[54]

The committee next turned its attention to the oft-rumored "whitewash" of the *Amerasia* case. Service was asked about his contacts with Lauchlin Currie, Ben Cohen, and Tom Corcoran. At first Service indicated that he knew Currie "only slightly." Later he admitted Currie had suggested he seek advice from Tom

Corcoran regarding his choice of a defense attorney. "Did he [Corcoran] give you any other advice?" queried Robert Morris. "No," replied Service. It was an answer which Morris and other critics would consider a deliberate falsehood. The FBI had undoubtedly briefed Morris about Corcoran's boast to "triple rivet" Service's grand jury appearance—and he now tried to show that Service was dissembling:

Morris: Did you know before you appeared before the grand jury, or did you have any reason to believe before you appeared before the grand jury, that you would not be indicted?

Service: I was confident that I was innocent.

Morris: Is it your testimony that you were *not* advised before you appeared before the grand jury that everything would be all right? I wish you would think very carefully on that . . . because it is an important question.

Service: Who was supposed to have made such a statement?

Morris: I asked you the question.

Service: I don't recall any such statement as that. Both my lawyer and Mr. Corcoran were extremely hesitant to allow me to appear. I suppose that lawyers naturally would hesitate to allow any person to waive immunity and appear. Mr. Munter finally agreed to allow me to appear.[55]

Morris refused to let the matter drop. Why, he asked, had Munter changed his mind and allowed the diplomat to appear? In replying, Service made a slip that delighted his critics: "I assume because he thought I was guilty, and therefore I would be all right—I'm sorry, that I was *innocent*, was not guilty, and would be all right."[56] Clearly, the diplomat was rattled and was reluctant to reveal very much about his interaction with Tom Corcoran.

* * *

Service's six-hour executive session finished at 4:30 PM on June 26, 1950. The Tydings Committee's loyalty investigation of State Department employees lasted three months and would generate a massive 2,509-page transcript. With members divided along party lines, no one expected a final report any time soon. But far from discrediting Senator McCarthy's outrageous charges, the highly publicized Tydings hearing had turned him into the leader of a national crusade against Communism—and John S. Service into one of its most prominent targets.

CHAPTER 20
LIVING IN LIMBO

In response to North Korea's surprise attack, President Truman ordered the U.S. Navy's Seventh Fleet into the Taiwan Strait—a decision that would impact American relations with the two Chinas for the next half century. Until that moment, both South Korea and Taiwan had been outside the U.S. strategic defense perimeter. The invasion of South Korea dramatically changed the geopolitical calculus.

"I told my advisors that what was developing in Korea seemed to me like a repetition on a larger scale of what had happened in Berlin," Truman explained in his memoirs. "The Reds were probing for weaknesses in our armor; we had to meet their thrust without getting embroiled in a world-wide war." To avoid a dangerous escalation—with its underlying threat of nuclear war with the Soviets—the United States would "neutralize" the Taiwan Strait to prevent "attacks by the Communists on Formosa, as well as forays by Chiang Kai-shek against the mainland . . . [to] avoid reprisal actions by the Reds that might enlarge the area of conflict."[1] American planes would patrol the China coastline to monitor cross-strait activity. The final status of Taiwan, said Truman, would be determined only after restoration of security in the Pacific.

U.S. forces in the Philippines were beefed up, and military aid to the French was increased to combat Indochina's revolutionary guerrillas. "The attack upon Korea makes it plain beyond all doubts," the president declared, "that Communism has passed beyond the use of subversion to conquer independent nations and will now use armed invasion and war."[2] It was a watershed moment that changed perceptions and strategic calculations on all sides. The United States now viewed the world through the prism of a monolithic Communism, bent on expansion and world domination.

Until now, the fall of Taiwan had been accepted as the inevitable outcome of China's civil war. Secretary Acheson had even raised the possibility of recognizing Mao's regime. The shocking aggression in Korea made it imperative that the Democratic administration not appear "soft" on Communism. Chiang Kai-shek, polishing his credentials as the region's strongest anti-Communist leader, dreamed of regaining the mainland with American help.

Mao Zedong again faced a hostile United States, allied with his archenemy. He had been aware of North Korea's invasion plan, but his army was mobilizing for a final assault on Taiwan to complete the "reunification" of China. Angrily, he denounced Truman's June 27 pronouncement as interference in the internal affairs of China, Korea, and other Asian countries: the American president had revealed America's "true imperialist face."[3]

"The fact that Taiwan is part of China will remain unchanged forever," declared an indignant Zhou Enlai, the People's Republic of China's new foreign minister. "This is not only a historical fact but has been affirmed by the Cairo Declaration, the Potsdam Declaration, and the existing conditions after Japan's surrender." Indeed, both the Nationalists and the Communists considered Taiwan a sacred part of China. But now the ultimate control of Taiwan could not be settled without American involvement.[4] And the thorny issues of Taiwan and North Korea remain unresolved into the twenty-first century.

* * *

Two days after crossing the thirty-eighth parallel, North Korean troops captured Seoul and moved rapidly toward the South Korean port city of Pusan. Gen. Douglas MacArthur, the newly named commander of the United Nations forces, rushed ill-trained and poorly equipped U.S. Army units from occupied Japan to stem the tide. The GIs were easily routed; stories of shocking defeats and heavy casualties filled American newspapers and frightened an already insecure public.

The Korean hostilities provided new ammunition to anti-Communist politicians and journalists. In a speech on July 6, McCarthy blamed the unfolding Korean disaster on "highly placed Red counselors" in the State Department, whose advice was proving "far more deadly than Red machine-gunners in Korea."[5] Now McCarthy's charges about blunders in China gained new credibility. Soon he was featured on the cover of *Time* magazine while the China hands morphed, once again, into scapegoats for the newest crisis in Asia.

"I can only thank God that our son is not yet of military age to be pulled into the Army to pay for the bungling, idiotic mistakes of as stupid and moronic a State Department as the country has ever known," a citizen wrote President Truman in July. "In fairness to the American parents whose children must be sacrificed, why can't you insist that the *Amerasia* case be honestly investigated and the traitors exposed for what they are?"[6]

"Some of you may be distressed by the line taken by the unfriendly press and Republicans," John Service wrote to family and close friends after his exhausting month of dual-track hearings. "If the worst they can say is that I was a dope (or a dupe) we can forget it." It had been three months since his return to Washington, and he was eager to clear things up and get on to India. Now it all seemed a waste of everyone's time—especially the Tydings hearings. "In a political show like this—and this is straight politics of the worst and most vicious variety," he wrote, "the answers are made up beforehand and depend on which side you are on." Sen. Bourke Hickenlooper of Iowa had acted as McCarthy's stand-in on the committee while Robert Morris, the minority counsel, leaked damaging versions of confidential testimony. The bureau's "leaked hints" always lacked context or substantiation. "A major part of our fight has been to get this out in the open, to get the cards on the table, and make them show their hand."[7] But decades would pass before the Bureau's thick *Amerasia* files were finally declassified. And it was only after the collapse of the USSR, when KGB and Venona files were opened, that Service fully understood the depth of suspicion created by his mere association with suspected Communists and sympathizers.

Now all he could do was await the verdict of the investigating panels. There were a few hopeful signs: the Tydings Committee had requested the full transcript of his loyalty board hearings as well as details about Hurley's favorable public comments regarding the Chinese Communists. Rhetts supplied Admiral Nimitz' public remarks about plans to land American troops on the China mainland, made in early 1945—before John Service was overheard telling Jaffe the same thing. "We can expect that we have not yet heard the last from Sen. McCarthy," Jack warned his family. "Please consider this letter confidential and only for family and intimate friends. And please destroy."[8]

* * *

The FBI kept the *Amerasia* case sizzling in the media. A Scripps-Howard cartoon depicted undertakers—one of them named "Mr. Fix"—carrying a coffin labeled "Amerasia," over the caption, "Trying to Bury It Alive." Radio commentator Fulton Lewis Jr. blasted the Tydings Committee for whitewashing its investigation of the case, excitedly alleging that, in secret testimony, Service had admitted meeting with Lauchlin Currie and Tommy "the Cork" Corcoran. Republicans on the committee wanted to call these two witnesses, but, Lewis reported, the political implications were "too explosive."[9]

John Service never knew of the duel between the FBI and Justice over how much to reveal to the Tydings Committee about the Corcoran wiretaps. Very few people knew about Corcoran's recorded conversations with Tom Clark—by now a Supreme Court justice—or that it was the White House that had ordered the FBI tap on Corcoran's phone. Such secrets would remain hidden for decades.

"Even if they go on investigating *Amerasia* forever," Caroline wrote her parents from India, "it must be clear by now that Jack did not take any documents from the government and that his involvement with the others was completely . . . innocent on his part. . . . America did not become great on any such basis of mutual suspicion and character assassination." She still hoped her husband would soon join the family in New Delhi.[10]

* * *

To Hoover, the case was clear: now that the country was engaged in a shooting war with Communists, John Service represented a serious security risk. Agents were assigned to interview General Wedemeyer's wartime staff to find out "whether any of them showed Service any secret military plans shortly before his return to the U.S. early in 1945."[11] Soon the bureau circulated a thick summary report on Service to security offices throughout the government and military. The dossier, organized into eleven sections, included "pertinent interviews" with Patrick Hurley, Milton Miles, Alfred Kohlberg, and Louis Budenz—and omitted all the favorable testimonials. It contained numerous allegations of his associations with "disloyal persons" or those with "known Communist connections"; one chapter was devoted to "indications of political manipulation in behalf of Service" in the *Amerasia* case.[12]

Hoover's suspicions about Service were reinforced by his knowledge of the top secret Venona cables project, Elizabeth Bentley's revelations, and ongoing counterespionage efforts. The FBI's growing watch list of suspected Soviet spies included several people associated with Service and his work in wartime China. By the time of Service's loyalty hearings, Sol Adler, after being called before the House Un-American Activities Committee (HUAC), had resigned and left the country to teach in his native Britain. Lauchlin Currie had moved to Colombia to oversee international economic development projects.

* * *

There was not an empty seat in the Senate gallery on July 20, 1950, when Millard Tydings of Maryland presented his subcommittee's findings to the Senate. For two hours he delivered a stinging indictment of Senator McCarthy and his "deliberate and willful falsehoods." John Service was among those who managed to get a seat at the showdown, and he enjoyed seeing Tydings go after McCarthy "hammer and tongs."

The *Christian Science Monitor* reported the scene in detail. "At one time, in towering passion, [Tydings] slammed his stick with full force against the face of the charts with a noise like a pistol shot." When Tydings offered sarcastic imitations of McCarthy's voice and of some well-known radio announcers, laughter and applause rippled across the gallery. The Maryland senator offered no resolution of censure against the Wisconsin senator but challenged other senators "to do something about it."[13] After his oration, Democratic colleagues applauded loudly, and many stopped at his desk to shake his hand.

Following a heated debate, the Senate voted along party lines to accept the committee's 313-page report and its conclusions: Senator McCarthy had used "the totalitarian technique of the 'Big Lie'" and perpetrated "a fraud and a hoax."[14] The Republican from Massachusetts, Henry Cabot Lodge Jr., accepted the report's finding that John Service was not a disloyal person, a pro-Communist, or a security risk, but he wrote in an appended note that Service had "showed himself to be gullible and indiscreet" and "completely failed to understand the human and political realities which he was confronting."[15] Other Republican committee members, complaining they had not seen a draft of the final report, threatened to issue their own minority report.[16]

The final report forthrightly criticized McCarthy's attack on John Service. The committee found "not one iota of evidence" that he was disloyal. "We have a picture of a blanket allegation being made against a man that his reports are 'pro-Communist.' Five years after the reports were written it is proposed to penalize a Foreign Service Officer by destroying his career and branding him as disloyal for writing what appears to have been the true facts as he saw them." The Tydings report also pointed out that it was Hurley—not Service—who spoke favorably of the Chinese Communists: "[Service] said repeatedly that the Chinese Communists were Marxists. . . . Thus it would appear that the shoe of 'pro-Communist' would appear to fit the foot of Patrick Hurley more snugly than it does John Service. Yet we reject . . . any suggestion that Patrick Hurley is anything other than a loyal American doing . . . his patriotic duty. . . . [This] illustration proves the fallacy of the method as well as the danger to the U.S. of hurling unfounded charges against a man's honest reporting."[17] McCarthy remained absent during Tydings' speech and the Senate vote, but he issued a press statement claiming that Tydings' impassioned speech was intended "to notify the Communists in the government that they are safe in their positions."[18]

* * *

"No doubt you are overjoyed to be exonerated, but I realize that this affair will leave scars on your soul as long as you live," Brooks Atkinson wrote to his beleaguered friend. "It must be hell to go through the public persecution that you have had and to be for so long at the mercy of rats and skunks, but you won by keeping your head and by not fighting back with the foul balls thrown at you. Your honesty, modesty and frankness turned out to be unassailable."[19]

John Service was disappointed that the Senate debate had not been thorough, systematic, or conclusive. Moreover, the release of the formal committee report did not dispel the cloud of suspicion. The Tydings Committee asserted it had found "not one shred of evidence to support the unwarranted charge that the *Amerasia* case was 'fixed' in any manner." But top officials at Justice and the FBI knew the secrets of Corcoran's tapped phone conversations—even if the committee and John Service did not.

More than fifty years later, a conservative commentator still harbored suspicions. "The obsession with whitewashing Service is apparent in every aspect of the record [of *Amerasia*]," wrote M. Stanton Evans in 2007. "In going after Service/*Amerasia,* McCarthy was tugging at the visible edges of an enormous network . . . that permeated the federal government and had objects more grandiose than the papers that made their way to Jaffe."[20]

* * *

In India, Caroline was growing impatient for her husband to rejoin the family. "When I stop to think about money, I could drive myself crazy," Caroline Service fumed in a letter to her parents. "We are in debt $2,000 to the Department for money we borrowed to get out here, and who is paying the lawyers, I don't know." If her husband remained stuck in Washington, she feared the State Department might soon stop paying his full salary. She concluded with the hope that "neither of my boys ever wants to go into government service or that Ginny marries into it."[21]

* * *

During the early weeks of the Korean conflict, the Joint Chiefs gave approval to Gen. Douglas MacArthur to fly to Taiwan for secret talks with Generalissimo Chiang Kai-shek—without consulting or informing either the State Department or the president. Then, without seeking even the Pentagon's permission, the general secretly stationed three squadrons of jet fighters on the island. News of his actions soon surfaced in the press, greatly embarrassing U.S. diplomats at the United Nations, who were already confronting PRC protests about American aggression in its territorial waters. In early August, MacArthur further inflamed the situation by sending an unauthorized message to the Veterans of Foreign Wars convention, expressing his strong personal views about the strategic importance of Taiwan. "By his words and by his actions," observed historian Warren Cohen, "MacArthur gave credence to the fears expressed by Mao and Chou En-lai of impending American attacks on the People's Republic, of an American effort to

Robert and Grace Service established the YMCA in Chengdu, Sichuan Province in 1906 where they raised three sons: John, Robert, and Richard (in front). *Courtesy of Service Family*

When Jack Service was growing up, it took ten days to travel by sedan chair from Chungking to Chengdu. *Courtesy of Service Family*

As captain of the Oberlin College track team, Jack Service won the all-conference mile championship three years in a row. *Courtesy of Service Family*

Jack and Caroline at his first consular post in Yunnanfu. *Courtesy of Service Family*

John Service being carried in a sedan chair down a typical "ladder street" in Chungking in 1941on his way to present his diplomatic credentials. He borrowed the top hat from a British diplomat and stuffed it with newspaper to make it fit. *Courtesy of Service Family*

In Yenan, John Service stands between the top Chinese Communist leaders: (left to right) Zhou Enlai, Chu Teh, Service, Mao Zedong, and Ye Jianying. *Courtesy of Service Family*

Jack Service working on the Yenan airstrip project in 1944. *Courtesy of Service Family*

Service and other members of the Dixie Mission in discussion with Mao Zedong. *Courtesy of Service Family*

Lin Biao briefs Service (in shorts and dark glasses) and other Americans at their Dixie Mission compound. *Courtesy of Service Family*

Dixie Mission Americans and Chinese Communist leaders at a special gathering of guerrilla forces in Yenan. *Courtesy of Service Family*

First meeting of Gen. Joseph Stilwell and Gen. Patrick Hurley in Chungking, before the Cairo Conference in 1943. *Western History Collections, University of Oklahoma*

Capt. Milton "Mary" Miles and Tai Li signing the unprecedented SACO agreement in 1942, which placed American trainers and intelligence operations under the control of China's secret police chief. *NARA*

Dixie Mission members pose in homespun suits—gifts from their Communist hosts in Yenan. (The photo later provided ammunition for zealous anti-Communists.)
Courtesy of Service Family

Capt. Milton "Mary" Miles reviews the American-trained troops of Tai Li's secret army at SACO headquarters outside Chungking. *U.S. Naval Institute Photo Archive*

At the Cairo Conference in December 1943, President Roosevelt and Prime Minister Winston Churchill sit between Chiang Kai-shek and his wife, Soong Mei-ling, who acted as interpreter. Gen. Joseph Stilwell stands directly behind FDR. *U.S. Naval Institute Photo Archive*

Gen. Joseph Stilwell (center, front) and Lt. Gen. Claire Chennault (center, rear) inspect aircraft. They bitterly disagreed over war strategy and priorities for precious supplies airlifted to China over the Hump. *NARA*

Fueling aircraft was a painstaking process in China. Fuel was first airlifted over the Hump, then transferred from barrels into five-gallon containers to be carried onto the wing and poured into fuel tanks. *NARA*

President Roosevelt relied upon Harry Hopkins, his closest aide and confidante, in conducting his personal style of diplomacy. *Library of Congress*

Left to right: T. V. Soong, Gen. Albert C. Wedemeyer, Generalissimo Chiang Kai-shek, and Gen. Patrick J. Hurley in November 1944, after Wedemeyer replaced Gen. Joseph Stilwell. *Western History Collections, University of Oklahoma*

Mao's chief of staff, Mao Zedong, Lin Tsu-han, General Hurley, General Chuteh, Zhou Enlai, and Col. David Barrett at the Yenan airstrip on November 7, 1944. *Western History Collections, University of Oklahoma*

Val Chao was a well-known actress in Chungking long before Jack Service fell in love with her. *Bancroft Library, University of California, Berkeley*

Diplomat John Paton Davies, a friend of John Service since boyhood in Sichuan, was fired by Secretary of State Dulles over the alleged "loss" of China. *NARA*

Diplomat John Carter Vincent was eventually forced to resign over the alleged "loss" of China by Secretary of State Dulles.
Library of Congress

At the conclusion of the Potsdam Conference in July 1945, President Harry Truman sits between Clement Atlee, the new British prime minister, and Joseph Stalin, the Soviet leader.
U.S. Naval Institute Photo Archive

Ambassador Hurley escorts Mao Zedong and Zhou Enlai to peace talks with Chiang Kai-shek in Chungking in August 1945. It was Mao's first airplane ride. *Courtesy of Service Family*

Bitter rivals Mao Zedong and Chiang Kai-shek toast each other at start of peace talks in August 1945 as Ambassador Hurley looks on. *U.S. Naval Institute Photo Archive*

Left to right: Emmanuel "Jimmy" Larsen, John Service, and Andrew Roth await arraignment following their arrest as suspects in the infamous *Amerasia* case in June 1945. *Copyright Bettmann/Corbis Images*

FBI Director J. Edgar Hoover kept a file on John Service for decades. *Library of Congress*

The House Un-American Activities Committee (HUAC) hearings of 1948 investigated Soviet spying in the United States. Elizabeth Bentley (left) was its "star witness," and diplomat Alger Hiss (far right) was a key suspect. *Library of Congress*

Secretary of State Dean Acheson surrounded by newsmen at a congressional hearing. Acheson was a key architect of U.S. foreign policy during the Cold War—and often a target of the anti-Communist crusade. *Library of Congress*

Aboard ship on their way to India in March 1950, the Service family (left to right) Virginia, Jack, Caroline, Robert, and Philip (in front) just before Service was recalled to Washington to face McCarthy's charges. The family remained separated for more than a year.
Courtesy of Service Family

Ben Cohen and Tommy Corcoran were influential New Dealers whose efforts to help John Service aroused suspicion of a political fix. *Library of Congress*

John Service, flanked by his lawyers, Ed Rhetts (left) and Gerald Reilly (right), testifies at his loyalty hearing before the Tydings Committee in June 1950. *AP Images/Herbert White*

This photograph, captioned: "Career Diplomat John S. Service (right) walks out of a Senate hearing room, on June 22, 1950, as his accuser, Senator Joseph McCarthy (R-Wis), grins in the background," appeared in newspapers around the country.
AP Images/Herbert White

Talburt's cartoon about the Amerasia case appeared in Scripps-Howard newspapers on June 2, 1950, during Service's loyalty hearings.
Scripps-Howard News Service/Talburt

In his Sarco office on June 17, 1957, John Service hears that the Supreme Court has ruled, in a 8–0 decision, that he was wrongfully fired in 1951. *AP Images/Marty Lederhandler*

In 1971 Jack and Caroline Service were invited to visit the People's Republic of China. After their private, three-hour meeting with Premier Zhou Enlai, Service sent a report to the State Department. *Courtesy of Service Family*

The handshake between U.S. president Richard Nixon and Mao Zedong, China's Communist Party chairman, changed the world's geopolitical landscape in February 1972. *Ollie Atkins/Special Collections & Archives, George Mason University Libraries*

In 1972 Henry Kissinger, Richard Nixon, Mao Zedong, and Zhou Enlai held the first substantive Sino-American diplomatic exchanges since John Service met with the Chinese Communist leaders in 1944–45. *Ollie Atkins/Special Collections & Archives, George Mason University Libraries*

Jack Service with the author in China in 1980. *Courtesy of Service Family*

Service received an honorary degree in Monterey, California, with both Caroline and Val Chao in attendance. *Courtesy of Val Chao Wu*

Yenan is now a tourist destination where Chinese can have their photos taken in rented 8th Route Army uniforms—and hearken back to a time when Communists seemed genuinely concerned with people's welfare and untainted by bribery or corruption. *Photo by Lynne Joiner*

turn the Korean crisis into an opportunity to return Chiang to the mainland."[22] President Truman was outraged to learn of the general's insubordination from a press release for a weekly newsmagazine.

* * *

On August 3, 1950, as John Service turned forty-one, he still had no clear idea when he could leave for India. More than five weeks had passed since his loyalty board hearing ended. "The worst way this affects me," he explained in a letter to his mother, "is that the State Department Loyalty Board cannot officially close its hearings and render its decision until it is notified by the FBI that the investigation is concluded and all information has been transmitted to the Board." Only at that point would his case be sent up to Truman's Loyalty Review Board for its approval.[23]

In August Jack accepted an invitation to take care of Ed Rhetts' rural Virginia household for a month while Rhetts and his wife vacationed in Wyoming. After nearly five months of living like a gypsy with various friends, the country sojourn must have been a welcome change—although not without its challenges. Service reported that he fixed the freezer that had gone on the blink, sent the broken cream separator to Sears for repair, and recovered Moozie the cow after she broke her tether and escaped for hours into the scrub pine woods across the road. His only complaint was "No news! No news! No news!" about his case. "I have started studying Hindustani in desperation," Service wrote his vacationing lawyer. "At least it gives the Dept a chance to say that I'm not doing nothing."

In a postscript, Jack mentioned that Senator McCarthy in a recent speech to the Milwaukee Retail Grocers "repeated practically all of the same old lies." Service had immediately written a polite letter to the head of the Wisconsin trade association, setting the record straight. Fortunately, "none of the press services carried [the speech] and apparently have decided not to give him any publicity as long as he merely repeats."[24]

During Service's sojourn on Rhetts' farm, the FBI received a confidential cable from U.S. military intelligence agents in Hong Kong: an informant claimed that an American diplomat named Service was doing espionage work for the Soviets in India. The bureau immediately requested more information on this encouraging lead—further delaying a decision by Service's loyalty board.

* * *

"The Ambassador has been wonderful about waiting for Jack and saying he would continue to wait," Caroline reported to her parents that August. But now she expressed a new and very real concern about her husband's limbo: "Is he going to be an election issue along with the other McCarthy victims?"[25]

"A man doesn't have to be a Communist to be dangerous," proclaimed broadcaster Henry J. Taylor in a September 4 radio program targeting John Service. "In spite of Korea—in spite of everything—the inside protection still exists, closing in around Service as it has around Alger Hiss and many others—and for so many years. . . . Now we have not a 'Red Herring,' but Red bayonets jammed down our throats. All we need is the truth."[26] At that moment, Congress was debating new internal security legislation. The White House had introduced a measure toughening the penalties for espionage and sedition, but Republicans countered with more drastic proposals. And now a conservative Democrat from Nevada, Pat McCarran, in alliance with Republican senators, had introduced a still more draconian bill.

A week after Taylor's broadcast, the infamous McCarran Act was passed by Congress. President Truman quickly vetoed the measure as endangering constitutional freedoms of speech, press, and assembly. It would, he told Congress, "spread a legal dragnet sufficiently broad to permit the prosecution of people who are entirely innocent or merely misguided."[27] His veto was easily overridden. The new law declared the U.S. Communist Party "a clear and present danger" to national security. Its members—and anyone linked to Communist-front organizations—were barred from national security jobs with the government or the defense industry, and even from holding a passport. Foreigners were barred from entering the country if they had ever been a member of a Communist or totalitarian political party. "Many legislators knew of the bill's perils," observed historian Richard Fried, "but declined to risk leaving an impression of lukewarm anti-Communism."[28]

* * *

When the secretary of defense resigned in early September, President Truman coaxed Gen. George C. Marshall out of retirement to take the post. But his confirmation hearings offered a new forum for crusading anti-Communists, who blamed Marshall for cutting aid to Chiang and suppressing Wedemeyer's 1947 report that recommended support, albeit with strings. The Republican senator from Indiana, William E. Jenner, declared Marshall was "either an unsuspecting stooge or an actual co-conspirator" and that he had been picked to provide "the front of respectability to the vicious sell-out not only of Chiang, not only of Formosa . . . but of the American GIs who are fighting and dying even now because of one treachery."[29] Marshall was eventually confirmed, but any hope for building bipartisanship in the conduct of the war and U.S. foreign policy ended.

In mid-September, the FBI finally received a supplemental report from intelligence agents in Hong Kong. "Fortunately, upon this occasion, the informant was not under the influence of liquor and therefore told his story clearly and logically," the G-2 interrogator reported. A Russian merchant seaman claimed to have heard a Russian cabaret singer in Calcutta boast that "an American Consul named Service had even been recruited" to work for Soviet intelligence. The informant proved unable to identify photos of either John Service or his brother, Richard (who was also a Foreign Service officer in China during the war). "Check his record," the Russian sailor told the investigator. "If he's been in China, that's the one."[30]

* * *

On September 15 General MacArthur launched a counteroffensive with a surprise landing of Marines at Inchon, forcing the North Koreans back across the border. But the campaign was taking a grim toll: already 11,000 South Koreans and nearly 7,000 Americans soldiers were dead; 106,000 South Koreans and nearly 14,000 Americans were wounded; and 57,000 South Korean fighters and close to 4,000 GIs were missing in action. Figures for North Korean casualties were never known.

As the Allied forces successfully pushed the enemy back toward the thirty-eighth parallel, the war objectives dramatically changed. Instead of merely reestablishing the old border, General MacArthur received permission to extend his offensive operations into North Korea itself with the ambitious aim of destroying the enemy force, reunifying the country, and holding elections under UN auspices. "This development came so naturally," observed one historian, "that American officials and the public gave very little thought to the risks and costs involved."[31]

* * *

"There is no progress here and we remain in this state of suspended animation," John Service told his mother, after reporting that his ears were covered with boils that "throb like the dickens, and feel like someone was turning a fork in the middle of my head." Now back in the city at John Davies' house, Service explained that he would soon move to the apartment of a vacationing Foreign Service officer, and then return to the attic bedroom of Tony Freeman's home, where her letters should be sent.[32]

* * *

By autumn five-year-old Philip was having trouble remembering what his father's face looked like, Caroline confided to her parents.[33] "I feel so sorry about Jack and this long, long delay I hardly know what to do." Six months had passed since the couple had last seen each other. "What is to keep people from jumping up for the rest of our lives telling lies that it is almost impossible to disprove?" She begged her parents to stop telling her they would "gain strength" through their ordeal. "Do you realize that Bob, who wants to get into the Foreign Service, would probably have no chance whatsoever in that line or in any other government job? This thing can easily affect their future schooling, their jobs, and their marriages. And that is no exaggeration."[34]

* * *

On September 29, 1950, Defense Secretary Marshall sent a top secret "eyes only" cable to General MacArthur: "We want you to feel unhampered strategically and tactically to proceed north of the 38th Parallel."[35] The plan to take the fight into North Korean territory had been approved, but with certain provisos. The offensive was not to be undertaken if there were any threat by Russian or Chinese Communists to counter our operations militarily in the north. No air or naval operations against Chinese or Russian territory or sanctuaries would be allowed; however, patrols along the Chinese and Russian coastlines were to be stepped up. This new era of limited war was the necessary response to the Cold War threat of nuclear annihilation. The United Nations began to debate a U.S.-sponsored resolution for holding elections in Korea, after reunification had been achieved by the American-led UN forces.

China did not intend to sit back and allow the Americans to destroy the North Korean Communist regime—or threaten its own national security. "The Chinese people absolutely will not tolerate foreign aggression, nor will they supinely tolerate seeing their neighbors being savagely invaded," warned Zhou Enlai. "Whoever attempts to exclude the nearly 500 million people from the United Nations and whoever would ignore and violate the interests of this one-fourth of mankind and fancy vainly to solve arbitrarily any Far Eastern problem directly concerned with China, will certainly break their skulls."[36]

In the United States, the warning was ignored. Few believed the Chinese would dare enter the war against the powerful American war machine. "I don't think that China wants to be chopped up," was the undiplomatic comment of one top State Department official.[37] On October 1 General MacArthur issued an ultimatum to the North Korean government: either surrender or face dire consequences. That same day South Korean army units—chasing enemy troops in retreat—crossed the thirty-eighth parallel into North Korea for the first time. Unintended consequences soon followed.

Zhou Enlai quickly summoned the Indian ambassador in Peking to a midnight meeting. The diplomat was asked to pass along an urgent message: if U.S. forces crossed the thirty-eighth parallel, China would be forced to intervene.

Unfortunately, the Indian ambassador held little credibility in Washington. Zhou's warning was interpreted as merely a gambit to influence the UN General Assembly's vote on a resolution authorizing American-led forces to "reunify and rehabilitate" Korea. And on October 7 the first American troops stepped across the thirty-eighth parallel, in hot pursuit of the enemy.

* * *

The State Department's loyalty board finally announced its decision in John Service's loyalty case on October 6, ruling that there were "no reasonable grounds" to believe the diplomat was disloyal. Despite a "single serious indiscretion in the handling of classified information" during the *Amerasia* episode, the board concluded Service "does not constitute a security risk to Department of State." Moreover, his wartime China reports were found to be "objective, and extraordinarily accurate, as political forecasts of what was to come." Rather than detecting any sympathy for Russia or Communism, the loyalty board determined that his dispatches contained "only a clearly expressed fear that the policy of the Chinese Nationalist Government and of the U.S. Government as a supporter of Chiang Kai-shek alone was headed for a major disaster that would throw all of China into the hands of the Soviet Union." John Service was "neither a Communist nor pro-Communist."[38]

"New 'Clean Bill' On Loyalty Given to John Service—Rumor from Orient Caused a Delay in Issuing Clearance," headlined the *Washington Star* story. Service quickly arranged to meet with the State Department official reviewing the board's findings. Carlisle Humelsine assured him that he would be off to India as soon as he completed his review in a few weeks. In the meantime, Service was finally granted permission to visit family in California. "He dismissed the possibility of my not going to New Delhi," Service happily wrote his wife, "and said 'Scripps-Howard isn't making our assignments for us.'"[39]

"I'd been waiting for it so long," Caroline Service confessed in a letter to a friend, "I could hardly take it in when I saw it." She had spotted the news of her husband's clearance in the English-language newspaper even before his cable arrived. Caroline now believed he would arrive by Thanksgiving—her forty-first birthday—when the older children would be home for school break. "If Jack is here nothing more could be asked," she wrote. "I'm very, very proud of my husband. Heaven only knows what the future will hold for us as regards his career, but I think he has proved himself during this terrible persecution."[40]

Many Americans held a very different view of her husband. "Until the *Amerasia* case is fully and *publicly* explored Robert [sic] Service is NOT cleared, in the opinion of this family or a single human being this family knows or has talked to since this scandal became a public issue," wrote Edith Dickey Moses of Blufton, South Carolina, to the White House. "We think Service's part in the fatal China policy—his pro-Communist sympathies and endeavors which influenced that fatal trend absolutely disqualifies him for work in the State Department."[41]

* * *

On October 15, President Truman flew to Wake Island for a private conference with General MacArthur. The general apologized for any embarrassment his unauthorized remarks about Taiwan to the VFW might have caused the president. "He said he wanted me to understand he was not in politics in any way," Truman later recalled.[42] The tall, pipe-smoking MacArthur exuded tremendous optimism, declaring the war was won and belittling the possibility that Chinese Communist troops might join the fray. A secret CIA intelligence report had similarly concluded Chinese intervention was improbable. "We are no longer fearful of their intervention. We no longer stand hat in hand," the general later declared to the president's delegation. "Now we have our Air Force in Korea [and] if the Chinese tried to get down to Pyongyang, there would be the greatest slaughter."[43] MacArthur promised that all resistance would end by Thanksgiving, and the GIs would be withdrawn by Christmas.

Soon after that Wake Island meeting, the first Chinese Communist forces crossed into North Korea. Before sending his "volunteer" fighters, Chairman Mao had cabled Stalin an urgent appeal for military aid. "If we allow the U.S. to occupy all of Korea, we must be prepared for the U.S. to declare war with China." The Russian dictator agreed to send some materiel and pilots to fly MiG-15 missions, but he never sent as much support as promised—and Soviet pilots were forbidden to fly within sixty miles of the battle front, to avoid confrontation with the Americans.

The first engagement of Chinese and American-led forces came on November 1. Using guerrilla tactics perfected during the Chinese civil war, the Chinese repelled the UN troops as they approached the Yalu River, separating Korea from China. But when the Chinese attackers withdrew, General MacArthur interpreted their disengagement as a retreat, again boasting, "American boys will be home by Christmas."[44]

* * *

The three-week road trip to California in his sister-in-law's borrowed car was a wonderful tonic for John Service. He relaxed for the first time since his recall. Just as it began to seem that his long ordeal was over, then came the news of China's entry into the Korean conflict—and vicious personal attacks began again. A *New*

York Times article highlighted the irate protest a Republican representative sent to the secretary of state.[45] Declaring that John Service had betrayed the nation's trust "while others were serving," Edith Nourse Rogers of Connecticut objected to his recent assignment to New Delhi. When Service found out the State Department planned no rebuttal, preferring to keep a low profile, he wrote directly to Rogers. His exasperation is evident:

> Your statement . . . that I have "betrayed" a trust is one, frankly, that I find baffling. It is an unwelcome distinction to be, as some have called me, "the most investigated man in the government." But I have cooperated voluntarily, whole-heartedly, and even gladly with those repeated investigations because nothing is more important to me than the clearing of my name. Is it too much to hope that the unanimous favorable result of those investigations eventually may be accepted? . . . There is a principle involved here; the right of an American to defend himself against charges and, after his innocence has been established, to be allowed to devote his best efforts for his government in a career . . . in the non-political, merit-based Foreign Service.[46]

Service sent copies to Undersecretary Carlisle Humelsine and other State Department officials, accompanied by a memo informing them that, if the congresswoman failed to take "favorable action within a reasonable time," he intended to let the *Times* publish his letter.[47]

The unfriendly fire from angry politicians and the worsening news from the war front apparently forced the State Department to hunker down—and Service's assignment was again held hostage. More than a month had passed since Humelsine's promise of a quick review. Fulton Lewis again targeted Service, announcing to his national radio audience that he had "new and hitherto undisclosed information" about John Stewart Service and the infamous *Amerasia* case. He blasted the Tydings Committee, attacked Service's "pro-Communist leanings and activities," alleged "thousands" of government documents were stolen for *Amerasia*, and insinuated a cover-up. And he named those involved in the political fix: Lauchlin Currie, "one of the most extreme leftish advisors to the late President Roosevelt"; Tommy "the Cork" Corcoran, "generally regarded as one of the greatest powers behind the Washington scene"; former Attorney General Tom Clark, "now a justice of the Supreme Court," and his former top assistant, James McGranery, "now a federal judge in Philadelphia"; and James McInerney, "the person in immediate charge of the *Amerasia* case." The FBI gleefully reported the broadcast had "a devastating effect."[48]

To address the revived allegations of political influence, Rhetts instructed Service to write down everything he could recall about his contacts with Currie and Corcoran at the time of his arrest. The result was a typewritten three-and-a-half-page, single-spaced memo. By now Service was aware of the suspicions about Currie, triggered by Elizabeth Bentley's HUAC testimony in 1948 and reinforced by his refusal to testify in Service's behalf. "LC is worse medicine than I had any idea of," Service would later confide to a close friend.[49]

Service wrote his memo in the third person, as if analyzing someone else's activities: "Service insisted that what he wanted and the only thing that was desirable for effective clearance was advice but not 'influence.'" After several meetings, "Service formed the impression that Corcoran had . . . concluded that the case against Service was weak and that an indictment was unlikely." The detailed memo explained that Corcoran had offered to take direction of his case without a fee, and that he was reluctant to have the diplomat appear voluntarily before the grand jury. But there was no mention of their many phone calls debating whether he should appear—or of Corcoran's comment that he was going to make sure a deal with Justice officials was "triple riveted." Was this a failure of memory, or did Service choose to overlook these details? When the FBI transcripts of Corcoran's tapped telephone calls were finally declassified, thirty-five years later, John Service would once again face questions about a political fix in the *Amerasia* case.

* * *

On November 7, 1950, the Republican Party won a landslide victory in the mid-term elections. The legend of Joe McCarthy's political invincibility grew exponentially as Democrats he had targeted were defeated. Sen. Millard Tydings of Maryland, chair of the committee that had cleared Service of disloyalty, lost his bid for a sixth term by 400,000 votes after McCarthy circulated a doctored photograph allegedly showing the senator talking with the head of the American Communist Party. The Democrats lost a total of twenty-eight seats in the House and seven in the Senate.

One of those Senate seats went to a two-term Republican representative from California named Richard Nixon, who had campaigned against his rival's "strong left-wing tendencies and sympathies." Nixon first gained national attention as a strong anti-Communist during the Alger Hiss hearings, and recently he had called for new loyalty hearings for employees of the State Department.

Gloom stalked the hallways at Foggy Bottom after the catastrophic elections. No one expected Dean Acheson to last much longer as secretary of state—and no one could say when the review of John Service's loyalty case would be completed.

"I have not told Caroline because absolutely nothing is certain, but privately, I think it extremely unlikely that I will ever get to India on this assignment," Jack confided in a letter to his mother. "It seems probable that they will try to avoid some trouble by finding a completely innocuous and quiet post and hope that no one objects to it." Such a course would "only whet the appetite of the jackals, who are now on the rampage as never before. . . . And the voters of Maryland have proved by majority vote that Tydings did a 'Whitewash.'"[50]

"If Acheson is to go down, he should not slink away like a craven but pass on his feet, fighting," replied Grace Service. "If he lets a man such as you down, what can others look for? Throughout this whole 'trial' you have been as a representative of many other Department men also accused by McCarthy." Grace, ever her son's moral compass, advised him to remember Lincoln's "marvelous, bull-doggish hold on ways of truth and honesty "—rather than imitate the department's timid "white rabbits."[51]

* * *

On November 24, 1950, the Chinese renewed their attack, catching the American-led forces by surprise. Three hundred thousand fighters, many of them ethnic Koreans, had infiltrated into North Korea, determined to push the Americans out.[52]

The shocking news from the warfront cast a pall over the annual Thanksgiving holiday dinner dance at the U.S. Army War College. Among the guests was diplomat Tony Freeman, who struck up a conversation with Carlisle Humelsine, the State Department official responsible for reviewing Service's clearance. Humelsine casually mentioned that he planned to uphold the loyalty board's finding, but he had decided to cancel Service's assignment to India. Given the glare of recent publicity, it seemed unwise to assign him to such a high-profile post, even though he clearly posed no security risk and certainly was not a Communist. Freeman made sure to share this startling news with his houseguest later that night.

Early Monday morning John Service went to the State Department to confront Humelsine. Unable to get an appointment, he sought out the director of personnel. "Our talk was friendly, but what you might call frank," Service reported to Caroline: "What it all boiled down to was this: did I have any idea of resigning? No. I was not going to quit under the shadow of false accusations. . . . Wasn't there any loophole in the retirement law? No. Earliest voluntary retirement is at 50. . . . This could be shortened to 3 years, . . . if I am put in the bottom 10% of the class by three successive selection boards. However my work has never caused any low ratings." The bureaucrat—whom Grace Service would no doubt have described as a "white rabbit"—asked Service if he might consider taking a leave of absence, to work outside the department for a couple of years while maintaining his pension eligibility until the controversy died down. In the current political atmosphere, Service objected, "no other government department would dare touch me." A year earlier, Harvard had offered him a position, but with universities now under attack from the anti-Communists, he doubted he could obtain any academic post. The personnel chief then suggested assigning him a low-profile post some place in Africa. "I said I thought the transfer from New Delhi unnecessary and unwise," Service explained in his letter to Caroline, "but if the department was convinced that there had to be a shift, 'let's get it quick.'"[53]

On December 6 the *Washington Star* carried the news that Service's assignment to India was dead, calling him "one of this country's most-investigated and most-cleared career diplomats." To cover itself, the State Department announced that the cancellation was because the embassy could no longer delay filling the post of political counselor.[54] Service would later reflect, "I became a scapegoat in a sense, a whipping boy [who] turned out to be an easy, vulnerable target for McCarthy and for the China lobby and for KMT and for Kohlberg."[55]

The Service story was overshadowed in the press by bigger news: convicted spy Judith Coplon had been released on a technicality. A federal appeals court judge ruled her arrest was made without a proper warrant, and the evidence found in her purse was therefore inadmissible. In fact, a senior Justice official had assured the FBI that if there were "probable cause" to suspect they were witnessing a felony, the street-corner arrest could be made.[56] Also not reported was the fact that crucial evidence of Coplon's espionage had been gleaned from supersecret Venona decrypts, which could not be introduced in court. Once again FBI agents looked like bunglers. Furious over the outcome, Hoover secretly ordered changes in FBI procedures: records of technical surveillance would henceforth be kept separate from general criminal case files to shield them from court-ordered discovery motions, congressional subpoenas, and requests from the Justice Department.[57] To an angry American public, the news of December 6 meant that a convicted spy had escaped a long prison term—and a suspect diplomat remained on the payroll at Dean Acheson's State Department.

* * *

The cancelled assignment came as a bitter blow to Caroline. Her depression deepened and her health deteriorated, much to the alarm of Ambassador

Henderson. Her father quietly offered to pay for Jack's flight to surprise his family for the Christmas holidays, but the skittish State Department refused Service's leave request. "I am sorry that there is just nothing I can do about getting out to help you pack up and travel," Jack wrote his wife. "Christmas will not occur, as far as I am concerned, until we all get together."[58]

CHAPTER 21
THE FIRING SQUAD

When the cable from Jack arrived, Caroline was devastated. Her distress was so evident that an embassy staffer immediately took her to see Loy Henderson. "The ambassador took one look at me and said, 'you poor child . . . sit down and tell me what you have heard.' I showed him the telegram and his immediate reaction was that you should be coming out here." Alarmed at her growing anxiety and depression, Ambassador Henderson cabled Humelsine to say that a decision on the family's fate needed to be made soon. "I read [your telegram] over and over," she wrote to Jack, "and cannot understand why the Dept. after leaving me out here all this time should now show such a spineless attitude—even considering the election results."[1]

* * *

Christmas Day marked nine months since Caroline had last seen her husband in Tokyo. Christmas 1950 was a grim holiday for many other Americans. MacArthur's troops did not come home from Korea by the holidays. Instead, they were involved in the longest retreat in the history of the U.S. Army: 105,000 soldiers, 98,000 civilians, 17,500 vehicles, and 350,000 tons of supplies were being evacuated from North Korean territory by an improvised flotilla of ships and fishing boats. After stopping the UN forces' drive to the Yalu River, Chinese "volunteers," in a ferocious series of surprise nighttime attacks, were pushing the Americans and their allies back across the thirty-eighth parallel.

Fear and anxiety replaced holiday cheer. The shocking news of mounting battlefront defeats and rising casualty figures filled the front pages. A *New York Herald Tribune* editorial demanded an explanation from Washington officials: "[How could] armies of well over 100,000 men, still retaining every modern weapon and full power of maneuver . . . be so completely overwhelmed even by superior masses of foot troops?"[2] On the home front, more stories about domestic spies added to the nation's insecurity. Not long after Judith Coplon's conviction was overturned, Harry Gold—one of the A-bomb spies—was sentenced to a thirty-year prison term.

McCarthy and the reinvigorated China Lobby whipped up their anti-Communist crusaders, outraged that John Service, the man they blamed for the "loss" of China, had again been exonerated while Mao's soldiers were killing American boys. Chiang Kai-shek attained new stature for his steadfast opposition to the Communist menace, and Service again became a convenient scapegoat.

* * *

Service focused on putting one foot in front of the other—as he had always done since trekking at his father's side in Sichuan. For weeks he tried to get answers to three key questions: What would be his next overseas post? How soon could the family be reunited? And when would the president's Loyalty Review Board (LRB) consider his case?

"How is the battle going?" Grace Service wrote from California. "I hope you have not given an inch. You are right and they are wrong."[3] But the news was not promising: the LRB would not take his case until the end of January; until then, officials refused to assign him to a new overseas post. His family would remain in limbo, ineligible for travel allowance to return home. John Service feared that being assigned to a "thumb-twittling job" in Washington would simply play into the hands of the department's critics.

Disappointed, Jack perhaps found solace in memories of a happier Christmas long ago, when his mother gave him a framed print of the Kipling poem that had helped the family endure hard times:

> If you can keep your head when all about you
> Are losing theirs and blaming it on you; . . .
> If you can wait and not be tired by waiting,
> Or being lied about, don't deal in lies,
> Or being hated, don't give way to hating . . .
> If you can bear to hear the truth you've spoken
> Twisted by knaves to make a trap for fools,
> Or watch the things you gave your life to, broken,
> And stoop and build 'em up with worn-out tools; . . .
> If you can fill the unforgiving minute
> With sixty seconds' worth of distance run,
> Yours is the Earth and everything that's in it,
> And—which is more—you'll be a Man, my son![4]

"My one great New Year's wish is that we will be together as soon as possible, and that this next year will be better than last," Caroline wrote Jack after Christmas. "Please, don't let them keep you from coming here to get us. I just keep thinking if I could only see you and feel you near me. All my love darling, for the New Year and for all the years to come, and let us hope we can be together, because it seems to me that is the thing that matters most."[5]

* * *

In early January 1951, the North Koreans and their Chinese allies recaptured Seoul, awakening fears of a Communist tide rolling across Asia, just as Stalin had swept through Eastern Europe. Mao's China was providing inspiration, training, and limited supplies to insurgencies erupting in French Indochina, British Malaya, the Dutch East Indies, and the Philippines.

For Chiang Kai-shek, these alarming developments presented an opportunity. Despite Truman's announced policy of neutralizing the Taiwan Strait, the CIA had secretly been given a green light to train and equip Chinese commandos. The Generalissimo's dream of recapturing the Chinese mainland once again seemed possible. "The CIA started to receive virtually unlimited funding for its collaborative efforts with Taiwan's intelligence and special operations units," wrote former CIA operative and diplomat James Lilley. As the war in Korea progressed, Taiwan became the principal base for launching secret operations against the mainland. "The hope was that robust clandestine efforts would sap China's resources and force it to divert manpower from the war in Korea."[6] The United States was again involved in China's civil war, which now became deeply entwined with the effort to oppose Communist aggression in Korea and Asia.

Taiwan became a major training base for Nationalist commandos and CIA activities. The CIA was dropping operatives off boats in the Taiwan Strait and parachuting agents into mainland territory to cause disruptions and gather intelligence. They airlifted arms and supplies to Chiang's forces, hiding along PRC borders. Aircraft for these missions were supplied by China Air Transport, the airline covertly funded by the CIA and operated by retired Gen. Claire Chennault—whose general counsel in Washington was Corcoran.[7] A "Chinese Third Force" of former Chinese military men was secretly trained at CIA bases on Okinawa and Saipan, hoping eventually to incite a popular revolt against Mao's government.[8]

* * *

Early in 1951 Chiang Kai-shek started using his newly enhanced credentials to settle old scores. A special target, of course, was John Service as both an instigator of the "Dixie Mission" and the unwelcome messenger carrying Roosevelt's bluntly worded cables. Those humiliating incidents had never been forgotten.

Chiang's intelligence service now provided its contacts at FBI and U.S. military intelligence with a confidential twenty-one-page report detailing the "pro-Communist" actions of fourteen individuals. (The translated title of the report is "Information on the Activities of U.S. and Foreign Nationals Assisting the Chinese Communist Party in an Attempt to Overthrow the Chinese Nationalist Government or Chinese Communist Elements Participating in the U.S. Communist Organs.") In the version declassified under a Freedom of Information Act appeal in 2003, most of the names in its table of contents were still blacked out (with the notable exception of Service and John Carter Vincent)—but it was easy to identify many of them as well-known critics of Chiang's regime. Number one on the enemies' list was clearly Owen Lattimore, the Asian scholar named by Senator McCarthy as the Soviet Union's top spy in America. Vincent and Service took second and third place respectively, and John Paton Davies was listed not far behind.

The secret report rehashed the false charges and flagrant distortions that had long been peddled by the China Lobby, but it also included some outlandish new charges. It claimed that Lattimore and Vincent had accompanied Vice President Wallace on his 1944 mission to China in order "to strengthen the power of the Chinese Communist Party." The Wallace delegation held "secret conferences" in Chungking to discuss "a treacherous plan" for sending arms and supplies to the Communists, plotting with John Service, John Paton Davies, and Gen. Joseph Stilwell—even though Stilwell was actually in Burma at the time. Wallace's confidential trip report to FDR was "obviously not in favor of our Government because of the influence of these persons mentioned above."

John Service was described as "the most active person in supporting the Chinese Communists." Following the conspiratorial meetings with Wallace, Service had been sent to the Chinese Communist Party headquarters in Chungking to tell officials about the decision to provide direct support. The proof of this nefarious mission was that on June 23, 1944, Service was observed arriving at Zhou Enlai's office in an army jeep with license plate number #2070. "By order of Stilwell, Mr. Service personally went to Yenan to confer with the Communist leader Mao Tse-tung, and he also showed Mao State Department documents favoring the Chinese Communists." As further proof of his pro-Communist activities, the report cited Service's October 10, 1944, memo to General Stilwell claiming its primary aim "was to hold down the Nationalist Government in order to let the Chinese Communist or third parties take its place." Service was also reported to have sent copies of his dispatches to Jaffe's *Amerasia* office from China, even before they were transmitted to the State Department!

The most salacious charge made against Service was that he consorted with female Communist agents, who used their "charms and physical attraction to lure foreign diplomats" into revealing important information. Zhou Enlai's female press secretary in Chungking, Kung Peng, had supposedly been "on very intimate terms with John Service."[9] Hoover disseminated the sensational dossier of disinformation to key government officials and politicians, explaining in his cover memo that it came from "intelligence files of Generalissimo Chiang Kai-shek in Formosa."[10]

Meanwhile, the FBI office in New Haven reported that an informant now identified a woman named Val Chao as the "mother of an illegitimate child whose father was John Service of the United States State Department." Although the actress never expressed any pro-Communist sympathies on campus, she was assumed to be a sympathizer "inasmuch as she returned to China in the summer of 1949 and presently is teaching at the Central College of Drama at Peiking [sic], China." In scouring her immigration file, agents located a copy of the child's birth certificate—originally naming a "John Hsieh" as the father—and Immigration and Naturalization Service (INS) records indicating that Chao left the United States on September 7, 1949.[11] Hoover sent a memo detailing Chao's activities to the Justice Department, the State Department, and the Civil Service Commission (the home agency of the Loyalty Review Board). The FBI director noted that a June 1950 letter from Val Chao to a friend in New Haven bore a Peiping, China, return address.[12] In his eyes, this detail confirmed that the woman was a Communist.

Hoover's memo repeated the new allegation that Service had an affair with Zhou Enlai's wartime press aide, Kung Peng. Within no time, the story was leaked to the press. "This Mata Hari wandered from bar to bed all over China concentrating on Americans who looked like soft touches for the Chinese Communists," wrote Fulton Lewis Jr. in his syndicated column. Lewis disclosed that U.S. officials had recently received a secret report from Taiwan providing new information about the pro-Communist activities of certain Americans, including John Service—showing, Lewis crowed, that he had lied to the Tydings Committee when he denied sending confidential information from China to *Amerasia*.

Lewis also reported that Service had sent a confidential memo to Stilwell, proposing a plan to support the Communists and undermine the Nationalist government. "Korea never would have happened in the first place if the State Department hadn't sold Truman on the idea that Chiang was through," Lewis wrote. "The dizzy part of it is that the same 'experts' are still working under Secretary Acheson's wing, helping the UN keep a damper on Chiang's forces right now."[13] The series of articles was inserted into John Service's file at the FBI. Service dismissed them as "silly garbage," but he nevertheless searched out the government translator of the Taiwan report. "I wanted to get either copies of the Chinese originals, or copies of the translations," Service recalled. "He was very sorry, but . . . it was something that he couldn't let me have."[14]

McCarthy gave another Lincoln Day speech attacking John Service with the old, disproved allegations. But he also added a new claim: Acheson had put Service in charge of personnel promotions for officers in Asia. "We finally forced them to call him home," he bragged. "Tydings and the loyalty board said Service had been 'indiscreet,' but that there was no evidence that he was not a loyal American." After a meaningful pause he added, ominously, "Service is now holding a higher paid job in the State Department."[15]

* * *

"I really see no end in sight what with new investigations on all sides," Caroline confided to her parents in February. McCarthy now sat on the State Department appropriations committee. The new chairman of the Senate Judiciary Committee, Patrick McCarran, had launched a new Senate Internal Security Subcommittee (SISS), and HUAC was once again hunting for disloyal Americans. Several of John Service's colleagues from wartime China were undergoing hearings or filling out background questionnaires as a preliminary step for their loyalty board investigations. Meanwhile, the LRB still had not ruled on Jack's case. "I look in absolute amazement at people who tell me to be cheerful," Caroline wrote. "I can be calm and resolute yes, but cheerful hardly."[16]

On February 13 and 14 the full LRB met behind closed doors and discussed John Service's case. The new chairman was Hiram Bingham, a former Republican senator from Connecticut who was determined to expand the board's influence in the hunt for subversives, especially inside the State Department. Whereas the Commerce Department and the post office had fired (on average) 8 percent of screened employees, according to new data, the State Department had never fired anyone on loyalty charges—although some suspects had been allowed to resign.

The LRB was under increasing political pressure to find and dismiss more suspect federal employees. According to the declassified minutes, Bingham told the board he had met with Secretary Acheson to remind him that HUAC was asking departments to provide the number of employees fired for disloyalty, and that SISS would be reviewing those records as well. Acheson, he reported, paid "very great attention."

A major weakness of the loyalty program regulations, Bingham believed, was their wording. Instead of seeking "reasonable *grounds*" for a disloyalty determination, the board should only be required to find "reasonable *doubt*" of an individual's loyalty. He proposed presenting that change to the Civil Service Commission and President Truman.

One board member expressed frustration at the State Department's laxity. "On this loyalty business—now take the Service case, where the record shows that the man living over there with a Chinese woman who we know and the record shows was under the pay of the Russian Government, and he's in love with that woman, and you say that he can be loyal, perfectly loyal to this Government, and he's a safe employee for the State Department, when we know that he's living with a woman who's under the pay of the Russian Government."

"In this particular case," commented another board member, "he came over to this country with the intention of divorcing his wife who had borne him two children so that he could marry this Chinese girl."[17]

Not one member disputed the false contention that John Service's lover was a Soviet spy, and they were appalled at the idea that the diplomat contemplated leaving his American wife and children. In light of recent media revelations, the board voted to return the Service case to the State Department, expecting its loyalty board to reverse the favorable ruling.

The board then passed a motion authorizing Chairman Bingham to propose an amendment changing the standard for judging loyalty cases to "reasonable doubt." When word leaked out that the Civil Service Commission was considering Bingham's proposal, the *Washington Post* denounced it in an editorial: "The only inference that can be drawn from Mr. Bingham's desire for a change is that he wishes to bring about the discharge or rejection of employees on *mere suspicion*."[18] There could be no surer way to wreck the Civil Service, the paper warned, and its effect would be "to inaugurate the very sort of witch-hunt which the loyalty boards have, in the main, avoided until now."[19] Nevertheless, later that spring, Truman amended his original executive order: the witch-hunters obtained the desired ammunition.

* * *

Directed by the LRB to reevaluate the Service case, the State Department security unit launched a new investigation. After concluding that Chao's illegitimate child must have been conceived in January 1946, the zealous chief security officer, a former FBI agent, decided that John Service's "physical whereabouts for the winter of 1945–46 becomes of interest." He assigned investigators to find out if there had been a secret rendezvous while Service was assigned to Tokyo and Chao was still in China.[20]

"The entire last two weeks has been a frantic effort to find out what was happening and where we stood," Jack wrote Caroline on February 27. The latest FBI report might contain anything—"a newspaper clipping, the flimsiest gossip or rumor, or even the absurd ravings of Fulton Lewis." His new overseas posting was being cancelled, he told her, and a new loyalty hearing had been ordered—but two of the three board members were on assignment in Europe. "There is nothing we can do about these delays, except, as I have said so many times until I know you are tired of hearing it, be patient and quiet and make the best of things."

In the interim, Jack was being assigned a low-profile administrative position. He expressed no bitterness: the State Department itself was a prisoner of the loyalty program's "ill-conceived machinery." As he explained to Caroline, "It is practically impossible for the Dept. to use me in Washington in any job even approximating my pay, rank and experience." Even his "innocuous assignment" might become the subject of attacks.

On the bright side, the job meant he was being officially transferred to department headquarters, and the family could finally receive travel orders and funds to return from India. He outlined several travel options: (1) "hop on the first plane"; (2) return by ship via Europe for some sightseeing; (3) keep the older children at boarding school until the school year ended; or (4) all remain in India, because "if they want to shoot me out of Washington, I could probably still come out and pick you up." But the decision would be Caroline's.[21]

* * *

Despite the upbeat letter, John Service was frustrated and increasingly worried. In early March he approached his friend Haywood "Pete" Martin, now the chief of personnel for the Foreign Service. He described the pressure of his unresolved situation, his family's continuing separation, and the ill effects on his wife's health. If he resigned—for the good of the department—before reaching retirement age, he would get no pension. And, given his notoriety, he wondered whether he could find a job to support his family. Martin suggested taking temporary leave from the State Department for a few years, to volunteer for a "mission impossible" assignment with the CIA. But after checking with his contacts there, Service glumly reported that the CIA's security people would not allow his consideration for any position.

Throughout his long ordeal, Service had refused to implicate high administration officials or his own superiors, even though they had encouraged and approved of the activities in China and Washington that led to his involvement in the *Amerasia* scandal. Now, he confided to his friend for the first time that Lauchlin Currie had encouraged him to send information from China and to talk freely with reporters, and how officials at State had arranged his White House back channel and had distributed his China reports throughout Washington's political and press circles. He refused, however, to mention any names. After all, Davies and Vincent faced loyalty investigations of their own. Vincent had already been shifted from an intended posting as U.S. minister to Switzerland to a consular job in Morocco that did not require Senate confirmation—with a substantial cut in pay as well as prestige.

Martin advised Service to provide all this information—including names—to the department's loyalty panel, but Jack decided that would only confuse the issues. Although Service considered their conversation confidential, Martin felt duty-bound to mention it to his boss, Carlisle Humelsine, who was responsible for reviewing all loyalty case outcomes for forwarding to the LRB. On March 21 Humelsine met with Hoover and formally requested the FBI to investigate this new information.

The next day two FBI agents showed up at the State Department to question John Service. He politely requested permission for his stenographer to take notes during the session but was turned down. They asked about Lauchlin Currie and his assistant, Michael Greenberg. Service refused to provide any information except that he knew Greenberg was a China specialist who had worked for Currie at the Board of Economic Warfare. "Nothing which occurred involving Mr. Currie constituted violation of the law, misconduct or a question of loyalty, and in no way concerned the FBI or the Loyalty Board," Service told them. He could not know that Greenberg had also been mentioned by Elizabeth Bentley in 1945 and identified in decoded Venona cables.

The FBI agents drilled the diplomat with questions about his association with a long list of suspicious people: Sol Adler, Chi Chao-ting, Duncan Lee, T. A. Bisson, Alger Hiss, Phillip Jaffe, Tung Pi-wu, and Dr. Ma Hai-teh (George Hatem). Why had he visited Hatem's brother when he returned to the United States in the spring of 1945? Simply to deliver a family letter, Service explained: Hatem ran a field hospital in remote Yenan and mail was disrupted during the war, so he had offered to act as mailman.

Next the interrogators turned their attention to Val Chao. Service freely admitted that at one time he thought he was "violently in love with her" and had asked his wife for a divorce, but he vehemently denied that she was a spy. Had Chao ever visited him in Japan during the winter of 1945–46? Why did the birth certificate of her illegitimate baby initially give John Hsieh as the name of the father? Service flatly denied any conjugal visit had occurred and said he knew nothing about the birth certificate.[22]

"The FBI finally broke precedent by talking to me directly," Service reported to his mother on March 23, after nearly two full days of grilling. "It was a revealing experience because it enabled me to see (better than before) how unsubstantial the stuff they pick up is . . . [and] how helpless they are, because of the nature of the gossip and rumors they pick up, to do very much about proving or disproving them."[23]

But the insubstantial rumors were being taken very seriously. The day after his FBI interrogation ended, Service received official notice that the State Department loyalty board was looking into new charges lodged against him: that he was a Communist or in sympathy with them, and might "voluntarily or involuntarily, divulge classified information without authority."

* * *

Ever since Fulton Lewis first publicized the spy lover tale, Jack had himself been trying to solve the mystery of the paternity of Val's child. Through friends, he now learned that the father was a U.S. Army Air Force major who had met Val at an embassy party during Marshall's mission to China.

"I've been wanting to apologize to you for four years now for not answering that letter you wrote me from NZ asking about Val. I still thought, then, that you were [the child's] father," wrote Annalee Jacoby Fadiman, the former war correspondent. Fadiman had befriended Chao when she arrived in America, three months pregnant. She had arranged for the baby to be taken care of by her gardener's wife, so Val could attend Yale.[24] For a long time, Val never corrected Fadiman's romantic assumption that Service was the father of her "love child." It had been her own fantasy as well, but eventually she confessed.

Fadiman attached to her letter a detailed affidavit about Chao, the child's father, and the difficulties that had forced the actress to return to China. Service sent the affidavit, along with his own ten-page letter, to the head of the State Department loyalty board. He described the wartime romance, defended Val Chao against the rumors that she was a Communist spy, and debunked the notion that he had fathered her illegitimate child. Pointing out that the child was born seventeen months after they had last seen each other, Service provided names of three people to whom she had revealed the father's name. He also addressed the confusion over the crossed-out name on the birth certificate: while it was true that his Chinese surname was Romanized as "Hsieh," Fadiman's affidavit revealed that the name was chosen "because it was the family name of Val's widowed mother."

"I understand that Miss Chao's return to China in 1949 has been interpreted as an indication that she may have been Communist or pro-Communist," his letter continued. "I am certain that any such interpretation is unfounded." She had experienced difficulties with her visa and in earning a livelihood as an actress in the United States. Service also strongly countered suspicions that his former mistress had been a spy. "In the first place, she was continuously in good standing with the Government and Kuomintang (Nationalist Party) during a period of close political surveillance." She would not have been issued a passport had she been suspected by Chiang's government. "In fact, if it is necessary to accept the absurd assumption that every woman in Chungking in 1944–45 was an 'agent,' the only conclusion could have been that Miss Chao was an agent of the Kuomintang. . . . Despite my careful and continuous observation I did not find, and have not since found, reason to consider that my relationship with Miss Chao was dangerous or undesirable from any security or loyalty point of view."[25]

Just as his new loyalty investigation was getting under way, Service learned that his name was probably on the list of Foreign Service officers being recommended for promotion. "I realized this could make a real problem for the State Department," Service remembered years later, "because under the regulations if they cut my name out, no one below me would be able to be promoted." He accordingly wrote the Secretary of State requesting his name be removed from consideration. "Under the current circumstances," Service explained, "I would consider it would be inappropriate to accept promotion." But he also expressed hope that his request would not prejudice any future chance for promotion after he gained "the clearance which I am morally certain will eventually be given me by the Loyalty Review Board."[26]

* * *

On April 11, 1951, Gen. Douglas MacArthur was dismissed as commander of Allied forces in Korea. "It was with the deepest personal regret that I found myself compelled to take this action," President Truman told the nation. "General MacArthur is one of our greatest military commanders. But the cause of world peace is more important than any individual." MacArthur had challenged the president's authority once too often. He disregarded orders not to use American troops near the Chinese border and repeatedly complained about being unable to unleash Chiang's forces in the fight against the Communists. But the last straw came when the general sent a letter criticizing Truman's policy of limited war to the leading Republican in Congress—who immediately publicized it. MacArthur wrote that the only way to win the war was to bomb protected Chinese bases in Manchuria—a suggestion all the more reckless because he had obtained secret approval to activate nuclear bombs for possible use against the enemy. Furious, Truman understood he could no longer entrust the general with a nuclear option.

"I believe that we must try to limit war to Korea for these vital reasons," Truman explained to the nation: "to make sure that the precious lives of our fighting men are not wasted; to see that the security of our country and the free world is not needlessly jeopardized; and to prevent a third world war."[27]

Reaction to Truman's announcement was swift. Senator McCarthy publicly called the president "a sonofabitch"; his decision to fire MacArthur was "a Communist victory won with the aid of bourbon and Benedictine."[28] The White House was swamped with 100,000 telegrams. Outraged politicians and journalists launched attacks on the familiar suspects who had "lost" China to the Communists and were now giving away Korea. Resolutions in support of MacArthur were passed by several state legislatures, and the general returned home to a hero's parade in San Francisco. Truman's popularity dropped to 23 percent.

On April 19, 1951, General MacArthur ended his fifty-two-year military career with a farewell address to a joint session of Congress that drew a standing ovation from teary admirers. "War's very object is victory, not prolonged indecision," he declared. "Under no circumstances" should Taiwan be allowed to fall under Communist control. "Such an eventuality would at once threaten the freedom of the Philippines and the loss of Japan, and might well force our western frontier back to the coast of California, Oregon and Washington."[29]

McArthur's speech triggered an outcry for a new investigation. "Washington is seething, of course, with Republican oratory over the MacArthur affair," John Service reported to his mother. "I assumed that it would be only a matter of time until we were thought of and sure enough . . . the *Times Herald* got around yesterday to giving us the credit. What a laugh! I have now been blamed for causing Stilwell to get thrown out by Chiang Kai-shek, for causing Hurley's resignation, for being the cause of Grew's resignation—and now finally MacArthur."[30] "Do not be shaken in your integrity," Grace Service replied. "Men like you are the nation's final hope and trust."[31]

* * *

The story of John Service's renewed loyalty investigation broke on May Day. A *Washington Star* story reported that a "new rumor" was delaying final clearance. The next day an obscure representative from Illinois named Fred E. Busbey declared that the first man to be dismissed under the new standard of "reasonable doubt" should be John Service—"fired before he has a chance to resign."[32]

"Since nothing is more important to me than clearing my name," John Service wrote to Busbey, "I am glad to cooperate with and await the outcome of any investigations, however prolonged or repetitious." He pointed out that under the American justice system, in contrast to congressional and administrative proceedings, a person could only be tried in court one time on the same charge. "Knowing my own innocence of any disloyalty, and proud of my record of 18 years as a member of the American Foreign Service, I have no intention of resigning."[33] Representative Busbey did not respond to Service's request for a meeting.

* * *

After fourteen months in India, Caroline and Phillip finally returned and settled into a small rented apartment near Dupont Circle. Ambassador Henderson reassured her he would "keep an eye" on the older children, still at boarding school, and expressed confidence that "in spite of the setbacks and discouragements which you and Jack have had, opportunities will again present themselves to Jack to perform distinguished service for the U.S."[34] But Caroline could not shake her depression. Shortly before leaving New Delhi she got word that her father had died. And she was now experiencing firsthand the nastiness of the newest American witch hunt, a new kind of culture shock. "How Jack stands all of this I simply can't imagine, because it has already made me feel completely dead," she confided to a friend. It saddened her to think that her brilliant husband might end up marking time until retirement. "He had been completely pushed out of the life that is food and drink to him."[35]

* * *

By early summer, under the command of Gen. Matthew Ridgway, UN forces succeeded in pushing the North Koreans and their Chinese allies back across the thirty-eighth parallel. Back-and-forth fighting for control of hilltops with names like "Pork Chop Hill" and "Heartbreak Ridge" set the bloody pattern of conflict that would last another two years. Efforts to begin peace negotiations were under way, but progress was slow.

Bitter political battles intensified. The so-called MacArthur hearings, jointly held by the Senate's Armed Services and Foreign Relations Committees, focused on alleged failures of American military policies in Asia while HUAC and the McCarran Subcommittee targeted alleged subversion from within. The left-liberal Institute of Pacific Relations was now painted as a hotbed of subversion.

During a McCarran Subcommittee hearing, General Wedemeyer was asked whether he considered former political advisers like John Service "disloyal." The general replied: "I would never accuse anyone of disloyalty. But I do know that, if I had followed their advice, Communism would have run rampant over China much more rapidly than it did."[36] Sensational headlines followed. Service was never called to respond, but the State Department finally rose to his defense by releasing Wedemeyer's 1945 letter of commendation, along with evidence that the general had insisted on keeping the diplomats on staff, following Stilwell's recall.

A few weeks later, *The Foreign Service Journal* published an essay by John Service discussing current threats to the integrity and independence of Foreign Service reporting. Service cited Wedemeyer's recent testimony as an example of "investigative autopsies" that ignored the actual context of field reports, ascribing "a meaning completely unwarranted or opposite to the writer's intent and language." He demonstrated how Robert Morris, now chief counsel of the McCarran Subcommittee, had used three fragmentary excerpts from one of Service's memos—written nine months before Wedemeyer even arrived in the war zone—to elicit Wedemeyer's damaging testimony. "The memo was made to appear to have a meaning the precise opposite of what it actually said."[37]

Service's careful commentary had little effect on the firestorm. Many other China Service officers were undergoing loyalty investigations and being subpoenaed by congressional committees, including John Paton Davies and John Carter Vincent. Another colleague, Edmund Clubb, resigned rather than respond to an absurd charge stemming from a 1932 visit to the offices of the *New Masses*, where he had briefly encountered Whittaker Chambers. As the United States' last consul-general in Beijing, Clubb's final official act had been to haul down the American flag and carry it safely home.

In mid-October Service received a letter from Hiram Bingham, the chairman of the president's LRB. The State Department loyalty board had again reaffirmed Service's loyalty and dismissed the latest FBI charges, but in the public interest, the LRB had decided to hold its own hearing into his case. Bingham said the new hearing would be based upon "the charges heretofore issued to you" in prior hearings. To prepare, Service and Rhetts reviewed the documents and evidence accumulated in his previous hearings. "We just sort of went in and said, 'Here we are,'" Service remembered. "We didn't prepare a case."[38]

The six-hour hearing began at ten o'clock on Thursday morning, November 8, 1951. The panel was composed of three veteran lawyers from well-known firms in Boston and New York, who had evidently studied his record meticulously. "Ed's professional reaction was that short of the Supreme Court, it would not be possible to assemble a more experienced and capable group, whose fairness and objectivity could be more relied on," Service wrote to his mother.[39] Although not an official member of the panel, the LRB chairman, Hiram Bingham, roamed in and out throughout the morning. Service never forgot his "forbidding, scowling presence" in the hearing room.

The panel of lawyers assumed the defendant had seen the same information they possessed, such as the FBI report on his arrest in June 1945. "Would you mind just letting me scan that report?" Rhetts asked at one point, and later explained, "Our difficulty here is that we don't have a copy of the same transcript you have." "You don't?" asked George Alger, the chairman. "Why not?" That question was easier to ask than to answer.

The LRB panel next asked about "the military plans" Service had discussed with the *Amerasia* editor in the recorded hotel room conversation. Service again explained that his choice of words had been inappropriate. "It was a very loose and really mistaken use of the word 'plans.' . . . This policy recommendation that if we landed in areas controlled by the Communists we should have to expect to work with them, was the only, quote, 'plan' that I saw. It wasn't a military plan in any sense." "Why not?" queried one board member. "Well," replied Service patiently, "a military plan, in the strict sense of the word, is detailed and specific plans for operations."

Service's personal copies of his China reports became another issue of contention:

Shattuck: You constantly refer to all these copies that you had as your own personal copies, and you refer to it as something that you could use in any way you chose, as if it were your own. . . . It was no different as to its confidential nature from any copies you sent to the State Department, was it, or to the Army?

Service: Yes, I believe they were different.

Shattuck: One was the carbon and the other was the original.

Service: But the character of the other copies was changed by the Army's or Embassy's comment or evaluation.

Clark: Did you see it? Did you see it after its transmission?

Service: No, sir.

Clark: Well, how do you know, then? . . . My point is that he should be just as careful about disseminating what he calls his personal copy as he would be about disseminating any other copy of the same document. . . .

Service: I would say it depends upon the nature of the material.

Shattuck: Yes, but the fact that it was what you call your personal copy has nothing to do with the question of whether you should circulate it, does it?

Alger: Does it?

Shattuck: That's a simple question. You ought to be able to answer it.[40]

In that sedate hearing room in 1951, John Service found it difficult to convey the peculiar environment of wartime China: intrigue, censorship, clashing personalities and contentious policy disputes, played out against a backdrop of revolution and Japanese aggression. To the board members, who had no experience of that turbulent era, his seemingly cavalier approach to his confidential reports and casual relations with members of the press suggested that the State Department had indeed been too lax about security matters. "What we got was an extremely rigorous 'expert' interrogation," Service later wrote his mother. The grilling, while not hostile, left him "exhausted" and feeling as though he had been "run over—and back and forth—by a bulldozer."[41]

Service and Rhetts were told they would receive a transcript of the proceedings in about two weeks. They would then be allowed to submit a brief to supplement the oral testimony. "Neither Ed nor I feel that this will have any effect on the outcome," Service advised his mother. "These men know the case so thoroughly that their mind is made up—we think favorably."[42]

Only when the transcript arrived did Service realize that the LRB panel had focused on the wrong section of the regulations. Instead of the section under which charges had "heretofore been issued" against him, the panel was evidently investigating a new charge: "willful disclosure of confidential information." When Rhetts informed the board of the mix-up, its members were highly embarrassed. Legally, Rhetts could have insisted upon a new hearing. Instead, he agreed to stipulate that his client waived that right and would allow the hearing to stand as if Service was aware of this new charge. "Ed said that his reaction was, as a lawyer, that these people would not use a technicality like this to hang [someone]." Service recalled. "Therefore, it must mean that they were going to decide in my favor."[43]

But on Thursday, December 13, 1951, a letter was delivered to Secretary of State Acheson from Hiram Bingham informing him that "based on the intentional and unauthorized disclosure of documents and information of a confidential and non-public character," the Loyalty Review Board panel had indeed found "reasonable doubt" in the case of Service's loyalty. Acheson was instructed to "remove the employee from the rolls of the Department."[44]

PART III
VINDICATION

CHAPTER 22
THE LONG FIGHT

The same morning that Hiram Bingham's letter was being delivered to the secretary of state, John Service dropped by the department's loyalty board office. The clerk froze when he saw him. "How did you know?" he asked. "Know what?" asked Service. "The Loyalty Review Board has just ruled against you!" the man blurted out.[1] A letter had been prepared advising Service that his employment in the Foreign Service would be terminated the next day.[2]

Service phoned Rhetts and went straight to his office. By the time he arrived, the attorney had already called Secretary Humelsine to schedule a meeting for late that afternoon. "I was incredulous at first," Service recalled. "When Ed Rhetts confirmed it, I was shocked, and then there was an initial period of hopelessness that this was final, that this was the end of everything."[3]

When Jack called, Caroline and her mother were preparing homemade baked beans for a supper with friends. She rushed downtown to find Jack and his lawyer sitting and staring at each other in silence. She began to weep. "Jack and I sat in Ed Rhetts' office, and there seemed no place to go and nothing more to do, just as though we had gone down a large black hole."[4] "There was a period of despair, why try to deny it?" Service admitted. "But, right then, Ed said he was going to try to take the case to court. I think at that moment, he was the only person who thought there was even a ghost of a chance that a case could be gotten into court."[5]

Caroline stayed about an hour. Then she marched over to the administrative offices of the Loyalty Review Board (LRB) and demanded to see the chairman, Hiram Bingham. "If I'd come from another planet, [the receptionist] couldn't have been more shocked," Caroline recalled with a chuckle. An assistant appeared and said Senator Bingham was in conference and unable to see her. "He spent a lot of time on my husband's case and I think that he can give me a few minutes of his time," Caroline replied. "I have nothing that I have to do, and I will just sit here. The conference must be over sometime. I will just stay here till Senator Bingham is free." Within five minutes, Mrs. John Service was ushered into a spacious office. "[Senator Bingham] took me by the hand and said, 'What can I do for you little lady?' I could have screamed." Caroline said she thought he had done a great injustice to a very worthy man. "His reply, which I will never forget, was that many people have had grave injustices done to them."[6]

* * *

Secretary Humelsine refused their request for a delay, explaining to Rhetts and Service that the State Department was bound by the opinion of the LRB. A press conference had been scheduled for 6:00 PM, and they were shown the extraordinary eighteen-page press packet, including Bingham's letter to Secretary Acheson, the findings of the LRB panel, and the overturned favorable opinion of the State Department loyalty board.

The LRB report acknowledged there was no evidence that Service was a member of the Communist Party or any subversive organization on the attorney general's list, and there was no reasonable doubt about his loyalty while stationed in China and Japan. "It was part of his duty to confer with the Communists and report upon what he found, and his conclusions as to what should be done." But in his dealings with *Amerasia*'s editor during a six-week period in the spring of 1945, the three-member panel found evidence of "intentional, unauthorized disclosure" of confidential government information. Although there was "no evidence that the employee stole or abstracted from the official files and transmitted to Jaffe or any other person any official files," his relationship with Jaffe created a reasonable doubt about his loyalty. The board ruled that several of Service's reports were "of a nature which no discreet person would disseminate without express authority."[7]

Of greatest concern had been the conversations in Jaffe's hotel room. "Service talked very freely, discussing, among other things, troop dispositions and military plans which he said he had seen and which he said were 'very secret.'" Although Service had asked his associates whether Jaffe were a Communist, the board felt he never took seriously enough the warnings that Jaffe was "bad medicine." "We find in the conversations . . . as reported by the F.B.I. . . . no indication of any caution by Service in the continuous line of answers he made to Jaffe's 'nosey' inquiries on State Department matters." The board decided such behavior stood in sharp contrast to his relations with war correspondents in China. Brooks Atkinson had stated that Service never showed him any classified materials—that he was "too punctilious about State Department security and declined to tell me everything he knew."[8]

John Service's indiscretion with Jaffe became a paramount issue for the LRB:

> To say that his course of conduct [with Jaffe] does not raise a reasonable doubt as to Service's own loyalty would, we are forced to think, stretch the mantle of charity much too far. . . . For an experienced and trusted representative of our State Department to so far forget his duty to his trust as his conduct with Jaffe so clearly indicates, forces us with great regret to conclude that there is reasonable doubt as to his loyalty. The favorable finding of the Loyalty Security Board of the Department of State is accordingly reversed.[9]

This finding was contrary to the State Department's loyalty board, which—while acknowledging that Service committed "two serious indiscretions"—had ruled there was no reason to doubt his loyalty. They discounted Service's hotel-room talk about secret military plans: "As a matter of fact, he was not advised of any secret information at all concerning the military plans of the United States." The department's board considered it a "mark of prudence" for a diplomat talking about "military speculations" with journalists in wartime "to refer to the subject matter as secret or confidential, in order that no conclusions may be attributed by the press to government sources."[10]

Service and Rhetts welcomed the comprehensive press packet as "ammunition to fight with."[11] Service quickly prepared a personal statement for distribution at the news conference:

> The Loyalty Review Board's decision is a surprise, a shock and an injustice. I am not now and never have been disloyal to the United States. The Board expressly states that it does not find me disloyal.
>
> What it has done is to base a "reasonable doubt" on a single episode which occurred six and a half years ago, which has been freely admitted by me and known to all responsible quarters since that time and for which I have been tried and unanimously acquitted at least nine times. . . . I am confident that my record of 18½ years' service to the American government and the testimony of the many people who have worked with me during that period will support me in my conviction that there is no doubt of my loyalty.[12]

A few years later, Dean Acheson revealed the president's role in Service's case. "We had to fire Jack because the fellow turned over some secrets to someone. It was a silly thing to do. But the President said 'no; this is wrong.' . . . You have to accept it. The boy was wrong. . . . So I fired him."[13] Both Truman and Acheson were under intense political pressure—and neither of them had reviewed the entire case, including the State Department loyalty board's records and the thick Tydings transcript. Truman simply reviewed a Justice Department case summary based on information from the FBI.

Out of the 3 million employees on the federal payroll, 14,000 cases had been investigated by the FBI. John Service was one of only 212 federal employees dismissed under Truman's loyalty program between 1947 and 1951.

* * *

Caroline's baked bean supper that evening was "like a wake" as the gathering listened to the news of Service's dismissal on the radio. "We were flattened out," she remembered. "This didn't exactly come out of the clouds because it had been building up for years. But, still, we couldn't believe it." The children were told they could stay home from school, but they decided to attend and met no hostility. The next morning the phone began to ring. Soon, cables and letters began arriving from around the world.[14]

From his new post in Teheran, Loy Henderson wrote: "I hope you will not allow yourself to be discouraged by what has happened, but will continue to make use of your talents on behalf of family and U.S. We know that you possess the courage and the vitality not to allow the gloom to enshroud you."[15]

George Kennan reflected upon the larger significance of Service's firing. "While you are the person most deeply and tragically affected, this is a blow to all of us who have at heart the interests of a good Foreign Service and a successful foreign policy," he wrote. "What has happened is the result of the first fumbling efforts of rather thoughtless people in Government to adjust to a problem of great complexity and delicacy. You have happened to get under the wheels of the somewhat ponderous and unsound machinery they have set up and have been injured as you might have been if you had walked into the path of a truck." Kennan even offered his country home as a retreat for the family. "I hope you will be able to find some sort of life in which there will be pleasure and satisfaction, even though it means starting all over again and forfeiting the chance to make the most of some of your talents."[16]

The next morning, Service went in to clear out his office and settle affairs. He was surprised to discover that the Equitable Assurance Company would not convert his cancelled group insurance to a term policy. Asked why, the agent bluntly explained that the company feared the ex-diplomat "might jump out of a window or something." Service felt "practically bare with no job, no retirement, no pension, nothing, no insurance."[17] But unlike the terrible night he spent in jail in 1945, he felt no sense of shame or disgrace.

* * *

"John Service, was, and is, a completely loyal American citizen," declared CBS radio news correspondent Eric Sevareid in his evening broadcast after Service's firing was made public. "It is my personal conviction, based on much firsthand knowledge, that the American diplomatic service contained no more brilliant, devoted, self-sacrificing field agent." He had known Service for eight years. "Even though no new evidence had been produced, [under the new rules] mere doubt can destroy a reputation, a career, all that makes life worth living for a citizen who happens to be in the federal service."[18] Sevareid was severely criticized at CBS and its affiliates for his commentary but did not tell Service for many years.

The controversial firing generated news stories at home and abroad. A pro-Chiang newspaper in Hong Kong described Service as one of the American officials "advising Chiang Kai-shek in the prosecution of defensive war against Japan [who] were actually plotting behind his back either to force him to collaborate with the Communists or to have him cast aside." The article declared that anyone "willing to deliver classified information to Russia is definitely unworthy of trust" and predicted "other dismissals would have to follow if the cleaning process is to produce the desired effect."[19]

A *Washington Post* editorial bemoaned the "tragic end" of Service's career and the growing "blight of McCarthyism." "The Foreign Service will find in Mr. Service's experience a grim warning against any deviation from the most pallid and sterile conformity in reporting on developments abroad."[20] Indeed, the State Department started to feel the chilling effects of the LRB verdict almost immediately as morale plummeted.

Ed Rhetts was especially outraged that the LRB ruling had relied upon the stipulation he had accepted—waiving the right to another hearing on the new charges. The LRB, he concluded, had no legal authority to overrule a favorable ruling by a departmental loyalty board. It would be a long battle to overturn its decision, working first through the civil service system and then in the federal courts, but Rhetts was determined to try—if Service only had the heart to keep battling.

"Don't let Rhetts persuade you to keep up the kicking," advised Grace Service. "Your friends know you. Show you can take a defeat and meet the world and its challenge with your head up. I am still proud of you." Her advice was to focus on the future: "Things may look dark for a few days—not for long. Get out and hunt for a job and I think you will find one." She enclosed a check for six hundred dollars to help with expenses.[21]

"I appreciate your feeling on this subject and am inclined to agree," Service replied. "No use in prolonging the already over-long affair if the struggle is to be hopeless." But he had allowed Rhetts to take steps to prepare for possible further actions—including a lawsuit—because "there was strong and deep feeling among Foreign Service and State Department people that this involves much more than just my case." Jack thanked his mother for the check and told her that friends had started a legal defense fund. "All China people, of whatever slant, and particularly people who have devoted a life to it . . . have had their world tumble. . . . The fact is that China has become a sort of a tragedy for everyone connected with it."[22]

* * *

By the end of 1951, loyalty investigations had engulfed many of Service's colleagues, including Davies, Ray Ludden, and Edmund Clubb. On December 17, John Carter Vincent, Service's former boss and mentor, returned from his post in Tangiers to face his first hearing before the State Department's loyalty board. It was becoming obvious that the real issue was not their loyalty or security but their political reporting and policy recommendations. At stake was the integrity of the Foreign Service itself.

After meeting several times, the group raised their concerns with the American Foreign Service Officers Association, but their plight was deemed "too delicate a political issue" for the organization to tackle. "So the hard fact was that we were on our own," Service concluded. "The Foreign Service Association averted its eyes and walked by on the other side of the road."[23]

* * *

Christmas 1951 was a quiet affair for the Service family, but at least they were together. Service was busy pursuing leads for a job with an international company or organization. New Year's Eve had always been Jack's favorite holiday, and despite their dismal situation, the Services decided to throw a party. "The day before, we called up people, and said if anybody wanted to drop in," Caroline remembered, "please come after eight o'clock." Her mother cooked a turkey for the buffet, and people kept dropping in all night long. Twenty years later, memories of all the loyal friends who came to celebrate with the outcast ex-diplomat still brought tears to John Service's eyes.[24]

* * *

By January Ed Rhetts had gathered vital ammunition for the civil service appeal. In response to his query, Secretary Humelsine had sent a letter confirming that the LRB's finding was the only reason Service had been fired. The *Foreign Service*

Journal published a strong editorial expressing "grave concern" over the LRB's conclusion: "There is a great deal at stake here for Service, the individual; for the Foreign Service as a group of dedicated government employees; for the Department in its heavy responsibility of diplomacy; and for the American people and their heritage of justice." It urged a court fight if necessary, "to make certain that justice prevails."[25]

Foreign Service officers around the world had begun to send contributions for Service's legal battle. From New Zealand, Amb. Robert Scotton sent a one-thousand-dollar check and a consoling thought: "With the passage of time, your recent difficulties will assume the proportions of a bad dream which is past and forgotten."[26] John Reid, a friend from Oberlin and a Washington attorney, acted as treasurer of the defense fund. He kept the list of contributors completely confidential, in case Service was ever called before a congressional committee and asked under oath to provide names.

* * *

On January 6, 1952, a *Washington Post* story reported that McCarthy had released the confidential minutes of a LRB meeting held the previous February. Board members were quoted complaining that the State Department loyalty program was "completely ineffective" in ferreting out disloyal employees, unlike such agencies as the post office. A follow-up story reported that the Civil Service Commission had immediately ordered an investigation to find the leaker—and "now the Loyalty Review Board is placed in the embarrassing position of facing accusations that its own records are not secure."[27]

These disclosures helped Rhetts in his petition for presidential review of the case. "The minutes disclosed by McCarthy indicated the Loyalty Review Board is not 'impartial' in handling cases, but apparently seeks a statistical quota of dismissals."[28] Because there was no formal machinery to hear appeals of LRB decisions, Rhetts requested that the president appoint an impartial individual or panel to review Service's case. And he asked that his client be given copies of all the FBI reports and transcripts that had been considered by the loyalty board.

McCarthy then raised the stakes by disclosing new excerpts from the LRB minutes dealing with Service's alleged wartime affair with a Communist spy. Service fired off a letter to Hiram Bingham, pointing out that such charges had never been mentioned during his LRB hearing and demanding a copy of all meeting minutes in which his case had been discussed. Otherwise, he was unable to defend himself "against this further character assassination by Sen. McCarthy" or to respond to "any further personal vilification based upon deliberations of your Board." Bingham took nearly four months to reply, and then he denied

Service's request on grounds of confidentiality. Several decades would pass before those minutes were declassified under the Freedom of Information Act.

In a letter to her dear friend Lisa Green, Caroline confided, "J. keeps his calm exterior, but he has been hurt to the depths of his soul—and it is a hurt I doubt if he'll ever completely get over."[29] Jack had yet to find a decent job. After hearing Sevareid's broadcast, one listener offered to give him a small boat supply business, and someone else offered a secondhand book business. But employment that would use his talents was proving hard to find. "No one would touch me," Service recalled. "I went around to all the companies I had done business with out in the Far East. . . . 'Oh, you're a fine guy, but sorry, what will the stockholders say?'" Nonprofit organizations and foundations, also under fire, were likewise unwilling to hire "the guy that lost China."[30]

Then, out of the blue, there arrived a letter from a businessman named Clement Wells. "I think you have been unfairly treated after your long connection with the Government and it has occurred to me that possibly you might be interested in entering commercial life." Wells owned Sarco, a company that manufactured steam traps in the United States, Britain, and France. "Early next year we expect to incorporate a small company entitled Sarco International, Ltd. and if it would be of interest to you to join us as a director and officer, perhaps it would be possible for us to meet."[31] Service immediately went to the public library to learn about industrial steam traps, and he asked friends to check out the firm. A Dun & Bradstreet report indicated the private company had a very good credit rating. State Department friends ascertained there was no taint of subversive activities or Communist associations attached to Wells or the company's officers.

On January 21 Service took the train to New York to meet Mr. Wells—a small, old-fashioned gentleman seated behind a roll-top desk in a corner office in the Empire State Building. "I suppose you don't know the difference between a steam trap and a mousetrap," Wells declared cheerfully. "But never mind. . . . We'll show you." He suggested that Service spend a week at their factory in Bethlehem, Pennsylvania. A few weeks later, with no other job prospects, Service agreed to visit the Sarco plant. Clement Wells would pay his travel expenses, and if Service decided to join the company, he would be paid for time spent learning about the business.

"So I had two weeks working on the assembly line in the factory, doing odd jobs. They moved me around a bit, but I was regarded as sort of a curiosity." He soon discovered that steam traps were essential in any industry that used steam as a source of power. Thousands of them were needed for factories, oil refineries, and even ships to run efficiently. "You don't want to waste that water," Service later explained, "but you've got to have some sort of an automatic valve in there that lets the water go back to the boiler, but holds the steam in the equipment."[32] John Service gratefully accepted Mr. Wells' job offer—to develop the company's export business—with a starting salary of nine thousand dollars a year, a cut of more than 20 percent from his Foreign Service salary.

Once again the family would endure a separation. Service moved to New York in March, again camping out with friends to save money. Caroline and the children would stay in Washington, D.C., until the school year ended.

* * *

The witch hunt continued in Washington. John Carter Vincent was subpoenaed by the McCarran Subcommittee for an investigation of the Institute of Pacific Relation's influence on the State Department. He spent twenty-eight hours on the witness stand. "I have never been to anything that disgusted me quite so much," Caroline reported to Lisa Green after attending a session. "The senators and their counsels brow-beat, ridiculed, and attempted to trap J. C. in every way they possibly could. . . . The man was made to answer yes and no to questions that could not be answered that way. . . . Any and every action and thought was made to appear part of a plot."[33] Once, when Vincent's memory failed him, counsel Robert Morris sneered, "Do you think it is possible you may have been a member of the Communist Party in 1945 and now have forgotten it?" Vincent's wife remarked that, by comparison, childbirth had been fun.[34]

"Nothing at all has been heard from [Rhetts'] appeal to the President," Caroline's letter explained. "People who know us or know anything about the Foreign Service . . . know that Jack is a man of integrity and loyalty. People who don't know him, but believe in fairness and decency also think well of him." And she remained convinced that "time and history" would eventually vindicate her husband—although she knew he did not want to wait that long.[35]

Having received no reply to his presidential request, Rhetts sent a second letter in early February, raising the issue of McCarthy's most recent revelations about Service's association "with a person alleged to be in the pay of the Russian government." This issue had not been raised at his LRB hearing, and Service had never had an opportunity to defend against it.[36] On February 23 Rhetts received the discouraging reply from the president's special counsel: "After discussion of this matter with the President, I regret to advise you that the requests you have made cannot be granted."[37]

Gen. Joseph Stilwell's widow also wrote to the president. Were her husband still alive, he too would have been "called upon to defend his honor" against McCarthy's "scurrilous attacks." "I am writing to you to ask a great favor in the name of Gen. Stilwell," she petitioned. "Not that you re-instate John Service, but that you talk to him and learn for yourself what a very fine young man he is, truly devoted to his country." Truman wrote in response, "I am trying to get things worked out so that justice can be done to the two men you named. The time isn't right now for me to see either one of them, but I believe we will get the situation straightened out before we get through."[38]

* * *

On March 23 the Senate subcommittee with oversight of the State Department budget—including Senators McCarthy and McCarran—met in closed-door session to enforce their anti-Communist agenda. Undersecretary Carlisle Humelsine was called on the carpet for repeatedly giving clearances to John Service. The senators were especially outraged about Service's alleged wartime affair with a Soviet spy lover, but their discussion was considered so scandalous that it was stricken from the official record and kept secret until the actual transcript was discovered twenty-five years later.

That excised exchange reveals that the central concern in Service's case may have had less to do with his alleged doubtful loyalty than his alleged immorality. Sen. Homer Ferguson asked Humelsine how the State Department's loyalty board could have possibly ruled in Service's favor "when he was living with a Communist who was not his wife?" Although never mentioned in the official findings on Service's loyalty case, this was apparently the charge that mattered most.

Senator McCarthy cited an allegation in the minutes of the LRB that the Chinese woman was "under the pay of the Russian government." Humelsine responded that the board had considered this allegation, but the investigation never substantiated it. "All Chinese are not Communists," he observed meekly. Ferguson persisted: "Can you say a man is not a security risk when he is living with a woman from a foreign country . . . and has a wife in this country?" Sen. Leverett Saltonstall asked, "Was his wife in this country still faithful to him?" "Senator," replied an embarrassed Humelsine, "I do not know. . . . Mrs. Service, I understand, is a very fine lady."

Saltonstall hastily attempted to clarify his intent: "If he was leading a double life, that is one thing. If he was leading this life with a Chinese woman, with his wife's knowledge because she had decided he no longer was any good, that is another thing." Senator McCarthy added to the outrageous discussion by injecting a unique understanding of the term "evidence":

Senator McCarthy: Is there any question about these facts [in the Service case]: number one, living with a Chinese woman; number two, evidence that she was a Communist; number three, evidence she was receiving pay as a spy. I am not saying whether you were convinced the evidence was true, but is there any question about the fact that evidence is in the files?

Mr. Humelsine: I will have to check whether I have authority to discuss that.[39]

* * *

At the time, John Service was trying hard to learn how to be a Sarco salesman. "The job just seemed to be a dead-end job, not really getting anywhere," he remembered.[40] On weekends, Jack returned to Washington, D.C. To Caroline, he seemed a fish out of water. "It is a pity that the thing that Jack is best fitted for in the world he can no longer do," she wrote her mother. "I often wonder if he will ever do anything again that he likes half so well or is so well fitted for."[41]

By the end of April, the Sarco International Company was officially incorporated. For his first trip abroad, to Mexico to drum up export business, Service eagerly studied Spanish. He telephoned home from Monterrey, Mexico, enthusiastic about the positive reaction his sales pitch received. "He sounded more cheerful than he has in ages," Caroline reported.[42]

Rhetts had by now exhausted all possibilities of executive review and reconsideration of the LRB ruling. The family faced a difficult decision: whether to take the case to court. There was no hesitation in Service's response to his lawyer: "This is a 'green light' to you for any plans or action which you consider desirable in my case. . . . Caroline and my brother . . . concur. It is our desire to fight the case and to seek restoration of my good name and reputation." Jack assured Rhetts of his commitment to see the case through: "We place ourselves in your hands. You need not fear, therefore, that we will pull out on you midway or abandon support which you or others may organize. . . . Of course I do not expect to sit idly by as a mere spectator."[43]

* * *

In early July, Senator McCarran released his subcommittee's report on the Institute of Pacific Relations. "But for the machinations of the small group that controlled and activated the IPR, China would be free and a bulwark against a further advance of the Red hordes into the Far East," the Nevada senator proclaimed. "Government agencies have been infiltrated by persons whose allegiance is with Communist Russia."[44] The usual suspects were repeatedly mentioned in the thick document. The *Washington Post* editorialized, "The McCarran Subcommittee has given us not a report, but a revision of history . . . a revision compounded out of McCarthian bigotry, McCarranesque spleen and MacArthurian legend. It is an attempt to perpetrate another fraud and hoax on the American people."[45]

President Truman was outraged. He ordered his new attorney general, James McGranery, to investigate the actions of the subcommittee. "From what I know of this case," the president wrote, "I am of the opinion that Davies and Lattimore were shamefully persecuted by this committee." Truman did not know, however, that McGranery himself had committed perjury in his confirmation hearing when he claimed under oath that he had "no connection" to the *Amerasia* case. Hoover knew, of course, and he made sure that McGranery understood his vulnerability. He sent his new boss a 1945 memo that described in detail one of those taped conversations with Corcoran.[46]

* * *

The Republican Party held its July convention in sweltering Chicago, where it nominated retired general Dwight "Ike" Eisenhower as its standard-bearer. Among the featured speakers was retired general Patrick Hurley, who spoke of his World War II efforts to help the heroic Chiang Kai-shek while fending off the sabotage of disloyal Foreign Service officers. Determined to win back the White House after twenty years, the GOP faithful were eager to attack the Democrats' triple failures: "Korea, Communism, and Corruption." On the campaign trail, Ike always drew applause by referring to "the mess in Washington," assuring enthusiastic audiences that a top priority of his administration would be to ferret out Communist spies, traitors, and security risks in the government.

* * *

By the time John Service celebrated his forty-third birthday on August 3, he had found a small apartment for the family in the Fordham Hill section of the Bronx: a twelfth-floor flat with two bedrooms and a view of the Hudson River. But after giving the manager checks for the security deposit and rent, he was informed that his application had been rejected by the Equitable Life Assurance Company, owner of the building. Company investigators had called to verify his employment at Sarco and had pointedly asked whether he was "*the* John Service." When his phone calls were not returned, Service confronted the manager: "If the reason back of the Equitable head office decision was the McCarthy and Loyalty Board publicity they should note the fact that the Loyalty Board decision specifically stated that I was not a Communist, that I had not stolen any official files and that I was not disloyal." Service gave the manager a copy of the State Department's press packet about his firing and asked to meet with his supervisors. On August 13 he got a letter saying that the company regretted that the apartment he had applied for was "not available." Service fired off a letter to the manager, calling attention to the current newspaper advertisement of that and similar apartments. He documented the "unhappy episode" in a seven-page memo for his attorney. The evident discrimination was ammunition for the lawsuit they had decided to file against the government.

Within a few weeks Service found another apartment, making sure to check in personally at the landlord's main office to head off trouble. The high-rise apartment house was located in Queens, and most of their neighbors were Jewish refugees with their own histories of persecution. Jack was reminded of his wrenching experiences handling Jewish immigration problems in wartime Shanghai.

To his parents' delight, fifteen-year-old Bob won a scholarship to attend high school in England that year and soon sailed off on his first solo adventure abroad. His older sister, Virginia, stayed in Washington, D.C., with friends to finish her last semester of high school. Only six-year-old Phillip shared the cramped two-bedroom apartment with his parents, attending school across the street. Whenever Ginny came home to visit, Phil gallantly gave up his bedroom and slept on the living room sofa. "There was a bit of floor sleeping when we were all there," Bob recalled.[47]

For Caroline Service, who had always known the security of her father's army posts or of the close-knit diplomatic community, the move was traumatic. "In many ways, New York and everything about it was more foreign to me than living abroad." Eventually she took a part-time job, first as a typist and later as a clerk in a neighborhood discount store, where she earned $1.25 an hour. "Every cent" was saved for her children's education.[48]

* * *

On October 31, 1952, Ed Rhetts filed a civil lawsuit on behalf of John Service against U.S. government officials, including Secretary of State Dean Acheson, Hiram Bingham, and other members of the LRB. It asked that the review board's findings be declared invalid, that statements reflecting on his security be expunged from the records, and that his job be restored with full back pay. The suit demanded that the LRB decision be set aside on the basis of the Fourteenth Amendment's guarantee of due process of law. If not, then plaintiff requested his entire loyalty case—and the LRB's finding of reasonable doubt—be fully reviewed in court. There was, however, no remedy of law for "the irreparable damage [Service] has suffered and continues to suffer as a result of his unlawful discharge," Rhetts' brief noted.

Service and Rhetts knew that their case rested on technical arguments about due process, particularly their claim that the LRB lacked authority to reverse State's favorable finding. Nevertheless, their 146-page petition was packed with exhibits, including media and congressional references to the FBI evidence that Service had never been allowed to see. Government lawyers successfully objected to some of the material, and the complaint had to be amended four times.

In 1955 their persistence began to pay off. The federal district court in Washington agreed to hear their latest amended complaint. The judge ruled that the LRB had indeed acted illegally, and he ordered its finding of "doubtful loyalty" stricken from all government records. But he refused to order Service's reinstatement, ruling that the secretary of state had acted legally in firing him under the discretionary power granted by the McCarran Act.

Even so, the victory against the illegal LRB finding was the occasion for a celebration with friends at Ed Rhetts' home that lasted until four in the morning. "Back in December '51, you may remember that I had little confidence that we would ever get this far," Service reminded Rhetts. "In fact, it was only your urging that made me willing to even start the suit."[49]

Dean Acheson had already acknowledged in an affidavit that the "sole reason" for Service's dismissal was the LRB ruling, giving Service strong grounds for an appeal. One year later, the appeals court upheld the lower court ruling, but its adverse ruling on Service's reinstatement left the door open for a final appeal—to the United States Supreme Court.

The entire family returned to Washington, D.C., in early April 1957 to hear Ed Rhetts argue Service's case before the highest court in the country. Sadly, Grace Service had died by then, and many of Jack's old China colleagues had been fired or forced to resign. But Joe McCarthy had finally been censured by the full Senate at the end of 1954; he would soon die of cirrhosis of the liver.

The presentation before the Supreme Court narrowed the case down to a single issue: "If a government department has regulations, is it required to follow its own regulations?" In his affidavit, former secretary Acheson had admitted that he had never reviewed Service's case, as State Department's regulations required at the time. Rhetts' task was to prove that those regulations were indeed in force—and that both the Tydings Committee and the full Senate had accepted that fact. Service spent many evenings at the New York Public Library after finishing Sarco work. "I went back to the *Congressional Record* and got all of the debates in the House and showed the number of hours that had been spent, pages in the *Congressional Record*, the number of senators who had taken part in the debate."[50]

His research proved invaluable when Rhetts argued their brief. "Justice Frankfurter and Justice Black wanted to know how the government could now say that Jack was not fired for these reasons when Mr. Acheson said it was *solely* the reason," Caroline reported in a letter to family members.[51] The justices listened to arguments from both sides—and then began the excruciating wait for the Supreme Court decision.

The call came at 1:40 PM on June 17, 1957, from a news reporter. "I literally held my breath," Caroline wrote Lisa. "The [reporter] could hardly get the words out for stuttering. After a few agonizing seconds he managed to say that the Supreme Court had just announced an 8–0 decision in 'your husband's favor.'" The decision was reported on all the news broadcasts. "The phone began to ring and didn't stop before midnight."[52] Twelve years had passed since Service's arrest in the *Amerasia* case—and nearly six since his dismissal from the State Department.

Although confident of victory in the Supreme Court, Service and Rhetts never expected they would get a unanimous verdict. Justice Tom Clark, the former attorney general, had recused himself from the decision. Only a few Washington insiders—J. Edgar Hoover, James McGranery, Tom Corcoran, and Clark himself—understood all the circumstances that made that recusal necessary.

"Almost as soon as the Supreme Court decision was announced, TV people descended on us, both in my office and then later on out at our apartment," Service recalled.[53] He had prepared a statement for this extraordinary moment, and proudly stepped in front of the cameras and microphones to deliver his message:

> I am thankful for the Court's decision and for our judicial system which gives each American the means to protect his rights and reputation.
>
> For almost nineteen years I was proud to make my career in the American Foreign Service. Every chief under whom I worked and every competent and authorized review of the facts found my service useful and loyal.
>
> In December 1951, the world was informed that I had been summarily dismissed for "doubt of loyalty." Administrative appeal was refused, and legal action became my only recourse. Through it, the unfounded action of the Loyalty Review Board was declared illegal and expunged. The Government eventually conceded that my discharge was not based upon doubt of my loyalty or security and that its sole basis had been the illegal action of the Loyalty Review board. Now the discharge has been declared illegal and the slate is clean.
>
> My debt is great: to my attorney, Mr. Charles Edward Rhetts, who accepted the case of a stranger more than seven years ago and, without regard for his own interests, has since devoted his great ability to clearing my name; to the several attorneys who in association with him have contributed to this outcome; to a courageous employer who was willing to give a job to a man publicly defamed; and to hundreds of friends whose unshaken confidence supported my family and me in this long fight for vindication.[54]

CHAPTER 23
RELUCTANT RETIREE

It was nearly seven o'clock in the evening when John Service got home from the office on the day of the Supreme Court decision. For their celebratory supper, Caroline fixed hamburgers and milk shakes while Phil monitored the television news, happily shouting to his parents whenever his father appeared.

All evening, the phone kept ringing. General Stilwell's widow called from California. Ray Ludden called from Germany, the wife of the new UN secretary-general (who knew Caroline in India) sent roses, and some friends arrived with champagne around nine o'clock. For Caroline, June 17, 1957, became "circled in red in my mind for the rest of my life."[1]

The morning commute to Manhattan presented a surreal scene. "People all through the subway car were reading about me," Jack recalled. "Out on the sidewalk, I could see people looking at the picture of me in the papers. But not one recognized me."[2] In her weekly column, Eleanor Roosevelt wrote: "Just at this time, when many of us have felt that the individual was losing many of his rights . . . I am also glad that, after his long fight, John Stewart Service, former Foreign Service officer, won a reversal of the judgment of the Court of Appeals."[3]

The Supreme Court now remanded the case back to the district court to issue new orders regarding Service's reinstatement. "It rather looks as though, after a bit more hassling, that we may be able to go back to the old job in the State Dept.," Jack wrote to his aunt. "It's the best public evidence of vindication."[4]

In late June Service traveled back to Washington for a discreet and informal Saturday meeting with the director general of the Foreign Service. The assumption was that he would be restored to the Foreign Service, and there were many details to be worked out regarding back pay, salary, and his new duties. Service was assured he would be given "a real job" but in a "non-sensitive position." But there would have to be yet another departmental investigation—under the new, even stricter standard of "positive loyalty" decreed by Secretary of State John Foster Dulles. This security review could be avoided, he was told, if he chose to resign. "[Service] had not fought this case for all these years with the intention of giving up now," the director reported in a memo, "and was determined to see the matter of his clearance through."[5]

On the Sunday following his court victory, the *Washington Star* ran a long article in which John Service finally talked publicly. "Yes, I'm bitter sometimes," the ex-diplomat confessed. "They kept changing the rules. I was cleared and cleared and cleared. Things kept changing."[6] Caroline told a friend, "I am convinced that very few people could have made the fight that Jack has made and come out so unscarred, but it has taken a toll none the less."[7]

On July 3, nearly six years after he had been illegally fired, a federal district court judge ruled that the firing was invalid and ordered John Service restored to the Foreign Service with "the benefit of all rights, emoluments and privileges flowing from a continuity of service." Six days later, the State Department officially reinstated him. Once again the family was swamped with letters, cables, and phone calls from well-wishers. Caroline happily wrote a friend, "For once 'good news' has traveled as far and as fast as 'bad news'. . . and I can't begin to tell you how all this simply makes my heart sing."[8]

John Service commuted from New York on his first day back in the Foreign Service. He officially requested six weeks' leave without pay to wrap up his business affairs, assuring the personnel chief, "Nothing will be permitted so far as I can avoid it to jeopardize my position in the Foreign Service." To the treasurer of his legal defense fund he wrote, "All indications so far seem to be good—almost too good, but I can't find the booby trap."[9]

John Service was by then a successful executive with Sarco. He had negotiated a new contract with the steelworkers union at the Bethlehem, Pennsylvania plant, managing to avoid a costly strike. And he had helped design—and patent—a more efficient "thermodynamic" stainless steel steam trap that prompted a boom in export sales. In 1955, when Clement Wells retired, he had appointed Service president of Sarco International. Wells also allowed him to purchase a small share in the manufacturing company itself, to the dismay of some of the veteran shareholding executives.

Wells had contributed to Service's legal defense fund, and he heartily congratulated him when the Supreme Court handed down its decision. But the timing of his resignation could not have been worse. Without a ready candidate to run Sarco International, Wells decided to sell the fast-growing export company to a British company he owned. Service flew to London to work out the details of the deal, which required approval of the British Treasury; he "quite gladly gave them a commitment not to go back into the steam trap business as competition."[10]

* * *

Tom Estes, the assistant secretary of state for operations, became Service's new boss. "I can assure you of a very warm welcome," he wrote. Service's first assignment would be to conduct a yearlong study aimed at resolving shipping problems for Foreign Service officers. Caroline called it a "coffee and pencil-sharpening job," but Service replied to Estes that he was "rarin' to go."[11]

John Service started his new job on September 3, still very much a "hot potato." A number of unfriendly stories publicized his new assignment and salary, which (though well below his rank and seniority) prompted a spate of letters from irate citizens that wound up in his personnel file. "While the Supreme Court said he had to be rehired, it does not mean he has to be retained," one angry taxpayer wrote. "Let's get that Service off the federal payroll soon. I will be watching."[12]

Sen. James Eastland of Mississippi, chair of the Senate Internal Security Subcommittee (SISS), was also watching. He queried Secretary Dulles about Service's salary, his new duties, and whether the question of security had been properly addressed by the court decision. The State Department responded that Service's security case was currently under review. State's security office chief proposed giving Eastland verbal reassurance that Service had been placed in a "selected" position but—due to the court order—that fact could not be disclosed "officially or for the record."[13]

The new security investigation would be another administrative proceeding. This meant that all the evidence in Service's file—including old FBI reports—could be reconsidered and reevaluated. A new FBI investigation was ordered, and a State security officer named Otto Otepka prepared an extensive summary and analysis, coupled to an appendix filled with memos from various government agencies, including the FBI and reports from Chiang's secret police. More than forty-five years later, the Otepka file was finally opened under a Freedom of Information Act appeal. This treasure trove—amounting to twenty-five boxes of unredacted material—provided critical information for piecing together Jack Service's story.

* * *

By the spring of 1958, John Service had completed his shipping study, reorganized the State Department's moving and transport operations, and become the de facto chief of a newly streamlined Division of Transport Management. "Service performed his duties in a highly commendable manner and never by action or word has he given less than the full measure of his ability," Estes wrote in his performance evaluation. "The normal observer would find it difficult to believe that Mr. Service had ever been away from active duty." Estes, nevertheless, hesitated to recommend a promotion: "It is felt that both he and the Department would prefer that there be no possible indication of bias in any direction. Hence, the rating officer has refrained from a natural inclination to allocate the highest rating in the belief that he is doing a greater service . . . trusting to the wisdom & equity of Selection Board to establish the proper place for Mr. Service on the list of officers [for promotion]." Estes concluded, "I should be happy to serve with this officer at any time."[14]

* * *

In mid-August 1958 Chinese Communist forces began an intense artillery bombardment on the Taiwanese-held islands of Quemoy and Matsu. It was the second crisis involving the tiny offshore islands. Four years earlier, Chiang had installed 70,000 troops to fortify them as part of a "return to the mainland" campaign endorsed by the CIA. That triggered a sustained artillery barrage against the islands accompanied by a Communist propaganda campaign to "liberate" Taiwan. President Eisenhower, resisting advice to use tactical nuclear bombs against China, signed a Mutual Defense Treaty with Taiwan in December 1954. Both houses of Congress passed a "Formosa Resolution," pledging to defend Taiwan against any armed attack in the future.

As a result, the stakes were much higher in 1958. "A Western Pacific Munich would not buy us peace," declared President Eisenhower, ordering the U.S. Seventh Fleet to provide escorts for Nationalist Chinese supply convoys within three miles of Quemoy. Two more aircraft carriers and additional bombers were dispatched to signal American resolve. The shelling continued sporadically until after the U.S. congressional elections in November, when the Communists shifted tactics—now proposing to resolve differences between the two "Chinese brothers" through dialogue.

The unresolved dilemma over the two Chinas had again roiled American politics, making John Service's return to normal duty virtually impossible. In late November, he appeared before a three-man panel of State Department security officers. For six days, without benefit of legal counsel, Service was grilled about his past associations: Phil Jaffe, Lauchlin Currie, Sol Adler, Chi Chao-ting, Kung Peng, and Val Chao. With his career at stake, Jack was to discover some unpleasant truths about some of his associations—and about himself.[15]

The panel focused on Service's apparently careless disregard of security regulations. For the first time in his thirteen-year ordeal, Service began to understand why his reporting about wartime China's tumult might have raised alarm bells for security officials focused on the threats of Communist conspiracies and Soviet espionage. At issue was not a question of his loyalty, Otto Otepka assured him, but whether his continued employment might constitute a risk to the national security given his past disregard for security regulations.

Questioner: We are rather astonished as security officers at the great pains that you went to in attempting to explain that none of this information you gave to Mr. Jaffe was classified. Yet the regulations make the originator of every document . . . responsible for its classification.

Service: We never contended that I was not in violation, technically speaking, of the regulations.

Questioner: Are you now of the same opinion that there were mitigating circumstances as to why you did this in 1945, and . . . that you should be excused for what you did?

Service: No, I don't think so. If the State Department had told me in 1945 . . . 'we consider you a security risk,' I would have had really no defense. . . . If the board had felt in 1951 that I had so violated regulations that I was not worthy of trust and confidence, I would have had little defense.

Another major concern centered on Service's distinction between personal copies and confidential official copies of his reports. "Do you maintain that that distinction still exists insofar as the classified nature of the material is concerned?" asked Otepka. To counter the charge that he had stolen official documents from State Department files, Service explained, he had emphasized that Jaffe was allowed to see only a careful selection of his personal copies. "I am questioning the validity of your contentions there in the light of the regulations," Otepka countered. "In the light of the regulations, there is no validity, sir," Service wearily conceded. "I quite agree with you."

For the first time, Service was read passages from FBI transcripts of conversations between Jaffe and his colleagues in which the editor boasted he had made copies of nineteen reports loaned him by Service, and "there is not a single one of them that Jimmy [Larsen] gave me." Another excerpt included the statement, "Jack Service was in solid." The director of the security office, Tomlin Bailey, interpreted that to mean he was "cooperating with them to their utmost satisfaction." "I haven't heard [the phrase] used that way," Service responded, "and I deny the truth of it."

Most distressing was the evidence that Sol Adler, his former housemate in Chungking, had sent copies of Service's reports to his boss at Treasury, Harry

Dexter White—and that both men were suspected of ties to a Soviet spy ring operating in Washington during the war years. "I must say that [Adler's] going off to England is something which I personally can't explain," admitted Service. "It is something which, as I say, disturbed me, just as Mr. Currie's going away is something that is disturbing."

When asked if he ever suspected Chi Chao-ting of being a Communist mole in 1944, when they lived in the same apartment house, Service said there had been no reason to be suspicious: Chi held a high position in Chiang's finance ministry. He only surfaced as a top official in Mao's Bank of China in the early 1950s. Service had been "dumbfounded" when Jaffe told him that Chi was married to his niece, and now he was surprised to be informed that Jaffe and Chi had worked together on leftist journals in the 1930s. Asked whether he had provided Chi with copies of his reports, Service immediately denied the charge—without mentioning the occasional late night talks that he and Adler shared with their upstairs neighbor.

The dots were being connected in ways that Service had never imagined. "Everybody who comes into the picture," Otepka observed, "seems to have had some sympathy for Communism, most persons with whom you were associated, that is." Service said he associated with many others as well, but "the emphasis, unfortunately, is on these people." He pointed out that during the war, the public Communist view was "practically indistinguishable from that of the liberals." He was asked if it were now clear that he had been used by the Communists and their sympathizers. "It's not a pleasant thing to say but, yes, I was certainly being used," John Service admitted. "I don't like the impression that I am just a complete dope. . . . Inevitably I am afraid it's the conclusion that is to be drawn."

Service was then asked to explain why his critics were convinced he had "contributed to the eventual triumph of Communism in China." Were his reports "heavily biased"? "No, I don't believe that they were," Service retorted. "What I said and advocated is a matter of record and we can hardly select from all that what it is that gave these people . . . many years afterward, the idea that I was trying to overthrow the Nationalist government."

"And do you believe," asked another questioner, "[those reports] are right today?" "My interpretation nowadays would be very, very different," Service replied. "I think I would have been far more skeptical about some of the facts which I then was willing to believe." His sober conclusion was balanced: "The general body of my reporting I think has been borne out . . . but] I would be silly to sit down here and argue that I was never influenced at all by the people around me or whom I talked to."

Service was asked if he had any final comments for the panel. "I wish we had had this kind of a proceeding long before," he told the panel. "I think that this is a very, very much more useful way of getting to the bottom of things than a formal sort of adversary hearing. I frankly am very much impressed, in fact, a little horrified at some of the things I have gotten glimpses of here." After thanking the security officers, he added, "It has been a useful experience for me."

* * *

Two weeks later the director of the security office submitted his report. Service had indeed been influenced by his association with leftists and Communists: "His judgment was bad, but there was no intention to betray the national security," Bailey concluded. "Nor do I think that his action did damage the national security." He also pointed out that in early 1945, when the FBI was called in to investigate State Department security, agents had found it inadequate and lacking proper coordination and procedures.[16]

But on the day after Christmas, Bailey's boss, Roderick O'Connor—with concurrence from Otepka—drafted a seven-page memo with a very different conclusion: "There is reasonable doubt as to whether John Service's continued employment is clearly consistent with the interests of national security." He recommended that Service be immediately suspended from duty and removed from government service. "To this day, [Service] either does not understand or will not admit the extent to which he and others were 'used' by Communist interests to further Communist ambitions in China," he asserted. Service's false distinction regarding his personal copies of official documents indicated he was "not reliable or trustworthy." If Service were now granted a security clearance, O'Connor argued, it would "make a mockery" of current security regulations and would "cast doubt on the validity of a whole series of earlier decisions."[17]

The memo went to the undersecretary of state for administration, who had final responsibility in security cases—and who happened to be Loy Henderson, who had watched over Service's family when ambassador to India. On August 11, 1959, nearly two years after Service's return to the State Department, Ambassador Henderson issued a security clearance to John Service. In a lengthy memo of his own, the undersecretary dismissed O'Connor's conclusions. "I find it difficult to conclude that Service has not made a convincing showing that he has not continued intentionally to disclose classified info without authority," wrote Henderson. "There is an absence of indiscretion for 14 years." As for O'Connor's charge that a clearance would mock security regulations, Henderson firmly rejected the inference that "anyone reaching a conclusion favorable to Service would be contemptuously disregarding the regulations."[18]

There was another jubilant celebration when Service got word of his security clearance. It meant he would finally be sent overseas. To avoid a fight over Senate confirmation, the State Department assigned him to head the consulate at Liverpool—but without the associated title or pay grade.

* * *

Once a thriving port city of the British Empire, Liverpool retained a large diplomatic community and nearly forty consulates. "Local people invariably called me consul-general," Service recalled with a smile, "simply because they couldn't conceive of anyone except a consul-general occupying the post."[19] And the United States' unofficial consul-general would eventually become president of Liverpool's consular corps.

So, in the autumn of 1959, the Services moved into a lovely Liverpool residence owned by the American government. The summer after they arrived, Ginny was married and the wedding reception was held at their home. "Our life in Liverpool was very happy," Caroline recalled. Apart from an endless round of diplomatic parties and civic events, they had few official duties to perform, especially since "no congressional people came roaring through."[20]

John Service's work drew commendations, and his Liverpool office received favorable comments from a State Department inspection team. He also spent nine months in London, filling in for the supervisory consul-general in charge of eight consular offices throughout the United Kingdom. But he was never promoted, and he later admitted to "a period of depression."[21]

The election of John F. Kennedy brought new hope. Secretary of State Dean Rusk talked about rectifying the wrongs of the McCarthy period. And by 1961 the schism between Russian and Chinese brands of Communism—which Service had reported in the forties—was official: Soviet advisers were withdrawn from China, and Nikita Khrushchev denounced Mao and his followers as "madmen."

During a home leave that fall, John Service talked to personnel officials about getting out of "the deep freeze" and being promoted. "I found out that a summary had been written for the record saying that because of all I had gone through, it could be assumed or expected that I would be unwilling to take responsibilities and make decisions," Service recounted. "Obviously, this had been put in to really prevent, to forestall, any board that wanted to promote me."[22]

Service knew that whatever his confidential file contained must have been put there at the direction of Loy Henderson. But Jack never saw the actual "booby trap," which had been inserted in the file by Henderson himself: "Although Mr. Service's activities during the period 1943–1945 have been determined not to constitute a security risk at this time, there is no question that his action in the Amerasia Case was reprehensible and has brought serious discredit upon the Foreign Service. This fact should be given proper consideration by any Selection Board considering Mr. Service's performance record."[23]

Henderson had saved Service's job, but his memo destroyed his career prospects. His memo was apparently the price to be paid for restoring Service's position in the diplomatic corps in the face of political pressure from anti-Communist politicians, Chiang Kai-shek's supporters, government security officers, and the FBI. Otto Otepka, one of Hoover's loyalists inside the State Department, made sure that a confidential 108-page summary of Service's case was always provided to any selection board considering his promotion. He also made sure it found its way to Senator Eastland's Senate Internal Security Subcommittee on Capitol Hill.

* * *

With no prospect of promotion, John Service reluctantly decided to retire. "He said something this week I've never heard him say before during all the hard years: 'I can't bear staying in Liverpool any longer and doing nothing,'" wrote Caroline to Lisa Green. "He has worked his heart out and beaten his brains out during the years . . . and I cannot blame him now for saying 'enough.'"[24]

In May 1962 John Service retired from the Foreign Service, and at age fifty-two he enrolled as a graduate student at the University of California in Berkeley. "My hope is to spend the next two decades (three, if I'm lucky) in studying, writing and teaching," he wrote to Clement Wells. "My first book shall certainly be dedicated to "CW—who made it possible." Service had sold his stock in Wells' steam trap company for more than $300,000, which enabled him to buy a home in the Berkeley hills and to reimburse his attorneys more than $70,000 for expenses.

In his letter to Wells, Service recalled the Englishman's unexpected job offer during his darkest days more than a decade earlier. "It was a wonderful thing you did! Perhaps I can't quite say that you saved my life, though that wouldn't be far off the mark, but you have certainly changed it immensely for the better—and, despite my unreasonably good fortune in that direction, I do not mean only financially."[25]

CHAPTER 24
RENAISSANCE

John Service arrived at Berkeley in September 1962. After the first lecture in his U.S. Far Eastern policy course, he introduced himself to the assistant professor. "When I ascertained that he was none other than *that* John S. Service, 'our man in Yenan' during 1944 and 1945," Chalmers Johnson recalled, "I could only mumble, 'Pleased to meet you. I think I'll go home and work on my lectures on Stilwell.'" Two years later, in July 1964—at the age of fifty-four—Service had earned an M.A. degree in political science and accepted a position at Berkeley's Center for Chinese Studies. "Not the least of his activities," Johnson noted, "were major efforts to build the Center's library of research materials on Communist China into one of the best in the world."[1]

Just as Service began his new job, a reporter called, asking whether the university knew of his background and whether he had undergone any sort of a loyalty check. In fact, an investigator from Washington had been sent by Senator Eastland's internal security subcommittee to check out the career track and responsibilities of Service's new position, but the university administration was not intimidated.

Over the next decade, John Service enjoyed a congenial and stimulating association with the university. He became editor of the center's research monograph series—and a living folk hero to graduate students, who turned to him as their "Ph.D. thesis doctor." Most importantly, Service said, Berkeley gave him the opportunity to connect again "after a long enforced absence, with the eternally absorbing and important subject of China."[2]

* * *

When John Service reluctantly retired from the Foreign Service in 1962, John F. Kennedy was president. The following year the president was assassinated, and five years later America was again shaken by momentous events: the assassinations of Kennedy's brother, Robert, and of Martin Luther King; the Tet offensive and the massive anti–Vietnam War protests; and Lyndon Johnson's decision not to run for reelection. On November 5, 1968, Richard Nixon was elected president—with surprising consequences for U.S.–China relations.

A year before his election, Nixon, always known as a tough anti-Communist, had written an influential piece in *Foreign Affairs*, arguing that it was now too dangerous to keep China isolated. In his inaugural address on January 20, 1969, Nixon subtly repeated the same message: "We seek an open world . . . a world in which no people, great or small, will live in angry isolation."[3]

Within ten days of entering the White House, the new president sent a memo instructing his national security adviser to find a way to get in touch with Chinese leaders. In his memoirs, Henry Kissinger admits that the administration had "no precise idea how to do this"—especially given the domestic realities, "not the least of which was Nixon's traditional support among the conservative 'China lobby' that had never forgiven Truman and Acheson for allegedly betraying Chiang Kai-shek."[4] Nevertheless, in a toast to a visiting Eastern European, Nixon dared to refer to the mainland as the "People's Republic of China." "This sounds unexceptionable now," recalled Winston Lord, a former Kissinger assistant, "but at the time no American official and certainly no president ever used that official designation. . . . We had always said 'Red China,' 'Communist China'. . . or something like that."[5]

In July 1969 the new administration quietly lifted some travel and trade restrictions on the People's Republic of China. By that time, violent clashes between the Soviet Union and Mao's China had become alarming. Springtime skirmishes along the Ussuri River led to a massive Soviet troop build-up at the border. The Soviet threat prompted China to reevaluate relations with its archenemy. The possibility of using the United States as a counterweight to Soviet pressure had not been explored since Mao's talks with Jack Service twenty-five years earlier.

To avoid public scrutiny of his efforts to contact China's leaders, Kissinger decided to use an unofficial—and unorthodox—"back channel" to Beijing. One of his former students at Harvard was a well-connected Pakistani. Her two brothers—now Pakistan's ambassadors in Washington and in Beijing—were close friends of the president of Pakistan, who maintained cordial relations with the Chinese leadership. Kissinger felt he could trust Amb. Aga Hilaly to be "meticulous and discreet," and he quietly began to cultivate his secret diplomatic channel.[6] By the end of the year China and the United States announced plans to revive ambassadorial-level talks in Warsaw (where Korean POW issues had been discussed previously).

* * *

Just before the Warsaw talks got under way in early 1970, the U.S. Government Printing Office published "The *Amerasia Papers*: A Clue to the Catastrophe of China"—a massive two-volume report of Eastland's Senate Subcommittee on Internal Security (SISS). A bulletin distributed to 900,000 GPO subscribers included this promotional announcement: "This document reads like a spy thriller, but is all the more interesting because it is true. They [sic] contain hundreds of official documents, many hitherto unpublished, which reflect abundantly the tragic errors in the Far Eastern policy of the United States Government in the closing months of World War II. . . . Part III presents an analysis of some of the documents . . . which were written in 1943–1945 as official dispatches by one of the arrested six, John Stewart Service." Service recalled, "After its appearance, I began receiving inquires from far and near, friendly and not so friendly . . . [as] the only person mentioned in the blurb."[7] In a 113-page introduction, the editor, Dr. Anthony Kubek of Dallas University, claimed that John S. Service had played "a central role in the strange case of the purloined Government papers," and had written many of the documents found in *Amerasia*'s office. "The content of these documents may prove to be of even greater importance to the historical record than *the fact that they were stolen*," Kubek declared, "because herein the fall of China to Communism was anticipated and *espoused*."[8]

The *New York Times* called the publication "nothing more than a crude attempt by the remnants of the 'China Lobby' within the U.S. government and on Taiwan to prevent any improvement in Sino-American relations."[9] Undismayed, Sen. James Eastland, the subcommittee chair, sent a copy to FBI Director Hoover, who had originally provided the cache of confidential documents to that committee in the 1950s.

Service was surprised to discover that more than one hundred of the three hundred documents in the compendium were "from the pen of John Stewart Service"—and that most of them had not been seized from *Amerasia* suspects but rather were confiscated from his State Department desk by the FBI. Those personal copies had been returned to him in accordance with a judge's ruling that none of the material was stolen government property. "The Department of Justice may have been proper and punctilious about returning the originals to me," Service noted, "but it appears that somebody thought it might come in handy to keep copies."[10] Ironically, their publication gave him access to his reports for the first time in twenty-five years. His own copies, entrusted to the State Department when he was posted overseas, had somehow been lost.

"This is no doubt a futile exercise," Service wrote journalist Ed Snow, "but I have become tired after twenty years of seething passivity." He had finally decided to write his own account of this episode because this new attack was "a direct reversion to the days of Hurley and McCarthy, except that I am now given even higher billing as the man chiefly responsible for the loss of China."[11] Kubek had also denounced Service's postretirement position at Berkeley as "a convenient cockpit for further possible propagandizing of the beatitudes of the Communist regime."[12]

Chalmers Johnson (by then the chairman of Berkeley's Center for Chinese Studies) deplored Kubek's introduction to the documents as "disgraceful scholarship . . . clearly propagandistically motivated." The center agreed to publish Service's own monograph: *The Amerasia Papers: Some Problems in the History of U.S.–China Relations.* ("It's not a very good title," Service later explained, "but we wanted to have it next to Kubek in the library catalog file."[13]) Service's treatise would be "an indispensable guide" to the historical documents in the SISS publication, and, as Johnson wrote in its foreword, future historians would benefit from both "his foresight and his hindsight."[14]

The first section of Service's 192-page monograph dealt specifically with the *Amerasia* case and the allegation that he had played a central role: "Dr. Kubek, without being able to offer the slightest scintilla of new evidence or information, blandly denies the validity . . . of a whole series of decisions conscientiously reached over the years by numbers of boards, grand juries, committees, and individuals, who had before them the whole record."[15]

In the second section, Service cited the historical record to counter Kubek's claim that the U.S. wartime policy toward China was "*to uphold in all possible ways* the central government of Generalissimo Chiang Kai-shek and to support his armies in the field against Japan."[16] He discussed his own reports and actions in the context of the official policy statements recently published in the authoritative State Department series *Foreign Relations of the United States.* Official American policy, he demonstrated, had prescribed flexibility toward the two Chinas and conditional support of Chiang. General Hurley's insistence on "personalized support of Chiang Kai-shek" only took hold after he became "mired down in the intransigent realities of Chinese politics."[17] Service also demonstrated Hurley's failure to grasp the complex issues: "[His] energy, persistence, and determination all proved of no avail in the face of the revolution, unseen by Hurley, which was already well started in China."[18] Naïvely, Hurley had assumed that a political settlement between leaders of the two Chinas should not be difficult to achieve because their aims seemed essentially the same. And after Yalta, Hurley—like Roosevelt himself—believed that the USSR would wholeheartedly support his own approach to the two Chinas. "Hurley apparently never could see the logical inconsistency between his conviction that the Chinese Communists were 'not Communists at all' and not supported, recognized, or encouraged in any way by the USSR," Service commented, "and his equally strong conviction that they would certainly and obediently accept the prompting, example, or dictation of the Soviet leaders."[19]

Kubek had also recycled Hurley's charge that Service had provided a confidential State Department document to Yenan, undermining his negotiations. It was, Service declared, an accusation without "the slightest iota" of truth, and an outrageous defamation of his character.[20]

Other important questions were addressed in Service's monograph: Why had Hurley remained ambassador? And why was it never made clear that the U.S. policy prescribed *conditional* support of Chiang? First, Service speculated, President Roosevelt preferred to conduct foreign relations personally—and it was likely that the mortally ill president was unable to comprehend the fluid situation in China. And, Service's monograph pointed out, no State Department representative was ever present when Hurley raged to Roosevelt over his rebellious staff's cable about deteriorating conditions.

But, Service wrote, there were significant clues that Roosevelt's support of Chiang was *not* unconditional. He cited the experience of journalist Ed Snow, an old friend of the president, who visited the White House while Hurley was still in Washington. "By 1945 Roosevelt was more than ever puzzled by Chiang Kai-shek as a man and a politician," Snow reported. "When I last saw him he had just heard about a breakdown in [China] negotiations, [and] said Chiang Kai-shek had 'raised some perfectly absurd objections' to the Communists' requests for certain guarantees along the lines of a bill of rights which appeared 'perfectly reasonable' to FDR."

"By now," Snow wrote, "[the president] recognized the growing strength of the Chinese Communists as the effective government of the guerrilla areas. He was considering giving them direct help against Japan, as a matter of military expediency." The president's comments surprised Snow who asked for clarification:

Snow: We can't support two governments in China, can we?
FDR: Well, I've been working with two governments there . . . I intend to go on doing so until we can get them together.[21]

Nevertheless, Service explained in his monograph, President Roosevelt was "keenly aware that China policy was a sensitive subject, that Chiang Kai-shek had a large and fervent band of American supporters, and that 'Communist' was a dirty word to important segments of the American public"—making the dilemma over the two Chinas "a thorny problem that Roosevelt preferred not to grapple with." The recent secret Yalta agreement with Stalin, Service suggested, was the principal reason why Roosevelt did not clarify his position, to Hurley or others. "Yalta seemed likely to Roosevelt to provide the answer to Chinese unity. In the meantime, Hurley was confident that his negotiations would be successful within the next month. There was no need, if this was true, to grasp the nettle of taking some other positive, and certainly unpleasant, action to end the deadlock in China. The Embassy and State Department proposal for direct military cooperation with the Communists was therefore set aside."[22]

To Kubek and the China Lobby, Hurley's tenure was "a high point" in Chinese–American relations. But to John Service, "Hurley's ill-advised stubbornness" had cost precious time and lost opportunities for both the United States and China. "The time lost was a ten month deadlock during the last, most critical months of the war. The opportunities lost were to seek a more realistic means of averting, or blunting, civil war and of preserving our relations with China, if not as the close friend and ally we once hoped for, at least on a basis better than bitter enmity."[23]

Service set forth his own alternate scenario. Had the United States implemented its plan to cooperate with Mao's forces, sending them supplies and assigning instructors, intelligence officers, demolition experts, and radio teams to work with guerrilla units in early 1945, the Japanese surrender would have evolved very differently. "There would have been no basis or arguable need for ordering that the Japanese surrender (in north China areas which the Communists had fought for and held for eight years) to be made only to Chiang's forces; nor for the strange orders for the Japanese to stand fast and resist the Communists until the Nationalists could find some way to reach them. Nor would it have been necessary for the U.S. to land . . . Marines to hold North China ports as proxy for the Nationalists."[24] And had American teams accompanied the Communists entering Manchuria, the Russians would have had no excuse for a protracted occupation. As Service explained:

> It seems clear that the implementation of an independent, uncommitted American policy in China . . . would have placed our relations with China at the beginning of the postwar period on an entirely different and much more realistically favorable basis. There probably would have been no civil

> war. But if there had been one, it would likely have been short and far less destructive. . . . And while we would certainly have had to give up our paternalistic, missionary attitude of wishing to shape China to our wishes, we might have found co-existence with a stoutly independent, nationalistic Mao Tse-tung not wholly impossible—and the world as a result considerably less complicated.[25]

To Kubek's final contention that Korea and Vietnam "became inevitable" because the United States "unwittingly assisted the wrong side in gaining control of China proper," Service offered a different appraisal:

> If the United States had been able to shed some of its illusions about China, to understand what was happening in that country, and to adopt a realistic policy in America's own interests, Korea and Vietnam would probably never have happened. . . . We would not still be confronted with an unsolvable Taiwan problem. . . . And Mao's China, having come to power in a different way and not thrust into isolation by a hostile West, might be quite a different place. It might be one, for instance, where Chinese–American ping-pong matches were normal occurrences instead of being a world-shaking event, unprecedented for more than twenty-one years.[26]

Just one month before the monograph's publication, the world was stunned to learn that the American table tennis team, competing in Japan, had been invited to visit China. On April 14, 1971, they were warmly received by Premier Zhou Enlai, who had never granted such access to Western diplomats stationed in Beijing. The Chinese team would later tour the United States.[27]

And then on July 15 a surprise announcement completely transformed the structure of international politics. In a joint communiqué, Beijing and Washington revealed that recently Kissinger had made a secret visit to China to prepare for an official visit by the president of the United States. "Of course, this was even more electrifying than the ping pong team," recalled Caroline Service. "I have hardly a good word to say for Nixon . . . yet, I suppose that only a Republican conservative . . . president could have done this."[28]

"We took even ourselves by surprise," Kissinger later admitted. "Originally we had not thought reconciliation possible. We were convinced that the Chinese were fanatic and hostile. But even though we could not initially see a way to achieve it, both Nixon and I believed in the importance of an opening to the People's Republic of China."[29]

Within a week of the dramatic announcement, John Service was back on Capitol Hill testifying about China. "It is the first Senate meeting where I have appeared without need for counsel," Service told the Senate Foreign Relations Committee. Sen. William Fulbright of Arkansas, the committee's chairman, replied, "It is a very strange turn of fate that you gentlemen who reported honestly about the conditions [in China] were so persecuted because you were honest about it."[30] The next day's newspapers and TV news carried stories about the witnesses (Service, John Paton Davies, and John K. Fairbank, another persecuted old China hand) who "fell victim to the McCarthy-era hunt for 'who lost China'" and had now emerged "from a quarter-century of obscurity."[31] This was the beginning of what Jack dubbed "the big turnaround." After the Nixon trip announcement and the Fulbright hearing, the media coverage became "astonishingly different in tone . . . even *Time* magazine just fell all over itself to be friendly."[32]

One month later, John Service was sitting in his Berkeley office when he got a phone call from a *New York Times* reporter with a stunning question: How did it feel to be invited to China by Premier Zhou Enlai? Apparently, in an interview with the Chinese premier, *Times* correspondent James Reston had suggested that it might be interesting for him to invite some of the Americans who had suffered because of their early reporting to return to China to see the changes. Zhou's response was immediate: John Service and three others he named would be warmly welcomed in China. "I collected my wits enough to [tell the *Times*] that I indeed would like to visit China."[33]

Service immediately contacted Marshall Green, now assistant secretary of state for East Asian affairs, to make sure the department would have no objection. "Nothing would give me more satisfaction," he wrote, "than to contribute (in any manner, however minor, directly or indirectly, openly or otherwise) to the success of the President's courageous moves toward relations with mainland China."[34] Green was an old friend from their days in New Zealand, and his wife, Lisa, had long been Caroline's dearest pen pal. He promptly replied that the department would be very pleased for Jack to visit and to report on his observations.

Service also contacted China's ambassador to Canada, Huang Hua, a friend from Yenan days, asking him to advise about visa and travel arrangements and to forward his personal response to Premier Zhou. "[Huang] wrote back saying that I was invited [and] was happy to tell me that we were to be guests of the Chinese government." Soon Jack traveled to Ottawa for a private dinner with Ambassador Huang and told him about his intention to report on his trip. "Jack just phoned to say that we've been granted a one month's visa to visit China," Caroline wrote Lisa Green. "Miraculous! . . . Impossible to believe."[35] To friends and colleagues, they might have been going to the far side of the moon.

Jack and Caroline Service arrived in Beijing on September 26, 1971, and were able to see many of his old friends—Dr. Ma, Sol Adler (who had moved there for medical treatment in the 1960s), and Kung Peng's widower, then China's deputy foreign minister. "The older people like Chu Teh, Tung Pi-wu and others were simply too high or too old," Service recalled. "I tried to see Madame Sun, but she wasn't very well, I was told."[36] He asked about Val Chao but was told that her theater troupe was on tour. The Services spent almost a month traveling in China, with stops in Shanghai, Yenan, and Chengdu, where they found the Service home now occupied by several families, and his father's YMCA turned into an epidemic-control bureau. In Chungking, the cemetery where his father and infant sister had been buried no longer existed. In late October they returned to Beijing.

Kissinger was back in Beijing as well to finalize details of Nixon's visit. When his aides learned that John Service was in town, they arranged a secret meeting. Kissinger asked Service how serious the Chinese were about Taiwan. "They're absolutely serious," he replied. "You don't think they're bargaining?" queried Kissinger. "On this question, they're not bargaining," the former diplomat answered. "It's a symbolic issue. They may be willing to accept some sort of a formula which would still not incorporate Taiwan, unified in the mainland, wholly. We have to recognize Chinese sovereignty, and that means we have to break off diplomatic relations with Taiwan." Kissinger was surprised. "My people are always telling [me] . . . they're like the Russians. This is just bargaining." "No, this is not a bargaining point," Service repeated.

Kissinger was even more surprised to learn about Service's early conversations with Mao. "Then the wheels went around for a little while," Service recalled, "and a moment later he said, 'Would you be willing to come to San Clemente?'" Kissinger asked Service to call his secretary as soon as he returned to the States, "and tell her . . . how we can get a hold of you anytime we want to." Kissinger repeated these instructions twice—and then again as he walked his visitor to the door. But when Kissinger returned to Washington, D.C., and was briefed about Service's controversial background, the invitation was dropped. Years later a former aide explained that the U.S.–China negotiations were so delicate, they had to be extremely careful not to inflame the China Lobby, even if it meant not talking to the only American diplomat who had ever held substantive talks with Chairman Mao.[37]

On the night of October 25, the United Nations General Assembly ended its annual fall debate over the two Chinas and, despite the United States' perennial opposition, voted to seat the People's Republic of China at the UN. The news reached Beijing just as Kissinger was packing to go home. "[Zhou] told me later that he had learned of the vote just before my departure," Kissinger later wrote, "but that he did not want to embarrass me by being the first to inform me." Although Kissinger knew that defeat was inevitable, no one had expected it as early as that autumn. Yet Zhou had told him that "Taiwan's status was more important to Peking than membership in the United Nations."[38]

On the day Kissinger flew back to Washington, D.C., Premier Zhou Enlai spent nearly three hours meeting with Jack and Caroline Service. "It was very, very warm and pleasant," Service said. "He remembered me very well [and] asked about old friends whom he'd known, Fairbank and Lattimore and various other people." Service hoped to talk about Hurley and the war years, but the premier brushed it aside: "That's all past. Let's talk about the present."[39] Service reported their conversation in a detailed eleven-page typewritten memorandum, dutifully sent to Assistant Secretary Green soon after their return.

"China being in the UN is not necessarily a great thing," Zhou Enlai had explained to Service. "We want, of course, to do what we can to contribute to world progress, but our first and major concern must be China itself: the changes in China are only beginning." President Nixon had proven to be a "man of courage, willing to take risks," but why, Zhou asked, was he "unwilling to be courageous" about Taiwan and Chiang Kai-shek? If Chiang accepted a peaceful reunification, he would be given an honorific position and furnished a comfortable life. "But there is little chance he will accept," Zhou told Service, "because he would have to abandon the image of himself that he has spent his life creating."

During the Japanese war, a coalition government in China had never really been possible, Zhou said, because "Chiang would never accept it." But a coalition government in war-torn Vietnam might still be possible. "If Nixon is able, before coming to China, to withdraw U.S. forces from Vietnam, he will be hailed by the people of China—and by all the peoples of the world."[40]

Secretary Marshall Green sent a "secret/sensitive" memo containing the gist of Service's report to the CIA, the National Security Council, and State's Bureau of East Asian Affairs. Their follow-up questions were channeled through Green, who discreetly raised them with Service on their long walks in the Berkeley hills during a private family visit.

In early 1972 Service was again invited to testify before the Senate Foreign Relations Committee, which was then reviewing the U.S. involvement in Vietnam and its shifting policy on China. He told the senators:

> My own recent visit to China has demonstrated to me, at least, that many of the roots of the Chinese present may be found in what we saw and reported

> from the Communist base in Yenan. . . . I think that our involvement in Vietnam, our insistence on the need to contain China and to prevent what we thought was the spread of Communist influence in South East Asia was based very largely on our misunderstanding and our lack of knowledge of the Chinese, the nature of the Chinese Communist movement and the intention of their leaders. . . . I think we got into Vietnam largely . . . through the misinterpretation and misfounded fear of China.[41]

Many Americans were still not ready to accept such an analysis, but years later, even former defense secretary Robert McNamara—the architect of LBJ's escalation of the Vietnam War—acknowledged that he had been wrong about China's intentions.[42]

In the weeks leading up to President Nixon's trip to China, Service's observations were eagerly sought by the media. The *New York Times* promoted a special four-part series authored by Service with an ad that proclaimed: "You can see [the] changes for yourself through his eyes." And when Nixon actually arrived in Beijing on Sunday, February 20, 1972, the cover of *Parade* magazine featured a photo of Jack and Caroline Service at the Forbidden City for its lead story, "Nixon's Trip to China: What Can We Expect?" The article included an exclusive interview with the former diplomat, who had "recently spent 46 days in China as a guest of his old friends, Chou En-lai and Mao Tse-tung." The *New Yorker* soon ran a glowing profile, and NBC produced a China documentary featuring Service and several other old China hands.

"Like millions of other Americans I saw you on the NBC program last week," wrote his old friend, Brooks Atkinson. "And one thing that delighted me is that the former traitors have become the national heroes, and if America had accepted what you were writing in 1945 . . . the world would have been spared a lot of trouble and misery. In the 1940s you were a traitor. In the 1970s you are a patriot and seer." Atkinson, now the *Times*' theater critic, perceived a streak of tragic irony—"except for one thing: you have lived to enjoy the dramatic climax."[43]

* * *

On February 28, 1972, the historic Shanghai Communiqué was signed by President Nixon and Premier Zhou Enlai, charting a new course for U.S.–China relations. Although the document noted the two countries' differences on a host of issues, the United States recognized that there is only one China:

> The United States acknowledges that all Chinese on either side of the Taiwan Strait maintain there is but one China and that Taiwan is part

> of that China. The U.S. government does not challenge that position. It reaffirms its interest in a peaceful settlement of the Taiwan question by the Chinese themselves. With this prospect in mind, it reaffirms the ultimate objective of the withdrawal of all U.S. forces and military installations from Taiwan. In the meantime, it will progressively reduce its forces and military installations on Taiwan as the tension in the area diminishes.[44]

The communiqué represented a significant transformation; but it would take nearly seven years to restore formal diplomatic relations between the two countries.

Meanwhile, the third major player in the geopolitical chess game—the Soviet Union—feared that the budding U.S.–China relationship would interfere with its own efforts to forge détente with the United States. A book published in Moscow—*The Affair 'Amerasia'*—blamed John Service and other veteran China-watchers for laying the groundwork in Yenan for the two countries' anti-Soviet collusion, and for influencing current public opinion in the United States.

In a way, the Russians were right. Within a few years of the Nixon–Mao handshake and the Shanghai Communiqué, all the veterans of the Dixie Mission were invited back to China for a reunion with former Yenan comrades, eager to rekindle the "Yenan spirit" of yesteryear. The conference provided grist for the Chinese propaganda mill, now eagerly promoting renewed Sino-American friendship after decades of bitter enmity.

John Service found himself much in demand as a speaker at American universities and at public forums urging normalization of relations with China. Although he turned down most requests, he did attend an extraordinary luncheon held at the State Department for the old China hands in 1973. When he rose to speak, Service was given a lengthy standing ovation. "Thank you, thank you," he repeated, trying to quiet the crowd—"and that is probably the biggest understatement of the year."[45]

Many guests at the luncheon felt the event had done more than anything they could remember to convince State Department officials that McCarthyism was really dead.[46] One retired diplomat, however, had placed antagonistic questionnaires on each table. And immediately, Sen. James Buckley protested to Secretary of State Rogers, questioning the "propriety" of the event—"if Service was indeed guilty of passing classified documents to a Communist agent."[47] Well aware that controversy still followed in his wake, Service wrote to thank the event organizers and added: "I only hope that the Association and those of you involved will not have cause to regret the magnificent gesture."[48]

"I was so pleased to see your face glowing with happiness as you sat at the table listening to Jack's talk and observing the sea of friendly faces surrounding you," Loy Henderson wrote to Caroline after the event. "May the future bring to you and Jack and to the other members of the Service family serenity and the kind of happiness that comes from the sense of worth-while accomplishments." Caroline responded, "You quite literally 'saved' us that year [in India] and I have never forgotten it."[49] Caroline Service never understood Henderson's significant role in ending Jack's career: both Caroline and Jack died years before his memo was finally declassified in 2003.

* * *

After his official retirement from Berkeley's Center for Chinese Studies in 1973, John Service's renaissance as a respected China expert continued. His workload increased. In theory he now worked only half time as editor of the center's modern Chinese dictionary project, but he continued to review Ph.D. manuscripts and still tutored Chinese scholars in English. In 1974 Random House published *Lost Chance in China: The World War II Despatches of John S. Service*, a collection of his wartime reports. And at several more appearances before Fulbright's committee, he took the opportunity to chide the government on its continuing ambivalence over China. "The Taiwan issue, if left long unsettled will be a time bomb ticking away for the future," he testified in September 1974. Although the Shanghai Communiqué stated Taiwan was merely a part of China, the United States remained the only major country that still recognized the regime on Taiwan as the Republic of China. "Even more paradoxical, we stand alone as the only country bound by military treaty to prevent a Chinese action . . . to bring about that territorial integrity and unity of China to which in the past we were so long and deeply committed."[50]

The tarnish on the Service escutcheon seemed to have been completely erased. Retirement, however, proved an elusive goal. Two big boxes of correspondence had piled up following his public appearances and publications. "I have made it a policy of refusing most invitations, but I can't refuse them all," Service wrote to a friend. "One particular chore is the number of scholars and graduate students . . . working on topics related to the war period, U.S–China, etc. . . . We've stopped doing things just for fun."[51]

Early in 1976 came the news that Premier Zhou Enlai was dead. China-watchers in the West—but not the Chinese public—knew that he suffered from a terminal cancer. His death was a tremendous shock to the Chinese people, who loved him and credited him with helping to halt the excesses of Mao's Great Proletarian Cultural Revolution.

"Few people who met Chou En-lai face-to-face were likely to forget him," John Service wrote in an article for the *Los Angeles Times*, recalling their intense wartime talks and their 1971 reunion in Beijing. As the two probed to understand each side's position, Zhou had always been the more "articulate and adroit. . . . And then, history played a trick," Service wrote. "The importance of the authoritative knowledge that Zhou and Mao Tse-tung gave us was not recognized by President Franklin Roosevelt and the American policy-makers. . . . Instead, Roosevelt and Stalin strangely found that their mutually unrealistic views on China coincided. So we had the Yalta agreement." This, in Service's view, had made civil war in China inevitable—with the U.S. tied firmly to Chiang Kai-shek—and "sealed the unhappy course of American-Chinese relations for the next 27 years."[52]

The death of China's premier touched off a renewed power struggle in Beijing: the ideologues, led by Mao's wife and her "Gang of Four," versus Zhou's allies, led by Deng Xiaoping. Within a month Deng was in disgrace. Two years later he returned to power to continue Zhou's unfinished efforts for economic recovery and an opening to the outside world.

* * *

In July 1976 John Service suffered a serious heart attack. That same month China experienced the deadliest earthquake recorded in the twentieth century: more than 240,000 were killed in Tangshan, and another 125,000 were injured. And in September China suffered another major upheaval—the death of Chairman Mao. The *New York Times* asked Service to write a commentary about the visionary leader of the Chinese Communists he had known in Yenan, who later led his people into disastrous turmoil.

* * *

Once fully recovered from his heart attack, Service continued working at Berkeley and advocating for normalization of relations with China. Normalization was finally announced on December 15, 1978, as Jack and Caroline were sailing from San Francisco on the first leg of a journey to visit Robert at his post in Chile. When their ship docked in Los Angeles, I joined them aboard for lunch. Toasting the occasion, Jack reminisced about his talks with Mao when the Communist leader first laid out his reasons for wanting friendly relations with the United States. Now, thirty-four years later, Mao's old Long March comrade, Deng Xiaoping, was coming to the United States for the official diplomatic recognition ceremonies.

Deng inaugurated a plan for China's "Four Modernizations" and had invited foreign executives to participate in the country's ambitious economic development. This bold new program was an echo of the vision Mao had first expounded to Service in his Yenan cave. Still, when some Chinese bravely demanded a "Fifth Modernization"—freedom of speech—they were ruthlessly silenced and sent to prison. "I may have fooled myself the first time I returned to China and been much too gullible," Service candidly admitted years later. "I was much too unquestioning [but I was] looking mainly at comparison with old China—people were being fed, clothed; the country was a functioning country which it wasn't before—[and] there was also a very dark side to China, as we all know or learned later on."[53]

On January 1, 1979, the United States officially transferred diplomatic recognition from Taipei to Beijing and again acknowledged there is only one China. Both sides tacitly agreed to accept the fact that the United States would continue unofficial relations with Taiwan. Congress passed the Taiwan Relations Act to provide for the continuation of commercial, cultural, and various other contacts; the American Institute in Taiwan (AIT) was established in Taipei to handle bilateral affairs and function as a virtual embassy—staffed by American diplomats on official leave. Agreeing to sell only "defensive" weapons systems to Taiwan, the U.S. removed its military bases and personnel from the island. But ambiguities remained—and the Taiwan issue continued to smolder.

* * *

In 1980 Jack and Caroline Service made their fourth return trip to China—and this time they met Val Chao. After Deng Xiaoping regained power at the end of the Cultural Revolution, Service was able to locate her and write a letter about their planned trip. "I really don't want to miss this chance to meet with you and I'm hoping from now on, you'll never lose touch with me," responded Val, in a six-page letter hand-written in Chinese. "When you visit my new home, you can taste my cooking and hear me play my *guqing* [a traditional seven-string instrument]. . . . The political battles of the last few years have made me feel very sad, but it is now getting better day by day. No outside power can stop friendship between the people of the U.S. and China—and our friendship can't be limited by time and space."[54]

Val then made a bold personal appeal to Zhou's widow for help in obtaining permission to meet with the foreigners. This was no minor matter. Val was forbidden to work during the Cultural Revolution, targeted as an "American whore." Red Guards joined by some of her theater colleagues had ransacked her home and seized all her furniture and possessions. Subjected to endless self-criticism sessions, Val was periodically banished to the countryside to "learn from the peasants." Still, she felt more fortunate than some of her artist friends who died during the series of vicious ideological campaigns that had characterized China's ongoing revolution since 1950.

The reunion took place in May at a banquet in Beijing hosted by Val's theater company. Amid many toasts to the friendship of the Chinese and American people, the Services and Chao were presented with albums filled with faded photographs of the actress in some of her most famous roles. Several days later Val accompanied Jack and Caroline on a memorable excursion into the hills outside the city. She talked about her persecution—and revealed that the theater company's lavish banquet signaled the official restoration of her reputation.

Caroline then shared a revelation of her own. She confessed to Val a fear that Jack still wanted to marry her. Together, the two women faced the fact that they loved the same man. "'I'm not going to divorce him,' Caroline told me," Val recalled more than twenty years later. "I said, 'why should you? I tell you the truth; we loved each other, and really cared for each other our whole life, but we do not belong to each other . . . we are very good friends and I will be your friend.'"[55]

There's an old Chinese saying, "May you live in interesting times." The aphorism certainly seems to fit the life of John Service who was an eyewitness and participant in one of the most tumultuous periods of the twentieth century.

EPILOGUE

Within six months of their meeting in Beijing, Val Chao was in North America visiting relatives. She managed to obtain a green card and got a job teaching Chinese in Monterey, California, only a two-hour drive from Berkeley. Occasionally she spent weekends with the Services, developing an uneasy friendship with Caroline. "She's nice lady, but she's always nervous," Chao recalled with amusement. "When she drives, I have to sit next to her, but when Jack drives, I have to sit in the back seat. So later, I see who's driving and I sit where I should."[1]

In 1983 the Pulitzer Prize–winning journalist Harrison Salisbury asked Jack Service to accompany him in retracing the Chinese Communists' eight-thousand-mile escape route in 1934–35—the legendary Long March. For several months they trekked through China's backcountry, interviewing old eyewitnesses and scouring the provincial archives. When Salisbury's *The Long March: The Untold Story* was published two years later, he and Service were both in demand on the lecture circuit. Around the same time, Service began work editing his mother's memoir, *Golden Inches.* Her published account of life as a Y missionary in the midst of China's turmoil was richly enhanced by his careful footnotes with pertinent historical references and his own anecdotes of growing up in Sichuan.

But the *Amerasia* case refused to die. In the spring of 1986 The *New Republic* published "Anatomy of a Fix: The Untold Story of the 'Amerasia' Case." Two college professors, Harvey Klehr and Ronald Radosh, had obtained recently declassified FBI files on the case—including the transcripts of Corcoran's wire-tapped telephone conversations. "The Chinese Nationalists and [John] Service indirectly collaborated to prevent courtroom proceedings that would have embarrassed them both," declared the authors. "And it was Tommy Corcoran, a former presidential aide who traded on his access to the powerful, who fixed the case." Corcoran's maneuverings, they claimed, were aimed at keeping the Chinese Nationalists out of harm's way. Thus, although there had indeed been "a high-level conspiracy to fix the case," the "right-wingers were wrong to conclude that the cover-up was orchestrated to protect Communists."[2]

There was "yet another ironic twist." In 1950 the FBI was threatening Justice officials with exposure of the embarrassing secret that Truman's White House had ordered the Corcoran wiretap. But later, wrote Klehr and Radosh, the FBI itself actually "maintained the Corcoran cover-up." Although the authors found no evidence that John Service was a spy, they concluded that he had dissembled: liberals were wrong "to think it was blind justice that secured Service's release."[3]

The article took Service by surprise. He had been contacted by the authors prior to its publication and told them he would "always be grateful" to Corcoran (who had died in 1981) and he hoped their article would not harm the lobbyist's reputation. "Any accusation that he was involved in a 'fix' is wrong," Service declared. "I was not guilty, and by the time the Grand Jury met, none of the concerned parties thought I was." Candidly, Service admitted that Corcoran had told him "very little of what he was doing." Consequently, Jack "always wondered about the Soong relationship to my case; I still do." Service said Corcoran was "conscientiously representing many interests: myself, the State Department and White House, Currie and Vincent, and at least T. V. Soong on the Chinese side." His behind-the-scenes operations "may look surprising, but I suggest that it wasn't actually sinister."[4]

After reading their article, Service was greatly disturbed by its interpretation of his connection to Corcoran. To set the record straight, he sent Klehr and Radosh another letter:

> Corcoran, I now realize, was not a man to leave well enough alone. He barged into the case on the pretext that he was acting for Ben Cohen, whom he described as an "awfully close friend" of mine, even though I had never met Cohen. Corcoran talked to the Justice people (to an extent not known by me until these transcripts); but I do not see that he fixed anything, because the people involved in handling the case at Justice were already making clear to . . . me that they did not expect an indictment. Corcoran is not the first person to claim that he had done more than he actually had; he just got caught by the wiretaps.[5]

In the early 1990s, after declassification of the secret Venona files, Radosh and Klehr expanded their article into a book about the *Amerasia* "spy case." They asserted that Phillip Jaffe intended to pass information to a Soviet intelligence agent—but provided no proof he ever did. Though John Service might be viewed as "the first victim of the Cold War," the authors still asserted he had not been completely truthful about the role Corcoran had played. They found it "difficult to explain how a man who was considered one of the best and brightest young diplomats of his generation could have been quite as naïve and unsuspecting as he portrayed himself as being in his own testimony."[6]

John Service was naturally upset by this characterization. "I realize that phrases like 'double-riveted' sound like a broad fix," he wrote to a friend. "But in the context of all that Corcoran had said in our previous conversations, I took this to mean only that I was not going to be surprised in the Grand Jury by new evidence. . . . Naïve? Yes. But I was a hillbilly from Chungking, not a cynical, sophisticated Washingtonian."[7] Nevertheless, Tommy the Cork's efforts to fix things only enmeshed Service deeper into the web of suspicion.

What if Corcoran and his pals had not meddled? Perhaps the *Amerasia* case would have gone to trial. Perhaps the sworn testimony of General Stilwell would have triggered a serious debate over the United States' China policy. Service might not have wasted all those years defending his reputation. And the chilling effects of his ordeal would not still haunt the United States' diplomatic and intelligence communities, where the group-think of those timid "white rabbits" so disdained by Service's mother still persists.

* * *

In 1994 Service's diplomat son Robert was confirmed by the Senate as an ambassador—without any questions raised about his father's controversial past, much to his mother's relief. That year, too, John Service was honored with a lifetime achievement award from the Diplomatic and Consular Officers, Retired (DACOR) at a special luncheon in the eighth-floor dining room of the State Department. Service's name was engraved on the prestigious Foreign Service Cup: "For service to his country, dignity in the face of injustice, and scholarship on China." With his wife and his three children and their families looking on, Jack Service accepted the official citation: "Diplomat, scholar, and editor, John S. Service has come to symbolize the triumph of justice over the indignities suffered by the American Foreign Service during the McCarthy period. . . . The life of John Service is a victory of intelligence, patience, and loyalty to country over political opportunism and hysteria—a dignified and important victory."

* * *

Over the past thirty years I have enjoyed many conversations with John Service and his family. In one conversation, he confided that he "was not, by any means, an ideal diplomat or foreign service officer." Jack said he had "clearly violated" Talleyrand's sage advice, that diplomats should never have "too much zeal." "I espoused views and when those views weren't accepted, I became committed to try to get them accepted."[8] Supremely confident that he possessed a special understanding of China, John Service admitted he had made it his mission to convince others of the proper policy to follow. He was even more passionate about China's desperate situation than he had ever been about Val Chao.

John Service was a tragically doomed messenger: the bearer of unwelcome tidings, first in China and later in Washington. His zeal got him caught up in the perfect storm of war and revolution, foreign intrigue and domestic paranoia that characterized the era. But he succeeded in getting his views in front of many key officials—who chose to ignore his insights.

After investing so much prestige in building up Chiang Kai-shek and China's image as a major power in the postwar world, Franklin Roosevelt wanted desperately to believe Ambassador Hurley's upbeat assessment of the desperate China situation—and he remained confident that he could make Stalin into a trusted partner in the postwar world.

What if Roosevelt had been able to give serious consideration to other alternatives—and to other actors besides Patrick Hurley? Was there in fact a window of opportunity in 1944–45, when the United States could have actively cooperated with Mao's forces and influenced China's revolution? Perhaps the tumultuous cycle of reciprocal misperceptions and violence might have been avoided, sparing millions of lives on all sides.

After decades of international isolation and violent internal upheaval, today's China favors an approach to modernization involving foreign economic investment that Mao first outlined to Service in Yenan more than sixty years ago. And now, in the twenty-first century—after the death of the bitter rivals Chiang and Mao—the two Chinas are taking pragmatic confidence-building steps toward a peaceful resolution of their conflict. But relations between the two Chinas and the United States remain delicate, with the potential, still, to trigger another international crisis.

* * *

John Service lived to be nearly ninety years old, yet he never completely shook free of the controversy that shadowed his life. But by the time of his death, he had earned the respect and warm admiration of many. When Oberlin College awarded Service an honorary degree, the professor who introduced him put it this way: "He was and is a man of integrity and great courage and high character. He did not allow the wrong that was done to him make him a lesser person."[9]

In early 1999, about three weeks before his death, Jack Service dined with me at one of his favorite Chinese restaurants in Berkeley. At the end of the meal, we opened our fortune cookies. Service's fortune read:

> Patience is precious, but truth is more precious than patience.

With patience and truth on his side, John Service saw his views vindicated by history and his good name publicly restored. He was, indeed, an honorable survivor.

NOTES

In citing works in the notes, short titles have generally been used. Works frequently cited have been identified by the following abbreviations:

Caroline Service Papers, Bancroft	Caroline Schulz Service Papers, 1919–1997 BANC MSS 99/237cz, Bancroft Library, University of California, Berkeley.
C. S. S. oral history	Caroline Schulz Service, "State Department Duty in China, the McCarthy Era, and After: 1932–1977," an oral history conducted by Rosemary Levenson (Berkeley: Regional Oral History Office, Bancroft Library, University of California, 1978).
FBI *Amerasia*	Federal Bureau of Investigation *Amerasia* File, Case #100-267360 (and specific report numbers when indicated).
John Service Papers, Bancroft	John S. Service Papers, BANC MSS 87/21cz, Bancroft Library, University of California, Berkeley.
J. S. S. oral history	John S. Service, "State Department Duty in China, the McCarthy Era, and After: 1932–1977," an oral history conducted by Rosemary Levenson (Berkeley: Regional Oral History Office, Bancroft Library, University of California, 1978).
Service memoirs	John Service, "Memoirs," Vol. I, "China Hand: Early Memories of John Service"; Vol. II, untitled.

	Unpublished manuscript. (Bancroft Library, University of California, Berkeley, 1988).
Service personnel file	U.S. Department of State Personnel File: John S. Service's Foreign Service Career, 1933–1962 (St. Louis, Mo.: National Personnel Records Center, a division of NARA).
Service security file	Department of State Security Case File relating to John Stewart Service, 1933–1973, A-1 (5543), RG 59, ENTRY A-1(5543), Lot #00D523, STACK 150, ROW 72, COMPTMT 7, SHELF 5 (College Park, Md.: NARA).
Tydings Hearings	State Department Employee Loyalty Investigation. Hearings before a subcommittee of the U.S. Senate Committee on Foreign Relations, 81st Congress, 2nd Session (Washington, D.C.: Government Printing Office, 1950).
Tydings Hearings, LSB	Transcript of State Department Loyalty-Security Board Hearing in the case of John S. Service printed as part of the Tydings Hearings Part 2, Appendix pp. 1958–2509.
Tydings Report	"State Department Employee Loyalty Investigation." Report of a subcommittee of the United States Senate Committee on Foreign Relations, 81st Congress, 2nd Session (Washington, D.C.: Government Printing Office, 1950).

Note on Materials Obtained under the Freedom of Information Act (FOIA)

In 1966 the Freedom of Information Act was passed to make U.S. government documents more accessible to citizens and federal bureaucracies more accountable. Unfortunately, the record of openness to government files has been disappointing. Tremendous backlogs of FOIA requests and problems locating records have occurred. In my research, I petitioned the FBI, the U.S. State Department, the U.S. Army, and U.S. Navy (for intelligence files from the OSS, CIA, and ONI) and waited more than four years to receive many files. Sometimes I was informed that a document originated with another agency, but I would not be told which one. On occasion I was told the papers were lost or simply misplaced. Even when I acquired documents, they were often heavily redacted. I then would petition for rereviews. Sometimes this resulted in obtaining important information, but I was still denied access to literally hundreds of pages of documents pertaining to John S. Service's case.

Prologue

1. *Congressional Record*, "Extension of Remarks" January 24, 1973, E409.
2. John Service Papers, Bancroft, copy of *Human Events* magazine from January 23, 1973.
3. Ibid.
4. David Biltchik, interview with author, May 2003.
5. John Service Papers, January 23, 1973 speech.
6. Ibid., copy of CBS News Report.

Chapter 1: The Knock on the Door

1. FBI *Amerasia*, #100-267360-1047-407, p. 31.
2. C. S. S. oral history, 83.
3. J. S. S. oral history, 314.
4. FBI *Amerasia*, #100-267360-1047-407.
5. Ibid., #100-267360-1047-335.
6. John Service, interview by author, tape recording, Berkeley, Calif., April 16, 1998.
7. J. S. S. oral history, 313a.

Chapter 2: The Road to Chungking

1. John S. Service, ed., *Golden Inches: The China Memoir of Grace Service* (Berkeley: University of California Press, 1989), 35, 218.
2. John Service, "Memoirs" (unpublished manuscript, 1988), I: 137 (hereafter, Service memoirs).
3. Service, *Golden Inches*, 132–34.
4. Ibid.
5. Service memoirs, I: 28.
6. Service, *Golden Inches*, 182.
7. Service memoirs, I: 91.
8. Ibid., I: 57.
9. Service, *Golden Inches*, 193.
10. J. S. S. oral history, 45.
11. The dramatic story of their trip on the smuggler's trail is told in Service memoirs, I: 150–63; J. S. S. oral history, 41–44; and Service, *Golden Inches*, 239–41.
12. Service memoirs, I: 154.
13. Ibid., I: 162.
14. Ibid., I: 174.
15. Ibid., I: 186.
16. John K. Fairbank, *The United States and China* (New York: Viking Press, 1961), 176.

17. J. S. S. oral history, 71.
18. C. S. S. oral history, 23.
19. Service memoirs, I: 279.
20. Ibid., I: 315.
21. John Service, letter to Caroline Service, January 1933 (John Service Papers, Bancroft).
22. C. S. S. oral history, 41.
23. J. S. S. oral history, 117.
24. John Service, letter to Caroline Service, October 10, 1935 (John Service Papers, Bancroft).
25. C. S. S. oral history, 55.
26. J. S. S. oral history, 128.
27. Sterling Seagrave, *The Soong Dynasty* (New York: Harper & Row, 1985), 349.
28. Ibid., 356.
29. J. S. S. oral history, 132.
30. C. S. S. oral history, 59.
31. Theodore White and Annalee Jacoby, *Thunder Out of China* (New York: Da Capo Press, 1980), 52.
32. This horrific episode is chronicled in Iris Chang, *The Rape of Nanking: The Forgotten Holocaust of World War II* (New York: Basic Books, 1997).
33. Kemp Tolley, *Yangtze Patrol: The U. S. Navy in China* (Annapolis, Md.: Naval Institute Press, 1971), 252.
34. White and Jacoby, *Thunder Out of China*, 53.
35. J. S. S. oral history, 157.
36. C. S. S. oral history, 71.

Chapter 3: China Odyssey

1. John Service, letter to Caroline Service and Grace Service, May 8, 1941 (John Service Papers, Bancroft).
2. Ibid.
3. J. S. S. oral history, 165.
4. Ibid., 166.
5. Gary May, *China Scapegoat* (Washington, D.C.: New Republic Books, 1979), 81.
6. Doris Kearns Goodwin, *No Ordinary Time: Franklin and Eleanor Roosevelt: The Home Front in World War II* (New York: Simon & Schuster, 1994), 265.
7. T. V. Soong collected papers (Stanford, Calif.: Hoover Institution, Stanford University).
8. Lauchlin Currie, "China Trip Report to President Roosevelt," March 15, 1942. Lauchlin B. Currie Papers: 1941–1993, Box 5 (Stanford, Calif.: Hoover Institution, Stanford University).
9. Barbara Tuchman, *Stilwell and the American Experience in China: 1911–1945* (New York: Bantam Books, 1970), 290.

10. Ibid., 292.
11. Goodwin, *No Ordinary Time*, 289.
12. J. S. S. oral history, 186.
13. Goodwin, *No Ordinary Time*, 290.
14. J. S. S. oral history, 187.
15. Ibid., 190
16. Ibid., 191
17. Goodwin, *No Ordinary Time*, 302.
18. Herbert Feis, *The China Tangle* (New York: Atheneum, 1965), 11.
19. Ibid.,12.
20. Tuchman, *Stilwell*, 251.
21. Affidavit of Col. Paul Jones, 1950 (John Service Papers, Bancroft).
22. Tuchman, *Stilwell*, 282–86.
23. Feis, *China Tangle*, 33.
24. Tydings Report, Testimony of Clarence E. Gauss before the State Department Loyalty-Security Board, May 1950, 2067. (Note: the transcript from John Service's State Department Loyalty-Security Board (LSB) hearing was made part of the record of the Committee transcripts. The LSB transcript is hereafter cited as Tydings Hearings, LSB.)
25. Service memoirs, II: ch. 1, p. 1.
26. J. S. S. oral history, 200
27. Service memoirs, II: ch 2, p. 8.
28. J. S. S. oral history, 209.
29. Service personnel file: Memo #505.
30. John Service, interview with author, June 9, 1998; Service memoirs, II: ch. 2, p. 11.
31. Service memoirs, II: ch. 2, p. 10.
32. J. S. S. oral history, 203.
33. Ibid., 215.
34. Ibid., 217, 218; and Service memoirs, II: ch. 2, p. 17.
35. Joseph W. Esherick, ed., *Lost Chance in China: The World War II Despatches of John S. Service* (New York: Vintage Press, 1975), 12.
36. Ibid., 9–19.
37. Service security file: Box 22, transcript of security interview, November 24–25 and December 1, 3, 4, 1958.
38. Service memoirs, II: ch. 5, p. 6.

Chapter 4: China Romance

1. Herbert Feis, *The China Tangle,* (New York: Atheneum, 1965), 51.
2. Maochun Yu, *The OSS in China: Prelude to Cold War* (New Haven, Conn.: Yale University Press, 1996), 67–69.
3. Ibid.
4. Joseph E. Persico, *Roosevelt's Secret War: FDR and World War II Espionage* (New York: Random House, 2001), 210.

5. Lauchlin Currie memo to Roosevelt, August 24, 1942, Box 5, Lauchlin B. Currie Papers (Stanford, Calif.: Hoover Institution, Stanford University).
6. J. S. S. oral history, 225.
7. Loyalty Review Board transcript, John S. Service–Edward Rhetts Papers, Box 1, p. 20, Harry S. Truman Library, Independence, Missouri.
8. Joseph W. Esherick, ed., *Lost Chance in China: The World War II Despatches of John S. Service* (New York: Vintage Press, 1975), 170–73.
9. Ibid.
10. Ibid., 169–76; J. S. S. oral history, 225–28b; and Service memoirs, II: 3–4.
11. Gary May, *China Scapegoat* (Washington, D.C.: New Republic Books, 1979), 91.
12. Ibid., 92.
13. OSS files, entry 92, box 24, folder 24, RG 226 (College Park, Md.: NARA).
14. Service personnel file: PER #504, Department of State.
15. Service security file: William Kimbel memo February 8, 1943.
16. Sterling Seagrave, *The Soong Dynasty* (New York: Harper & Row, 1985), 384.
17. Barbara Tuchman, *Stilwell and the American Experience in China: 1911–1945* (New York: Bantam Books, 1970), 44.
18. C. S. S. oral history, 76–77.
19. E. J. Kahn Jr., *The China Hands: America's Foreign Service Officers and What Befell Them* (New York, Viking Press, 1975), 18.
20. "Davies LSB testimony," Service security file: "Summary and Analysis," 319 (College Park, Md.: NARA).
21. J. S. S. oral history, 227–28.
22. Ibid., 235.
23. "FDR–Hopkins–Sherwood manuscript, 7 Chinese Affairs," Box 325, Franklin Roosevelt Presidential Library, Hyde Park, New York.
24. Map Room files, Box 165, Franklin Roosevelt Presidential Library, Hyde Park, New York.
25. Feis, *China Tangle*, 60.
26. Charles R. Romanus and Riley Sunderland, *U.S. Army in World War II: The CBI Theater: Stilwell's Mission to China* (Washington D.C.: Office of the Chief of Military History, Department of the Army, 1953), 283.
27. J. S. S. oral history, 238.
28. Ibid., 235.
29. Service memoirs, II: ch. 3, p. 7.
30. Kahn, *China Hands*, 68, 74.
31. Service memoirs, II: ch. 3, p. 13.
32. Ibid., II: ch. 3, p. 7, 13.
33. J. S. S. oral history, 245
34. Service memoirs, II: ch. 4, p. 7.
35. J. S. S. oral history, 247–50.

36. Tang Tsou, *America's Failure in China: 1941–50* (Chicago: University of Chicago Press, 1963), 64.
37. Army Chief of Staff folder, Map Room files, Franklin Roosevelt Presidential Library, Hyde Park, New York.
38. Tuchman, *Stilwell*, 509.
39. Quoted in Feis, *China Tangle*, 109.
40. Kahn, *China Hands*, 101.
41. Gen. Joseph W. Stilwell Papers, Box 15, File 184 (Stanford, Calif.: Hoover Institution).
42. Service memoirs, II: ch. 5, p. 1.
43. J. S. S. oral history, 257; and John Service, interview with author, August 1998.
44. Esherick, *Lost Chance in China*, 93.
45. Val Chao, interviews with author, January 2000 and July 2002.
46. C. S. S. oral history, 74–75.
47. J. S. S. oral history, 255.
48. John Service, interview with author April 14, 1998.
49. Val Chao, interviews with author, January 2000 and July 2002.
50. John Service, interviews with author, April–August 1998; Val Chao, interviews with author, July 2002.
51. John Service, letter to Conrad Snow, April 10, 1950 (John Service Papers, Bancroft).
52. J. S. S. oral history, 264.
53. Charles Romanus and Riley Sunderland, *The CBI Theater: Stilwell's Command Problems* (Washington, D.C.: Office of the Chief of Military History, Department of the Army, 1955), 326.
54. Theodore White and Annalee Jacoby, *Thunder Out of China* (New York: Da Capo Press, 1980), 178.

Chapter 5: The Generalissimo

1. John Service, letter to David Barrett, 1970 (John Service Papers, Bancroft); J. S. S. oral history, 270; and Service memoirs, II: ch. 6, p. 10.
2. John Service, letter to David Barrett, 1970 (John Service Papers, Bancroft); and E. J. Kahn Jr., *The China Hands: America's Foreign Service Officers and What Befell Them* (New York: Viking Press, 1975), 111.
3. Tang Tsou, *America's Failure in China: 1941–1950* (Chicago: University of Chicago, 1963), 163.
4. "Notes of Vice President's Conversations with President Chiang," June 21–24, 1944; and Henry Wallace Folder; Presidential Secretary's Files (Hyde Park, New York: Franklin Roosevelt Presidential Library).
5. Currie letter files: folders 43–50, Carton #2 (John Service Papers, Bancroft).
6. Joseph W. Esherick, ed., *Lost Chance in China: The World War II Despatches of John S. Service* (New York: Vintage Books, 1975), 138–57.
7. Ibid.

8. Tsou, *America's Failure in China*, 196n67.
9. Esherick, *Lost Chance in China*, 138–57.
10. Ibid.
11. Service security file: Box 23.
12. John Service, interview with author, August 13, 1998.
13. Gary May, *China Scapegoat* (Washington, D.C.: New Republic Books, 1979), 105.
14. Ibid., 104–7.
15. Herbert Feis, *The China Tangle* (New York: Atheneum, 1965), 149; and May, *China Scapegoat*, 107.
16. Kahn, *The China Hands*, 111.
17. Tsou, *America's Failure in China*, 165.
18. May, *China Scapegoat*, 107.
19. Charles Romanus and Riley Sunderland, *The CBI Theater: Stilwell's Command Problems* (Washington, D.C.: Office of the Chief of Military History, Department of the Army, 1955), 380.
20. Barbara Tuchman, *Stilwell and the American Experience in China: 1911–1945* (New York: Bantam Books, 1970), 600.
21. Service memoirs, II: ch. 6, p. 15.
22. For details about the exchange of cables, see Feis, *China Tangle*, 172.
23. John Service interview with author, May 27, 1998; Tydings Hearings.
24. David Barrett, *Dixie Mission: The United States Army Observer Group in Yenan, 1944* (Berkeley: Center for Chinese Studies, University of California, 1970), 27.
25. Maochun Yu, *The OSS in China: Prelude to Cold War* (New Haven, Conn.: Yale University Press, 1996), 161.
26. Barrett, *Dixie Mission*, 28.

Chapter 6: Chairman Mao

1. Carolle J. Carter, *Mission to Yenan* (Lexington: The University Press of Kentucky, 1997), 28; and David Barrett, *Dixie Mission: The United States Army Observer Group in Yenan, 1944* (Berkeley: Center for Chinese Studies, University of California, 1970), 14.
2. Gunther Stein, *The Challenge of Red China* (New York: McGraw-Hill, 1945), 347.
3. Barrett, *Dixie Mission*, 30.
4. John Service, interview with author, August 18, 1998.
5. John Paton Davies, *Dragon by the Tail* (New York: W. W. Norton, 1972), 345. Even though Davies did not arrive in Yenan until October 1944, his comment is apt.
6. Harrison Forman, *Report from Red China* (New York: Henry Holt, 1945), 46–47.
7. Zhang Baijia, "Chinese Policies toward the United States 1937–1945," in *Sino-American Relations, 1945–1955: A Joint Reassessment of a Critical*

Decade, eds. Harry Harding and Yuan Ming (Wilmington, Del.: Scholarly Resources, 1989), 21.

8. J. S. S. oral history, 270.
9. Service memoirs, II: ch. 7, pp. 14–15.
10. Tydings Hearings.
11. For details, see Service memoirs, II: ch. 7, p. 3; and Barrett, *Dixie Mission*, 30–31.
12. Service memoirs, II: ch.7, p.17.
13. Theodore White and Annalee Jacoby, *Thunder Out of China* (New York: Da Capo Press, 1980), 229.
14. Service memoirs, II: ch. 7, p. 2; and J. S. S. oral history, 276.
15. Michael Schaller, *The U.S. Crusade in China, 1938–1945* (New York: Columbia University Press, 1979), 186.
16. Joseph W. Esherick, ed., *Lost Chance in China: The World War II Despatches of John S. Service* (New York: Vintage Press, 1975), 290.
17. Service memoirs, II: ch. 7, pp. 6–7; and J. S. S. oral history, 277.
18. Stuart Schram, *Mao Tse-tung* (Harmondsworth, England: Penguin, 1966), 220–21. For more on the Soviet role in China during the 1920s, see Conrad Brandt, *Stalin's Failure in China* (New York: W. W. Norton, 1966).
19. Esherick, *Lost Chance in China*, 179.
20. Service memoirs, II: ch. 7, p. 4; and J. S. S. oral history, 272.
21. Esherick, *Lost Chance in China*, 182.
22. Service memoirs, II: ch. 7, p. 8; and J. S. S. oral history, 279.
23. E. J. Kahn Jr., *The China Hands: America's Foreign Service Officers and What Befell Them* (New York: Viking Press, 1975), 119; and Michael M. Sheng, *Battling Western Imperialism: Mao, Stalin, and the United States* (Princeton, N.J.: Princeton University Press, 1997), 78, 83.
24. Service's report of this meeting, quoted in the following passages, is found in Esherick, *Lost Chance in China*, 291–307.
25. Gary May, *China Scapegoat* (Washington, D.C.: New Republic Books, 1979), 117.
26. William P. Head, *America's China Sojourn: America's Foreign Policy and Its Effects on Sino-American Relations, 1942–48* (Lanham, Md.: University Press of America, 1983), 103.
27. See various sources including Sheng, *Battling Western Imperialism*; Esherick, *Lost Chance in China*; Kahn, *The China Hands*; Davies, *Dragon by the Tail*; and Steven I. Levine, "On the Brink of Disaster: China and the United States in 1945" in *Sino-American Relations 1945–1955: A Joint Reassessment of a Critical Decade*, eds. Harding and Ming (Wilmington Del.: Scholarly Resources, 1989).
28. Charles Romanus and Riley Sunderland, *The CBI Theater: Stilwell's Command Problems* (Washington, D.C.: Office of the Chief of Military History, Department of the Army, 1955), 416–17.
29. Barrett, *Dixie Mission*, 34.

30. OSS files, "Dixie," RG 226, Entry 148, Box 7, Folder 36, (NARA).
31. Milton E. Miles file, OSS files, Box 39 "War Dept. Military Intelligence Div. G-2"; OSS files, "Dixie," RG 226, Entry 148, Box 7, Folder 36, (NARA).
32. OSS files, "Dixie," RG 226, Entry 148, Box 7, Folder 36, (NARA); Barrett, *Dixie Mission*, 43.
33. Ibid.; Maochun Yu, *The OSS in China: Prelude to Cold War* (New Haven, Conn.: Yale University Press, 1996), 41–43, 166–69.
34. Esherick, *Lost Chance in China*, 322–26.
35. Service letter to John Davies, August 8, 1944, Box 2, "Davies" Folder 51, (John Service Papers, Bancroft).
36. Romanus and Sunderland, *The CBI Theater: Stilwell's Command Problems*, 416.
37. Ibid., 421.
38. May, *China Scapegoat*, 112.
39. Stein, *The Challenge of Red China*, 441.
40. Romanus and Sunderland, *The CBI Theater: Stilwell's Command Problems*, 421.
41. Barbara Tuchman, *Stilwell and the American Experience in China: 1911–1945* (New York: Bantam Books, 1970), 601.

Chapter 7: October Crisis

1. Val Chao, interview with author, January 3, 2000.
2. David Barrett, *Dixie Mission*: *The United States Army Observer Group in Yenan, 1944* (Berkeley: Center for Chinese Studies, University of California, 1970), 34–35.
3. J. S. S. oral history, 272; Joseph W. Esherick, ed., *Lost Chance in China: The World War II Despatches of John S. Service* (New York: Vintage Press, 1975), 192–98.
4. Esherick, *Lost Chance in China*, 192–98.
5. Gary May, *China Scapegoat* (Washington, D.C.: New Republic Books, 1979), 120; and Stuart Schram, *Mao Tse-tung* (Harmondsworth, England: Penguin, 1966), 226.
6. Memo from Whittlesey to Commanding Officer, AGAS-China, September 9, 1944, OSS files, RG 226 (NARA).
7. Ibid.
8. John Service, memo to Commanding General, Fwd. Echelon USAF-CBI, October 15, 1944, RG 226 (NARA).
9. Charles Romanus and Riley Sunderland, *The CBI Theater: Stilwell's Command Problems* (Washington, D.C.: Office of the Chief of Military History, Department of the Army, 1955), 433.
10. Esherick, *Lost Chance in China*, 234–38.
11. Ibid., 318–21.
12. Ibid., 200–201.
13. Ibid.

14. Ibid., 248.
15. Ibid., 248–49. For more on Communist views, see 283–87.
16. Barbara Tuchman, *Stilwell and the American Experience in China: 1911–1945* (New York: Bantam Books, 1970), 619.
17. Romanus and Sunderland, *The CBI Theater: Stilwell's Command Problems*, 427–30.
18. Herbert Feis, *China Tangle* (New York: Atheneum, 1965), 185.
19. Romanus and Sunderland, *The CBI Theater: Stilwell's Command Problems*, 434–36.
20. Ibid., 437.
21. "United States Relations with China, with Special Reference to the Period 1944–1949," Department of State Publications 3573, Far Eastern Series 30 (Washington, D.C.: Office of Public Affairs, 1949), 561.
22. Michael Schaller, *The U.S. Crusade in China, 1938–1945* (New York: Columbia University Press, 1979), 169.
23. Romanus and Sunderland, *The CBI Theater: Stilwell's Command Problems*, 445–46.
24. Joseph Alsop, "Why We Lost China 3: The Foredoomed Mission of General Marshall," *Saturday Evening Post*, January 21, 1950, 111.
25. Tuchman, *Stilwell*, 631.
26. Romanus and Sunderland, *The CBI Theater: Stilwell's Command Problems*, 455; Tuchman, *Stilwell*, 640.
27. Romanus and Sunderland, *The CBI Theater: Stilwell's Command Problems*, 463.
28. Ibid. 455–56.
29. Box 2, Folder 51, 1944 letter (n.d.) to John Emmerson (Service Papers, Bancroft).
30. Esherick, *Lost Chance in China*, 247–49.
31. John Service interview with author, April 16, 1998.
32. Esherick, *Lost Chance in China*, 159–66.
33. J. S. S. oral history, 292.
34. Barrett, *Dixie Mission*, 46.
35. John Service, interview with author, August 18, 1998.
36. John Paton Davies, *Dragon by the Tail* (New York: W. W. Norton, 1972), 344.
37. Feis, *The China Tangle* (New York: Atheneum, 1965), 230–32.
38. Davies, *Dragon by the Tail*, 347.
39. John S. Service, *The Amerasia Papers: Some Problems in History of U.S.–China Relations* (Berkeley: Center for Chinese Studies, University of California, 1971), 147n25.

Chapter 8: Washington's Darling

1. J. S. S. oral history, 292–93.
2. Stephen R. MacKinnon and Oris Friesen, *China Reporting: An Oral History*

of American Journalism in the 1930s and 1940s (Berkeley: University of California Press, 1987), 141–43.
3. J. S. S. oral history, 293.
4. Joseph W. Esherick, ed., *Lost Chance in China: The World War II Despatches of John S. Service* (New York: Vintage Press, 1975), 331; and E. J. Kahn Jr., *The China Hands: America's Foreign Service Officers and What Befell Them* (New York: Viking Press, 1975), 133.
5. Esherick, *Lost Chance in China*, 332.
6. John Service, interview with author, August 18, 1998.
7. Herbert Feis, *The China Tangle* (New York: Atheneum, 1965), 201.
8. J. S. S. oral history, 293.
9. Quoted in Tydings Hearings, LSB, 1753–55.
10. Ibid.
11. "Soong and Hurley" Folder: Hopkins, Harry; Map Room files, Franklin Roosevelt Library, Hyde Park, New York.
12. J. S. S. oral history, 294.
13. Esherick, *Lost Chance in China*, 160.
14. John Paton Davies wrote four memos (November 1944) laying out the geopolitical considerations behind the group's efforts for a change in U.S. policy. See *Foreign Relations of the United States: Diplomatic Papers, 1944* Vol. VI, *China* (Washington, D.C.: Government Printing Office, 1944); and OSS files, "Dixie," Entry 148, Box 7, Folder 36, RG 226 (NARA).
15. Drew Pearson, November 29, 1944, column, "Drew Pearson's Washington Merry-Go-Round" (John Service Papers, Bancroft).
16. J. S. S. oral history, 294.
17. Feis, *The China Tangle*, 258n4.
18. John Service, interview with author, February 13, 1998.
19. John S. Service, *The Amerasia Papers: Some Problems in History of U.S.–China Relations* (Berkeley: Center for Chinese Studies, University of California, 1971), 165n45; and J. S. S. oral history, 299.
20. Sterling Seagrave, *The Soong Dynasty* (New York: Harper & Row, 1985), 401.
21. David Barrett, *Dixie Mission: The United States Army Observer Group in Yenan, 1944* (Berkeley: Center for Chinese Studies, University of California, 1970), 56.
22. Ibid., 61–62.
23. Ibid., 62–64.
24. Feis, *The China Tangle*, 214–16.
25. John Paton Davies, *Dragon by the Tail* (New York: W.W. Norton, 1972), 367–68.
26. Theodore White and Annalee Jacoby, *Thunder Out of China* (New York: Da Capo Press, 1980), 250–51.
27. Davies, *Dragon by the Tail*, 367.
28. Barbara Tuchman, *Stilwell and the American Experience in China: 1911–1945* (New York: Bantam Books, 1970), 621.

29. W. Averell Harriman and Elie Abel, *Special Envoy to Churchill and Stalin: 1941* (New York: Random House, 1975), 371.
30. Russell D. Buhite, *Patrick J. Hurley and American Foreign Policy* (Ithaca, N.Y.: Cornell University Press, 1973), 174.
31. Charles Romanus and Riley Sunderland, *U.S. Army in World War II: Time Runs Out in CBI* (Washington, D.C.: Office of the Chief of Military History, Department of the Army, 1958), 72–74, 249; and Barrett, *Dixie Mission*, 70–73.
32. OSS files, Entry 148, Box 7, Folder 104, RG 226 (NARA).
33. Service security file: Box 25, vol. 2, 1954–73, 2 of 3, A-1(5543) (NARA).
34. Barrett, *Dixie Mission*, 70–75.
35. Ibid., 75.
36. C. S. S. oral history, 76.

Chapter 9: The Ambassador's Paranoia

1. J. S. S. oral history, 300.
2. Val Chao, interview with author, January 3, 2000.
3. Wedemeyer Memorandum for the President, December 3, 1944, Map Room files, Box 165, Franklin Roosevelt Library, Hyde Park, New York.
4. Herbert Feis, *The China Tangle* (New York: Atheneum, 1965), 218; Russell D. Buhite, *Patrick J. Hurley and American Foreign Policy* (Ithaca, N.Y.: Cornell University Press, 1973), 178.
5. E. J. Kahn Jr., *The China Hands: America's Foreign Service Officers and What Befell Them* (New York: Viking Press, 1975), 149.
6. John Paton Davies, *Dragon by the Tail* (New York: W. W. Norton, 1972), 383.
7. Charles Romanus and Riley Sunderland, *U.S. Army in World War II: Time Runs Out in CBI* (Washington, D.C.: Office of the Chief of Military History, Department of the Army, 1958), 249.
8. OSS files, "Dixie," RG 226, Entry 148, Box 7, Folder 36 (NARA); Maochun Yu, *The OSS in China: Prelude to Cold War* (New Haven, Conn.: Yale University Press, 1996), 185–87.
9. Davies, *Dragon by the Tail*, 347–48.
10. Joint hearing by Senate Foreign Relations and Armed Services committees May 3, June 25, 1951: the so-called MacArthur Hearings.
11. "Yenan Trip" memo, January 24, 1945, OSS files, RG 226, Entry 148, Box 7, Folder 36 (NARA).
12. Maochun, *OSS in China*, 185–89.
13. John S. Service, *The Amerasia Papers: Some Problems in History of U.S.–China Relations* (Berkeley: Center for Chinese Studies, University of California, 1971), 125.
14. OSS files, Entry 148, Box 7, Folder 104, RG 226 (NARA).
15. "United States Relations with China, with Special Reference to the Period 1944–1949," Department of State Publications 3573, Far Eastern Series 30 (Washington, D.C.: Office of Public Affairs, 1949), 77.

16. Michael Schaller, *The U.S. Crusade in China, 1938–1945* (New York: Columbia University Press, 1979), 204.
17. David Barrett, *Dixie Mission: The United States Army Observer Group in Yenan, 1944* (Berkeley: Center for Chinese Studies, University of California, 1970), 76–77.
18. Romanus and Sunderland, *U.S. Army in World War II: Time Runs Out in CBI*, 52.
19. Kahn, *China Hands*, 145.
20. Ibid., 146.
21. Schaller, *U.S. Crusade in China*, 208.
22. John P. Davies, Box 2, Folder 15–17 (John Service Papers, Bancroft).
23. Joseph W. Esherick, ed., *Lost Chance in China: The World War II Despatches of John S. Service* (New York: Vintage Press, 1975), 341.
24. Barbara Tuchman, "If Mao Had Come to Washington: An Essay in Alternatives," *Foreign Affairs* 51 (October 1972): 44–64.
25. Schaller, *U.S. Crusade in China*, 204–5.
26. Map Room files, Box 165, Folder 11, Franklin Roosevelt Library, Hyde Park, New York.
27. Feis, *The China Tangle*, 222.
28. Maochun, *OSS in China,* 192–93.
29. Ibid., 74.
30. J. S. S. oral history, 301.
31. Tydings Hearings, LSB, 1984–88.
32. J. S. S. oral history, 302.
33. Romanus and Sunderland, *U.S. Army in World War II: Time Runs Out in CBI*, 253.
34. Service security file: Security interview, December 3, 1958, p. 39.
35. Val Chao, interview with author, July 25, 2003.
36. Service personnel file: Memo #495.
37. John Service, interview with author, August 18, 1998.
38. Doris Kearns Goodwin, *No Ordinary Time: Franklin and Eleanor Roosevelt: The Home Front in World War II* (New York: Simon and Shuster, 1994), 572–73.
39. Feis, *China Tangle*, 253–54.
40. Esherick, *Lost Chance in China*, 344.
41. Goodwin, *No Ordinary Time*, 583, 585.
42. Esherick, *Lost Chance in China*, 349.
43. John Service, "Chou En-lai, as Seen by an Old China Hand," *Los Angeles Times*, January 14, 1976.

Chapter 10: Farewell to China

1. Joseph W. Esherick, ed., *Lost Chance in China: The World War II Despatches of John S. Service* (New York: Vintage Press, 1975), 354.
2. Herbert Feis, *The China Tangle* (New York: Atheneum, 1965), 223.
3. J. S. S. oral history, 306.

4. Wedemeyer, letter to John Davies, February 1945, "Papers of John S. Service and Charles Rhetts," State Department Loyalty Investigation, Box 1, Truman Library, Independence, Missouri.
5. John S. Service, *The Amerasia Papers: Some Problems in History of U.S.–China Relations* (Berkeley: Center for Chinese Studies, University of California, 1971), 184.
6. Esherick, *Lost Chance in China*, 357.
7. J. S. S. oral history, 306a.
8. Service, Letter to John Carter Vincent, February 1945 (John Service Papers, Bancroft).
9. Service, *Amerasia Papers*, 184–85.
10. Service letter to John Davies, February 19, 1945.
11. J. S. S. oral history, 306.
12. Esherick, *Lost Chance in China*, 358–63.
13. Service, Letters to Grace Service, March 8, 1945 (John Service Papers, Bancroft).
14. Secret cable, Gross to Wedemeyer, March 21, 1945, Department of State. Released through author's FOIA rereview request on May 5, 2004, by U.S. Army Intelligence.
15. Esherick, *Lost Chance in China*, 370.
16. Ibid., 351–53.
17. J. S. S. oral history, 308.
18. Esherick, *Lost Chance in China*, 375–78.
19. Ibid., 378.
20. "Translation of Chu Teh letter," January 23, 1945, OSS files, RG 226, Entry 92, Box 24, Folder 24 (NARA).
21. Letter from Adolf Suehsdorf, Folder 4, Box 8 (John Service Papers, Bancroft).
22. Service, *Amerasia Papers*, 150.
23. Esherick, *Lost Chance in China*, 371–78.
24. Ibid., 372.
25. Service, *Amerasia Papers*, 182–83.
26. Ibid., 189.
27. Esherick, *Lost Chance in China*, 349.
28. Doris Kearns Goodwin, *No Ordinary Time: Franklin and Eleanor Roosevelt: The Home Front in World War II* (New York: Simon & Schuster, 1994), 586.
29. Ibid., 586–87.
30. David McCullough, *Truman* (New York: Simon & Schuster, 1992), 337.
31. Goodwin, *No Ordinary Time*, 571.
32. Feis, *China Tangle*, 271; and E. J. Kahn, Jr., *The China Hands: America's Foreign Service Officers and What Befell Them* (New York: Viking Press, 1975), 153.
33. Service, *Amerasia Papers*, 108.
34. Charles Romanus and Riley Sunderland, *U.S. Army in World War II: Time Runs Out in CBI* (Washington, D.C.: Office of the Chief of Military History, Department of the Army, 1958), 159.

35. Service, *Amerasia Papers*, 124–27.
36. Ibid., 125–26.
37. Russell D. Buhite, *Patrick J. Hurley and American Foreign Policy* (Ithaca, N.Y.: Cornell University Press, 1973), 212.
38. Harry Harding and Yan Ming, editors, *Sino-American Relations 1945–1955: A Joint Reassessment of a Critical Decade* (Wilmington, Del.: Scholarly Resources, 1989), 92.
39. Gross to Wedemeyer cable, March 21, 1945.
40. Feis, *China Tangle*, 273n11; and Gross to Wedemeyer cable, March 21, 1945.
41. Esherick, *Lost Chance in China*, 381.
42. Ibid., 384.
43. Ibid., 383.
44. Gross to Wedemeyer cable, March 21, 1945.
45. Service, *Amerasia Papers*, 163.

Chapter 11: The FBI Trap

1. Tydings Hearings, 930–31.
2. Ibid., 934.
3. Ibid., 1186.
4. Harvey Klehr and Ronald Radosh, *The Amerasia Spy Case: Prelude to McCarthyism* (Chapel Hill: University of North Carolina Press, 1996), 32.
5. FBI *Amerasia*, memo March 20, 1945.
6. Other illegal searches took place on March 26 and 27, April 23 and 24, and May 14, 1945. See White House Central Files for Justice Department and FBI security reports, Truman Library, Independence, Missouri.
7. Klehr and Radosh, *Amerasia Spy Case*, 83.
8. Ibid., 49–50.
9. FBI *Amerasia*, File #100-267360-468, June 14, 1945, memo, 8–9 ("Summary").
10. Klehr and Radosh, *Amerasia Spy Case*, 52.
11. "Battle for Iwo Jima," U.S. Marine Corps, www.geocities.com/Pentagon/7338/usmc.html.
12. History Learning Site, http://www.historylearningsite.co.uk.
13. E. J. Kahn, Jr., *The China Hands: America's Foreign Service Officers and What Befell Them* (New York: Viking Press, 1975), 157.
14. Tang Tsou, *America's Failure in China: 1941–50* (Chicago: University of Chicago Press, 1963), 185.
15. Kahn, *China Hands*, 157n13.
16. J. S. S. oral history, 311.
17. Doris Kearns Goodwin, *No Ordinary Time: Franklin and Eleanor Roosevelt: The Home Front in World War II* (New York: Simon and Shuster, 1994), 602.
18. Ibid., 605.
19. David McCullough, *Truman* (New York: Simon & Schuster, 1992), 372.
20. Ibid., 355.

21. John S. Service, *The Amerasia Papers: Some Problems in History of U.S.–China Relations* (Berkeley: Center for Chinese Studies, University of California, 1971), 164.
22. Ibid., 162.
23. Ibid., 163.
24. "Hurley to Truman 1945," Staff Members and Office Files: Naval Aide to President Files, 1945–53 Communications File, Truman Library, Independence, Missouri.
25. Klehr and Radosh, *Amerasia Spy Case*, 62.
26. J. S. S. oral history, 310.
27. Service, *Amerasia Papers*, 166.
28. FBI *Amerasia*, File #100-267360-105 memo, D. M. Ladd to Hoover, April 18, 1945.
29. Service personnel file: Memo #494.
30. Service security file: John Service, Security interview November 24–December 11, 1958, p. 60.
31. Tydings Hearings, 1272.
32. Ibid.
33. Service security file: FBI Transcript of hotel conversation April 19, 1945, Appendix D, Box 5.
34. Ibid.; Service, Security interview, November 24–December 11, 1958; and Phillip Jaffe, unpublished autobiography, Jaffe Papers (Atlanta: Emory University, 1979), 26.
35. Service security file: Service, Security interview, November 26–December 11, 1958.
36. Ibid.: "Loyalty Review Board" transcripts, Appendix C, Box #2, p. 35.
37. McCullough, *Truman*, 370–73.
38. Charles F. Romanus and Riley Sunderland, *Time Runs Out in CBI* (Office of the Chief of Military History, Washington, D.C.: 1958), 337.
39. Tydings Hearings, 1273.
40. Service security file: Security interview, November 26–December 11, 1958, Box 22.
41. Tydings Hearings, 1285.
42. Klehr and Radosh, *Amerasia Spy Case*, 62.
43. John Service interview with author April 16, 1998.
44. FBI *Amerasia*, File #100-267360-1287, summary memo June 5, 1950.

Chapter 12: Convergence

1. FBI *Amerasia*, #121-13347-101 memo attachment, J. S. S. statement to FBI, June 6, 1945.
2. Ibid., #121-13347-101 memo, May 16, 1950; and ibid., attachment J. S. S. statement to FBI, June 6, 1945.
3. John Service, letter to family, April 28, 1945 (John Service Papers, Bancroft).

4. John S. Service, *The Amerasia Papers: Some Problems in History of U.S.–China Relations* (Berkeley: Center for Chinese Studies, University of California, 1971), 92.
5. Russell D. Buhite, *Patrick J. Hurley and American Foreign Policy* (Ithaca, N.Y.: Cornell University Press, 1973), 207–8; see also John Paton Davies, *Dragon by the Tail* (New York: W. W. Norton, 1972), 395.
6. Buhite, *Patrick J. Hurley*, 212–13.
7. For Hurley comment, see Service security file:"Summary and Analysis," 36; see also FBI *Amerasia*, memo to J. Edgar Hoover, August 20, 1945; and ibid., June 14, 1945 memo re: interview with Anna Lamberton.
8. FBI *Amerasia*, memo #100-267360-652 (with Hoover comment handwritten at bottom of page).
9. Theodore White and Annalee Jacoby, *Thunder Out of China* (New York: Da Capo Press, 1980), 249.
10. David McCullough, *Truman* (New York: Simon & Schuster, 1992), 377.
11. Harvey Klehr and Ronald Radosh, *The Amerasia Spy Case: Prelude to McCarthyism* (Chapel Hill: University of North Carolina Press, 1996), 63.
12. McCullough, *Truman*, 383.
13. FBI *Amerasia*, memos #121-13347-236 and #121-13347-221, May 17, 1945; and Klehr and Radosh, *Amerasia Spy Case*, 67–68.
14. McCullough, *Truman*, 381–82.
15. Service security file: Box 5, Appendix D, from FBI record 13, pp. 1–2.
16. Ibid., from FBI record 17, p. 1.
17. FBI *Amerasia*, #121-13347-101 memo, May 16, 1950, attachment: "Service signed statement to FBI, June 6, 1945."
18. Tydings Hearings, LSB, 2477.
19. Service, *Amerasia Papers*, 129.
20. Ibid., 130 and 128.
21. Tydings Hearings, 1274.
22. Klehr and Radosh, *Amerasia Spy Case*, 75.
23. J. S. S. oral history, 312.
24. Joe Ball, letter to Truman, May 15, 1945, File-208b, Truman Library, Independence, Missouri.
25. Tang Tsou, *America's Failure in China: 1941–50* (Chicago: University of Chicago Press, 1963), 259; and Herbert Feis, *The China Tangle* (New York: Atheneum, 1965), 308.
26. Davies, *Dragon by the Tail*, 398.
27. Tsou, *America's Failure in China*, 259.
28. FBI *Amerasia*, #100-267360-1276 memo, June 9, 1950, re: Forrestal diary, entry from May 28, 1945.
29. Service security file, Box 5, Appendix D, FBI memorandum and transcript of May 29, 1945, recordings.
30. FBI *Amerasia*, #100-267360-260 memo, May 29, 1945.
31. Ibid., #100-267360-1407 summary memo, May 11, 1950.

32. Ibid., memo #100-267360-283, memo to Hoover from Gurnea, May 29, 1945; Klehr and Radosh, *Amerasia Spy Case*, 85–86.
33. FBI *Amerasia*, #100-267360-285, memo to Hoover from Gurnea, May 31, 1945.
34. Klehr and Radosh, *Amerasia Spy Case*, 89.
35. FBI *Amerasia*, #100-267360-277, memo from Gurnea to Hoover, June 2, 1945.
36. Tydings Hearings, 1169.

Chapter 13: Case Corked

1. *The New York Times*, June 8, 1945.
2. FBI *Amerasia*, #100-267360-242 memo, June 11, 1945, and attached I. F. Stone article in *PM Daily*, June 8, 1945, with Hoover comment written on bottom.
3. John Service, letter to Grace Service, June 7, 1945 (John Service Papers, Bancroft).
4. C. S. S. oral history, 87.
5. Service Memo, November 1–3, 1950, Edward Rhetts File (John Service Papers, Bancroft).
6. J. S. S. oral history, 319.
7. Harvey Klehr and Ronald Radosh, *The Amerasia Spy Case: Prelude to McCarthyism* (Chapel Hill: University of North Carolina Press, 1996), 99.
8. Blind carbon copy of Paul L. Jones letter to Prof. Harvey Klehr, January 20, 1985, Correspondence File (John Service Papers, Bancroft).
9. *New York Post*, "Spies or Victims?" June 8, 1945.
10. Woltman, Frederick, "Reds Caused Stilwell and Chiang Break," *San Francisco News*, June 8, 1945.
11. J. S. S. oral history, 316.
12. *New York Herald Tribune*, June 8, 1945.
13. FBI *Amerasia*, File #100-267360, memo #420.
14. Editorial, "Try It in Court," *Cincinnati Post*, June 12, 1945, attached as FBI *Amerasia*, Files #100-267360-419 to 100-267-360-420 memo, June 14, 1945, to Hoover and Gurnea from Conroy.
15. John Service, letter to Grace Service, June 11, 1945, family correspondence (John Service Papers, Bancroft).
16. Grace Service, letter to Uncle Fred, June 11, 1945, family correspondence, Box 1 (Grace Boggs Service Papers, BANC MSS 87/22cz, The Bancroft Library, University of California, Berkeley).
17. Corcoran transcripts, June 10–September 24, 1945, in J. Edgar Hoover's "C&O" File #2 Part 1, Section 2, Federal Bureau of Investigation, 94–96. The Corcoran transcripts were kept in Hoover's special confidential files. However, copies of Corcoran's conversations also wound up in the Truman Library and became open to the public long before the existence of Hoover's secret "C&O" files was known.

18. Klehr and Radosh, *Amerasia Spy Case*, 114. J. Edgar Hoover's "C&O" File #2 Part 1, Section 2, Federal Bureau of Investigation; transcript June 11, 1945, Currie and Corcoran, 6–10.
19. FBI *Amerasia*, #100-267360-384 memo, June 11, 1945.
20. Service Memo, November 1–3, 1950, Edward Rhetts File (John Service Papers, Bancroft).
21. FBI *Amerasia*, #100-267360-366 memo, June 12, 1945, Hoover to Tolson,
22. Klehr and Radosh, *Amerasia Spy Case*, 105.
23. Tydings Hearings, 1014.
24. FBI *Amerasia*, memo #100-267360-523x lists the articles found in Service's office desk.
25. Richard Service letter to John Service, June 19, 1945, Box 10 (John Service Papers, Bancroft).
26. Klehr and Radosh, *Amerasia Spy Case*, 100.
27. Tang Tsou, *America's Failure in China: 1941–50* (Chicago: University of Chicago Press, 1963), 193.
28. *New York Times*, "Arrests on 'Leaks' Defended by Grew," June 16, 1945.
29. J. S. S. oral history, 317–18.
30. C. S. S. oral history, 87.
31. David McCullough, *Truman* (New York: Simon & Schuster, 1992), 400.
32. Ibid.
33. FBI *Amerasia*, #100-267360-428 memo, June 18, 1945, Hoover to Gurnea.
34. Ibid., #100-267360-468 memo, June 19, 1945, furnished to Hitchcock.
35. Ibid., #100-267360-459 memo, June 22, 1945, Gurena to Hoover.
36. Service memo November 1–3, 1950, Edward Rhetts File (John Service Papers, Bancroft).
37. FBI *Amerasia*, #100-267360-505 memo, June 29, 1945, Gurnea to Hoover.
38. Ibid., #100-267360-452 memo, June 22, 1945, Ladd to Tamm.
39. Klehr and Radosh, *Amerasia Spy Case*, 117–18.
40. J. S. S. oral history, 319.
41. Service Memo to Ed Rhetts, November 1–3, 1950, Edward Rhetts File (John Service Papers, Bancroft).

Chapter 14: FBI Person of Interest

1. David McCullough, *Truman* (New York: Simon & Schuster, 1992), 404.
2. John Service, interview with author, August 13, 1998.
3. Tang Tsou, *America's Failure in China: 1941–50* (Chicago: University of Chicago Press, 1963), 142.
4. Harry S. Truman, "Notes on the Potsdam Conference," July 17–30, 1945, Presidential Secretary's File, Truman Library, Independence, Missouri.
5. McCullough, *Truman*, 424.
6. FBI *Amerasia*, #100-267360-570 July memo to Hoover from Gurnea.
7. John Service, Memo to Ed Rhetts, November 1–3, 1950, Edward Rhetts File (John Service Papers, Bancroft).

8. FBI *Amerasia*, #100-267360-1000, summary memo p.16.
9. Ibid., #100-267360-643 memo, August 1, 1945; Corcoran Conversations, July 21–31, 1945, Presidential Secretary's File, Truman Library, Independence, Missouri (hereafter, Corcoran Transcript, HST); Corcoran Transcript, FBI, in J. Edgar Hoover's "C&O" File #2 Part 1, Section 2, Corcoran transcripts: June 10–September 24, 1945 (hereafter, Corcoran Transcript, FBI).
10. McCullough, *Truman*, 442; Harry S. Truman, *Memoirs by Harry S. Truman*, Volume I: *Year of Decisions* (Garden City, N.Y.: Doubleday, 1955), 419.
11. McCullough, *Truman*, 423.
12. Corcoran Transcript HST; Corcoran Transcript FBI.
13. Ibid.
14. Service Memo to Edward Rhetts, November 1–3, 1950, Edward Rhetts File (John Service Papers, Bancroft).
15. Harvey Klehr and Ronald Radosh, *The Amerasia Spy Case: Prelude to McCarthyism* (Chapel Hill: University of North Carolina Press, 1996), 110.
16. Corcoran Transcript HST, July 31, 1945.
17. Ibid., August 1, 1945.
18. Ibid.; FBI *Amerasia*, #100-267360-631x memo, August 2, 1945, Gurnea to Ladd re: Corcoran-McGranery conversations.
19. FBI *Amerasia*, #100-267360-491, memo June 11, 1945.
20. John S. Service, *The Amerasia Papers: Some Problems in History of U.S.–China Relations* (Berkeley: Center for Chinese Studies, University of California, 1971), 37.
21. FBI *Amerasia*, memo #100-267360-643, August 1, 1945, from Gurnea to Ladd.
22. Service security file: FBI memo from Denver office, June 3, 1950, re: Chronology of *Amerasia* Case, Box 4, Appendix C, p.18.
23. Corcoran Transcript, FBI, 203.
24. Ibid., August 2, 1945, 227–28.
25. Wilbur Peterkin papers, 1943–94, Hoover Institution Archives, Hoover Institution on War, Revolution and Peace, Stanford University, Stanford, California.
26. OSS–China File Entry 148, Box 7, Folder 104, RG 226 (NARA); Carolle J. Carter, *Mission to Yenan* (Lexington: The University Press of Kentucky), 173–74.
27. Stuart Schram, *Mao Tse-tung* (Harmondsworth, U.K.: Penguin, 1966), 231–32.
28. Gary May, *China Scapegoat* (Washington, D.C.: New Republic Books, 1979), 130.
29. Klehr and Radosh, *Amerasia Spy Case*, 390.
30. Michael Schaller, *The U.S. Crusade in China, 1938–1945* (New York: Columbia University Press, 1979), 232, 243.
31. Ibid., 243–45.
32. Ibid., 231.

33. Maochun Yu, *The OSS in China: Prelude to Cold War* (New Haven, Conn.: Yale University Press, 1996), 223.
34. OSS files, RG 226, Entry 148, Box 11, Folder 161 (NARA).
35. Ibid., Folder 163.
36. Service security file: "The grand jury transcript," Appendix C, Box 4/4. After fifty-eight years, the confidential transcript of John Service's secret grand jury testimony was declassified and released at the author's request under the Freedom of Information Act in 2003.
37. Ibid.
38. Ibid., 495.
39. McCullough, *Truman*, 455.
40. FBI *Amerasia*, #100-267360-651 memo, August 4, 1945, Hoover to Clark re: *Amerasia* case rumors.
41. Ibid., #100-267360-650 memo, August 10, 1945, Gurnea to Hoover.
42. Grace Service, diary entry, August 10, 1945 (Grace Boggs Service Papers, BANC MSS 87/22cz, The Bancroft Library, University of California, Berkeley).

Chapter 15: Clean as a Whistle

1. Service security file: Nathaniel Davies, diary entry, August 13, 1945, Appendix F.
2. John Service, letter to Grace Service, August 21, 1945 (John Service Papers, Bancroft).
3. Service security file: Nathaniel Davies, diary entry, August 13, 1945, Appendix F.
4. Herbert Feis, *The China Tangle* (New York: Atheneum, 1965), 341; Tang Tsou, *America's Failure in China: 1941–50* (Chicago: University of Chicago Press, 1963), 305, 236.
5. Stuart Schram, *Mao Tse-Tung* (Harmondsworth, England: Penguin, 1966), 236.
6. Michael Schaller, *The U.S. Crusade in China, 1938–1945* (New York: Columbia University Press, 1979), 247.
7. David McCullough, *Truman* (New York: Simon & Schuster, 1992), 460–62.
8. John Service, letter to Grace Service, August 21, 1945 (John Service Papers, Bancroft).
9. Tsou, *America's Failure in China*, 283.
10. See Rhetts File for notes regarding meetings with Tung Pi-wu in summer of 1945 (John Service Papers, Bancroft).
11. OSS files, RG 226, Entry 148, Box 6, Folder 87 (College Park, Md.: NARA).
12. John Service, *The Amerasia Papers: Some Problems in History of U.S.–China Relations* (Berkeley: Center for Chinese Studies, University of California, 1971), 190.
13. Service personnel file, memo #489.

14. C. S. S. oral history, 93.
15. John Service, letter to Grace Service, August 21, 1945 (John Service Papers, Bancroft).
16. FBI *Amerasia*, #100-267360-652 memo, August 21, 1945, Hoover to Attorney General Clark.
17. Service file, RG 59, File 123, Box 904, Note from Atty. Gen. Clark to Secretary of State, re: grand jury decision, August 24, 1945 (College Park, Md.: NARA).
18. *Oberlin News Tribune*, August 16, 1945.
19. John Service, letter to Grace Service, August 25, 1945 (John Service Papers, Bancroft).
20. Service personnel file: Memo #354.
21. J. S. S. oral history, 331.
22. John Service, letter to Grace Service, October 1, 1945 (John Service Papers, Bancroft).
23. Russell D. Buhite, *Patrick J. Hurley and American Foreign Policy* (Ithaca, N.Y.: Cornell University Press, 1973), 237.
24. John Service, interview with author, May 27, 1998.
25. Naval Aide to the President Files 1945–1953, "Chiang from Truman: 1945–46," Staff Members and Office Files, Box 7, Truman Library, Independence, Missouri.
26. J. S. S. oral history, 337.
27. Harvey Klehr and Ronald Radosh, *The Amerasia Spy Case: Prelude to McCarthyism* (Chapel Hill: University of North Carolina Press, 1996), 131.
28. FBI *Amerasia*, #100-267360-671 memo, August 28, 1945 to Hoover from Gurnea.
29. Ibid., #100-267360-1000 summary memo, April 3, 1950.
30. Ibid., #100-267360-671 memo, August 28, 1945.
31. Curt Gentry, *J. Edgar Hoover: The Man and the Secrets* (New York: W. W. Norton, 1991), 342.
32. *Congressional Record*, 79th U.S. Congress, 1st Session, Vol. 91 (1945): pt. 7: 9552–53; and Klehr and Radosh, *Amerasia Spy Case*, 136–40.
33. Klehr and Radosh, *Amerasia Spy Case*, 132.
34. Robert J. Lamphere and Tom Shachtman, *The FBI-KGB War: A Special Agent's Story* (New York: Berkeley Publishing Group, 1987), 38–40. After the fall of the Soviet Union, Soviet intelligence files revealed a number of plots to kill Bentley.
35. Lauren Kessler, *Clever Girl* (New York: HarperCollins, 2003), 128–32.
36. Ibid., 129, 135–36.
37. Lamphere and Shachtman, *FBI-KGB War*, 40.
38. Tsou, *America's Failure in China*, 304.
39. Schram, *Mao Tse-tung*, 236–37.
40. Theodore White and Annalee Jacoby, *Thunder Out of China*, (New York: Da Capo Press, 1980), 286, 288.

41. Tsou, *America's Failure in China*, 305.
42. White and Jacoby, *Thunder Out of China*, 289.
43. "Civil War in China: Editorial Opinion on Policy We Should Pursue Toward Rival Governments." *New York Times Overseas Weekly*, November 11, 1945.
44. Michael M. Sheng, *Battling Western Imperialism: Mao, Stalin, and the United States* (Princeton, N.J.: Princeton University Press, 1997), 110.
45. Ibid., 110.
46. Buhite, *Patrick J. Hurley*, 263–64.
47. Feis, *China Tangle*, 400.
48. Ibid., 397.
49. John Service, letter to Grace Service, November 26, 1945 (John Service Papers, Bancroft).
50. Buhite, *Patrick J. Hurley*, 260–65.
51. Harry S. Truman, *Memoirs by Harry S. Truman*, Volume II: *Years of Trial and Hope* (New York: Signet Books, 1956), 85.
52. McCullough, *Truman*, 475.
53. Service security file: "Summary and Analysis," Part II, Box 1.
54. For Hurley resignation letter, November 26, 1945, see "United States Relations with China: with Special Reference to the Period 1944–1949," Department of State Publications 3573, Far Eastern Series 30 (Washington, D.C.: Office of Public Affairs, August 1949), 581–84. For photo and caption, see *Los Angeles Examiner*, "Senate to Probe Hurley Charges; Ex-Envoy Says U.S. Arms Wrongly Used," November 29, 1945.
55. J. S. S. oral history, 338–39.
56. Service security file: "Summary and Analysis," Part II, Box 1, 342.
57. John Service, letter to Secretary of State James Byrnes, December 8, 1945 (John Service Papers, Bancroft).
58. Service security file, Summary and Analysis, Box 1, p. 110.
59. Buhite, *Patrick J. Hurley*, 275.
60. Service security file: "Summary and Analysis," Part I, Box 1.
61. Tydings Hearings, 1266, quoting from Secretary Byrnes testimony at hearings before Senate Foreign Relations Committee, December 5, 6, 20, 1945.
62. *The New Republic*, December 10, 1945.
63. FBI *Amerasia*, #100-267360-759 memo, December 6, 1945 from Hoover to Clark.

Chapter 16: The Storm Gathers

1. Val Chao interview with author, January 3, 2000.
2. John Service interview with author, August 18, 1998.
3. Val Chao interview with author, January 3, 2000.
4. Zhao Wenru (Val Chao), *Dreams Across the Seas: My Path in Exploring Drama* (Shanghai: China Drama Publishing House, 2005), 91; and Val Chao interview with author, January 3, 2000.
5. *Washington Post*, February 18, 1946; and Harvey Klehr and Ronald Radosh,

The Amerasia Spy Case: Prelude to McCarthyism (Chapel Hill: University of North Carolina Press, 1996), 134.

6. FBI *Amerasia*, #100-267360-759 and #100-267360-1000 memos.
7. Klehr and Radosh, *Amerasia Spy Case*, 141.
8. FBI *Amerasia*, #100-267360-846 memo.
9. Service security file: Appendix F.
10. Ibid.: Appendix V, Box 21.
11. Ibid.: "Summary and Analysis," Box 1, Pt. II, p. 381.
12. Klehr and Radosh, *Amerasia Spy Case*, 144.
13. Tydings Hearings, 1268.
14. C. S. S. oral history, 104.
15. David McCullough, *Truman* (New York: Simon & Schuster, 1992), 520.
16. J. S. S. oral history, 342.
17. FBI *Amerasia*, #100-267360-911 memo, April 3, 1950; and ibid., #100-267360-1000 memo.
18. "White House Justice/confidential file," George Elsey folder 7, Truman Library, Independence, Missouri; and FBI *Amerasia*, #100-267360-909 memo.
19. Klehr and Radosh, *Amerasia Spy Case*, 149–51.
20. J. S. S. oral history, 242–44.
21. C. S. S. oral history, 106.
22. United States House of Representatives Elections, 1946, http://www.answers.com/topic/united-states-house-elections-1946.
23. Tang Tsou, *America's Failure in China: 1941–50* (Chicago: University of Chicago Press, 1963), 438.
24. Russell D. Buhite, *Patrick J. Hurley and American Foreign Policy* (Ithaca, N.Y.: Cornell University Press, 1973), 318.
25. Tang Tsou, *America's Failure in China: 1941–50*, 420.
26. Harry Harding and Yang Ming, *Sino-American Relations 1945–1955: A Joint Reassessment of a Critical Decade* (Wilmington, Del.: Scholarly Resources, 1989), 126.
27. "United States Relations with China, with Special Reference to the Period 1944–1949," Department of State Publications 3573, Far Eastern Series 30 (Washington, D.C.: Office of Public Affairs, 1949), 688.
28. Tsou, *America's Failure in China*, 413.
29. "United States Relations with China," 688.
30. Tsou, *America's Failure in China*, 387.
31. "Recommendation for Assistance to Greece and Turkey," Harry S. Truman Administration, Elsey Papers, Truman Library. www.trumanlibrary.org/whistlestop/study_collections/doctrine/large/documents/index.php?documentdate=1947-03-12&documentid=5-9&pagenumber=1.
32. Tsou, *America's Failure in China*, 449.
33. Harding and Ming, *Sino-American Relations*, 109.
34. C. S. S. oral history, 109.
35. McCullough, *Truman*, 553.

36. Ibid.
37. Curt Gentry, *J. Edgar Hoover: The Man and the Secrets* (New York: W. W. Norton, 1991), 319.
38. C. S. S. oral history, 110.
39. Tsou, *America's Failure in China*, 451.
40. Ibid., 454.
41. "United States Relations with China," 257.
42. Tsou, *America's Failure in China*, 455.
43. Ibid., 459–60.
44. Ibid., 483.
45. Ibid., 443.
46. John Service, letter to Michael Green, December 5, 1986 (John Service Papers, Bancroft).
47. Service personnel file: Memo #481.
48. J. S. S. oral history, 345–46.
49. Service security file: "Summary and Analysis," Box 4, appendix C.
50. Chennault interview April 22, 1949, in Shanghai; released by Department of State on FOIA appeal, May 4, 2004.
51. Lauren Kessler, *Clever Girl* (New York: HarperCollins, 2003), 187.
52. Klehr and Radosh, *The Amerasia Spy Case*, 150.
53. Kessler, *Clever Girl*, 172.
54. Ibid., 187.
55. Federal Bureau of Investigation, "Venona," http://foia.fbi.gov/foiaindex/venona.htm.
56. Robert J. Lamphere and Tom Shachtman, *The FBI-KGB War: A Special Agent's Story* (New York: Berkeley Publishing Group, 1987), 100.
57. C. S. S. oral history, 111.
58. Service personnel file: Memos #473 and #474.
59. Service security file: "Summary and Analysis," Appendix D.
60. E. J. Kahn Jr., *The China Hands: America's Foreign Service Officers and What Befell Them* (New York: Viking Press, 1975), 199.
61. J. S. S. oral history, 350.
62. C. S. S. oral history, 104.

Chapter 17: The Hurricane Strikes

1. Tang Tsou, *America's Failure in China: 1941–50* (Chicago: University of Chicago Press, 1963), 495.
2. Ibid., 501–2.
3. Ibid., 495.
4. E. J. Kahn Jr., *The China Hands: America's Foreign Service Officers and What Befell Them* (New York: Viking Press, 1975), 201.
5. "Taiwan's 228 Incident: The Political Implications of February 28, 1947," A Foreign Policy and Center of Northeast Asian Policy Studies, Brookings Institution conference, February 22, 2007, http://www.brookings.edu/

events/2007/0222taiwan.aspx.

6. John S. Service, *The Amerasia Papers: Some Problems in History of U.S.–China Relations* (Berkeley: Center for Chinese Studies, University of California, 1971), 132.
7. J. S. S. oral history, 353, 355.
8. "United States Relations with China, with Special Reference to the Period 1944–1949," Department of State Publications 3573, Far Eastern Series 30 (Washington, D.C.: Office of Public Affairs, 1949), annex, 564–76.
9. Ibid., xvi.
10. J. S. S. oral history, 353; and Robert P. Newman, "The Self-Inflicted Wound: The China White Paper of 1949," *Prologue* 14 (1982): 141–56.
11. *New York Times*, August 21, 1949.
12. Russell D. Buhite, *Patrick J. Hurley and American Foreign Policy* (Ithaca, N.Y.: Cornell University Press, 1973), 293.
13. Newman, "Self-Inflicted Wound," 148.
14. Buhite, *Patrick J. Hurley*, 293.
15. Lyman Van Slyke, ed., *The China White Paper: August 1949* (Stanford, Calif.: Stanford University Press, 1968), 8.
16. Ibid., 9.
17. *Foreign Relations of the United States: 1949*, Vol. VIII, *The Far East: China* (Washington, D.C.: Government Printing Office, 1949), 357–60. Available at http://digicoll.library.wisc.edu/cgi-bin/FRUS/FRUS-idx?type=header&id=FRUS.FRUS1949v08.
18. Harry Harding and Yuan Ming, eds., *Sino-American Relations, 1945–1955: A Joint Reassessment of a Critical Decade* (Wilmington, Del.: Scholarly Resources, 1989), 144.
19. Newman, "Self-Inflicted Wound," 153–54 and n9.
20. Tsou, *America's Failure in China*, 505.
21. J. S. S. oral history, 355.
22. Val Chao, interviews with author, January 1, 2000, and July 25, 2003; John Service, interview with author, August 18, 1998.
23. Stuart Schram, *Mao Tse-tung* (Harmondsworth, England: Penguin, 1966), 251.
24. Kahn, *China Hands*, 206n12.
25. Service security file: Appendix F.
26. Memo to Hoover from S. D. Boykin, director, Office of Controls, February 25, 1949. Released to author under FOIA appeal on December 9, 2003.
27. Service security file: FBI report in Appendix C, 373.
28. May 13, 1949, report of Statford B. Duke in Tokyo. Released by Army Intelligence CIC under author's FOIA appeal in 2004; and Service security file, Appendix B, July 3, 1949, interview with Laing Duncan in Tokyo (memo from Hoover to Hatcher to Chief of State Dept. Security).
29. Service security file: June 28, 1949 report of interview with W. F. Davies Gebhart in Shanghai, Appendix B, Box 4.

30. Tsou, *America's Failure in China*, 531.
31. Eben Ayers Papers, diary entry January 5, 1950, p. 336, Truman Library, Independence, Missouri.
32. Kahn, *China Hands*, 212.
33. J. S. S. oral history, 358.
34. Caroline Service, letter to parents, January 14, 1950, reprinted in C. S. S. oral history, 235.
35. Joseph Alsop, "Why We Lost China 1: The Feud Between Stilwell and Chiang," The *Saturday Evening Post*, January 7, 1950, 17.
36. Service security file: "Summary and Analysis"; and Security interview November 26–December 11, Box 22, Folder, December 3, 1958.
37. McCullough, *Truman*, 759.
38. Robert Louis Benson and Michael Warner, eds., *Venona: Soviet Espionage and the American Response 1939–1957* (Washington, D.C.: National Security Agency and Central Intelligence Agency, 1996), xxiv; John Earl Haynes and Harvey Klehr, *Venona: Decoding Soviet Espionage in America* (New Haven, Conn.: Yale University Press, 2000), 156; and Allen Weinstein, *Perjury: The Hiss-Chambers Case* (New York: Alfred A. Knopf, 1978).
39. J. S. S. oral history, 359.
40. C. S. S. oral history, 113–15.
41. David M. Oshinsky, *A Conspiracy So Immense: The World of Joe McCarthy* (New York: Free Press, 1983), 105.
42. George Elsey Papers, Truman Library, Independence, Missouri.
43. Oshinsky, *A Conspiracy So Immense*, 106.
44. Tydings Hearings, 1756–58; see also Oshinsky, *A Conspiracy So Immense* 108–9; and McCullough, *Truman*, 765.
45. Ibid.
46. *Wheeling Intelligencer,* February 10, 1950.
47. Oshinsky, *A Conspiracy So Immense*, 112.
48. Schram, *Mao Tse-tung*, 254–55.
49. C. S. S. oral history, 115.
50. Curt Gentry, *J. Edgar Hoover: The Man and the Secrets* (New York: W. W. Norton, 1991), 378–79.
51. Oshinsky, *A Conspiracy So Immense*, 114.
52. Ibid., 119.
53. Ibid., 122.
54. Robert J. Lamphere and Tom Shachtman, *The FBI-KGB War: A Special Agent's Story* (New York: Berkeley Publishing Group, 1987), 118, 142.
55. J. S. S. oral history, 361.
56. Oshinsky, *A Conspiracy So Immense*, 128.
57. Tydings Hearings, 140. McCarthy's full remarks on Service are found in pp.130–40.
58. FBI John Service Loyalty Investigation file #121-13347, March 16, 1950 letter from Col. John O. Beaty to McCarthy.

59. John Service, interview with author, August 8, 1998; J. S. S. oral history, 361.
60. Kahn, *China Hands*, 217–18.
61. Caroline Service, letter to parents, March 17, 1950 (Caroline Service Papers, Bancroft).

Chapter 18: The Inquisition Begins

1. John S. Service Foreign Service File: March 24, 1950, press statement, RG 59, Box 904, File 123, 59.
2. J. S. S. oral history, 362.
3. Remarks of Herve J. L'Heureux, March 29, 1950, in ibid, 367a. Caroline Service, letter to parents, March 31, 1950, re: Jack's reception (Caroline Service Papers, Bancroft).
4. Service security file: Henry Taylor March 20, 1950, broadcast. Placed by Sen. Lawrence Smith (Wis.) in *Congressional Record*, 81st Congress, 2nd Session, Vol. 96 on May 1, 1950, for March 20, 1950; see p. A3322 legislative day p. A4266.
5. Caroline Service, letter to parents, March 31, 1950 (Caroline Service Papers, Bancroft).
6. David M. Oshinsky, *A Conspiracy So Immense: The World of Joe McCarthy* (New York: Free Press, 1983), 148.
7. *Washington Post*, "Loyalty Files Denied Probe By Truman-President Orders Board to Review At Once All Cases Cited by McCarthy," March 28, 1950.
8. Robert Griffith, *The Politics of Fear: Joseph R. McCarthy and the Senate* (Amherst: University of Massachusetts Press, 1970), 75.
9. *Congressional Record*, 81st Congress, 2nd Session, Vol. 96 (March 30, 1950): 4438, 4440, 4454. See also Service security file, Appendix C.
10. Robert P. Newman, "Self-Inflicted Wound: The China White Paper of 1949," *Prologue* (1982): 214.
11. J. S. S. oral history, 364.
12. Ibid., 365.
13. John Service, letter to John Vincent, May 16, 1951 (John Service Papers, Bancroft).
14. J. S. S. oral history, 365–67.
15. John Service, letter to family, July 4, 1950 (John Service Papers, Bancroft).
16. FBI *Amerasia*, #100-267360-1001 memo, April 10, 1950.
17. Service security file: J. Edgar Hoover, letter to Service, April 12, 1950, Appendix C, Box 4.
18. Joseph Grew, letter to Service, April 17, 1950 (John Service Papers, Bancroft).
19. Eric Sevareid, letter to LSB chair Brig. Gen. Conrad Snow, April 21, 1950 (John Service Papers, Bancroft); and Service personnel file: Memo #459, Wellington Embassy to Department of State, April 3, 1950, re: "Reaction of New Zealand Government Officials to Sen. McCarthy's attack on Mr. John S. Service."

20. Arthur Ringwalt, letter to Service, April 20, 1950 (John Service Papers, Bancroft).
21. Caroline Service, letter to John Service, April 13, 1950; and letter to parents, April 16, 1950 (Caroline Service Papers, Bancroft).
22. Grace Service, letter to John Service, April 12, 1950 (John Service Papers, Bancroft).
23. FBI Service Loyalty File #121-13347, May 1, 1950, memo to J. Edgar Hoover from Guy Hottel (SAC Washington Field Office).
24. FBI *Amerasia*, #100-267360-1032, May 1, 1950, memo re: Fred Woltman articles in *New York World-Telegram*.
25. Ibid., #100-267360-1017 memo, April 17, 1950, re: Sokolsky articles on OSS break in *New York World-Telegram*, April 7, 1950.
26. Caroline Service, letter to parents, May 4, 1950 (Caroline Service Papers, Bancroft).
27. John Service, letter to Caroline Service, May 2, 1950 (John Service Papers, Bancroft).
28. Theodore White, letter to Service, May 1, 1950 (John Service Papers, Bancroft).
29. *New York Herald Tribune*, May 4, 1950.
30. Oshinsky, *Conspiracy So Immense*, 153.
31. FBI *Amerasia*, #100-267360-1080 memo, May 22, 1950 Nichols to Tolson with Hoover handwritten comments.
32. Oshinsky, *A Conspiracy So Immense*, 156.
33. David McCullough, *Truman* (New York: Simon & Schuster, 1992), 769–70; and Oshinsky, *Conspiracy So Immense*, 157.
34. John Service, letter to Richard Service, May 19, 1950; and Caroline Service letter to John Service, May 8, 1950 (John Service Papers, Bancroft).
35. John Service, letter to Caroline Service, May 17, 1950 (Caroline Service Papers, Bancroft).
36. Caroline Service, letter to parents, May 17, 1950 (Caroline Service Papers, Bancroft).
37. Service security file: Box 4, Appendix C.
38. J. S. S. oral history, 370.
39. Service security file: Box 4, Appendix C: Denver FBI report April 26, 1950 by Joseph Learned.
40. FBI Service Loyalty File, memo #121-13347-125, and May 29, 1950, report from agents Leece and Lanman.
41. FBI *Amerasia*, memo #100-267360-1133; and FBI Service Loyalty File #121-13347-127, May 29, 1950, letter of Agent Howard Fletcher on Hurley interview.
42. Harvey Klehr and Ronald Radosh, *The Amerasia Spy Case: Prelude to McCarthyism* (Chapel Hill: University of North Carolina Press, 1996), 181.
43. FBI *Amerasia*, #100-267360-1209 memo, May 22, 1950, Nichols to Tolson; ibid., Hoover May 23, 1950, letter to Assistant Attorney General Peurifoy

re: response to State Department on "100 percent" remark; and Klehr and Radosh, *Ameriasia Spy Case*, 181.
44. Tydings Hearings 974, 998–99.
45. Ibid., 1067.
46. FBI *Amerasia*, #100-267360-1186 memo, May 29, 1950; ibid., #100-267360-1497 memo, April 7, 1952.
47. Fred Woltman, "Tydings Says He'll Tell Whole Story of Amerasia Case," *Washington Daily News*, May 23, 1950.

Chapter 19: The Hearings

1. Tydings Hearings, LSB, 1959.
2. Ibid., 1960.
3. John Service, interview with author, August 13, 1998.
4. Tydings Hearings, LSB, 1961–62.
5. Ibid., 1970–71.
6. Ibid., 2020.
7. Ibid., 2022.
8. Ibid., 2031.
9. FBI *Amerasia*, memo #121-13347-172 to J. Edgar Hoover, June 19, 1950. (The informant can be identified as a Madame Koo, wife of the Chinese ambassador to the United States. Her name was blacked out in the declassified FBI memo, but the censors missed one reference.)
10. John Service, letter to Grace Service, June 3, 1950 (John Service Papers, Bancroft).
11. Tydings Hearings, LSB, 2064.
12. Ibid., 2066.
13. Ibid., 2120–22.
14. Ibid., 2121.
15. Ibid., 2118.
16. Ibid., 2215, 2223.
17. Tydings Hearings, 1063.
18. Tydings Hearings, LSB, 2235. The published transcript incorrectly used the word "usual." In his personal copy of the transcript, John Service neatly underlined the word and penciled in the margin "error," adding, "unusual," with an exclamation point. He made many other corrections to his copy of the published transcript.
19. John Service, letter to Grace Service, June 3, 1950 (John Service Papers, Bancroft).
20. Ibid.
21. Fred Woltman, "Amerasia Got F.D.'s China Plan to Make Stilwell Boss," *Washington Daily News*, June 6, 1950.
22. Tydings Hearings, LSB, 2417–23.
23. Caroline Service, letter to parents, May 25, 1950 (Caroline Service Papers, Bancroft).

24. John Service, interview with author, May 27, 1998.
25. FBI Service Loyalty File #121-13347-157 memo re: John S. Service loyalty investigation. This memo was only obtained through a supplemental FOIA request by the author for rereview of Service's FBI file.
26. FBI Service Loyalty File #121-13347-172.
27. Val Chao, interview with author, July 25, 2003.
28. FBI Service Loyalty File #121-13347 memo May 1, 1950, to J. Edgar Hoover from Guy Hottel, SAC Washington Field.
29. John Service, letter to Grace Service, June 11, 1950 (John Service Papers, Bancroft).
30. Tydings Hearings, LSB, 2452–53.
31. *Washington Evening Star*, June 20, 1950.
32. J. S. S. oral history, 371.
33. Tydings Hearings, 1267.
34. J. S. S. oral history, 372.
35. Tydings Hearings, 1263.
36. Ibid., exhibit: letter of commendation from General Wedemeyer, 2477.
37. J. S. S. oral history, 372.
38. Tydings Hearings, 1329.
39. Lisa Green, letter to Colonel and Mrs. Schulz, June 24, 1959 (Caroline Service Papers, Bancroft).
40. Editorial "What Service Did," *Washington Post*, June 24, 1950.
41. John Service, letter to Caroline Service, May 2, 1950 (John Service Papers, Bancroft).
42. FBI *Amerasia*, memo #1080, May 22, 1950, from Nichols to Tolson.
43. Tydings Hearings, 1355.
44. Ibid., 1376.
45. Ibid., 1386, 1384.
46. Ibid., 1387.
47. Tydings Hearings, LSB, 2457.
48. Ibid., 2458.
49. Ibid., 2474.
50. John Service, letter to "Mother and Father [Schulz]," July 4, 1950 (John Service Papers, Bancroft).
51. Tydings Hearings, 1400.
52. Ibid., 1403; FBI John Service Loyalty File #100-267360-1133 memo, January 28, 1953. Released to author under FOIA appeal in May 2004.
53. Tydings Hearings, 1408–9.
54. Ibid., 1417.
55. Ibid., 1423–29.
56. Ibid., 1429.

Chapter 20: Living in Limbo

1. Harry S. Truman, *Memoirs by Harry S. Truman*, Volume II: *Years of Trial and Hope* (New York: Signet Books, 1956), 384.

2. David McCullough, *Truman* (New York: Simon & Schuster, 1992), 780.
3. Stuart Schram, *Mao Tse-tung* (Harmondsworth, England: Penguin, 1966), 264
4. Tang Tsou, *America's Failure in China: 1941–50* (Chicago: University of Chicago Press, 1963), 562; and Schram, *Mao Tse-tung*, 263.
5. Arthur Herman, *Joseph McCarthy: Reexamining the Life and Legacy of America's Most Hated Senator* (New York: Free Press, 2000), 122.
6. President's Personal File, Box 562, citizen letters re: Korean conflict, Truman Library, Independence, Missouri.
7. John Service, letter to family, July 4, 1950 (John Service Papers, Bancroft).
8. Ibid.
9. FBI *Amerasia*, #100-267360-1302 memo, June 29, 1950, from Nichols to Tolson re: Fulton Lewis broadcast.
10. Caroline Service, letter to parents, July 8, 1950 (Caroline Service Papers, Bancroft).
11. FBI *Amerasia*, #100-267360-1306 cable, June 27, 1950, to Tolson, Ladd, and Nichols.
12. FBI Service Loyalty File #121-13347-190 memo, June 26, 1950, from C. H. Stanley to A. H. Belmont re: summary of John Service case.
13. *Christian Science Monitor*, "Tydings Offers Records to Back McCarthy Perjury Charge," July 20, 1950.
14. Richard M. Fried, *Nightmare in Red: The McCarthy Era in Perspective* (New York: Oxford University Press, 1990), 128.
15. Tydings Report, 92, 332–33.
16. M. Stanton Evans, *Blacklisted by History* (New York: Crown Forum, 2007), 234–36.
17. Tydings Report, 78–80.
18. Herman, *Joseph McCarthy*, 135.
19. Brooks Atkinson, letter to Service, July 22, 1950 (John Service Papers, Bancroft).
20. Evans, *Blacklisted by History*, 269, 373–74.
21. Caroline Service, letter to parents, July 8, 1950 (Caroline Service Papers, Bancroft).
22. Warren Cohen, *America's Response to China* (New York: Columbia University Press, 1990), 170.
23. John Service, letter to Grace Service, August 5, 1950 (John Service Papers, Bancroft).
24. John Service, letter to Edward Rhetts, August 14, 1950 (John Service Papers, Bancroft).
25. Caroline Service, letters to parents, August 17 and 24, 1950 (Caroline Service Papers, Bancroft).
26. Taylor broadcast, September 4, 1950 (John Service Papers, Bancroft).
27. Truman speech on the veto of the McCarran Internal Security Act, September 22, 1950, Teaching American History, http://teachingamericanhistory.org/library/index.asp?document=859.

28. Fried, *Nightmare in Red*, 117.
29. Tsou, *America's Failure in China*, 568.
30. "Memo August 31, 1950 From Lt. Col. Arthur K. Harrold, U.S. Army Liaison Office, American consulate, Hong Kong; To: Asst. Chief of Staff, G-2, Dept of the Army, Washington DC." Note: Forwarded to Hoover from Brig. Gen. John Weckerling, Chief, Intelligence Division of U.S. Army in September 1950. This information was finally declassified by the U.S. Army Intelligence on December 17, 2003, under author's FOIA request.
31. Tsou, *America's Failure in China*, 571.
32. John Service, letter to Grace Service, September 15, 1950 (John Service Papers, Bancroft).
33. Caroline Service, letter to parents, September 9, 1950 (Caroline Service Papers, Bancroft).
34. Ibid., September 23, 1950.
35. McCullough, *Truman*, 799; and Truman, *Memoirs*, II: 411.
36. Tsou, *America's Failure in China*, 572–73.
37. Ibid., 574.
38. Service security file: "Summary and Analysis," Box 1-3-LSB, folder 4, 410–13.
39. John Service, letter to Caroline Service, December 10, 1950 (John Service Papers, Bancroft).
40. Caroline Service, letter to Lisa Green, October 20, 1950 (Caroline Service Papers, Bancroft).
41. Service security file: "Summary and Analysis, October 12, 1950 letter to CON-Bayliss.
42. Truman, *Memoirs*, II: 416–17.
43. Tsou, *America's Failure in China*, 575.
44. "People's Volunteer Army," www. answers.com/topic/people-s-volunteer-army.
45. *New York Times*, November 2, 1950.
46. John Service, letter to Edith Nourse Rogers, November 10, 1950 (John Service Papers, Bancroft).
47. John Service, memo to Humelsine, November 13, 1950 (John Service Papers, Bancroft).
48. FBI *Amerasia*, #100-267360-1397 memo, November 3, 1950, Nichols to Tolson.
49. John Service, letter to John Carter Vincent, May 16, 1951 (John Service Papers, Bancroft).
50. John Service, letter to Grace Service, November 17, 1950 (John Service Papers, Bancroft).
51. Grace Service, letter, November 22, 1950 (John Service Papers, Bancroft).
52. Korean War, http://www.answers.com/topic/korean-war.
53. John Service, letter to Caroline Service, December 7, 1950 (John Service Papers, Bancroft).
54. *Washington Star*, "Humelsine Approves Clearing Of Service 'Disloyalty'

Charges . . . Now Goes to President's Loyalty Review Board for a 'Post-Audit,'" December 6, 1950.
55. J. S. S. oral history, 391.
56. Robert J. Lamphere and Tom Shachtman, *The FBI-KGB War: A Special Agent's Story* (New York: Berkeley Publishing Group, 1987), 127. For Coplon case and Venona, see ibid., 102–29.
57. Curt Gentry, *J. Edgar Hoover: The Man and the Secrets* (New York: W. W. Norton, 1991), 373.
58. John Service, letter to Caroline Service, December 7, 1950 (John Service Papers, Bancroft).

Chapter 21: The Firing Squad

1. Caroline Service, letter to John Service, December 2, 1950 (Caroline Service Papers, Bancroft).
2. Editorial, "MacArthur Blunders in Korea," *New York Herald Tribune*, November 27, 1950.
3. Grace Service, letter to John Service, December 17, 1950 (John Service Papers, Bancroft).
4. Rudyard Kipling, "If," in *The Writings in Prose and Verse of Rudyard Kipling* (New York: Charles Scribner's Sons, 1910), 200–201.
5. Caroline Service, letter to John Service, December 27, 1950 (Caroline Service Papers, Bancroft).
6. James Lilley and Jeffrey Lilley, *China Hands* (New York: Public Affairs, 2004), 79.
7. The author's FOIA appeal to obtain files on Corcoran and Chennault was denied by the CIA.
8. Lilley and Lilley, *China Hands*, 78; E. J. Kahn Jr., *The China Hands: America's Foreign Service Officers and What Befell Them* (New York: Viking Press, 1975), 241.
9. U.S. Army Intelligence G-2 memo January 9, 1951, re: Nationalist Chinese intelligence report. Author obtained under FOIA appeal on December 17, 2003; see also Service security file, Appendix D for copy of Chinese report.
10. Service security file: J. Edgar Hoover, letter to Hatcher, March 5, 1951, Appendix D.
11. FBI Service loyalty file #121-13347-197, memo to J. Edgar Hoover from New Haven FBI, January 8, 1951.
12. FBI Service loyalty file #121-13347-198, Hoover memo to Boykin, January 25, 1951; and Hoover memo to McInerney, February 14, 1951.
13. FBI File #121-13347, memos to Hoover from New York SAC, February 26, 1951, re: Lewis articles.
14. J. S. S. oral history, 382–84.
15. McCarthy file (John Service Papers, Bancroft).
16. Caroline Service, letter to parents, February 4, 1951 (Caroline Service Papers, Bancroft).
17. Transcript excerpts of meeting of LRB, February 13–14, 1951 (John Service

Papers, Bancroft); Harvey Klehr and Ronald Radosh, *The Amerasia Spy Case: Prelude to McCarthyism* (Chapel Hill: University of North Carolina Press, 1996), 209.

18. *Washington Post*, February 18, 2008, emphasis added.
19. Kahn, *The China Hands*, 228.
20. Service security file: State Department Security Office Confidential Memo, February 19, 1951, Appendix D.
21. John Service, letter to Caroline Service, February 27, 1951 (Caroline Service Papers, Bancroft).
22. FBI memo by agents Zander and Taylor, March 23, 1951, John Service State Department Loyalty File, p. 539; see also Appendix D, "Investigations," for Hoover's memos to Hatcher (March 30, 1951) and Humelsine (April 2, 1951). For more on Soviet spying see also John Earl Haynes and Harvey Klehr, *Venona: Decoding Soviet Espionage in America* (New Haven, Conn.: Yale University Press, 2000), 113, 145–50.
23. John Service, letter to Grace Service, March 23, 1951 (Grace Boggs Service Papers, BANC MSS 87/22cz, The Bancroft Library, University of California, Berkeley).
24. Annalee Jacoby Fadiman, letter to John Service, March 23, 1951 (John Service Papers, Bancroft).
25. John Service, letter to Conrad Snow, April 10, 1951 (John Service Papers, Bancroft).
26. John Service, letter to Secretary of State, March 23, 1951 (John Service Papers, Bancroft); J. S. S. oral history, 384–384a.
27. U.S. State Department, Department of State Bulletin, April 16, 1951, http://usinfo.org/docs/democracy/58.htm.
28. Arthur Herman, *Joseph McCarthy: Reexamining the Life and Legacy of America's Most Hated Senator* (New York: The Free Press, 2000), 155.
29. American Rhetoric, Top 100 Speeches, General Douglas MacArthur, Farewell Address to Congress, April 19, 1951, http://www.americanrhetoric.com/speeches/douglasmacarthurfarewelladdress.htm.
30. John Service, letter to Grace Service, April 13, 1951 (John Service Papers, Bancroft).
31. Grace Service, letter to John Service, April 16, 1951 (John Service Papers, Bancroft).
32. *Congressional Record*, 82nd Congress, 1st Session, Vol. 97 (May 1, 1951): 4814.
33. John Service, letter to Representative Busbey, May 6, 1951 (John Service Papers, Bancroft).
34. Loy Henderson, letter to Caroline Service, April 21, 1951, C. S. S. oral history, 131a.
35. Caroline Service, letter to Lisa Green, May 8, 1951; and letter to parents, February 18, 1951 (Caroline Service Papers, Bancroft).
36. Wedemeyer testimony September 19, 1951, before the Senate Internal

Security Subcommittee at its hearings regarding the Institute of Pacific Relations (IPR). His remarks are mentioned in Service security file, "Summary and Analysis," 416.
37. John Service, "Pertinent Excerpts," *The Foreign Service Journal*, October 1951; reprinted in J. S. S. oral history, appendix VI, 537–39.
38. J. S. S. oral history, 386.
39. John Service, letter to Grace Service, November 10, 1951 (John Service Papers, Bancroft).
40. United States Civil Service Commission Loyalty Review Board Hearing, November 8, 1951, Papers of John S. Service and Charles E. Rhetts, Truman Library, Independence, Missouri.
41. John Service, letter to Grace Service, November 10, 1951 (John Service Papers, Bancroft).
42. Ibid.
43. J. S. S. oral history, 388.
44. Service security file: Appendix F.

Chapter 22: The Long Fight

1. J. S. S. oral history, 392.
2. Carlisle Humelsine, letter to John Service, December 13, 1951 (John Service Papers, Bancroft).
3. John Service, interview with author, April 16, 1998.
4. Caroline Service, letter to Lisa Green, June 19, 1957 (Caroline Service Papers, Bancroft).
5. John Service, interview with author, April 16, 1998.
6. C. S. S. oral history, 141–42.
7. Service security file, Appendix F: "Department of State for the Press," December 13, 1951, No. 1088.
8. Ibid.
9. Ibid.
10. Ibid.
11. John Service, letter to Grace Service, December 22, 1951 (John Service Papers, Bancroft).
12. "Personal Statement of John S. Service," December 13, 1951 (John Service Papers, Bancroft).
13. Dean Acheson, oral history transcript, February 17, 1955, p. 35, Truman Library, Independence, Missouri.
14. C. S. S. oral history, 144–45.
15. Loy Henderson, letter, December 21, 1951 (Caroline Service Papers, Bancroft).
16. George Kennan, letter, December 14, 1951 (John Service Papers, Bancroft).
17. J. S. S. oral history, 395.
18. Eric Sevareid, CBS news report, December 14, 1951 (John Service Papers, Bancroft).

19. "The Case of John Stewart Service," *Hong Kong Standard*, December 17, 1951 (John Service Papers, Bancroft).
20. Editorial, "The Long Shadow," *Washington Post*, December 15, 1951.
21. Grace Service, letter to John Service, December 14, 1951 (John Service Papers, Bancroft).
22. John Service, letter to Grace Service, December 22, 1951 (John Service Papers, Bancroft).
23. E. J. Kahn Jr., *The China Hands: America's Foreign Service Officers and What Befell Them* (New York: Viking Press, 1975), 304.
24. Ibid., 240.
25. "The Service Case," *Foreign Service Journal* January 22, 1952 (John Service Papers, Bancroft).
26. Robert Scotton, letter to John Service, January 4, 1952 (John Service Papers, Bancroft).
27. Editorial, "Distortions of History," *Washington Post*, January 9, 1952.
28. Ed Rhetts first appeal to President Truman, January 7, 1952 (John Service Papers, Bancroft).
29. Caroline Service, letters to Lisa Green, January 12 and 23, 1952 (Caroline Service Papers, Bancroft).
30. John Service, interview with author, August 18, 1998.
31. Service security file, Clement Wells, letter to John Service, December 18, 1951, Appendix B, Box 22.
32. J. S. S. oral history, 409.
33. Caroline Service, letter to Lisa Green, February 4, 1952 (Caroline Service Papers, Bancroft).
34. Gary May, *China Scapegoat* (Washington, D.C.: New Republic Books, 1979), 228; Kahn, *The China Hands*, 273.
35. Caroline Service, letter to Lisa Green, February 4, 1952 (Caroline Service Papers, Bancroft).
36. Ed Rhetts, letter to President Truman, February 4, 1952 (John Service Papers, Bancroft).
37. Charles S. Murphy, letter to Ed Rhetts, February 20, 1952, Loyalty Investigation of John S. Service file, Truman Library, Independence, Missouri.
38. Winifred Stilwell, letter to President Truman, February 24, 1952; Truman, letter to Winifred Stilwell, February 29, 1952, Loyalty Investigation of John S. Service, Truman Library, Independence, Missouri.
39. Newman file, transcript of Appropriations Subcommittee meeting, March 23, 1952 (John Service Papers, Bancroft).
40. John Service interview with author, May 27, 1998; J. S. S. oral history, 411.
41. Caroline Service, letter to mother, April 17, 1952 (Caroline Service Papers, Bancroft).
42. Caroline Service, letter to Lisa Green, April 11, 1952 (Caroline Service Papers, Bancroft).
43. John Service, letter to Ed Rhetts, April 1952 (John Service Papers, Bancroft).

44. Report of the Special Subcommittee to Investigate the Administration of the Internal Security Act and Other Internal Security Laws, July 1951, on its investigation of the Institute of Pacific Relations, July 1952, RG46, 13.94, NARA.
45. Editorial, "McCarran's Revenge," *Washington Post*, July 4, 1952.
46. Harvey Klehr and Ronald Radosh, *The Amerasia Spy Case: Prelude to McCarthyism* (Chapel Hill: University of North Carolina Press, 1996), 211.
47. Robert Service, interview with author, August 9, 2008.
48. C. S. S. oral history, 159, 161, 163.
49. John Service, letter to Ed Rhetts, July 3, 1955 (John Service Papers, Bancroft).
50. J. S. S. oral history, 433.
51. Ibid., 434c.
52. C. S. S. oral history, 178.
53. J. S. S. oral history, 435.
54. Ibid., 435a.

Chapter 23: Reluctant Retiree

1. Caroline Service, letter to Lisa Green, June 17, 1957 (Caroline Service Papers, Bancroft).
2. Service interview in *Providence Evening Bulletin*, July 1, 1957.
3. Eleanor Roosevelt, "My Day" column, *New York Post*, June 20, 1957.
4. John Service, letter to Aunt Lynda, June 25, 1957 (John Service Papers, Bancroft).
5. Service personnel file: Memo #244, June 29, 1957.
6. Isabelle Shelton, "Twelve Years under a Loyalty Cloud," *Washington Star Sunday*, June 23, 1957.
7. Caroline Service, letter to Lisa Green, June 29, 1957 (Caroline Service Papers, Bancroft).
8. Ibid.
9. John Service, letter to Leon Cowles of personnel office, July 10, 1957; and letter to John Reid, July 13, 1957 (John Service Papers, Bancroft).
10. J. S. S. oral history, 438.
11. John Service, letter from Tom Estes, July 16,1957; Service letter to Tom Estes, August 5, 1957 (John S. Service Papers, Bancroft); and J. S. S. oral history, 441.
12. Service personnel file: Burke, letter to Dulles, July 31, 1957, PER #220; and Dinen, letter to Kennedy, September 11, 1957, PER #206.
13. Service personnel file: Eastland, letter to Dulles, October 12, 1957, memo #204; State, letter to Eastland, November 18, 1957, #205; and Roderick O'Connor memo, n.d.
14. Service personnel file: John Service Fitness Report, May 28, 1958, #391.
15. The material in this passage is drawn from Service security file: November 24–December 4, 1958, security interview, Box 22, Investigations Vol. 2, 1954–73.

16. Service security file: Bailey memo to Roderick O'Connor, December 19, 1958, Box 25, Investigations Vol. 2, 1954–73.
17. Service security file: Roderick O'Connor, memo to Loy Henderson, December 26, 1958, Box 25, Investigations Vol. 2, 1954–73.
18. Service security file: Loy Henderson memo to Roderick O'Connor, August 11, 1959, Box 25, Investigations Vol. 2, 1954–73.
19. J. S. S. oral history, 449.
20. C. S. S. oral history, 189–91.
21. J. S. S. oral history, 451–52.
22. Ibid., 453.
23. Service personnel file: Loy Henderson memo, August 11, 1959, memo #433.
24. Caroline Service, letters to Lisa Green, March 26 and April 13, 1962 (Caroline Service Papers, Bancroft).
25. John Service, letter to Clement Wells, April 15, 1962 (John Service Papers, Bancroft).

Chapter 24: Renaissance

1. Chalmers Johnson, "Foreword," in John S. Service, *The Amerasia Papers: Some Problems in History of U.S.–China Relations* (Berkeley: Center for Chinese Studies, University of California, 1971), 8–10.
2. Ibid., 13.
3. Henry Kissinger, *White House Years* (New York: Little Brown, 1979), 168.
4. Ibid., 167.
5. Quoted in Nancy Bernkopf Tucker, ed., *China Confidential: American Diplomats and Sino-American Relations, 1945–1996* (New York: Columbia University Press, 2001), 227.
6. Kissinger, *White House Years*, 181.
7. Service, *Amerasia Papers*, 17–18.
8. U.S. Senate, Committee on the Judiciary, Senate Internal Security Subcomittee, "The Amerasia Papers: A Clue to the Catastrophe of China" (Washington: Government Printing Office, 1970), 70; see also Service, *Amerasia Papers*, 18, italics in original.
9. Service, *Amerasia Papers*, 10.
10. Ibid., 23.
11. John Service, letter to Edgar Snow, February 11, 1971 (John Service Papers, Bancroft).
12. Service, *Amerasia Papers*, 70.
13. J. S. S. oral history, 475.
14. Service, *Amerasia Papers*, 10–11.
15. Ibid., 51.
16. Ibid., 55, italics in original.
17. Ibid., 56.
18. Ibid., 95.

19. Ibid., 87.
20. Ibid., 104–7.
21. Ibid., 125–26.
22. Ibid., 127.
23. Ibid., 95.
24. Ibid., 190.
25. Ibid., 191.
26. Ibid., 191–92.
27. For details, see Kissinger, *White House Years*, 709–10.
28. C. S. S. oral history, 201.
29. Kissinger, *White House Years*, 163.
30. E. J. Kahn Jr., *The China Hands: America's Foreign Service Officers and What Befell Them* (New York: Viking Press, 1975), 290.
31. *Daily News Wire Services*, "Two 'McCarthy Victims' to Testify on Red China," n.d.
32. J. S. S. oral history, 487.
33. Ibid., 479.
34. John Service, letter to Marshall Green, August 12, 1971, Marshall Green Papers, 1947–1998, Hoover Institution, Stanford University, Stanford, California.
35. J. S. S. oral history, 479; and C. S. S. oral history, 202.
36. J. S. S. oral history, 480.
37. Ibid., 484–85; Richard Solomon (former assistant to Kissinger at the National Security Council), interview with author, May 2003.
38. Kissinger, *White House Years*, 770, 784.
39. J. S. S. oral history, 481–82.
40. Confidential Memo, December 2, 1971, RE: John Service talk with Zhou Enlai, Marshall Green Papers 1947–1998, Hoover Institution, Stanford University, Stanford, California.
41. Kahn, *China Hands*, 294.
42. Robert McNamara with Brian VanDerMark, *In Retrospect: The Tragedy and Lessons of Vietnam* (New York: Vintage, 1996), 33.
43. Brooks Atkinson, letter to John Service, February 20, 1972 (John Service Papers, Bancroft).
44. "The Joint U.S.-China Communiqué, Shanghai, February 27, 1972," http://usinfo.org/docs/basic/shanghai_e.htm.
45. Kahn, *China Hands*, 301.
46. David Biltchik (former Foreign Service Officer), interview with author, May 14, 2003.
47. Service security file: Letter James Buckley to William Rogers, February 1, 1973, Box 25.
48. John Service, letter to David Biltchik, January 31, 1973 (John Service Papers, Bancroft).
49. Henderson, letter to John and Caroline Service, February 7, 1973; Caroline

Service, letter to Loy Henderson, February 2, 1973 (Caroline Service Papers, Bancroft).

50. Hearings on "Prospects for Normalizing Relations with Communist Countries," September 25, 1974, before the Committee on Foreign Relations, United States Senate, 93rd Congress, 2nd Session (Washington, D.C.: U.S. Government Printing Office, 1974), 348, 447.
51. John Service, letter to Martin Wilbur, October 27, 1975 (John Service Papers, Bancroft).
52. John S. Service, "Chou En-lai, As Seen by an Old China Hand," *Los Angeles Times*, January 14, 1976, 5.
53. John Service, interview with author, August 13, 1998.
54. Val Chao, letter to John Service, November 21, 1979 (John Service Papers, Bancroft).
55. Val Chao, interview with author, July 25, 2003.

Epilogue

1. Val Chao, interview with author, July 25, 2003.
2. Harvey Klehr and Ronald Radosh, "Anatomy of a Fix: The Untold Story of the 'Amerasia' Case," The *New Republic*, April 21, 1986, 18 ff.
3. Ibid.
4. John Service, letters to Radosh and Klehr, November 25 and 27, 1985 (John Service Papers, Bancroft).
5. John Service, letter to Radosh and Klehr, June 22, 1986 (John Service Papers, Bancroft).
6. Harvey Klehr and Ronald Radosh, *The Amerasia Spy Case: Prelude to McCarthyism*, (Chapel Hill: University of North Carolina Press, 1996), 12.
7. John Service, letter to Joe Esherick, May 6, 1996 (John Service Papers, Bancroft).
8. Service memoirs, I: Prologue, "Too Much Zeal," and Service interview with author August 18, 1998.
9. J. S. S. oral history, 513a, b.

GLOSSARY AND ACRONYMS

228 Incident	When the Taiwanese protested on February 28, 1947, against Nationalist misrule and corruption, the government reacted with mass shootings, arrests, and the imposition of a repressive martial law rule that lasted for decades
8th Route Army or *Ba Lu Jun*	The larger of the two Chinese Communist-controlled units of the National Army of the Republic of China; fought the Japanese from 1937 to 1945 (see also New 4th Army)
CCP	Chinese Communist Party
China Lobby	An influential group of businessmen, politicians, and journalists who strongly promoted Nationalist China's interests in the United States
Dixie Mission	The code name for the American Observers Group sent to Yenan to learn about Mao and his Communists
FOIA	Freedom of Information Act; the legislation allowing citizens to petition for access to confidential government documents
Formosa	Portuguese name for Taiwan, in wide usage in 1940s and 1950s

G-2	U.S. Army Intelligence
HUAC	House Un-American Activities Committee
The Hump	Nickname for the treacherous Himalayan mountain range that pilots flew over to deliver supplies to China during World War II
Ichigo	Code name of Japanese offensive in China during the spring of 1944
IPR	Institute of Pacific Relations, an international organization for the exchange of views on nations of the Pacific Rim; accused of harboring Communists during the McCarthy era
KGB	Russian abbreviation for "Committee for State Security," the umbrella agency for intelligence gathering and security; disbanded in 1995, it was succeeded by FSB, the "Federal Security Service"
Kuomintang, or KMT	Nationalist Party of China, founded by Sun Yat-sen and headed by Chiang Kai-shek after 1926
Lend-Lease	The American aid program (1941–45) that provided munitions and supplies to Britain, Russia, China, and other allied nations
Long March	The legendary eight-thousand-mile retreat of the Communist Party partisans to escape capture by the pursuing Nationalist Army in 1934–35, which ended in Yenan, Shaanxi Province
LRB	Loyalty Review Board set up by President Truman as a civilian appeals board for federal employees accused of disloyalty
LSB	The State Department's Loyalty Security Board, established by President Truman as part of the loyalty program for federal employees in 1947

Manchukuo	The puppet state set up in Manchuria and part of Mongolia in 1932 by Japan with the last Qing emperor, Puyi, installed as the nominal regent and emperor
Manhattan Project	The United States' supersecret program that developed the atomic bomb
Marshall Plan	Innovative economic recovery aid program established in 1947, named for Secretary of State George Marshall, for rebuilding Western Europe and repelling Communist influence
New 4th Army	The smaller of the two major Chinese Communist-controlled military forces operating behind enemy lines (see also 8th Route Army)
ONI	Office of Naval Intelligence
OSS	Office of Strategic Services
OWI	Office of War Information
PRC	People's Republic of China
ROC	Republic of China
SACO	Sino-American Special Technical Cooperative Organization
Sarco	The private company manufacturing industrial steam traps that hired John Service
SISS	Senate Internal Security Subcommittee
Tydings Committee	A subcommittee of the Senate Foreign Relations Committee, chaired by Millard Tydings, charged with investigating Senator McCarthy's charges of Communist infiltration of the State Department

Venona Project	Supersecret decryption program of the U.S. Army Signal Corps to break the Soviet code during World War II, in diplomatic cables between Moscow, New York, and Washington, D.C.
VFW	Veterans of Foreign Wars Association
V-J Day	Victory over Japan Day; applied to both August 14, 1945, the date surrender was announced, and September 2, 1945, the date of formal surrender ceremonies

INDEX

ABOUT THE AUTHOR

Lynne Joiner is an Emmy award-winning broadcast journalist, news anchor, and documentary filmmaker who knew John Service for more than twenty years. Her work includes assignments for: CBS, NBC, ABC, CNN, NPR, and Christian Science Monitor Radio. After graduating from Cornell University, Joiner first traveled to Asia and studied Chinese in Taiwan. In December 1975, she filmed her first documentary in China and has returned frequently on assignments, including work as a Shanghai Television news consultant. She directed the international journalism awards program at Johns Hopkins SAIS and has taught at Stanford University and at a high school. She lives in San Francisco and has one son.

The Naval Institute Press is the book-publishing arm of the U.S. Naval Institute, a private, nonprofit, membership society for sea service professionals and others who share an interest in naval and maritime affairs. Established in 1873 at the U.S. Naval Academy in Annapolis, Maryland, where its offices remain today, the Naval Institute has members worldwide.

Members of the Naval Institute support the education programs of the society and receive the influential monthly magazine *Proceedings* or the colorful bimonthly magazine *Naval History* and discounts on fine nautical prints and on ship and aircraft photos. They also have access to the transcripts of the Institute's Oral History Program and get discounted admission to any of the Institute-sponsored seminars offered around the country.

The Naval Institute's book-publishing program, begun in 1898 with basic guides to naval practices, has broadened its scope to include books of more general interest. Now the Naval Institute Press publishes about seventy titles each year, ranging from how-to books on boating and navigation to battle histories, biographies, ship and aircraft guides, and novels. Institute members receive significant discounts on the more than eight hundred Press books in print.

Full-time students are eligible for special half-price membership rates. Life memberships are also available.

For a free catalog describing Naval Institute Press books currently available, and for further information about joining the U.S. Naval Institute, please write to:

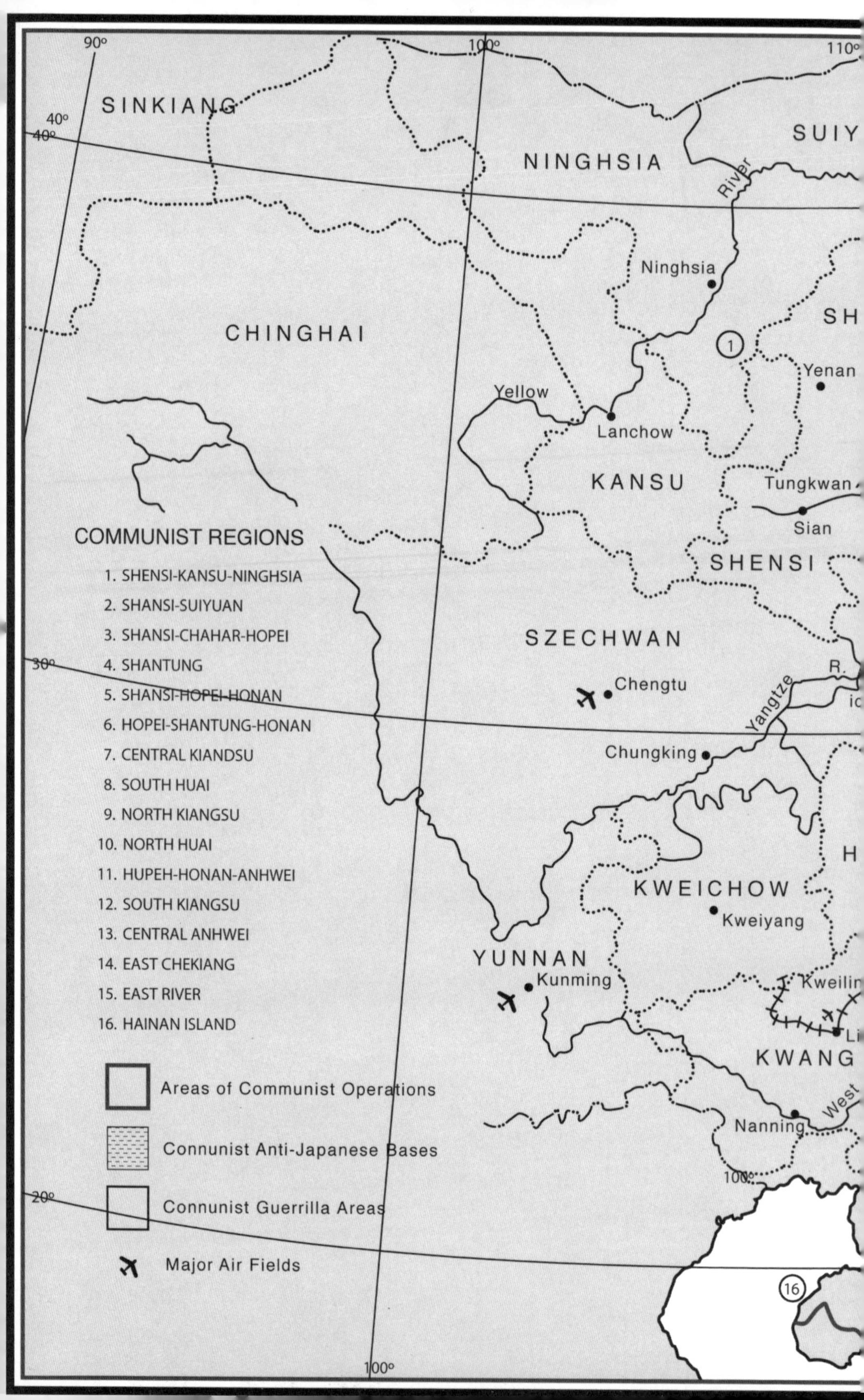

90°
100°
110°
40°
40°
30°
20°
100°
100°
SINKIANG
NINGHSIA
SUIY
River
Ninghsia
SH
CHINGHAI
1
Yenan
Yellow
Lanchow
KANSU
Tungkwan
Sian
SHENSI
COMMUNIST REGIONS
1. SHENSI-KANSU-NINGHSIA
2. SHANSI-SUIYUAN
3. SHANSI-CHAHAR-HOPEI
4. SHANTUNG
5. SHANSI-HOPEI-HONAN
6. HOPEI-SHANTUNG-HONAN
7. CENTRAL KIANDSU
8. SOUTH HUAI
9. NORTH KIANGSU
10. NORTH HUAI
11. HUPEH-HONAN-ANHWEI
12. SOUTH KIANGSU
13. CENTRAL ANHWEI
14. EAST CHEKIANG
15. EAST RIVER
16. HAINAN ISLAND
SZECHWAN
R.
Chengtu
Yangtze
Chungking
H
KWEICHOW
Kweiyang
YUNNAN
Kunming
Kweilin
KWANG
Areas of Communist Operations
West
Nanning
Connunist Anti-Japanese Bases
Connunist Guerrilla Areas
Major Air Fields
16